CORPORATIST IDEOLOGY IN
KEMALIST TURKEY

Modern Intellectual and Political History of the Middle East
Mehrzad Boroujerdi, *Series Editor*

OTHER TITLES IN MODERN INTELLECTUAL
AND POLITICAL HISTORY OF THE MIDDLE EAST

Cultural Schizophrenia: Islamic Societies Confronting the West
Daryush Shayegan; John Howe, trans.

Freedom, Modernity, and Islam: Toward a Creative Synthesis
Richard K. Khuri

God and Juggernaut: Iran's Intellectual Encounter with Modernity
Farzin Vahdat

Iranian Intellectuals and the West: The Tormented Triumph of Nativism
Mehrzad Boroujerdi

Localizing Knowledge in a Globalizing World: Recasting the Area Studies Debate
Ali Mirsepassi, Amrita Basu, and Frederick Weaver, eds.

Mysticism and Dissent: Socioreligious Thought in Qajar Iran
Mangol Bayat

The Genesis of Young Ottoman Thought: A Study in the Modernization of Turkish Political Ideas
Serif Mardin

The Story of the Daughters of Quchan: Gender and National Memory in Iranian History
Afsaneh Najmabadi

CORPORATIST IDEOLOGY IN

KEMALIST TURKEY

Progress or Order?

TAHA PARLA *&* ANDREW DAVISON

Syracuse University Press

First Edition 2004

04 05 06 07 08 09   6 5 4 3 2 1

Title page: Mustafa Kemal Atatürk giving a speech in Mersin on 17 March 1923.
From *Dahi Kutarıcı: Mustafa Kemal Atatürk, 1881–1938*
(Istanbul: Ata Basın Yayın, 2000), front cover.

The paper used in this publication meets the minimum requirements
of American National Standard for Information Sciences—Permanence
of Paper for Printed Library Materials, ANSI Z39.48–1984.∞™

Library of Congress Cataloging-in-Publication Data
Parla, Taha.
  Corporatist ideology in Kemalist Turkey / Taha Parla and Andrew Davison.— 1st ed.
    p. cm. — (Modern intellectual and political history of the Middle East)
  Includes bibliographical references and index.
  ISBN 0-8156-3054-9 (hardcover : alk. paper)
  1. Kemalism. 2. Corporate state—Turkey. I. Davison, Andrew, 1962– II. Title. III. Series.
HD3616.T872P37 2004
322'.3'09561—dc22   2004017122

Manufactured in the United States of America

CONTENTS

TAHA PARLA completed his graduate work at Columbia University. He is a professor of political science at Boğaziçi University in Istanbul.

ANDREW DAVISON completed his graduate work at the University of Minnesota. He is an associate professor of political science at Vassar College.

PREFACE

In this study, we develop a theoretically and comparatively informed account of the ideological content of Kemalism—the name given to Mustafa Kemal Atatürk's and his party's political thought and practice and the persistently official and semiofficial, hegemonic ideology of the Turkish Republic, formally founded in 1923. Through a textual and contextual analysis of Kemalism's primary expressions in Atatürk's speeches and the official documents of the ruling Republican People's Party during the founding period, material that we believe has been inadequately and selectively considered in existing literature, we offer interpretations of the political, economic, social, and cultural goals of the Kemalist version of Turkish nationalism, of the power and authority relations that Atatürk and his colleagues believed were necessary to achieve their implementation, and of the actual practices, relations, and institutions created in that process.

Concomitant with this goal is our desire to situate and critically evaluate Kemalism within the comparative, theoretical landscape of late capitalist, modern, and secular political ideologies. Emerging in part from within the tradition of Comtean scientific positivism in the Turkish context, Kemalism celebrated the construction of political futures according to human, rather than divine, design. Kemalism's "secular" and "modern" reputation has led many observers to see it as an example of the fulfillment of many political goals of European modernity in a Muslim context, goals such as individual freedom, citizen equality, and rational and accountable educational and governing structures. Interpretations of Kemalism vary depending on focus, but the most prominent accounts of its political and ideological content suggest that it may be understood as exemplifying secular, democratizing liberalism in some respects and state socialism in others. The first claim—of Kemalism's presumed democratic liberalism—derives from its celebrated, but we think overstated, commitment to populist and nonreligious bases of governance and education. The latter claim—of its presumed state socialism—derives from its commitment to economic statism.

We believe that these accounts mistake Kemalism's ideological content and that such misinterpretation may be demonstrated through a reading of Kemalism's founding documents, in which its ideological aims, interests, and presuppositions are very clearly articulated. Our reading of the primary documents suggests to us that Kemalism's ideological character is best understood not in terms of liberalism or socialism, but in terms of corporatism. Kemalism is best seen as an early variant of rightist, Third Way (*tertium genus*) political ideologies that pursue capitalist modernity and societal transformation but reject both an individualist vision of liberalism and a class-based vision of society and social transformation of socialism.

Far from containing liberalism and socialism, Kemalism opposes and, indeed, undercuts them. The fact that it exhibits antitheocratic tendencies does not render it either secular or liberal. The fact that it promotes "populism" does not render it democratic. The fact that it endorses a strong role for the state in the context of economic development does not make it socialist.

As a corporatist ideology with goals of "national" social and economic mobilization, Kemalism is not anticapitalist, but it is antiliberal and antisocialist, regarding the individualist premises of liberalism and the radicalism of socialism as divisive.

Of course, each of these ideological traditions—liberalism, socialism, and corporatism—encompasses various subtraditions, as well as very different historical articulations. Corporatism, for example, encompasses both solidaristic and fascistic versions. Given this, we further consider how different emphases within Kemalism illustrate these different possibilities within corporatism, contending that although Kemalism's priorities and aims strongly emphasize solidaristic corporatism, they also incorporate partialy fascistic characteristics here and there.

Under close scrutiny, then, and insofar as European modernism is associated with liberalism, Marxism, or both, Kemalism is neither properly modern nor properly secular, and its commitment to rational education and governance must be questioned. After unpacking the core of Kemalist corporatism in detail and delineating what we think are ultimately more general ideological issues related to modernity and secularity, we illuminate prospects for and barriers to a more democratic Turkey within the Kemalist legacy. We do not uncritically endorse the political ends of liberalism, socialism, modernism, or secularism in the Turkish context, but we do contest the assumption of their presence in and availability within Kemalism. Our conclusion, therefore, includes broader reflections of a comparative nature about contemporary ideologies as defined according to substantive, democratic criteria.

This work draws on previous, independently written work by the two authors: Taha Parla's three-volume study *Türkiye'de Siyasal Kültürün Resmî Kaynakları* (The official sources of political culture in Turkey), published in Turkish (first editions 1991–92, second editions 1994); and Andrew Davison's *Secularism and Revivalism in Turkey: A Hermeneutic Reconsideration* (1998). Parla's first two volumes consist of extensive, critical textual analyses of Atatürk's *Nutuk* (Great speech, 1927) and other collected statements. They are the first of their kind in the Turkish or anglophone social science literature. The third volume is a documentary analysis and explication of Kemalism's institutional documents, of which Atatürk was the primary architect, during the single-party period of 1923–47. Davison's book is an argument for hermeneutic (or interpretive), comparative inquiry in the study of secular-modern politics. It contains two substantive chapters on secular thought and laicist practice in Turkey. The present work combines elements from all of these works and extends the analysis beyond them.

NOTE ON TRANSLATED MATERIALS AND CITATION STYLE

The authors have translated all of the originally Turkish materials used and analyzed in this text. The title translations are the authors' as well. Citations to the sequentially numbered, three-volume edition of Mustafa Kemal Atatürk's *Nutuk* (Great speech) include the name Atatürk, the year of publication (1960, 1962, or 1963), and the page number. Official party programs are listed in the second part of the works cited section and are cited in text by the abbreviation for the Republican People's Party (RPP), the year of the program, and the section, article, or paragraph number. Citations for quoted materials from the six-volume collection *Atatürk'ün Söylev ve Demeçleri* (Atatürk's public addresses and statements) include the abbreviation *SD*, the volume number, the date of the original address or speech, and the page number of each translated passage. A full list of these quoted materials may be found in the third part of the works cited section, where the volumes are listed sequentially.

CORPORATIST IDEOLOGY IN
KEMALIST
TURKEY

1

INTRODUCTION

This study offers what we think is a long overdue, detailed account of the corporatist ideological content of Kemalism based on an interpretive study of the primary sources and original texts. As such, we think it contributes to two general areas of political inquiry: studies of contemporary Turkish politics and political history, and modern political ideological analyses of corporatism and secularism. In this chapter, we describe these contexts for this study. We begin by providing an account of how the ideological content of Kemalism is commonly interpreted within both anglophone and Turkish milieus and conclude by discussing both the importance of making Kemalism's corporatist and "secularist" dimensions the subject of serious attention in modern ideological analysis.

KEMALISM AND MODERN TURKISH STUDIES

Studies of contemporary Turkish politics display an arresting lack of interpretive interest in systematically and comparatively analyzing Kemalism's constituent ideological content, even as it is hailed as the preeminent modernizing ideology for a Muslim political context. Too often, this content is characterized in terms of Kemalism's famous six "arrows"—nationalism, republicanism, populism, laicism, transformationism, and statism—or in terms of its self-representations, such as with the words *modern, westernizing,* and *secular.* Used as substitutes for analysis, these terms oversimplify rather than clarify the substantive character and content of the ideology and the specific meanings that each of these concepts has within that framework. Important distinctions within nationalism, fundamental questions concerning Kemalism's specific understanding of republicanism or populism, and so on are left underconsidered.

The discernable tendency to employ Kemalism's selective, self-representations such as *modern, Western,* and *secular* as substitutes for ideological analysis pervades the literature, whether the portrayal appears to endorse those qualities or to criticize them. Indeed, the unanimity concerning Kemalism's secular, modernizing character is noteworthy.

Some studies, for example, depict Kemalism as a successful, westernizing, and modernizing ideology in part out of a basic agreement with its rightness in the Turkish context. They see Kemalism as essentially democratizing. This view has come to be called a "tutelary democratic" view, on which we elaborate in the next section. One of its variations even suggests that Kemalism, owing to its commitment to modernity, rationalism, and enlightenment, is actually nonideological. According to this view, "ideology" is illusion, whereas Kemalism reflects truth. Kemalism is seen accordingly as having brought an end to rule by Ottoman-Islamic illusion and ushered in rule "for and of" the people characteristic of modern, republican nation-states. This is truth, it is said, and thus Kemalism provides general guidelines for Turkish modernity—the six arrows—but not a rigid ideology. As we show, Mustafa Kemal contributed to this view when he declared to have based his decisions on worldly necessity, not on abstract theoretical guidelines. But the acceptance of Kemalism's "modern," "westernizing," and "secular" self-representation in accounts of its ideological content may be found in literature that is highly critical of Kemalism as well, wherein Kemalism is seen as inappropriate to the Turkish context. In various versions of this account, Kemalism is seen as imposing a set of strict, militantly secular and westernizing practices on a Muslim context. As such, it can hardly be considered to represent the people or their interests. In other words, either out of essential approval or out of essential disapproval, discussion over the ideological content of Kemalism most often remains at the level of large abstract categories such as "secular," "modern," "Western," and "authoritarian," which, in our judgment, obscure rather than clarify its ideological content. Let us take a close look at these common views.

THE TUTELARY DEMOCRATIC THESIS

For those who have interpreted Kemalism with approval, the usual estimation of Kemalism suggests that Atatürk was a realistic, pragmatic leader whose project of "tutelary democracy" contained only so much ideology—if any at all—as was necessary to bring Turkey out of the traditional slumber characteristic of the Ottoman Imperial-Islamic past and to make it into a modern, emancipated nation with secular, democratic, egalitarian foundations. Turkey's most renowned interpreters in both the anglophone and Turkish settings over the past half-century have described the goals of Atatürk, the "Kemalist Revolution," and Kemalism itself in essentially these terms. The concepts of various "tutelary democratic" accounts shift, but the idea of Atatürk as possessing a democratic intention and of Kemalism as a revolutionary-democratic ideology remains almost always the same.

In *The Emergence of Modern Turkey,* for example, the renowned historian Bernard Lewis describes the "Kemalist Revolution" as having "brought new life and hope to the Turkish people, restored their energies and self-respect, and set them firmly on the road *not only to independence, but to that rarer and more precious thing that is freedom*" (1961, 293, emphasis added)."[1] Political analyst Dankwart Rustow, equally renowned within twentieth-century studies of political development and modernization, describes Kemal himself as having "superseded the decadent elements of the Ottoman tradition and . . . propelled the Turkish nation from half-hearted into wholehearted Westernization and modernization" (1984, 351). In his view, "Atatürk's Revolution" contained some "distinctly democratic" elements: "Using every resource of communication and social mobilization to rally his countrymen and women to a desperate national defense, he established in the nascent Republic the principles of *government for the people and of the people,* and solidly prepared the ground for the subsequent phase *of government by the people*" (354, emphasis added). These are just two prominent examples from the literature, but they represent the common account of two of the most influential interpreters of modern Turkish history in the English-speaking world. (What we are mentioning is only illustrative, not exhaustive, given how large and profuse the mainstream is.) The main representatives of the orthodoxy in social science literature in Turkish are Tarık Zafer Tunaya and Suna Kili.[2] They, along with generations of interpreters, have described Kemalism as the "the birth of humanism" and "enlightenment" in Turkey, associating it with the "belief" in and the "hope" for "rational democracy."[3]

---

1. Lewis's book gathered material with similar emphases concerning the character of Kemalism that he had published throughout the 1950s. See Davison 1998, 138, 178, and 185, for further discussion.

2. See especially Kili 1969 and Tunaya 2002.

3. See especially Kili 1984a, 1984b, and 1996; Kışlalı 1996; Köker 1990; and Heper 2000, 71–72.

In the tutelary democratic accounts of Kemalism, both the cult of the hero status that sprung up around Kemal and the authoritarian measures taken by his regime are downplayed as having less to do with Kemal's personal ambition or with Kemalism's essential antidemocratic content than with the needs of the people in a heavily traditional context. Kemalism's early authoritarian elements were "tutelary" democratic—meaning, democratizing measures undertaken by a trustful and trustworthy guardian, a great leader prepared to set and capable of setting an extraordinary example in order to lay the foundations for democratic practice.

Mustafa Kemal is thus said to have been a "reluctant" charismatic leader, interested less in self-promotion than in creating a modern state based on law and respectful, competitive politics. In the anglophone literature, Lewis set the theme in *The Emergence of Modern Turkey,* saying that even though Kemal's contemporaries often called him a dictator, "he yet showed respect for decency and legality, for human and political standards" (1961, 290). Lewis asserts that Kemal "was not a revolutionary junior officer seizing power by coup d'etat"—a figure like Gamal Abdul Nasser of Egypt, who, at the time Lewis was writing, seemed (to Lewis) to personify illegitimate charismatic appeal—"but [was] a general and a pasha, taking control by gradual, *almost reluctant* steps in a moment of profound national crisis" (291, emphasis added). Similarly, Rustow describes Kemal as having "received, in his own day, some exaggerated adulation" and notes how "after his death was often referred to in worshipful phrases such as 'Our Dear Father,' or 'Eternal Chief' " (1984, 352). "Yet," Rustow writes, Kemal was a man of "personal modesty," "an organization man [who was] thrown into a charismatic situation" (1970, 212). Among his "historical achievements" can be counted "a recognition of the essential need for *broad and uncoerced support from below*" (1984, 350, emphasis added). Again, the idea is that in the early days of forming the republic Kemalism made "major decisive steps" toward "social and political liberation" (Lewis 1998, 134).

Any absolutist and authoritarian tendencies, in this view, are said to have been necessary to the tutelary requirements of the democratic vision. Democratic intent therefore is found in the short-lived experiments with opposition parties in 1924 and 1930, during the single-party period (1923–47).[4] That Mustafa

4. The two parties founded during these experiments were the Progressive Republican Party (PRP, Terakkiperver Cumhuriyet Fırkası, founded November 17, 1924) and the Free Republican Party (FRP, Serbest Cumhuriyet Fırkası, founded August 12, 1930). Less than nineteen months

Kemal permitted limited party competition is more important, in this account, than its abandonment, for the experiments showed Kemal's willingness to expand the arena of decision making. Democratic intent is also found by most of Kemal's and Kemalism's interpreters in what is known—incorrectly, we argue—as the movement's "secularism." By "separating" religion from politics and the state, "the Kemalists created," as Ergun Özbudun has put it, "at least a precondition for liberal democracy" (1988, 13–14). Such accounts reject any essentially ideologically rightist character in Kemalism, considering its oppressive content as tutelary: that is, as "purely pragmatic and temporary," in Özbudun's words, not "ideological" (1988, 12).

These important political theoretical categories—such as liberal democracy, secularism, pragmatism—are, from our point of view, too broadly cast over a more complex array of ideas and ideological commitments that defy, or, in some cases, only narrowly support, their application. Some of the descriptions in the literature on Kemalism's political thrust seem to depend, moreover, on global political circumstances, as Lewis's remark about Kemal being a pasha, not "some revolutionary junior officer," implies. We do not mean to insinuate that research on Turkish politics has been entirely politicized, but we do wish to point out how Kemalism's "democratic intentions" have been evaluated as such in relation to what have been taken as ideologically undesirable alternatives over the past century or so.

KEMALISM AS SECULAR, MODERN, AND RATIONAL: FOR AND AGAINST

In the early and mid-twentieth century, Kemalism was *not* Bolshevism or fascism, so it was frequently described in terms of liberalism and democracy (Lewis 1961, 291). Hans Kohn, for example, a renowned early theorist of modern nationalism, suggested in the early 1930s that the Republican People's Party (RPP, Cumhuriyet

---

after its founding, the former was charged with abetting "obscurantist reactionarism" (*irtica*) by the Independence Tribunals established during the Kurdish rebellion of 1925 and was dissolved (along with other forms of opposition, including media). In 1926, after a discovery of a plot on Mustafa Kemal's life (June 15, 1926), leaders of the PRP were put on trial. Some were incarcerated; seven were executed. The FRP leadership dissolved its party only four months after its founding in 1930, after being accused of treason for contesting the tightly controlled elections that year.

Halk Fırkası/Partisi) was "imbued with the spirit of secularism and liberalism which is making such headway today in all the countries of the East" (1933, 154–55). Similarly, since the Iranian revolution in 1979, Kemalism has been described as the "polar opposite" (Esposito 2000, 2) of theocratic politics. This is an extremely widely held belief in Middle East and international studies, one held both approvingly and disapprovingly. Lewis, for example, has approvingly described the "Kemalist secular democracy" as the binary alternative to Khomeinist Islamism: "Of the many movements and seizures of power that have claimed the name revolution in the Middle East in the twentieth century, two were of particular importance: the Kemalist revolution in Turkey and the Khomeinist Revolution in Iran, the one *seeking to establish a secular democracy,* the other an Islamic theocracy" (2000, 257, emphasis added).[5] Note the connection between Kemalism, secularism, and democracy.

Without defending Khomeinist theopolitics, many interpreters have nonetheless questioned Kemalism's democratic bases in part because of its "secularism." They argue that Kemalism's blows against the symbols and institutions of Islam—abolishing the caliphate; eliminating Islamic law; closing Islamic courts, schools, and local institutional spaces; and outlawing Sufi orders—demonstrate its antireligious excess, its "strict," "militant," or "authoritarian" secularism, not democracy. Kemalism, on this view, is neither "pluralist" nor "accommodating."[6] Nor is it truly secular because "true secularism" would guarantee "religious freedom," whereas Kemalism prohibits it. Culturally conservative political movements in Turkey have made this case for "true secularism"—against Kemalist authoritarian "secularism"—since the earliest days of the republic.[7]

The disapproval of Kemalism's "antireligious" militancy is quite prominent in the anglophone literature on Turkey. For example, John Esposito, a scholar of

5. The promotion of Kemalism as a model for progress and development in Muslim political milieus has been extensive throughout the century. At the time of this writing, it has gained even greater steam as a model for the reconstruction of the entire Middle East in the context of the global "war on terrorism." See Kongar 2001, 100–103, and the interview with James Woolsey, former director of the U.S. Central Intelligence Agency, entitled "Ortadoğu'ya Atatürk modeli" (The Atatürk model for the Middle East). Woolsey states that President George W. Bush is, "ideologically speaking, a follower of George Washington and Kemal Atatürk" ("Ortadoğu'ya Atatürk" 2003, 22). See also interviews with prominent establishment figures in Ozankay 2000.

6. See, for example, Göle 1996.

7. For the range of interpretations applied to Kemalist laicism, see Davison 1998.

Islam and Islamist movements, speaks matter-of-factly about Atatürk's "principle of secularism" and his "legacy" of a "strong secular state," noting that "Atatürk created and shaped modern Turkey as a secular state, the only totally secular state in the Middle East" (2000, 4–6). To this extent, Esposito's account registers partial agreement with Lewis, but, unlike Lewis, Esposito does not find Kemalism's "secular" and "modern" identity very democratic. He calls it "secular fundamentalism." "Secularism is not simply the separation of religion and politics," he asserts, "but, as past and current history demonstrate, an antireligious and anticlerical belief" (9).

We argue that these depictions of Kemalism—as either secular or too secular, modern or too modern, liberal democratic or not liberal and pluralist enough—are not entirely inconsistent with some of Kemalism's own self-representations, but they do little to advance understanding of its core political ideological content. But first another dominant interpretation must be briefly outlined, that which sees Kemalism as lacking ideology altogether.

KEMALISM AS NONIDEOLOGICAL

When analyses of Kemalism's ideological content are not either explicitly or implicitly assigning democratic intent to it, they sometimes emphasize its pragmatic, nearly nonideological quality. In such accounts, the six arrows of Kemalism are conceptualized as loose prescriptions for the general direction of Turkish development; they are not rigid and specific ideological guidelines for exact and precise action. There is a "big tent"—and hence democratic—element to Kemalism, it is argued, one that has made possible several particular political programs, as evidenced by the fact that movements from both the so-called left and right, within the state and outside of it, claim that they are the rightful heirs of Kemal's mantle. From this perspective, Kemalism has been judged to be either a very flexible, hegemonic ideology or an ideology that is too flexible to be considered ideological at all.[8] According to Erik Zürcher, it is the latter. "As an ideology," he writes, Kemalism "lack[s] coherence." It is "best seen as a set of attitudes and opinions which were never rooted in any detail" (1993, 189).

The claim that Kemalism is nonideological rests additionally on the view that

8. See *Kemalizm,* the second volume of the İletişim Publishers series entitled *Political Theory in Modern Turkey* (İnsel 2001) for various applications of Kemalism across the political spectrum.

Kemalism prescribes science and circumstance-based reasoning as the "guides for life," in the words of the famous Kemalist maxim, rather than religious or other forms of a priori ideational thinking. Ergun Özbudun and Ali Kazancıgil write, "If it is possible to reduce Kemalism to a single dimension, it would not be wrong to single out rationalism, since it was a rationalist and positivist mentality that underlined all of Atatürk's speeches, thought, actions, and reforms" (1981, 4). "The new individual whom the Republican regime wanted *to bring out*," Kemal Karpat writes, "was a rationalist, antitraditional, anticlerical person, approaching all matters intellectually and objectively" (1959, 53, emphasis added). The revolution's "dependence on secular and positive thought" made it a national, "scientific and rationalistic" revolution, avers Suna Kili (1984b, 100–101). From this perspective, Kemalism offers a program of modern, realistic, and pragmatic worldly governance for Turkey, not "ideology." Indeed, countless interpreters in both social scientific and policymaking circles have said that Mustafa Kemal Atatürk offered precisely the mentality required for modern governance. Donald Webster declared in the 1930s that Mustafa Kemal was the "pragmatic" "alchemist" for the catalytic movement of Turkey from its "traditional" past to a "democratic," "modern" age (1939, 240 ff.). And although recent commentators have evaluated Kemalism's position on religion or ethnonational ideology with some critical attention, Atatürk's reputation as a pragmatic, modernizing leader committed to scientific reasoning above all else remains relatively stable. Indeed, for those who think that Kemalism is antireligious or ignores the role that local identities more generally play in political life, or both, the regime's commitment to positivist rationality is at the heart of the problem. In this work, we do not suggest that Kemalism lacks a commitment to positivism, only that its place within the ideological framework has been misstated or overstated.

Kemalism's alleged core scientific pragmatism is a major reason why, in the estimation of countless interpreters of the Turkish founding, political ideology was much less an effective force than Atatürk's tutelary democratic "realism." Those who speak of Atatürk's pragmatic realism suggest that if there was any relation between ideas and action, the latter shaped the former, not the reverse. "Kemalist principles grew out of action and in response to concrete needs and situations," Özbudun succinctly asserts (2000, 21). Kemalism as an ideology, that is, grew out of its "worldly focus," not from some abstract conceptions of how one ought to act, rule, or lead. Similarly, Daniel Lerner and Richard Robinson suggest that for the Kemalist founders of Turkey, "each policy and program was evaluated by what the ruling elite conceived to be the public welfare, not according to some *a priori* religious doctrine or political ideology" (1960, 24). This evaluation not only reiterates the dominant interpretation of Kemalism, but also registers basic agreement with what the dominant interpretation sees as Kemalism's nonideological path to democratic modernity. In their widely studied book on political development in the Middle East, James Bill and Robert Springborg similarly posit that "Atatürk was above all a realist. He understood power and had an unusual ability to bridge the gap between ideal and reality" (2000, 140). He "broke many of the traditional interpersonal patterns that had dominated Ottoman patrimonial rule," and the revolution that he led "stands as a revolution of modernization and a movement of substantial political development" (141). Such versions of the tutelary democratic thesis are consistently repeated and recycled in popular accounts. Atatürk's main anglophone biographers, Patrick Kinross and Andrew Mango, stress everything from Kemal's nonideological pragmatism to his democratic universalism. Kinross's account sees Kemal as a "a realist, who thought not in terms of gestures, but of actions," who "infused [the Turkish people] with a belief in the values of Western democracy" (1964, 504). Mango describes Kemal as "a democrat in theory" who "left behind him the structure of democracy, not of dictatorship" (1999, 536, 534). "He worshiped reason. . . . [H]is vision was humanist and universalist" (536).

As our study of the vision, formulation, purpose, and politics of Kemalism shows, we think that all of these accounts of Kemalism exhibit problems of what we call conceptual imprecision. Kemalism is not nonideological, liberal, socialist, and democratic, nor is it philosophically universalist, and its perceived commitment to rationalism and pragmatism needs to be reevaluated. Kemalism is, rather, a specific variant of rightist, corporatist ideology committed to a view of society, reason, and action that bears only slight resemblance to its rationalist and pragmatic reputation. Accounts of Kemalism that rely on the six arrows or on the oversimplified modern, secular, positivist, and pragmatic self-representations of Kemalism fail to capture adequately the explicit and implicit nonsecular and antidemocratic aims, interests, intentions, and presuppositions of the Kemalist corporatist ideological frame and of the politics constituted by it. These politics include the transformations *(inkılâplar),* as Atatürk called them, in political, legal, social, and cultural affairs implemented during the single-party period, as well as ongoing emplacements of the Kemalist ideology within the constitutional and legal structures of the state (e.g., the penal code, Labor Law, Law on Higher Education, and so on). The claims that Atatürk was a secular and modernizing tutelary democrat or authoritarian westernizer thus suffer, we argue, from a failure to consider and study the original expressions and contemporary ideological structure of Kemalism.

The interpretation of Kemalism as nonideological, or "above" ideology, is perhaps the most difficult to contest, not because it is more correct than the others, but because it is most enduring and, as we demonstrate in subsequent chapters, *most* incorrect. Such a claim constitutes a major defining element of Third Way ideologies: their practicality, their pragmatic opportunism, and their Bonapartist claim to an "above-class" status relative to the interests of particular classes or social groups. Third Way ideologies shield themselves from critical examination by claiming to represent the will of the whole. In the case of Kemalism, this self-protective ideological maneuver functions to mask the ideology inherent in its particular account of the nation, of the nation's goals and objectives, and of the political character of the Kemalist state. Kemalism's "nonideological" self-representation thus serves to insulate it from critical consideration of its authoritarian corporatist ideological core. One of the analytically troubling ironies of the history of Kemalism is that it is seen, on the one hand, as an "enlightenment" program ostensibly committed to ongoing self-scrutiny in relation to worldly experience and, on the other, as a project that should eternally stand above criticism because it embodies the truth. We view its claim to enlightenment status as a component of its ideological character, not a compelling description of it.

Implicit, then, in our examination of the ideological content of Kemalism is our assumption that Kemalist principles and Kemalism, as articulated and ratified primarily by Mustafa Kemal, constitute in and of themselves coherent objects for ideological analysis. In making this assumption, we are *not* suggesting, however, that Kemalism is monolithic, unique, original, or static. All ideologies contain internal differentiations and tensions, as well as nuances and ambivalences, and all ideologies emerge out of and develop within dynamic historical contexts. In this sense, historical and sociological analysis into the roots and trends of any ideology often proves as enlightening as interpretations of founding texts. Such indeed is the case with Kemalism. It contains a spectrum of trends and possibilities, populist romantics as well as bureaucratic conservatives, dangerous racists and less dangerous nationalists, greater and lesser laicists, and so on. Each trend expresses an emphasis on one or another element of Kemalist ideology. In addition,

Kemalism's historical sources reach significantly into the second constitutional period of the late Ottoman Empire and into nationalist trends forming both there and in Europe (Mardin 1983). Prefascistic republican and what Ernst Nolte (1965) calls the "critical liberal" (anti-French Revolution) trends in France are, for example, very important to the development of Kemalism.

In identifying and elucidating Kemalism's less well-known corporatist tendencies, therefore, we are not saying that these ideological emphases are unique or peculiar to Turkey. Nor are we suggesting that all Kemalists always subscribe to Kemal's particular formulations all of the time, although, given Kemalism's ongoing hegemony that we describe later, we are very hesitant to understate the depth of its influence in the form we interpret here. What we are saying is that when the Kemalists captured power, they implemented a view of the organization of power that they—again, especially Mustafa Kemal, but also those who joined in and promoted Kemalism—*intended* to be understood and appreciated (greatly, actually) as Kemalism and that the ideological character of this view is still in need of more analysis. Therefore, we concentrate our efforts here on beginning what has yet in our judgment to be adequately done: examining the original expressions of Kemalism that are constitutive of the politics associated with it and accounting for what was actually said, with what purposes, and with what significance to the actors themselves. These purposes capture the essence of our understanding of the interpretive approach to ideological analysis, and they allow us to demonstrate Kemalism's ideological content.

The primary texts for this project include: Mustafa Kemal Atatürk's *Nutuk* (Great speech) of October 15–20, 1927 (36.5 hours in length) and his *Söylev ve Demeçleri* (Public addresses and statements) covering his entire political career; the official party programs and documents of Atatürk's RPP through 1945; and explications of the goals expressed in these statements by high-ranking party officials and ideologues. In all, these texts comprise the most important, most representative, and most authoritative public expressions of Kemalism's ideological content.

KEMALISM AND MODERN IDEOLOGY

This study also aims to contribute to studies in comparative political ideologies and political practice. There are two dimensions to this contribution. Because Kemalism is often described in the residual, catch-all terms of democracy and secularism, it is clear that a serious shortcoming of the various existing accounts lies in the lack of familiarity with the corporatist lexicon. This deficiency points to a broader problem in studies of political ideology. Too often these studies are pitched solely at the level of the great "isms," such as liberalism, communism, socialism, conservatism, fascism, and religious revivalism, ignoring the existence and import of corporatist ideological possibilities in part because corporatism is frequently seen as nonideological relative to the other "isms." Corporatism has been understood in political science mainly as an alternative to pluralist and Marxist models of interest representation, institutional decision-making processes, and regime types, and most often in the context of Latin American political studies,[9] not as a more general ideological force in modern politics. Like the other main "isms," however, corporatism, at the most general level, posits a distinct interpretation and model of political, economic, and social action and of relationships under conditions of advanced or developing capitalism. Moreover, like the others, it consists of several variants. The two main species are solidaristic corporatism and fascistic corporatism—as distinct from the societal and state corporatism that are prevalent in the comparative literature on interest representation. (Equating corporatism with fascism, as some do, obscures alternative corporatist articulations, although equating societal corporatism with neoliberalism is not analytically sufficient to distinguish corporatism and liberalism either.)

Corporatism's distinction lies in its rejection of the categories of individual, class, and tradition as the core analytical categories of its political vision, though each may play some role within different corporatist articulations. Corporatist formulations derive models of society and forms of political and economic organization from "occupational groups," professional organizations, or corporations. These groupings compose the fundamental building blocks of its political vision. Thus, for example, different forms of corporatism—solidarist and fascist alike—reject the excessive individualism of liberalism and the divisiveness of class conflict. They do not, however, reject capitalism or even Marx's critique of it. In fact, corporatism appropriates Marx's analysis of alienation to its own logic by introducing the moral code of corporations as palliative settings within which the alienated individual can find social and moral refuge as well as political or

---

9. See, for example, Schmitter 1974; Stepan 1978, 2001; and Wiarda 1997. For such institutional discussions in the context of Middle East politics, see Richards and Waterbury 1996, and, in the Turkish context, Bianchi 1984.

economic representation or both. Subspecies of corporatism evince various categories, but what mainly distinguishes these subspecies is their interpretation of the relationship between the individual, society, and the state. Solidaristic corporatism, as we elaborate in chapter 2, conceives of corporations as buffers between the individual and the state, whereas fascistic corporatism assimilates all within the metaphysical corporatist state, denying all distinctions between state and society.

In Turkey, corporatism as an ideological phenomenon came via appropriations of solidaristic corporatism in Durkheimian positivism by the Young Turk ideologue Ziya Gökalp (1876–1924) (Parla 1985). It then underwent some changes within the ideological frame of the Kemalists, who maintained aspects of the solidaristic core articulated by Gökalp, but who also tinkered in part with certain protofascistic corporatist tendencies of the interwar period. The Kemalists jettisoned other, more pluralistic dimensions of Gökalp's thought in the process. Our discussion here focuses initially on bringing out the corporatist identity and nuances of Kemalism as the actors themselves articulated it. We also relate this identity to the broader category of corporatism in a conscious effort to contribute to studies of corporatism as a contemporary ideology constitutive of institutional and other praxiological dimensions of politics.

The second area of political ideological analysis to which our work aims to contribute is studies of secularism. As with the tendency to misconceptualize Kemalism in the limited vocabulary of the great "isms," studies of Kemalist laicism too often equate it analytically with "secularism," rather than consider alternative and more fitting analytical options. This is a problem to be found more generally in studies of "nontheocratic" understandings of the relationship between power and religion. That is, too often all nontheocratic options are conceptualized as "secular," as if nontheocratic governance is understood and practiced always and everywhere the same—say, in the "secular" state in India, the "secular" state in the United States, or the "secular" state in Turkey. As a growing body of recent literature forcefully demonstrates, this general classification obfuscates important differences between various specific so-called secular doctrines and forms of governance.[10] This tendency is aggravated further by a habit of seeing secularism more as a subcomponent of liberal democratic ideol-

10. For additional conceptual background in this context, see Davison 1998 and 2003, Parla and Davison forthcoming. For conceptual discussions outside the Turkish context, see essays by

ogy, as in the various accounts of Kemalism, than either as a subject of rigorous analytical attention in itself or as worthy of being interpreted variously within different ideologies.

Our study of what is understood as Kemalism's "secularism" suggests that the absence of rigorous attention to various analytical possibilities within the range of nontheocratic options has hindered the interpretation of Kemalism's understanding of the relationship between the state and Islam, of Islam itself, and of various secularizing possibilities in both contemporary Turkish politics and modern ideological discourse. The Kemalists described their project using the French word *laicisme,* which is translated into Turkish as *laiklik* and into English as *laicism.* Like secularism, laicism is one tradition and set of practices, itself with varying forms, subsumable within the broad category of nontheocratic modes of political, economic, and social organization. We do not equate laicism with secularism, although there are some areas of shared meaning and practice. Kemalist laicism is most often described throughout the literature as "secularism," leaving the impressions that Kemalist laicism achieves everything from a radical separation between state and tradition to the privatization or elimination of religion in the conscience. As we argue, Kemalist laicism is at odds with these ideals in both concept and practice. Kemalism is a partly anticlerical and even limited form of laicism that posits neither a thorough separation between religious institutions and the state nor the privatization of religion characteristic of liberalism. It contrasts rather obviously with alternative and more thorough secular practices, be they privatist, atheist, or antitheist. Thus, equating laicism with secularism entails, at least potentially, some conceptual confusion. In our discussion of Kemalist laicism, as in our discussion of Kemalist corporatism, we make a conscious effort to relate specific dimensions of Kemalism's laicism to the broader problematic of secular political thought and practice.

Strongly undergirding our study is the premise that the meanings of politics expressed in political ideologies are substantially constitutive of political action, practice, relations, and institutions. *Constitute* here means to make these elements of political life partly what they are. We take the interpretive analytical view that the language of politics is not simply instrumental, that it is not only used for purposes of mobilization and legitimation. It is also something that constitutes the

Rajeev Bhargava, Charles Taylor, Jean Bauberot, and Michael Sandel, in Bhargava 1998; Chadwick 1975; Connolly 1999; Mitchell 2000; and Stepan 2001, 245.

symbolic identity of political actions, relations, practices, and institutions. In this regard, the language of political life makes these elements of politics mean some things and not others. It defines areas for understanding and relating to political life by constituting it symbolically with some meanings and not others.[11] As such, we think that an account of the meanings constitutive of political experience— along with other complex social and political forces—is indispensable to any adequate explanation of that experience. Therefore, within the specific case of Kemalist politics, only by adequately accounting for the constitutive concepts of Kemalism is it possible to understand it and to make sense out of the politics constituted by it in Turkey, both during the founding of the contemporary Turkish Republic and in many arenas of political life today.

11. On the "constitutive" relation between meaning and practice, see Davison 1998, especially chapter 2 and the interpretive literature discussed therein.

Corporatism in Kemalist Turkey

2

IDEOLOGY AND
CORPORATISM

In this chapter, we describe the kinds of questions concerning ideological analysis that our discussion of Kemalism seeks to answer, outline the understanding of ideology that we employ throughout the study, and delineate in detail the characteristics of corporatism's solidarist and fascistic versions.

PROBLEMS OF POLITICS, FORMULATION,
AND CONTEXTUALIZATION IN THE STUDY
OF MODERN POLITICAL IDEOLOGIES

The study of politics involves several kinds of analytical problems that, from one point of view, plague the study of modern political ideologies, but, from another, make it an intellectually and politically stimulating area of political inquiry. This is not the place for an exhaustive analysis of such problems, but several of them are relevant to understanding the place and significance of this study in the context of modern political ideologies.

One such problem concerns the determination of the substantive political implications entailed by different ideologies. We may call this the problem of politics. Is liberalism, for instance, a democratic ideology, as ideological liberals understand it to be, or is it, as ideological Marxists view it, a justification for rule by one class over another? Is conservatism under rapidly changing conditions oriented toward stability or toward change?

Far from being mere quibbles over terms, a consideration of such questions helps to reveal the precise, substantive visions of politics posited by alternative ideologies. Answering such questions allows students of ideology to explore in finer detail both the ideas contained within such ideologies and the kinds of political practices they shape.

A second familiar problem in ideological inquiry concerns the determination of the specific beliefs and commitments of the founding fathers of various ideologies, or the "innovating ideologists," as Quentin Skinner (1978) has called them. Did Marx subscribe to a determinist understanding of the course and flow of history? Or was it Engels? Was Rousseau a totalitarian or a democrat? We may call this second problem the problem of formulation and purpose: "formulation" because it concerns grasping the mode and context of the founding expressions of the ideology (in such texts as essays, pamphlets, books, speeches, letters, and interviews); and "purpose" because it also concerns investigating the intentions of the founding ideologues, the specific meanings that their expressions had in the context of the problems that they sought to address. The contemporary debate over whether or not John Locke's account of natural rights and the role of government in the *Second Treatise* is protocapitalist is a good example of a pursuit within the problem of formulation and purpose.[1] Dissatisfied by one account of original purpose or another, interpreters return to the original utterances, seeking to grasp their identity and significance by reconstructing different aspects of the original linguistic, personal, social, economic, and political contexts.[2]

A third problem in the study of modern political ideologies is that of relating the concepts and terms of the "great isms" to particular, often more conceptually complex, local expressions of them or their variants. We call this the problem of conceptual locality and precision. How, for example, are the terms of classical Burkean conservatism to be applied to American conservatism, or those of Marxism to Chinese communism? Answering such questions requires exploring the specific context of local ideological formulations and articulating a more compelling and more precise account of their terms. American conservatism, for example, sometimes combines classical theories about the role and function of government typical of early liberal theorists with a reverence for traditional values typical of Burkean conservatism. Various versions of Marxism emphasize particular aspects of the larger ideology in principle and in practice, but then evince remarkable differences under differing political and historical conditions.

1. See Dunn 1969, Goldie 1983, Macpherson 1962, Ryan 1965, and Tully 1980.
2. For the important intellectual background and argument over these issues, see Tully 1988.

An extension of this problem emerges when the terms of the "great isms" are applied to contexts where, from an interpretive view, neither the ideas nor the practices associated with such "isms" or categories effectively apply. In such cases, for example, a specific ideological context may be (mis)described as "liberal" even though the ideas and practices constitutive of its politics evince analytically conservative or fascistic tendencies. Where the problem of conceptual precision is concerned, it remains the task for analysts of ideology to clarify more precisely the ideological terms that best account for given local formulations. The point of departure for this work, for example, is that Kemalism has been described as liberal, secular, democratic, and modernist, but its constitutive conceptual frame suggests other ideological categories. Indeed, critical analytical scrutiny of many highly cherished ideologies across the political spectrum frequently reveals a more complex picture of those ideologies.

All of these problems of politics are interrelated. More conceptual precision regarding local ideologies and practices may generate a better understanding of their original formulations as well as the political visions to which they may be related at the more general ideological level. A more refined study of the formulation and purposes of ideologists often enhances our understanding of different political visions and specific interpretations. In general, a better understanding of the histories of various ideologies in specific contexts yields far greater understanding of the general conceptual landscape of modern ideological possibilities. We are able to get a larger, genealogical sense of what has happened, what may happen, and what might still happen within the fold of liberalism, socialism, fascism, and so on. It is with each of these problems in mind that we offer the present study of Kemalist corporatism. We seek to provide a more compelling and precise account of Kemalist corporatism and enhanced clarity about both its founder's purposes and its place within the more general arena of modern "isms."

IDEOLOGY

The concept of *ideology* has many meanings and is associated with many different kinds of research and analytical agendas in political and social inquiry. While a comprehensive analysis of the concept is far beyond the scope of this book, for the purpose of our study, we understand *ideology* to mean a set of beliefs about social life in general and about politics in particular that constitute, undergird, and shape political thought, action, relationships, institutions, and policy.[3]

The relationship between ideology and practice implied here is, of course, not always very simple. Ideology and practice may not match each other one to one. "Liberals" sometimes violate rights, "socialists" sometimes perpetuate inequality, "conservatives" sometimes accelerate sociopolitical change, "theopolitical revivalists" sometimes collaborate with atheists, and so on. In such cases where a one-to-one correspondence between ideology and practice does not obtain, there may be found a mediated or perhaps an indirect relationship between the two, or, alternatively, an explanation for the practice or action by the ideology. In the case of the former, the gap between ideology and practice may be explained as a result of some calculation by ideologues in the context of strategic political competition, or, in the second case, justifications may be located within the nuances and details of the ideology's conceptual possibilities. That is to say, an apparently odd relation between ideology and practice may be resolved by looking more deeply into the range of interpretive possibilities within the political actor's ideological frame. Liberals, for example, may support government restrictions or violations of liberty (e.g., restrictions on smoking or on free and unfettered movement across borders) because liberalism legitimizes in principle the use of governmental power to "protect rights" (e.g., "life") and the general welfare, even liberty itself. Socialists may legitimize unequal patterns of power as necessary to promote rapid revolutionary change. Conservatives may carry out such change in order to restore prominent traditions that have been trodden over. So the existence of a situation whereby the practice ostensibly differs from the ideological intention is not reason for considering ideology unimportant. Ideology may be there as a constitutive, influential, undergirding ideological component of the situation and therefore must be analyzed.

In situations in which ideology does not appear to materialize in action at all—the first case given earlier, in which it appears as a weapon for competitive political struggle and strategic advantage—ideology itself is a presumption of intent or intended action, whether or not the intent is brought to a conclusion. And in such cases, the action cannot be adequately understood without accounting for the presumed intent. ("Unintended" actions, in fact, are understandable as such only by reference to some intent.) At minimum, then, the ideology provides the

3. For further discussion, see Ingersoll, Matthews, and Davison 2001.

general parameters within which political action and practice take place and are to be understood. It is a component of political experience even when the constitutive conceptual bases are largely strategic. At maximum, it may indeed comprise those bases and, in conjunction with other factors, explain why some actions or policies (and not others) have been taken, why some coalitions or institutions (and not others) have been built, and so on.

Beyond the relation between ideology and practice in general, we understand ideologies to be generated and perpetuated by individuals, acting either in concert or alone, who have some stake in constituting understandings about the political world and options available within it. The articulation of certain ideologies occurs when interested individuals enter into political discourse in order to fashion a novel view of the political world and the goals of human beings within it. The nature of the interest may vary according to ideology and context. What is significant at a general level is that ideologies offer accounts of existing social and political concepts and practices, as well as the ends to which politics should be directed. Ideologues may be variously located in the spheres of social life: they are not necessarily the economic or political elite. They may be members of a particular economic class, or they may be members of an autonomous or relatively autonomous intelligentsia, as was partly the case with Kemalism. As ideologues, they are engaged in an attempt to articulate new or to perpetuate old explanations of the world and justifications for particular kinds of political action in it.

These two components—explanation and justification—are central to all ideologies and link ideology with the idea of legitimacy. Ideologies seek both to make sense out of the world and to offer a rationale for living and acting in it. As such, they offer visions of legitimate thought and practice in the public world. These visions claim to be true in both conceptual and practical terms.

At the conceptual level, ideologies offer a "correct" or "right" way of understanding the political world. For example, some ideologies offer different views of capitalism. The normatively desired view one finds in certain forms of individualist liberal thought is at odds with the normatively critical view one finds in certain forms of Marxian thought. The differences between these views have radically profound implications for understanding much of political life in our time, from wars of national liberation against imperialist regimes to the structural readjustment polices of the International Monetary Fund. Views about the "rightness" or legitimacy of capitalism are embedded within various ideological frameworks.

At the practical level, ideologies are linked with legitimation because they offer guidelines for rightful action in social and political life. Ideological concepts and beliefs shape political action. The great majority of political action is therefore ideologically informed: it is action undertaken with an understanding of what constitutes good action and what constitutes bad action, desirable and undesirable objectives, worthy and unworthy plans, and so on. A question about action, such as whether a national flag should be flown or burned, for example, will be answered differently by different ideologies. Not all people answer this or other politically significant questions consciously, but whatever the answer and whatever the action, the action most often has ideologically discernable elements. All ideologies offer, in this sense, some prescription for legitimate and illegitimate action—and in this context, "prescribed action" is not limited only to radical or revolutionary action but may include action either against or in defense of an existing order, and that is either implicit or explicit. Liberalism does not, for example, explicitly dictate that persons should not think of society in terms of class divisions. It offers a view of society as composed of free individuals, a view that implicitly deemphasizes and in most cases *rules out* class-based concepts as desirable or necessary. Ideologies, in their explanatory and justificatory functions, thus offer views of both what is right and what is wrong, conceptually as well as practically.

The concept of *ideology* posited here does not require conscious understanding of a specific ideology among those whose political lives are constituted by it. A broad range of ideological expression characterizes the general public (those not necessarily attentive to matters of ideological formation). It is commonly the case that only the makers of ideologies—ideologues—and those who study them professionally are fully conscious of the concepts and implications of a particular ideology, although policymakers, politicians, activists, and pamphleteers may also attain a degree of conscious awareness. For such persons, ideologies normally constitute conscious blueprints for action. For many persons, however, ideologies exist only as loosely stated philosophies of life. One task in the analysis of ideology, therefore, is to clarify sociologically dominant ideological presuppositions and understandings of politics in the general public—however inchoate or partially expressed. This task may be carried out by analyzing an ideology's most refined articulations in the public expressions of the ideologues themselves. Analysts of ideology must therefore provide compelling accounts of the ideology's central logic—the concepts, meanings, and understandings that constitute it as it is articulated for public consumption and that distinguish it from other ideologies.

A perplexing question for all students of ideology concerns the relationship between the study of ideology and ideology itself. Is it possible to study ideologies without prejudice, in a nonideological way? We do not think that an absolutely objective viewpoint can be adopted in the study of ideologies. Nonetheless, we think that the study of ideology can be nonideological or objective relative to its subject matter in the sense that ideological analysis may delineate the concepts and political visions of alternative ideologies and present them for comparison, both on their own terms and in relation to substantive political concerns of various kinds. Political ideology analysis therefore offers comparative descriptions of the central tenets of various ideologies, of various conceptions of society or the human being, and of the role and function of leadership and government. It also enables evaluation of the particular visions in relation to substantive concerns, such as democracy or the preservation of traditions. Both analytical goals require analysts of ideology to make judgments and to suggest matters of emphases, but ideological analysis, if carried out with a sensitivity to the existence of the alternative and various interpretations, can offer comparatively informed explanations of a given ideology and its substantive implications. This, at least, is our central goal with regard to Kemalism: we delineate its central conceptual core and emphases, and we scrutinize it in relation to the concerns of democratic theory. Thus, we consider the study of ideology to operate on a slightly higher level than that of ideology itself, but we also maintain that some ideologies offer more democratic accounts and prescriptions than do others. We are quite aware that our study of Kemalism is driven not only by the analytical goal of situating Kemalism within a corporatist frame rather than the liberal and socialist frames, but also by an interest in analyzing the merits of the tutelary democratic thesis about Kemalism and thus in reinterpreting the relation between Kemalism and democracy, both at Turkey's founding and in the context of Kemalism's continued hegemonic status in Turkey today.

A THEORY OF CORPORATISM

Our purpose in this section is twofold: first, to delineate the conceptual contours of corporatist ideology as distinct from those "isms" it rejects, liberalism and Marxism; and second, to chart out the distinctions among several kinds of corporatism as well as the different capitalist and capitalizing contexts in which corporatism historically has been found.[4]

In his "Preface to the Second Edition" (1902) of *Division of Labor in Society* (1893), Emile Durkheim describes a society that is "aware of itself" as one that is organized into "occupational groups" or "corporations." Based on a conception of society and social organization that can be found in its essentials in Plato's *Republic*, Durkheim's concept of the "occupational group" was not new when he first proposed it. However, its appearance in the context of predominantly capitalist societies at the turn of the twentieth century marked a significant moment in the history of modern political thought. In the context of the analysis of modern ideologies, Durkheim's "Preface" articulates some themes central to corporatism, especially the solidaristic, nonfascistic variant one finds prevalent in capitalist and capitalizing societies throughout the twentieth century. Theorists of Turkish nationalism such as Ziya Gökalp at the turn of the century found these themes relevant to theorizing politics in the Turkish context. As such, the "Preface" may be considered the major manifesto of modern solidaristic corporatism in general and a central inspiration of modern Turkish political thought in particular. In it, Durkheim describes why corporate groups, acting in conjunction with the corporate state, are "destined" to play a fundamental role in creating order and morality in modern politics. It is useful to take a quick glimpse at the major themes in the "Preface" as an introduction to the finer details of a fairly complex corporatist political vision.

In formulating his concept, Durkheim analyzed what he saw as the "moral anomie" and "weakening" of "public morality" in modern capitalist societies, shaped increasingly by rampant individualistic norms, on the one hand, and by intensifying trends of functional specialization brought about by the division of labor, on the other.[5] He rejected the claim that the division of labor alone "can be held responsible" for the moral breakdown—the weakening of ties between members of society—and argued that the roots of such anomie lie not in society's failure to abolish that division, but rather in its failure to order institu-

---

4. These distinctions were originally introduced into the anglophone literature on Turkey in Parla 1985, which serves as the basis for this discussion.

5. By division of labor, he means basically the growth of distinguishable sectors of professional, industrial, and agricultural activities.

tional relations properly according to it. "For anomie to end," he wrote, "there must then exist, or be formed, a group which can constitute the system of rules actually needed."[6] Rather than seeing the capitalistic social-structural trends of dividing labor into huge, distinct sectors as threats to social equilibrium, we should see these trends as its basic, institutional foundations. Thus, the idea of structuring and regulating social relations by "corporate" or "occupational" groups came to Durkheim's mind: "An occupational activity can be efficaciously regulated only by a group intimate enough with it to know its functioning, feel all its needs, and be able to follow all their variations. The only one [group] that could answer all these conditions is the one formed by all the agents of the same industry, united and organized into a single body. This is what is called the corporation or occupational group."

For Durkheim, therefore, if anomie is to be overcome and public morality restored, members of society should be understood, for purposes of social and political organization, in terms of the occupational positions they fill. It is in those positions where they share their lifetime activities with others and where their needs from the perspective of the social whole are generated. If "all the agents of the same industry" are "united" and "organized" "into a single body," he maintained, social discord and fragmentation may be overcome. Corporations organized along the lines of the division of labor and not the "individual," therefore, should constitute the primary building blocks of any ethically sound vision and organization of modern political and social life.

Durkheim matched these proposals to transform society with others that would transform the role and function of the state. In place of the individualist, "hypertrophied state" that is "forced to oppress and contain" so-called free individuals, he envisioned a new kind of corporate state in which "the national corporations" would constitute "the elementary divisions." Existing states, he complained, are "too remote from individuals; [their] relations too external." Individuals need to be connected socially, and the state, by providing both the larger institutional frame and rationalization for the corporate schema, should perform this function. It should establish institutions that actively mold individuals to be proper participants in social and political life as members of specific functional units of society. Thus, the corporate state ought to "penetrate deeply into the in-

6. All quotes from Emile Durkheim come from Durkheim 1933, 1–31.

dividual consciences and socialize them within." It ought to lay the groundwork for a dynamic cooperative arrangement between politics, corporations, and individuals. As we shall see, this vision admits of a variety of different emphases, which we examine later. For his part, Durkheim believed that the essence of the arrangement provides the basis for a more ethically robust social and political existence in modern "nations": "A nation can be maintained only if, between the State and the individual, there is intercalated a whole series of secondary groups near enough to the individuals to attract them strongly in their sphere of action and drag them, in this way, into the general torrent of social life."

More specifically, corporatism should be understood as a system of thought and action with three distinct referents or levels: first, a theory-ideology about a model of society and economy; second, a set of economic and class policies about actual procedures for conducting the representation of interests; and third, a particular form of political institutionalization and authoritative decision making. These levels are logically related, though they may not necessarily be so in practice.

Society and Economy

Corporatism's distinction lies in its view of society as an organic whole consisting of mutually interdependent and functionally complementary parts. The major units, the molecules of society, are the occupational groups. Corporatism, therefore, opposes the central categories of the liberal and Marxian models of society. It views the individualism of the former as overly atomistic and consequently disruptive of social equilibrium, and it views the struggle and warfare, if not the sheer presence, of classes in the latter as detrimental to the maintenance of the social system.

In the corporatist model, society is not the mere sum of individuals, and the public interest does not result from individual pursuit of self-interest. Rather, the sum is greater than the numerical total of individuals; it has its own reality and prerogatives vis-à-vis individuals. The individual's pursuit of his or her own interests, especially those associated with private property, is considered legitimate insofar as it serves social solidarity and does not violate the public interest. Corporatism thus sees itself as providing a higher rationale than that provided by liberalism for understanding and securing the public good. From its point of view, neither the liberal conception of the minimal (or slightly expansive) state designed to protect individual rights of life, liberty, and property nor—as we shall see later—the Marxian view of the state as a regulator (in some form) of contradictions within capitalism offers a compelling account of the contemporary sociopolitical condition.

Still, as we noted earlier, the instantiation of particular ideologies in particular contexts may generate different forms of any given ideology. Thus, for example, just as certain forms of liberalism incorporate class terminology without diluting a central concern for the individual, corporatist articulations incorporate, to varying degrees, the concepts of individual and class. Each may play some role within different corporatist articulations. Variations on understanding the place of the individual within corporate, occupational groups give rise to two main species of actually existing corporatist theory and practice: solidaristic corporatism and fascistic corporatism.

What distinguishes the solidaristic and fascistic variants of corporatism is essentially the different ways in which they postulate the interrelationship between the individual, society, and the state. The fascistic variant assimilates the society and therefore the individual, at least in theory, within a metaphysicalized corporative state. Its motto is, "everything within the state, nothing outside the state." It sees the occupational groups and the corporations as the public organs of the state, to be used to control and dominate society, transmitting to the latter orders of the state concerning the duties and obligations of individuals who have no prior rights vis-à-vis the state.

By contrast, solidaristic corporatism views the occupational groups as buffers between the individual and the state. While imbuing otherwise egoistic individuals with public-spiritedness, corporations check and restrain the state from encroaching upon individual members' autonomous domain, thereby protecting them. In solidaristic political theory and jurisprudence, individuals still possess rights, although these rights are limited in comparison to those of the liberal model. But they also have duties or obligations to society—not to the state—in the interest of unity and solidarity. In the solidaristic variant, the state is but a regulatory and coordinating institution, with jurisdiction primarily in the intercorporational domain.[7]

The reason for this basic difference between the two species of corporatism

7. We are downplaying the stature of the state for heuristic purposes. Durkheim criticizes Hegel's "metaphysicalized State," but Durkheim's state, in some places, is still paramount.

is that fascism attempts to transcend the individual-centered, liberal model by radical negation, whereas solidarism tries to transcend it by modification, retaining certain political and cultural ideals of liberalism. The two forms do not always appear in practice as distinct. Both partially and fully articulated forms of corporatism can have, on the one hand, more pluralistic and libertarian solidaristic variants or, on the other, more totalitarian and autocratic fascistic variants.

During the interwar period in Europe, many corporatist theoreticians and ideologues argued that corporatism constituted a Third Way (*tertium genus*) ideology, lying somewhere between capitalism and socialism. This characterization is very misleading because corporatism is not anticapitalist as such. Corporatism neither rejects capitalism with its central elements of private property and enterprise nor offers a fundamental critique of it. Corporatist theory, as Durkheim's analysis of anomie suggests, does bear some resemblance to Marx's critique of alienation, but the resemblance is misleading. The end to which the corporatist critique is directed is not the abolition of human power differentials affiliated with capitalist class structure. The end of the critique is unity, harmony, and efficiency across differently situated, functional spheres of industrial society. Historically it has been the case that corporatism—in both its solidaristic and fascistic forms—has appropriated elements of the anticapitalist critiques into its own logic by introducing the moral code of corporations as palliative settings within which the alienated individual can find social and moral refuge. In general, however, corporatism seeks to replace liberalism as the superseding rationale of modern capitalism, but not to replace capitalism itself. The profit-maximization logic of capitalism in its competitive phase has been subordinated to, but not displaced by, another higher logic of capitalism—the logic of system maintenance and social morality.

Furthermore, corporatism offers an alternative rationale for capitalism in various capitalist contexts. We may define two primary capitalist contexts where corporatist theory and practice, in varying degrees, have taken hold: developmental capitalism and advanced capitalism. Developmental capitalism is distinguished by state policies designed to forward capital accumulation. In such a context, the corporatist formula serves economic development by providing a rationale and justification for a disciplined labor force and capital accumulation under neomercantilist policies of state capitalism. In advanced capitalism, corporatism serves to contain class polarization between numerically and organizationally advanced labor and monopolistic classes, under the perceived or actual threat of the former. In both contexts, corporatism may assume either solidaristic or fascistic forms.

We hasten to add that corporatism can exist in both capitalist contexts as a set of economic and class policies and of actual procedures for conditioning interest representation (level 2) and as a particular form of political institutionalization and authoritative decision making (level 3), whether or not a conscious theoretical articulation exists for those practices. Given the variability of contexts and the discernable absence of a corporatist vocabulary in a world that has had to justify itself in either liberal-democratic or socialist terms for the past fifty years, it is not always the case that one finds an explicit rationale for corporatist capitalism in contexts where it is practiced, especially in western Europe today. Policy indicators may be observed, but no *official* corporatist ideological expression need accompany them. This aspect of corporatist practice creates specific problems for any study of it, especially given the moral authority of liberal doctrines in the Western ideological sphere, wherein corporatists publicly conform to liberal rhetoric while concealing their policy and institutional initiatives that slight, rather than respect, the inviolable integrity of individuality (as, for example, liberal theory posits). Corporatism, then, may be expressed in the form of a well-formulated, programmatic political ideology, or it may remain as a loose worldview that needs to be analyzed in places other than official statements.

Policies for Interest Representation

At the second level of analysis, corporatism, as a series of coherent procedures, involves, first, distinct practices in the process of corporate-interest representation either outright by corporations or by interest groups organized on a corporate basis. It also involves distinct governmental, economic, and class policies, often but not necessarily accompanied by nongovernmental decision-making bodies such as economic councils or a miscellany of statist and mixed-economy structures. As distinct from the high dosages of state regulation and intervention in the economy in the liberal model, in which the economy and the state remain separate and the former primary, the distinction between the state and the economy in the corporatist model is blurred. In the fascist variant, state and politics become supreme over the economy and society. In the solidaristic variant, statism or etatism, the state not only encourages and advises the economy; it directs, supervises, and manages it. The state assumes the role of arbiter between labor and capital and between employer and employee by frequently legislating against both strikes and lockouts in the higher interest of the public good.

Corporatism also has its distinct traits—in theory and practice—as a model of political and legal organization. In the liberal paradigm, the main unit of political activity is the individual, with his and her legal prerogatives against the state. The main mechanisms of interest articulation and aggregation are groups and political parties. The groups may be latent or organized when separate individual interests coincide for a period of time. In principle, such groups dissolve when the common goal is achieved or ceases to unite distinct individuals. The accompanying major structure in the liberal model through which the articulated and aggregated interests are transformed into authoritative, central political decisions is the institution of parliament. The supremacy of the parliament—elected according to the territorial principle and functioning according to the majority principle and the principle of electoral mandate given for a specific period of time—is axiomatic in the liberal model. This is the principle of the primacy of the legislature or the principle of parliamentary legitimacy.

In the corporatist paradigm, by contrast, the major units of political activity and organization are not the atomistic individuals and the changeable groups, but the well-defined, constant occupational groups, whose relation to the state is predetermined through de jure or de facto structures. Accordingly, the major mechanism of interest articulation and aggregation is neither the group nor the political party, but the corporative organizations, such as various professional or industrial or agricultural or labor associations. The main mechanism of central political decision making, the governmental structures within which corporations or corporately organized interest groups and the state meet, is either a parliament, which is elected according to the corporative expectations and principles of functional representation, or outright corporative councils organized in pyramidal form, which displace the institution of parliament. Subspecies of the corporatist model are possible where there may exist a single corporative chamber (pure constitutional corporatism) or a combination of corporatively and territorially elected chambers (mixed constitutional corporatism), the weights of which may vary. Finally, corporatism may coexist with, not totally replacing, the political party system, which has now become subordinate to corporative interests, or it may be implemented by a single-party regime, where associations are made organs of the party.

Corporations, with their relative monopoly on the political representation of interests, may or may not be singular at all levels, merging employees and employers in a certain occupational sector (the number of categories differs according to the particular corporative scheme), but they must be so at the national level if corporative arrangements and structures have crystallized.

Corporatism is thus a larger category than *corporative state* or, for that matter, *corporationism,* and it is not always coterminous with *fascism,* with which it is too often equated (owing to their conjunction in the early-twentieth-century fascist contexts). Although historically the first implementations of the "corporative state" in its near-full crystallization were observed in the classical fascist countries of interbellum Europe, our analysis suggests that it is theoretically possible and historically demonstrable even for a fully corporative state to be solidaristic and not fascist. The reduction of corporatism to fascism occludes an appreciation not only for the nonfascistic corporatist elements of post-World War II advanced capitalist societies, but also for the corporatist formations, of both solidaristic and fascistic variety, in the nonindustrial world before and after World War II.

Politics

Finally, to speak of political corporatism it is not necessary that constitutional corporatism should exist. Even in a system where corporatism has not crystallized at the constitutional level, it may exist at other levels of political institutionalization, which again find their expression in subconstitutional laws and statutes. Inclusion or exclusion—or legalization or prohibition—may be effected informally, or semilegally, by granting or not granting particular political associations "public" status or by accepting or eliminating them outright. The differential weight that specific occupational organizations may carry even in the most inclusive form of corporatism is primarily a function of existing class structures, depending on the value (in qualitative or quantitative terms) that the corporatist leadership assigns to each group.

There may also be cases where corporatist political structures are not accorded constitutional or subconstitutional legal status, but where the main mechanism of political decision making, despite preservation of parties and parliaments, rests elsewhere and does not function according to the axiom of parliamentary legitimacy or supremacy. The party government, for example, may make its decisions not on the strength of its electoral mandate, as in the liberal model of representative parliamentary democracy, but on the prior approval of organized interest groups formally represented or informally effective in extragovernmental, deliberative, or bargaining councils and structures. This process may manifest itself, especially in times of so-called crises of democracy (i.e., liberal parliamentary democracy), in political and juridical theories or practices of "executive supremacy" or "executive legitimacy." Or it may take place, all the same, without such accompanying political-legal justification, in countries of long-established, but now actually passé, liberal parliamentary democracy, where full political institutionalization does not complement actual corporatist, societal, and economic practice. Hence, the creeping corporatism (at the expense of liberalism) in a given country may be less readily visible because of such lack of closure.

In Turkey, corporatism comes via appropriations of solidaristic corporatism in Durkheimian sociological positivism by the Turkish nationalist ideologue Ziya Gökalp. Generally egalitarian, populist, culturally pluralistic, and statist, Gökalp's corporatism underwent some transformations within the ideological frame of the Kemalists, who maintained the solidaristic core formulated by Gökalp while also tinkering partly, but consciously, with distinctly fascistic corporatist tendencies. Our discussion here focuses primarily on bringing out the solidaristic corporatist ideological identity and nuances of Kemalism (level one) as the actors themselves articulated it and as it has become a persisting feature of Turkish political culture since the founding of the republic.

3

SITUATING KEMALISM

In describing Kemalism as Turkey's hegemonic ideology, we mean to capture the way in which it has become the sole, most determinative, all-encompassing public philosophy embedded and enforced in the governing and socializing institutions of the Turkish Republic since Mustafa Kemal and his faction of the national liberation movement consolidated political power and established the modern Turkish state. In this chapter, we detail Kemalism's status as Turkey's hegemonic ideology and the historical context for its emergence as such.

KEMALISM AS A HEGEMONIC IDEOLOGY

A hegemonic ideology becomes so both in and through its conscious and unconscious production and reproduction in various spheres of political and social life (laws, constitutions, education, and media) and in its internalization by members of society. The latter occurs when individuals, though not necessarily in fully conscious ways, accept, assent to, and make use of the ideology as the sole legitimate understanding, interpretation, and vision of the political world.[1]

---

1. Our use of the concept *hegemony* bears resemblance to its use by the Italian Marxist theorist Antonio Gramsci (1891–1937), who originally developed it to describe the ways that dominant political and social institutions—for example, political parties, educational institutions, the media, the bureaucracy—produce consent and agreement throughout society to secure their control over it. That is, hegemony occurs when the ruling classes or strata manage to control and shape not only the relations of power and economy in a society, but also people's understanding about the rightness of those relations. Gramsci argued that the battle over the constitution of society is thus waged and must be waged over its members' understandings and consciousness. In this sense, "hegemony, in its most complete form," writes Robert Bocock, "successfully achieves its objective of providing the fundamental outlook for the whole society" (1986, 63). Gramsci's insight helps us to see a form of domination in the ideational content of people's understandings and to trace the

A hegemonic ideology is by definition monopolistic and exclusionary. It secures and reserves public space solely for itself by rejecting prima facie the legitimacy of existing alternative ideologies. In this regard, a hegemonic ideology
may be distinguished from what might be called a "pluralistic ideology." Although both hegemonic and pluralistic ideologies aim to capture hearts and
minds, the hegemonic ideology does so with the objective of eliminating the
condition of ideological pluralism. Where an ideology is pluralistic, other ideologies are not ruled out; owing their existence in part to the condition of pluralism,
pluralistic ideologies do not effectively deny institutional spaces for the expression of alternative ideological positions. Where an ideology is hegemonic, however, alternative ideologies are actively ruled out: for example, laws may prevent
the expression of terms inconsistent with the hegemon, or university curricula
policies may forbid some forms of ideological expression while enshrining others as topics of courses whose successful completion is necessary for graduation.
Graduates of such universities may be unwilling, either by virtue of conditioning
or as a result of calculated social strategies, to engage in either formal or informal
consideration of alternative interpretations. Similarly, the teaching of a single
truth in elementary schools may condition its adherents to believe that there is
no better way of viewing the world, that open ideological debate threatens soci-

---

sources of that content to particular centers of power. For Gramscian theorists, hegemony occurs
not only when understandings are restricted through ideological repression—say, in the classical
Marxist form of disseminating "false consciousness"—but when understandings are produced to
create consent to a given social formation. This view differs slightly from that of other contemporary critical social theorists, such as the political theorist Jürgen Habermas. For Habermas, ideologies are "illusions that are outfitted with the power of common conviction" (1986, 88) and are
created by strategic actors who manipulate systems of power to promote such illusions in order to
maintain their power base. Habermas maintains that critical social theory can enlighten people
about the forms of ideological formation and indoctrination and thus free them from these untoward constraints on their ability to generate legitimate, democratic forms of power. Both Gramsci
and Habermas, despite their differences, suggest that conceptual domination in the form of ideological domination is untoward relative to democratic possibilities. Hegemonic ideologies, in this
sense, must be understood and transcended for the particular kind of domination that is enacted
through them to end. Our understanding of a "hegemonic ideology" and its significance in democratic theory elaborates on this point in the context of more general ideological phenomena. See
Gramsci 1990 and Habermas 1986.

ety, or that there is no reason to think differently. The hegemonic ideology is hegemonic in part because it seeks to prevent the competition characteristic of ideologically plural contexts. Active prevention of pluralism occurs as both an intentional and an unintentional consequence of action carried out within the framework of the ideology.

When all of the major and minor institutions of political culture function to produce and reproduce the hegemonic ideology, and when individuals across generations collectively and continually act within that framework, that particular ideology secures itself as hegemonic. Although the state may provide great powers of enforcement to secure this status, the omnipresence of the hegemonic ideology in nonstate institutional spaces will also suffice to marginalize or eliminate alternative, emergent ideological beliefs. As the only "acceptable" understanding of the good and the bad, the desirable and the undesirable, the beautiful and the ugly, a hegemonic ideology monopolizes the social space for itself, and, when successfully internalized in a given body politic, it denies alternatives the opportunity for existence and expression.

In Turkey, the hegemony of Kemalism is preserved in a variety of legal, constitutional, practical-political, and sociocultural ways, covering nearly the entire gamut of social and political life. Among the most notable cultural forms are the ways in which the personality of Mustafa Kemal Atatürk occupies a preeminent presence in all sites of human social relations in Turkey. Kemalism is sustained by the promotion of Kemal as the "Eternal Chief," "the Grand Leader," and the "Father of us all." His image and his ideas adorn the landscape of social life; multiple portraits and posters of him hang in nearly every public meeting place, from local restaurants, grocery markets, and stationary stores to concert halls and libraries; statues, busts, and memorabilia such as calendars and buttons are everywhere; his epigrams appear on the frontal pieces of school buildings and state offices from postal services to the army barracks throughout the country; his extended "Message to the Youth" is memorized by every youngster early in his or her schooling and is hung or written on the walls in schools, universities, and other institutions of socialization (we analyze this message in chapter 6); other pithy loyalty oaths such as the popular "Atam izindeyiz" bumper sticker—"We are in your traces, our Ata"—pervade the everyday landscape. *Ata* is the prefix to "Atatürk," the surname Mustafa Kemal adopted when the law requiring that all Turks adopt surnames was passed in 1934. *Ata* translates literally as "ancestor" or "great father"; hence, the name "Atatürk" memorializes Mustafa Kemal as the great pater of the contemporary Turks (we have more to say about the ideological dimensions of this name in subsequent chapters).

Atatürk is present as well in the more official institutional spheres of Turkey's political culture, ensuring that, as one party official put it during the RPP's 1943 Party Congress, "the Eternal Chief [Ebedi Şef] Atatürk, who is the source of administration of the Turkish nation, lives and always will live among us."[2] Atatürk appears on all Turkish banknotes. His portrait is requisite in governmental offices and thus appears in ministry halls, official meeting places, schools, and universities. Government officials and leaders of a variety of other associations regularly visit his tomb (the Anıtkabır, or Monumental Mausoleum), frequently following official protocol by ushering visiting dignitaries to the site, where they pay homage to Atatürk. On republican holidays, leading political and economic figures from across the political spectrum visit the tomb to declare their indebtedness to the Great Leader (Büyük Önder) of the Turkish nation. On these days, television stations broadcast programs with a picture of Atatürk in a corner of the screen, and many Turkish newspapers distribute free posters, books of Atatürk's sayings, and even molded, plastic flags and busts to their readerships. With his picture on the front page of the newspaper, behind the cashier, in the train station, and on the office mantels of doctors, businesspersons, professors, teachers, and bank executives, Mustafa Kemal is forever a presence and topic of conversation and thought in contemporary Turkey.

Kemal and Kemalism are extremely powerful in formal structural terms as well. Kemalism is the constitutionally declared, official ideology of Turkey, and legal structures promote and protect Kemalism as the hegemonic ideology. Laws exist to "protect" Atatürk's personality and memory. They have been incorporated into various penal code regulations, including the restrictive 1972 and 1983 Association Laws, which were promulgated under the wings of Kemalist military governance. In the wording of the 1983 version of the law, "defaming or ridiculing the personality, activities, or memory of Atatürk" is illegal. The inclusion of "activities" is especially important because the line between "criticizing" activities and "defaming" them is one determined by the state courts. The law thus effectively prevents any criticism of Atatürk that may be interpreted by the judicial

2. See Şükrü Saraçoğlu, "Closure of the RPP Congress," June 15, 1943, in Jaeschke 1990, 87.

authorities as "improper." It explicitly rules out some forms of political discourse and induces, both implicitly and explicitly, a politics of homage and deference to Mustafa Kemal Atatürk. Moreover, insofar as Atatürk is protected as the "founder of the republic," these laws are implemented by the state as integral to preserving the integrity of the republic itself. Our documentary analysis in later chapters shows how it came to be that, in the official ideology of Kemalism, the person of Atatürk is identified with the state itself. Within the frame of Kemalism, attacking one is understood as attacking the other. Thus, protecting one is tantamount to protecting the other. These laws continue to structure the boundaries of legitimate public discourse and action in Turkey today.

Laws governing the practices of political parties and the content of education provide further contemporary examples of measures taken to preserve Kemalism's hegemonic status. The Political Parties Law requires that activities be "carried out in conformity with Atatürk's principles and reforms" (Article 4), and the Higher Education Law of 1981 (law 2547, November 4, 1981) empowers the Council of Higher Education[3] to "see to it that students are imbued with a consciousness of service in loyalty to Atatürk nationalism in the direction of Atatürk reforms and principles" (Article 5). This principle of instruction is also codified in Article 42 of the 1982 Constitution, instituted in the wake of the military coup of 1980, which employs both stronger language and the power of sanction. The text appears in the second part of the Constitution's third section, entitled "The Rights and Duties of Education and Instruction," under the noteworthy main heading "Social and Economic Rights and Duties":

> Education and instruction are conducted under the supervision and control of the state, according to contemporary principles of science and education, in the direction of Atatürk's principles and reforms. No education and instruction institutions contrary to these foundations may be opened. The freedom of education and instruction does not remove the obligations of loyalty to the Constitution. (Third Section, Article 42)

3. A constitutional body composed of various presidential (eight), bureaucratic (six), ministerial (two, by the Ministry of Education), and military (one) appointees, invested, inter alia, with the power "to regulate all higher education and direct activities of all institutions of higher education" (Article 6).

That the still effective Constitution of the Turkish Republic specifically forbids education contrary to "Atatürk's principles" constitutes another clear example of Kemalism's hegemonic status.

As our analysis shows, Mustafa Kemal Atatürk's own ideas as well as those ideas of the broader Kemalist ideology pervade the governing structures of the regime, but they do not always do so precisely in the name of Atatürk. During the single-party period, the de jure constitutions did not enforce the language of "Atatürk's principles and reforms," but the state was governed primarily according to the party programs, which did enforce it. The party programs and statutes constituted the de facto governing documents of the regime. Explicit Kemalist governance language emerged in the 1961 Constitution, brought about by the 1960 military coup, which declares loyalty to "Atatürk's reforms" as well as to various ideas associated with Kemal and Kemalism. The 1982 Constitution goes much further in this regard, declaring in the third paragraph of the preamble that the republic is founded on "the understanding of nationalism that was determined by Atatürk, the founder of the Turkish Republic, the immortal leader and unequaled hero, and [on] His reforms and principles." Furthermore, Article 58, "The Protection of the Youth" (the ninth part of the section "Social and Economic Rights and Duties"), states: "The State takes the measures for bringing and developing the youth, to whom our independence and Republic are trusted, under the light of positive science, in the direction of Atatürk's principles and reforms, and against the views that aim at destroying the indivisible integrity of the State and its territory and nation."

This statement specifies certain ideological principles (to be examined later) for cultivation of the youth. It also concisely expresses the perceived functionality of Kemalism ("Atatürk's principles and reforms") for the republican ruling elites and classes, who have found it strategically advantageous to promote, rather than to contest or question, the hegemonic ideology.

The ruling segments include the military, but are not limited to it, as is commonly thought. Beyond the military's special place in Kemalist ideological terms—something we analyze in detail later—its status as a contemporary defender of Kemalism is that it is organized and armed—that is, it possesses the power of decree and outright violence. Having used that power several times during times of crisis in the history of the republic (most notably in the coups of 1960, 1971, and 1980), it has induced compliance to Kemalist governance on the part of politicians from across the political spectrum, all of whom formally and independently continue to commit themselves to Kemalism. But the military alone does not preserve Kemalism. Its dominance is very desirable in part because it has also been functional for other strata that maintain Kemalist hegemony in the normal functioning of the state and society. In class-analytical terms, the elite or ruling class alliance of big business, the landed bourgeoisie, and the state and clerical bourgeoisie has changed only slightly since the 1920s and 1930s. The military has functional authority from the ruling classes and uses it in favor of preserving existing social stratifications. Therefore, the members of the clerical bourgeoisie—such as academics and state bureaucrats (ministry staffs, legal officers, etc.)—reproduce the ideology that the governing Kemalist elites and the military implement. The military is therefore not the only or the last bastion of Kemalism. It is one among many others. In everyday political terms, the officers are not the only ones to visit the Anıtkabır in homage to Atatürk, and, when they do, they do not go alone; they are accompanied by representatives of these other sectors. As such, Kemalism's hegemony is produced by various dominant social strata, not only the most ostensibly coercive ones.

The various sociocultural, political, legal, and constitutional ways in which Kemalism's hegemony is achieved and circulated manifest an officially declared, all-encompassing ideological standard and reference point for social and political life in Turkey. Kemalism, both in its societal omnipresence and in the imperative structures of legality, backed up by enforcement powers of the state, occupies nearly every public space for political thought and action in the Turkish Republic. From the moment persons are born into Turkish society, they are taught to view Mustafa Kemal as the unparalleled chief and savior of the Turkish nation and to devote themselves to preserving his accomplishments and legacy; he is the great leader of the nation, the one without whom they would not be what they are today. What is less understood by adherents and observers alike is how this reverence and the support for the tenets of the great leader's ideology also sustain a fairly coherent corporatist ideological frame of power and interest that shapes much of the landscape of political practice in Turkey today.

A HISTORICAL SKETCH

Turkish political folklore focusing on the personality of Mustafa Kemal Atatürk traces the origins of the national resistance movement to his famous landing at the Black Sea port of Samsun, where he began to unify disparate Anatolian resistance organizations in order to defend the nation against the military encroachments of conquering Western powers. Not uncoincidentally, Mustafa Kemal began his own history of the resistance movement there as well. He opened *Nutuk,* his famous speech of 1927, by saying, "Gentleman, I landed at Samsun on the 19th of May, 1919" (Atatürk 1960, 1).

This event is not necessarily a bad beginning for popular history concerned with the dynamics of leadership and liberation, for it occurred at an undeniably profound moment in Turkish political history: only four days earlier the Greek army had landed on the Aegean coast under the protection of the British and U.S. navies. The Western victors were in the process of dividing the Asian spoils of World War I (the Italians had already landed in Antalya, on the Mediterranean Sea, on March 29). Kemal's emergence as leader of the movement, however, did not arise sui generis, and although Mustafa Kemal came to enjoy his position to such an extent that he would claim most successes of the national movement to be his own, his embarkation at Samsun was not only his decision. Rather, this event, like other events in Anatolia at the time, occurred and therefore must be understood within the highly contested postwar political arrangements over the future of the Turkish Muslim populations of Anatolia and Thrace in particular. A comprehensive account of the history of the national struggle is beyond the scope of our concern here. Nonetheless, a brief sketch of the historical situation and power dynamics is necessary to understand the context of Mustafa Kemal's and Kemalism's definitive ideological statements.

Two general forces shaped national struggle: foreign imperial designs for the territory, on the one hand, and the contest over the leadership of the vanquished Ottoman Muslim populations, on the other. The leadership contest was waged between those who occupied positions of power in the Ottoman sultanate administration and its opponents in the disbanded Committee of Union and Progress (CUP). The former had pursued a policy of appeasement after British occupation of Istanbul in January 1920. The latter were the famous "Young Turks," who wrested power away from the palace in the so-called Young Turk Revolution of 1908 and governed until 1918. At the war's end, especially after early Greek victories and arrests or attacks on CUP members throughout the region by other occupying powers, the CUP rejected an appeasement strategy and reconstituted its organizational infrastructure to resist both the foreign invaders and the capitulating Ottoman regime. It was this movement that Mustafa Kemal came to lead after his landing at Samsun.

Imperialistic plans for the Ottoman territory were drawn up in a series of secret agreements between Allied powers during World War I (Constantinople Agreement, Treaty of London, Sykes-Picot Agreement). The plans were concretized in the Treaty of Sèvres of 1920, which carved the remaining territories of the empire in Anatolia and Thrace into spheres of influence among the British, French, Italians, Greeks, and Ottomans. The victorious powers, including the United States, envisioned an independent Armenia in eastern Anatolia as well as a plebiscite in Kurdistan in southeastern Anatolia. When the treaty was presented to the Istanbul regime in June 1920, the Italian and Greek militaries had already advanced to occupy regions allotted to them.

The Ottoman acceptance of the terms of Sèvres in August reflected differences of outlook between the imperial-palatial administration of the last Ottoman sultan, Sultan Mehmet VI Vahdettin, and the well-organized nationalist movement. Like Ottoman administrations facing defeat in the previous century, the sultan sought to place the empire's fortunes in the hands of the apparently more powerful. This strategy of appeasement also reflected the sultan's lack of sympathy for the organizing principles and political goals of the unionist and nationalist movement. One important reason for his view was that the CUP, while in power the previous decade, had undertaken reforms designed both to limit the power of the palace vis-à-vis the other institutions of rule and to demote Islam's institutional role, which the Ottoman sultans, claiming the caliphate or successor to the Prophet as leader of the Islamic community, had seen themselves responsible to ensure.

The nationalist movement in Anatolia was an ideologically diverse grouping, but the many different so-called nationalists were uniformly committed to a program of resistance to foreign rule. The CUP had prepared plans for resistance in Thrace and Anatolia prior to the end of the war. The CUP leadership asked Mustafa Kemal to take the helm of the fledgling Societies for the Defense of National Rights. He was known for having demonstrated heroic skills during the battle for the Dardanelles in World War I (at Gallipoli); and, having taken part in the 1908 regime change, he was also viewed as sympathetic to the CUP's general political tendencies.

When it became clear in midsummer 1919 that Mustafa Kemal was engaged in organizing for the nationalist cause, the sultan's regime recalled him. He refused to return to Istanbul, however, and then resigned from his official position just before he was to be dismissed by the sultan. Local activists in Anatolia declared their loyalty to him after his status was reaffirmed by more senior members of the nationalist military establishment, such as the other well-known officer, Kazım Bey (Karabekir).

Many historians agree that the one thing that could solidify the unity of the ideologically heterogenous national movement would be an external threat. The imperialistic plans of the Sèvres Treaty and the Italian and Greek invasions provided precisely the boosts necessary to enable rapid organization among many of the smaller resistance groups. The first major national congress was held in Erzurum, in eastern Anatolia from July 23 through August 6, 1919. As an indication of the broadening scope of the movement, the Society for the Defense of Rights of the Eastern Anatolia renamed itself the Society for the Defense of Rights of Anatolia and Rumelia (Thrace) when it met again at Sivas in September. Both congresses reaffirmed the indivisibility of the Ottoman-Muslim lands of the empire as well as the sovereignty of the nation, forming the core of what became known as the National Pact, the official statement of nationalist aims (promulgated in January 1920). Most important, the movement also declared its loyalty to the reigning Ottoman institutions. The National Pact, for example, announced the need to protect and liberate the sultan-caliph from foreign pressures. At both Erzurum and Sivas, a "representative committee" was elected, with Mustafa Kemal chosen as its president. In December, the representative committee met in Ankara, where several months later the new Grand National Assembly (GNA) would convene.

The fall elections for the Ottoman Parliament in October-November 1919 produced, unsurprisingly, a powerful majority favorable to nationalist aspirations. (Most candidates had been previously approved by the resistance movement.) This Parliament ratified the National Pact after attempts at rapprochement (the Amasya Accord) between the nationalists and the sultan failed in October 1919. The Parliament, in defiance of the British occupiers' attempts to silence it by arresting some prominent members, prorogued itself in April. Many parliamentarians, including prominent nationalists Ismet (İnönü) and Fevzi (Çakmak), then accepted Mustafa Kemal's invitation on March 19, 1920, to take their seats in the new Assembly in Ankara.

Denounced by the Istanbul government, whose grand mufti issued a religious decree declaring it permissible to kill the nationalist "rebels," pursued by various invading and occupying powers, and facing partition of the territory (the United States had already recognized the new Armenian Republic), the new

GNA met for the first time on April 23, 1920. Mustafa Kemal was elected president of the Assembly the next day. The Assembly then named its own Islamic authority, who opened the first session with a prayer and religious decree "to do all to liberate the caliph from captivity" and to carry out the objectives of the National Pact. On April 29, the Assembly passed the High Treason Laws and eleven days later declared the capitulating Ottoman grand vizier a traitor. In May, the Assembly also elected a council of ministers and eight months later promulgated the Constitutional Act. Among its measures, the act established the doctrine of popular sovereignty, two-tiered (or second-degree) parliamentary elections, collectively responsible ministries, and a president with extensive powers. To some, these events are the founding events of the new republic—one main reason why the founding of the state is sometimes dated 1920, not 1923. The latter was the year the republic was proclaimed, a topic we discuss later.

The National Struggle

It is significant to keep in mind that Ottoman acceptance of the Sèvres Treaty in August 1920 constituted the decisive break with the nationalists, who then proceeded to portray themselves as the only legitimate representatives of the local Muslim populations. They buttressed this claim by initially declaring their support for the Ottoman caliphate, for example, even as they sought to create more collectively representative mechanisms of governance. The nationalist movement was, after all, a coalition of many groups, some of which remained committed to the Ottoman state. In this sense, the legitimization strategy of the nationalist leadership was consistent with CUP governance from 1908 through 1918. The CUP had promulgated constitutionalist reforms—many that they turned into authoritarian tools—but they did not issue a fundamental challenge to Ottoman structural or symbolic legitimacy. As Feroz Ahmad has pointed out,

> As early as 1912, the Unionist-controlled Assembly had strengthened the constitutional position of the ruler, [Sultan] Mehmed V, now that they no longer feared him . . . [and] despite the existence of a strong Turkish faction in the CUP, the policies of the regime until the very end continued to be essentially Islamist. It is no accident that even after the defeat, the army that Enver Pasha led against the Bolsheviks in Turkistan was called "the Army of Islam." (1991, 4–5)

The nationalist struggle was not very different in this particular regard, even though Enver Pasha (1881–1922) did not lead it. (Considered by many to be a potential rival to Mustafa Kemal, Enver Pasha was prevented from entering Anatolia and died in August 1922 in a battle in Tajikistan.) Under Mustafa Kemal and other leading military officers, the Turks struggled, in the language of the movement, to "free Islamic lands" by "expelling the infidel invaders." In battle, the fallen were given the honorific titles of martyr (*şehit*). Mustafa Kemal himself was accorded the title *gazi*—the heroic title given to Ottoman fighters who distinguished themselves in battle—after the famous battle at Sakarya, where the Turkish army regrouped and routed the invading Greek forces (September 13, 1921). The identity of the national struggle as a struggle for Islamic freedom waged by Ottoman patriots was apparently so profound that, at war's end in October 1922, as Ahmad states, "many now became convinced that the Sultanate could be abolished and a constitutional system essentially Islamic in character maintained at the same time" (1991, 6). An important step in this regard was taken in November 1922, when the GNA declared the Ottoman government to have "passed into the domain of history" (as of March 1920, the date of the British occupation of Istanbul), while at the same time maintaining the caliphate and Islam as the religion of the state.

The First and Second Assemblies and
the Competition for Turkish Sovereignty

Important institutional and group power dynamics occurred in the "First" GNA (1920–23) that profoundly affected the character of Turkish politics and the Kemalist transformation in the years to come.[4] Several politically distinct groups emerged from the national movement and competed to define Turkey's new sovereign aims and objectives. It was a dynamic moment, reminiscent of the years immediately following the 1908 restoration of the Ottoman Constitution, when the politically active Turkish national community debated, formed parties, built coalitions, and actively vied for power. One participant in early republican politics who served as vice president of the Assembly for a short time noted in 1928 that the first GNA had "governed the country in such a manner that its democratic system was even admired in the West" (Adivar 1991, 31). For example, several

4. On the 1921 and 1924 Constitutions, see Parla 2001.

weeks after Istanbul's capitulation, and after Mustafa Kemal had established contacts with the Soviets for support against the British and Ottomans, a traditionalist group, fearful of being taken over to the communist camp, formed the Association for the Preservation of Sacred Institutions (Muhafaza-i Mukaddesat Cemiyeti) in July 1920. In response, Kemal formed his own Defense of Rights Group (Müdafaa-i Hukuk Grubu) the following May, consciously choosing the name of the original societies in order to enhance the group's claim as the nation's rightful representative. Mustafa Kemal's leadership position gave him and his loyal supporters a distinct advantage in shaping the outcome of these contests. He variously co-opted and crushed "leftist" forces oriented toward the Bolsheviks and then maneuvered to ensure the control of his group over the Assembly.[5]

Another group emerged in 1922 and 1923, in part to contest Kemal's authoritarian practices in the Assembly. What would come to be known as the Second Group (İkinci Grup) included former respected members of the national movement. Some of them, such as Adnan (Adıvar), had been elected to the Council of Ministers in May 1920, shortly after the establishment of the GNA. With an eye toward constraining Mustafa Kemal's influence over the political process, members of this group succeeded in passing a law ensuring that the Assembly would exercise prerogative over the selection of cabinet ministers (in July 1922).

A factor not unrelated to the increasing power of the Kemalist faction prior to the end of the war in 1922 was the creation of an inchoate judicial structure controlled by the Assembly and a cabinet to deal with crimes of high treason. In July 1922, prior to the final Turkish offensive against the Greek army, the Assembly passed a law establishing Tribunals of Independence, whose members were to be chosen from among the Assembly. The formation of these tribunals is significant, for they came to play an important part in Kemalist politics during the early years of the republic as the Kemalist faction consolidated its power.

At the end of 1922, with peace negotiations between the national movement and the various Allied powers underway at Lausanne, Mustafa Kemal declared his intention to transform the Defense of Rights Group into a political party. In April 1923, just after the dissolution of the Assembly, members of Kemal's group formed the People's Faction in preparation for upcoming elections. The People's Party (later the RPP) was officially formed that August. The climate sur-

5. See the discussion in Zürcher 1993, 164–72.

rounding these events suggested potential turmoil ahead. In March, a leader of the Second Group had been assassinated by persons suspected of having ties to Mustafa Kemal. Also, the Assembly dissolved itself, but only after amending the High Treason Law the previous day to make it illegal to campaign for a return to the sultanate. Such developments signaled that the defeat of the Ottoman Empire did not mean an end to conflict and intrigue in Turkish politics. Elections for a new Assembly, held in June and July, produced an overwhelming victory for delegates hand-picked by Mustafa Kemal, who, as we argue in the remaining chapters, had been pursuing quite self-consciously a strategy of self-aggrandizement. These new parliamentary members formally constituted the People's Party in August, two days before the Second National Assembly convened.

Its session between 1923 and 1927 was extremely tumultuous. It began with tremendous achievements: the ratification of the Lausanne agreement settling most of Turkey's border concerns;[6] the formal declaration of Ankara as the capital of the new state, and the proclamation of the new Turkish Republic. But the period was also characterized by tremendous political disagreement and violent conflict. Kemalist policies ranging from the dramatic abolition of the caliphate, the Shariah, and the *medrese* system in 1924 to the implementation of the sartorial regulations in 1925 (mandating brimmed caps for males wearing hats and prohibiting veils for women working in state institutions) and a new civil code in 1926 stirred opposition both to the particular policies and to the authoritarian elements of Kemalist rule. Over the course of several years (and arguably up to the present day), opponents of Mustafa Kemal and his RPP organized and attempted to challenge the latter's increasingly authoritarian rule and aims. This is not to say that the opponents were themselves necessarily more democratic, but to identify and to stress the emerging perception of Kemalist authoritarian tendencies within the domestic Turkish political arena.

For instance, members of the Second Group who had objected to the hasty and exclusive manner in which the Kemalist faction declared the republic—while the opposition was out of town—constituted themselves as the Progressive Republican Party (PRP, Terakkiperver Cumhuriyet Fırkası) in November 1924. The party was closed less than a year and a half later, however, after it was seen as con-

6. The exceptions were the Mosul Province, later incorporated into Iraq but still highly contested, and the Alexandretta (Hatay) Province, still claimed by Syria.

tributing to the Kurdish rebellion of 1925. The Independence Tribunals charged the party with abetting "reactionarism" (or "obscurantism").

The content of the opposition outside the Assembly during the founding period is still in the process of being clarified by historical research. Nonetheless, it is clear enough that both Kurdish and Turkish conservative national groups composed much of that opposition. Historians generally agree that the Kurdish rebellion of 1925 was motivated in part by national aspirations for greater political autonomy and in part by calls for the restoration of Islamic institutions. Ahmad aptly notes that "the Kemalists also recognized the significance of religion in the Kurdish revolt and the vital role played by popular Islam in the lives of the masses" (1991, 12). The Kemalists responded by imposing martial law on February 25 (which the PRP had supported), describing the rebels as "religious fanatics" and "obscurantists," amending the High Treason Law to prohibit the "political use of religion," and sanctioning the Law for the Establishment of Tranquility, which made it possible for the Independence Tribunals to ban "illegal" associations and to execute violators of the law without Assembly sanction.

Back in Ankara, the disbanding of the PRP did not deliver a decisive blow to the influence of its leadership. This would come only after prominent members of the PRP were charged in 1926 with participating directly and indirectly in a plot to assassinate Mustafa Kemal. These charges were fatal, both figuratively for opposition politics during the mid-1920s and literally for some members of the PRP (sixteen were sentenced to death). Their involvement and the authenticity of the charges have been questioned by many observers of the period, not to mention by participants in these events. Even one prominent and sympathetic observer of the regime, Dankwart Rustow, noted that "only few . . . had any prior knowledge of the plot," and "the charges that the Progressive Party had abetted the Kurdish uprising" were "even flimsier" (1968, 805). These trials were mock trials designed to liquidate the remnants of old CUP rivals, thus marking the end of an intra-elite struggle that had grown out of the national struggle.

The executions of some members of the opposition sent an unmistakable message to others who might consider inheriting their role. It also confirmed that if any political openings were to occur, the regime would determine the time and manner on its own. Change, like power itself, would flow from above, as an outcome of the will of the leadership. A second possible political opening occurred, in the late 1920s, when Turkey was hit by both the drought of 1927–28 and the global economic downturn. The regime looked to one of its loyalists, Fethi Bey, to found a loyal opposition party—the Free Republican Party (FRP, Serbest Cumhuriyet Fırkası). However, like the PRP, the FRP attracted opposition sentiments outside the Assembly that again alarmed the Kemalist regime. The FRP leadership voluntarily closed the party after provoking charges of treason when they questioned the validity of the 1930 elections.

The fact that the leaders of both the FRP and the PRP had been prominent, respected members in the nationalist movement suggests that what was really at stake in their demise was power. Without including the claim that the opposition held the promise for greater democracy (skepticism is warranted here), it is possible to note that the Kemalists set a precedent for a certain style of political behavior in the contemporary Turkish Republic. In their purges of a viable political opposition, the Kemalists effectively eliminated a certain practice of cooperative, consensus-building politics through which conflict could be institutionalized rather than suppressed. As we show later, the bases of this disposition were moreover not simply calculations of strategic interest in the context of a battle for power. Their bases were, we maintain, profoundly ideological as well. That is to say, we suggest that the view that political institutions are spaces to be dominated with a single truth rather than filled with a collision and exchange of ideas is embedded in the ideological framework of the Kemalist ideology itself. Ideologically, Kemalism sets the pattern that politics is about achieving total control over the state in order to eliminate rivals and press ahead with one's agenda. That successor parties to the RPP have promoted this pattern is not a mere fact of political circumstance; it is in part, we believe, an outcome of the hegemonic ideology.

INSTITUTIONAL AND CULTURAL REFORMS

As part of the regime's legal and sociocultural policies consistent with ideological objectives, it outlawed the folk Islamic brotherhoods; closed their meeting halls, lodges, and sacred tombs; and repressed their leadership. Many of these coercive measures were undertaken with the objective of "establishing tranquility" for the new regime by quieting some of its opposition. These policies were thus very much part of the ongoing political battle between opposing factions of the former national independence coalition. They also certainly entailed the suppression of one form of politicized Islam in Turkey, but, although these policies have been associated with the regime's interest in "secularization," it is important not to overstate their relationship to the regime's policies regarding the place of Islam within the state.

This point is borne out by taking into account the fact that what has been said to be the quintessential act of secularizing the state, the dramatic abolition of the caliphate, did not entirely entail an end to the regime's interest in institutionalized religion. The abolition of the caliphate was accompanied by the creation of a new office, the Directorate of Religious Affairs, whose head was to be appointed by the president and whose office was to be "attached" to the office of the prime minister. The functions of the new office include(d), in the words of the law that created it, "the dispatch of cases related to belief and ritual, administration of mosques and *tekke*s [religious lodges]."[7] The director was thus placed in charge of the appointment and dismissal of all mosque personnel, including imams and *hatip*s (roughly, preachers and prayer leaders). The office itself would be the "proper place of legal recourse." We examine the conceptual underpinnings of the Kemalist version of Islam in our section on laicism in chapter 5, but it is important here to note that policies commonly associated with the regime's secularization policies did not entail the dissolution of the religious establishment or its full separation from political power. Laicism integrated Islam in a new structure of governance.[8]

After securing dominance over the state during the mid-1920s and through the 1930s, the Kemalists promulgated many significant legal and cultural reforms that are the hallmark of its modernizing, westernizing, and nation-state-building image. Some of these reforms—such as the adoption of the Gregorian calendar and the Italian penal code and criminal code (1926), the Latin script in place of Arabic (1928), the metric system (1931), last names and the Sunday weekend holiday in place of Friday (1934), the Italian labor law (1936)—were both attacks on the traditional Muslim cultural order and efforts to integrate Turkey's economic life and prospects with those of the societies to its west. We discuss the ideological bases of these and other reforms, such as the extension of suffrage to women

---

7. The General Directorate of Religious Affairs was founded by the enactment of the Law on the Abolition of the Ministry of Shariah and Foundations and the Ministry of General Staff (Şer'iye ve Evkaf ve Erkanıharbïye-i Umumiye Vekaletlerinin İglasına Dair Kanun), number 429, on March 6, 1924. All quotations here are from this law.

8. For a more detailed discussion of interpreting the structural relations, see Davison 1998; compare Keddi 1988.

in the 1930s[9] and the regime's language-purification policies, in the context of our broader treatment of the ideological objectives of Kemalism in chapters 4 and 5.

Some of these reforms were logically continuous with the goals of previous Ottoman reform movements and hence were not objectionable to even some of the rival political elites who had been purged from the scene, but other reforms constituted a discernibly novel extension of the logic of institutional change. The implementation in 1926 of a slightly adapted version of the Swiss civil code illustrates the dynamic of both continuity and change. As Mahmut Esat, the justice minister at the time, explained, the new Turkish civil code was implemented to replace "outdated" and various religious laws with a new and unified "national" legal system.[10] Aspects of the reforms were, however, consistent with reform efforts in the late Ottoman period, including matters of women's rights and status, on which the new code is seen as having its greatest impact. The code continued a process of granting greater rights to women that had begun with the 1917 Family Law, promulgated during the CUP period. That law had granted women rights to divorce and increased the numbers of schooling and teacher-training opportunities for girls and women. It had also raised the nuptial age from twelve to seventeen for women and from fifteen to eighteen for men. The new 1926 code actually lowered the legal age for women to fifteen, but it also granted women divorce rights by repudiation, rights over surname after divorce, and rights to make inheritance and property claims, and it mandated male monogamy.

As our discussion suggests, these and other changes led to opposition to Kemalism from several different quarters. The Kemalists responded to these challenges with a variety of strategies intended to consolidate their power—from temporary appeasement to full repression. Against those who took up arms, the regime responded with the Law for the Establishment of Tranquility, initially supported by the formal opposition party and then used to disband it. Needless to say, there was much work for the High Treason Courts to do. The successful squelching of any opposition—in other words, the creation of the prized "tranquility" and "order"—provided an opportunity for the Kemalists to pursue their version of the Turkish transformation by implementing a series of cultural, legal,

9. Women were granted the right to participate in municipal elections in 1930 and the right to vote in general elections in 1934.

10. See the full text and analysis in Davison 1998.

and economic policies that gave fuller clarity to Kemalist objectives for the nation. Along the way, the regime, led by the charismatic Mustafa Kemal, endeavored to establish its vision of governance and its version of Turkish national modernity as hegemonic. We turn now to examining the terms and strategies of this ideological activity and how Kemalism came to be, and to be seen so widely as, the incontestably true and correct path for modern Turkey.

4

KEMALISM AND
IDEOLOGY

As we noted in chapter 1, when the ideological content of Kemalism is not explained away, it is commonly explained in terms of the RPP's famous "six arrows": republicanism, nationalism, populism, laicism, transformationism, and statism. Throughout the literature on Kemalism and modern Turkish politics, one finds some variation in the English translation of the original Turkish names for these arrows. The words for *populism, laicism,* and *transformationism,* for example, are sometimes translated as *peopleism, secularism,* and *revolutionarism.* We think that the former terms are more fitting because they capture the ideological ends and purposes of the politics associated with them, as understood within the Kemalist frame. In this chapter, we begin to show why this is the case by detailing the limits of relying upon the arrows for understanding Kemalism and by demonstrating that Kemalism, contrary to its nonideological reputation, consciously posits what its foundational expressions describe as particular "ideas" and "principles" as standards for governance and social transformation. These principles include the regime's corporatist commitments, commitments that are not evident in the official definitions of the six arrows but are prominent in other spaces of formal expression, including Atatürk's speeches and official RPP documents.

THE RECEIVED VIEW AND ITS LIMITS:
KEMALISM'S SIX ARROWS

The six arrows, announced in their complete form in the 1931 RPP program, were intended to describe the political goals of Mustafa Kemal and the RPP in a shorthand form. The "arrow" symbolically alludes to the historic accouterments of the Central Asian Turkish peoples and metaphorically suggests the image of a projectile—Turkey—being shot through space and time, traveling swiftly and directly on a clear path, or on six clear paths, determined by its grand marksman, Mustafa Kemal.

It is true that the six arrows provide a window into Kemalism's ideological content. They were at work both in how the Kemalist project was described publicly and in the minds of the actors who implemented them. Apt, too, is the metaphor of arrows shot by a grand marksman and his party. Kemal and the other party ideologues were quite proud to declare that they had launched Turkey in a new direction. One may even, with certain qualifications, say that understanding the meanings and central importance of the six arrows is necessary to understanding the politics of the entire republican period. These arrows were fired with such "success" that, with very few exceptions, Turkish politics has ever since been practiced within their ideological range of flight.

We think, however, that the routine descriptions of the six arrows common in the literature on Turkish politics miss other important aspects of Kemalism that should be central concerns of ideological analysis. Such descriptions of the arrows tell us very little, for instance, of the Kemalist view of the role and function of the state vis-à-vis society, of power relations in general, or of the power and authority relations that the Kemalist leadership believed were necessary to implement their various republican, nationalist, populist, laicist, statist, and transformationist policies. Indeed, analysis that does not see the larger ideological frame of Kemalism falls short in understanding the political ideological meanings of the six arrows themselves.

When it comes to understanding the "republican" arrow, for example, observers of Turkish politics are well aware of the Kemalist objective to replace the absolutist, imperial, monarchical governing structures of the Ottoman Empire with a state based on republican principles of governance. And indeed, much textual evidence—in both Kemal's and the RPP's public statements—can be marshaled to support this account of the meaning of *republicanism*. The section of the 1931 program that describes this arrow, for example, reads: "The Party believes that Republic is the form of state that best and in the surest way represents and implements the ideal of national sovereignty. The Party, with this unshakable conviction defends the Republic by all means against danger" (Section 2, Article 1, Paragraph A). From our perspective, however, such an account of the "republican" arrow fails to provide answers to other, more fundamental questions about the nature of Kemalist republicanism that are central to the study of ideology.

For example, what was the leadership's particular understanding of republican governance? How did Atatürk and the RPP depict the practices and institutional power relations associated with republicanism? What kind of republic did they seek to create? How, in fine, was republicanism constituted, with what specific meanings and concepts in power terms and in the context of Kemalism's other specific governing and transformative objectives?

Similar questions can be raised with regard to the other arrows. We are aware, for instance, that the pursuit of nationalism, when painted with a broad analytical brush, indicated Kemalism's rejection of, for example, monarchicalism and cosmopolitanism. This view was articulated well before the 1931 program, wherein it is stated that "the source of will and sovereignty is the nation" (RPP 1931, Section 2, Article 1, Paragraph C). It can be found in numerous speeches and statements of many different persons and groups involved in the national struggle. One of Kemal's more colorful moments on this theme occurred in a speech in Dumlupinar in 1924. *"Efendiler* [Gentlemen, countrymen]," he declared, "national sovereignty is such a light that, in front of it chains melt, crowns and thrones burn and perish. Institutions built on the basis of enslavement of nations are everywhere condemned to collapse" (*SD* 2: 1924a, 179). As in the case of republicanism, however, knowing that Kemal was a nationalist leaves unanswered many questions concerning the particular understandings of "the nation" present in his and the broader Kemalist discourse. For example, how did the Kemalists portray the character of the Turkish nation? Did their expressed understandings exhibit a uniform understanding of "nationalism," or did they vary from time to time? How did the leadership understand and publicly describe the history of the Turkish nation, its internal character, and its relation to other nations?

So, too, with populism, statism, laicism, and transformationism. The first, populism, is well known as the principle through which the Kemalists declared sovereignty to rest with "the people," as opposed to the sultan. Thus, as early as 1922, Mustafa Kemal declared that "in our language, this government is called 'People's government' " (*SD* 3: 1922a, 51). But how did the leadership understand this entity referred to as "the people"? Was it, for instance, an aggregate of individuals or social classes? Or was it some kind of social whole? Moreover, how did the political leadership understand its role and hence its relationship to the people?

Statism, we know, means giving the state an active role in directing national economic development. The 1931 program describes the arrow in this form: "Although it considers individual work and activity as basic, it is one of our important principles, to have our nation attain prosperity and our country a high level of development in the shortest time possible, to engage the State actively in those affairs—especially in the economic field—that are necessitated by the general and high interests" (RPP 1931, Section 2, Article 1, Paragraph Ç).

Despite the clarity of this statement, however, many questions remain open. For example, how exactly did the regime view its role regarding the relation between state and economy, or between individual, class, or corporate economic pursuits and national development? What priority was given to economic development relative to other political or cultural objectives?

Laicism is well known as the principle through which the Kemalists sought to describe their policies regarding the place of Islam and Islamic institutions in the new republic. These policies were tied, as much of the literature makes clear, to the RPP's commitment to reorganizing political and educational affairs according to the methods and concepts of the natural sciences. Thus, the 1927 party statutes and the 1931 program linked the elevation of science to the demotion of Islam from politics and "worldly affairs." This shift, according to the Kemalist program, was necessary to the "nation's success." The 1931 document reads as follows:

> The Party has accepted as a principle that, in the administration of the State all laws, regulations, and procedures should be made and applied according to the principles and forms that the sciences and technologies have secured for contemporary civilization according to the needs of the [contemporary] world.
>
> Since the view of religion is a matter of conscience, the Party sees it as the main cause of our nation's success in contemporary progress to keep separate religious ideas from the affairs of the state and the world and from politics. (RPP 1931, Section 2, Article 1, Paragraph D)

As we have noted, this policy did not entail separating religion and state by removing all religious institutions and officials from the state. Rather, it entailed creating the Directorate of Religious Affairs and making its new officers paid employees of the state. But again, many questions about the substance and aims of the laicist doctrine remain unanswered. For example, what was the leadership's officially stated view of religion itself? What was the relation between religion and national identity in the laicist doctrine? If there was an expressed commitment to protecting the freedom of religious conscience, how did Kemal and the RPP conceptually square this commitment with their practices designed to control the place and content of religion?

Finally, transformationism meant altering Turkey's political, social, and cultural dynamics in order to set them in tune with similar dynamics in societies to its west. A long set of cultural policies helps to grasp aspects of the ideological nature of this goal, but some important questions remain to be explained. How, for example, did the principal actors understand the policies, practices, and institutional reforms associated with the idea of a transformation? Why transformation and not revolution—a distinction that Mustafa Kemal himself made? What were the transformation's distinguishing accomplishments in his eyes? And, more important, how did he and the party understand each of these policies, practices, and reforms? The scientific outlook, for example, is often said to be at the center of the Kemalist reforms. To what extent is this the case, and how are the reforms associated with scientific thinking related conceptually to reforms associated with the nationalizing project?

This is an admittedly cursory summation of each of these principles, and we do not deny that answers to some of these questions have been offered in the existing literature on Turkish politics. Nevertheless, a more exhaustive, comparative, ideological analysis of the original expressions of Kemalism remains necessary. Such analysis requires, moreover, in-depth consideration of the relationship, for example, between populism and republicanism or between populism and nationalism or between nationalism and laicism. To what extent were "the people" and "the nation" related or distinct in the terms of the official ideology? How did the ideology's doctrine of nationalism influence its understanding of laicism and the status that the Kemalists were willing to assign to Islam? It obviously becomes difficult to answer such questions without adequate answers to our previously stated question: What sort of republic did the Kemalists aim to create? These questions cannot be answered by studying the six arrows in isolation or by letting them or the relatively simply official definitions of them stand for ideological analysis.

The arrows restrict the analysis of Kemalism so narrowly that, beyond the contours of the arrows themselves, other and even more fundamental questions related to the study of Kemalism as an ideology go unanswered. These questions concern the leadership's understandings of political power itself and of the roles and functions of particular institutions of the republic (assembly, army, education, press, opposition parties, and so on). They also include questions concerning the Kemalist view of the Turkish transformation and its relationship to other forms of transformation. What were Mustafa Kemal's expressed understandings of the roles and functions of the RPP? What was his conception of his own role? Given the continuing impact of the cult of the hero created by Atatürk and his followers, it is imperative that studies of Kemalism attend to more than the patent statements of the six arrows and examine other aspects of the public ideology.

KEMALISM AS AN IDEOLOGY

Part of the reason many interpreters have relied on the arrows as sufficient analytical categories lies in the widespread impression, described earlier, that Mustafa Kemal and the leading political organs of Kemalism lacked an ideology at all during the 1920s, at least until the arrows were announced in the RPP's 1931 program. Until then, so the argument goes, whatever ideological content Kemalism had, it emerged slowly, if at all, as the Kemalists pragmatically cleared away their conservative opponents in order to take the reins of the state unto themselves. Kemal himself reinforced this interpretation when, in *Nutuk* in 1927, he depicted his political activities as "practical" (*amelî*) during the years of national struggle and institutional creation (Atatürk 1960, 15). He claimed to have acted only according to the circumstances of the moment, rather than from some ideological directive, preferring "actions and deeds over words and theory" (Atatürk 1963, 718). The period of the 1920s is thus said on some accounts to be the quintessential period of Mustafa Kemal's political pragmatism, during which he announced his intentions, purposes, and motives only when he knew he was certain to succeed in implementing his goals. On this account, the only effective ideas during the 1920s were those related to Mustafa Kemal's superior foxlike and lionlike strategic skills, which he employed with great acumen in order to defeat Turkey's wartime enemies, to capture power, and to launch Turkey's transformation. Many interpreters have concluded that there is thus little reason to look to the documents of the 1920s to find ideology because none is said to exist.

This view, however, misses many developments at the level of ideology beginning as early as 1920, including speeches and public statements made as matters of governance by Mustafa Kemal himself. It also selectively accepts Kemal's own professions, ignoring others and, more important, ignoring how political ideas he expressed were not only instrumental for problem solving, but also symbolically crucial in constituting and shaping understandings of nearly all matters of political importance. Mustafa Kemal's main goal in the *Great Speech*—as we detail later—was to promote his own position in the national struggle and the ultimate rightness of his plans for the new Turkey. His professions of sheer political pragmatism should be seen in this legitimizing context as creating a particular image essential to the role he was justifying. This is especially relevant regarding his view that he acted according to the circumstances of the moment alone: consider that in the early 1920s Kemal gave speeches that illustrate his early commitment to the ideological tendencies that are said to emerge only after 1927 or 1931.

In 1923, for example, he offered a distinct view of the nation that is not captured in rote analysis of Kemal's obvious commitment to the "nationalist" arrow. Speaking to journalists at a special gathering in Izmir, during a time when he was balancing Turkey's interests vis-à-vis the capitalist West and Soviet Russia during the first Cold War, he explicitly rejected the idea that the Turkish nation comprised classes with conflicting interests: "In my view, our nation does not possess various classes that would follow very different interests from one another and because of this be in a state of struggle with one another. The present classes are in the nature of being necessarily complementary of each other" (*SD* 2: 1923h, 82). This is a very significant statement, one that quite confidently rejects the Marxian understanding of society in favor of the corporatist vision.

Evidence for early ideological development can be found in other party ideologues and orators' texts as well. From our perspective, the early years constitute the formative years of Kemalist solidaristic corporatism, and the early statements—statements that illustrate a clear continuity with those found well into the 1930s and 1940s—comprise the foundational, ideological texts of the regime. They illustrate clear solidaristic corporatist ideological dimensions of Kemalist "pragmatic" politics from its inception, and they are the texts that have set the basic ideological contours for Turkish political thought and practice since its founding. It is thus incorrect, we think, to consider Kemal's statements—like the one rejecting a Marxist vision of society—to be "pragmatic" gestures, for the evidence suggests a continuity of commitment and practice consistent with these central ideological premises. Consider, for example, the following texts from 1923 through 1943. We quote these texts at length in order to provide evidence for our claims, especially the claim that central ideological continuities exist in the content of Kemalism's public expressions.

The texts selected here cover many concepts in Kemalist thought and practice that we analyze in detail in subsequent chapters. Here, it is important to keep in mind the ideological context of the Cold War. Many of the statements appear to be aimed explicitly at rejecting the idea that Turkey sought to join the Marxist-Leninist camp. In this process, the Kemalists clarified their own solidaristic corporatist outlook. Thus, important to notice in these texts are several recurrent and characteristic themes on the leadership's commitment to a corporatist conception of society: an emphasis on social solidarity within a society composed of occupational groups; a rejection of economic class as a relevant category for understanding Turkish society; a stress on the role of capital and private property in national economic development; an articulation of the different duties of each occupational group in the social whole; and a stress on the active role of the state in shaping the relations among these so-conceived corporations.

Text 1 is an excerpt from Mustafa Kemal's 1923 "Speech with the People in Balıkesir." In it, Kemal explained the new RPP's conception of the Turkish nation and its role therein:

This nation very often was [in the past] pained by political parties. Let me put to you that in other countries parties have been formed and are being formed on the basis of economic objectives, to be sure. Because there are various classes in those countries. In return for a political party that is formed to protect the interests of a class, another party is formed with the purpose of protecting the interests of another class. This is very natural. Well known are the consequences that we witnessed thanks to political parties that have been formed as if there existed in our country separate classes. Whereas when we say People's Party, not only parts but the whole of the nation is included. Let us first review our people.

As you know, our country is a country of farmers. Therefore, the great majority of our nation are farmers and herdsmen. This being the case, one is also reminded of owners of large lands and farms. How many of us possess large lands? On what scale? Upon examination, it will be seen that nobody possesses large lands in proportion to the area of the country. Therefore, the landowners, too, are people who should be protected.

Then come the artisans and the small merchants who carry out commerce in small towns. Surely we are obliged to ensure and protect their interests, their present, and their future. Just like the large landowners we presume to exist against the farmers, there are no people who possess large capital vis-à-vis these merchants. How many millionaires do we have? None. Therefore we are not going to be enemies also of those who have little money. On the contrary, we shall see to it that many millionaires, even billionaires, grow up in our country.

Then comes the worker. In our country today, institutions such as factories, manufacturing shops, and so forth are very limited. The number of our present workers would not exceed twenty thousand. Whereas we need many factories to elevate our country. And workers are necessary for this. Therefore, it is necessary to protect and care for the workers who are no different from the farmers who till the land.

And then come the persons who are called the intellectuals and the ulema [religious leaders]. Gathering by themselves, can these intellectuals and ulema be hostile to the people? The duty that falls to them is, penetrating the people, to guide and elevate them and to lead them in progress and becoming civilized. It is thus I see our nation. Therefore it is not possible to separate into classes practitioners of various occupations because their interests are compatible with one another, and all of them comprise the people. (*SD* 2: 1923f, 97–98)

Text 2, an excerpt from Mustafa Kemal's 1925 "A Talk in Akhisar," continues this theme:

A nation, a social collectivity, cannot take even a single step with the effort and work of an individual. . . . The country needs a solidary unity. (*SD* 2: 1925a, 224)

Text 3, the entire Article 2 of Section 2 of the 1931 RPP program, directly follows the sections on laicism quoted earlier and expounds on the role of occupational groups in Turkish society:

It is one of our fundamental principles to consider the people of the Republic of Turkey not as composed of fully separate classes but as a body that is differentiated into practitioners of various activities from the point of view of the division of labor for social life.

(A) Small farmers, (B) Small manufacturers and traders, (C) the worker and the laborer, (D) Free professionals, (E) Industrialists, the large landowners, and businessmen and merchants of the major occupational groups that form the Turkish community. The work of each of these is requisite for the life and happiness of one another and of the general body social. The objective that our party aims at attaining with this principle is to provide or secure social order and solidarity instead of class struggle and to establish harmony of interests in a manner that would not be mutually contradictory. Interests are proportional with the degree of ability and effort. (RPP 1931, Section 2, Article 2)

Text 4, an excerpt from Section 3, Article 5, of the same program, entitled "Economy: Agriculture and Industry, Raw Minerals and Forests, Commerce, Public Works," explains Kemal's understanding of the state's role in creating interoccupational harmony:

We shall take into account the lives, the rights, and the interests of the nationalistic Turkish workers and laborers. Establishment of harmony between labor and capital and enactment of stipulations adequate to the need by a labor law are considered among the important affairs of the Party. (RPP 1931, Section 3, Article 5)

Text 5 is the entire Section 3, Article 6, of the same program:

In the development of the country, all commercial activities are important. All capital owners who work normally and who rely on technology are entitled to encouragement and protection. (RPP 1931, Section 3, Article 6)

Text 6 is Mustafa Kemal's 1935 speech "Opening the 4th Great Congress of the RPP," on the division of labor:

In our program, the private and general interests of the citizens positioned in each department of the division of labor have been taken into consideration without any bias. It is very important that this truth should be plainly known by all citizens. (SD 1: 1935, 383)

Text 7, taken from Section 4, Articles 14 and 16, of the 1935 RPP program, entitled "Agriculture, Industry, Minerals, Forests, Commerce, and Public Works," again describes interoccupational relations:

ARTICLE 14

No economic enterprise can be contrary to the public interest as it cannot be against the harmony between national and all other private activities. This harmony in the unity of work between employers and the employees, too, is fundamental. Mutual relations between the workers and employees shall be regulated by the labor law. Labor disputes shall be settled by our arbitration, and if that proves not possible, by the instruments of arbitration formed by the state.

ARTICLE 16

All commercial activities are important in the country's development. Those capital owners who work normally and who rely on technology shall be protected and encouraged. (RPP 1935, Section 4, Articles 14 and 16)

Text 8, an excerpt from Mustafa Kemal's 1937 speech opening the third convening year of the Fifth Assembly, outlines his commitment to the corporatist vision of society:

I should immediately inform you that I, when economic life is mentioned, I consider activities of agriculture, commerce, industry, and all public works as a totality that it would be incorrect to be thought of as separate from one another. I should also remind you on this occasion that, in the machine of political existence that gives a nation independent identity and value, the mechanisms of the state, the idea, and economic life are so interrelated and so interdependent with and on one another that if these apparatuses are not operated in full harmony and in reciprocal accord, the motive force of the government machine will have been wasted, and the full yield expected of it cannot be realized. (*SD* 1: 1937a, 394)

Text 9, which is the entire text of Section 1, Paragraphs C and D, of the 1943 statement "The RPP after Twenty Years," offers a justification for state involvement in "harnessing" occupational groups to promote "civilizational advancement":

PARAGRAPH C

Organizing classes, allowing class struggle that would bring into relief the contradiction between their interests would serve nothing but wasting the energy of the society for naught and spoiling the tranquility of enterprise and employers. One should not consider the Turkish nation as consisting of various classes, but view it as a coming together of occupational groups, and should never give way to the formation of classes that would exploit one another.

PARAGRAPH D
In order to secure the Turkish nation's rapid advancement in civilization as well as to prevent classes that would exploit others contrary to the manner that populism requires, it is necessary in the economic field to utilize all means that individuals and legal entities possess and the power of the State both at the same time and in a harmonious way. (RPP 1943b, Part 1, Section 1, Paragraphs C and D)

In the same document, the RPP reiterates succinctly its corporatist alignment:

It has been clearly shown to everybody that there can be found a way of not giving way to the formation of classes and occurrence of class struggle although the principle of individual property is preserved. (RPP 1943b, Part 2, Section 4)

These texts illustrate a commitment on the part of the Kemalist leadership to a distinctly solidaristic corporatist ideological conception of society and of the role and function of political institutions therein, from the earliest days through the immediate period after Mustafa Kemal's death. This commitment is an ideological commitment that cannot be gleaned through the official accounts of the meanings of the six arrows. Shifts in circumstances and in other Kemalist emphases did not alter this central ideological element, and recognizing these commitments constitutes a start to offering some answers to the kinds of questions we raised earlier. To be sure, other particular aspects of the Kemalist frame depicted in these texts need to be explored. One may observe, for example, in Text 8 Mustafa Kemal's articulation of a characteristically mechanical view of the role and function of politics and in Text 9 indications that the RPP leadership not only rejected the conception of Turkey as a class society, but was also concerned to prevent a class struggle from taking place therein ("allowing a class struggle"). These statements only underscore the need to account more precisely for the ideological character of Kemalism and indeed for the deeper meanings of the six arrows themselves.

THE "IDEAS" AND "PRINCIPLES" OF KEMALISM

Given the tight relationship between the ideas of Mustafa Kemal as expressed in his speeches and the ideas found in the party documents, he was surely their chief, if not their sole author. And it is in these RPP official programs that one also finds the "ideas" that constituted the practices associated with the Kemalist transformation. The 1931 program, for example, begins: "The main ideas that constitute the foundation of the program of the RPP are evident in the actual deeds and implementations from the beginning of our transformation up to date" (RPP 1931, Introduction). This partial reinforcement of a so-called pragmatist mode—the notion that one should look to the RPP's deeds to understand its ideas—does not *deny* a role for ideas or suggest that *no* ideas shaped RPP practice. "Moreover," the program continues, "the major ones of these ideas have been determined in the general principles of the Statute accepted by the Great [RPP] Congress of the year 1927 and in the declaration of the General Presidency approved by the same congress and in the declaration announced on the occasion of the 1931 elections to the Grand National Assembly."

The party issued another program four years later that opens with a similar refrain, mentioning "the main ideas that constitute the foundation of the program of the RPP," and it adds one crucial feature: it names the ideas as the "principles" of "Kamâlism." "All the principles pursued by the party are principles of Kamâlism" (RPP 1935, Introduction). The spelling of the doctrine suggests some experimentalism vis-à-vis Turkish language-purification reforms. The 1943 program spells the doctrine in its current form ("Kemalism") and adds the arrow-born trajectory image of a "path," a concept that permeates Kemalist discourse: "All these principles that are the foundations of the Party are the path of 'Kemalism'" (RPP 1943a, Introduction; see also RPP 1947, Introduction).

Thus, apparently as early as 1931 the official party saw a coherence to ideas that it would shortly thereafter baptize as Kemalism. It is significant that the 1931 statement itself glances back to the year 1927 as its own benchmark. In particular, it notes that the "major" "ideas" of "our transformation" had been "determined in the general principles" of the statutes of the 1927 party Congress and in the declaration of the "general president." This is a clear statement showing that the most significant ideas shaping the Turkish transformation were those ideas articulated by the RPP structure and by its leader, Mustafa Kemal. To the extent that the RPP had by this time eliminated potential rivals and consolidated its power, the institutions and leadership role of the new state took on secondary importance to the party institutions and leadership.

Moreover, a glance back at the 1927 statutes serves to remind us of the continuity between them and even previous official declarations by the party and its leader. The "major" "ideas" that were "determined" in 1927 were articulated much earlier, not to mention evident in actions and deeds. Thus, we submit that Kemalism, ostensibly born in the 1930s, was the effective political ideology of the properly labeled Kemalist movement as early as 1922 in some of its aspects and 1919 in others. The proof of this claim is established in our fuller analysis of the original documents in the next chapter. To say that Kemalism exhibited some coherence between roughly 1922 and 1947 is not, however, to say that the ideas of which it was composed were fixed in their meaning throughout this entire period. There were indeed important alterations. The important point is that the early Kemalists, despite some of their most famous declarations emphasizing the primacy of action over thought, acted upon what they themselves considered specific "ideas" that they had about the future of "modern Turkey." This means that Kemalism's ideological content must be examined rather than ignored.

5

RETHINKING KEMALISM'S "SIX ARROWS"

The benchmark 1927 statutes declared the republic to be a "nationalist, populist republic." Notably present here are three of the six arrows: nationalism, populism, and republicanism. Significantly, the first two are presented as descriptive features of the republic. Notably absent are the three other arrows, laicism, transformationism, and statism, even though by 1927 the policies consistent with those aims had begun to unfold. In this chapter, we unravel the ideological content of the Kemalist conception of the Turkish Republic by analyzing in detail the meanings of all six of the Kemalist arrows.

NATIONALISM

Nearly all participants in the politics of the early republic were committed nationalists in some sense of the term. They differed, however, regarding the ends, purposes, and specific understandings of the "nation." An issue of much concern in recent scholarship on national identity concerns the affiliational terms of Turkish national identity within Kemalism, especially whether Kemalism's account of Turkish national identity is inclusive and pluralist vis-à-vis other identities, including so-called ethnic ties, or whether it is exclusive. Much has been said, for example, about Kemalism's construction of Turkish national identity in relation to Kurdish identity. The documentary evidence suggests to us that, although the official discourse of Turkish republicanism may stress an inclusive conception of national affiliation under the banner of Kemalism, there is evidence in Mustafa Kemal's own discourse for narrower criteria. There are "two faces" of Kemalist Turkish nationalism, one inclusive and one exclusive (Parla 1992a, 176–211).

As early as 1919, Mustafa Kemal was defining a distinct Turkish national identity with what he considered exemplary and, in some cases, superior qualities vis-à-vis others. To be sure, such descriptions aimed to boost the image of the Turkish nation in both the eyes of his local audience as well as those of the colonial powers in the post-Ottoman lands. It was well known at the time that the occupying powers believed that they had both the legal and moral authority to govern the former subject populations of the Ottoman Empire and to see them become "fit" for "modernity." Article 22 of the Covenant of the League of Nations (1919), for example, upon which the colonial mandates for governance of the former Ottoman Empire were based, states the following: "To those colonies and territories which have ceased to be under the sovereignty of the States which formerly governed them and which are inhabited by peoples not yet able to stand by themselves under the strenuous conditions of the modern world, there could be applied the principle that the well-being and development of such peoples form a sacred trust of civilization and that securities for the performance of this trust should be embodied in the Covenant."

Kemal's nationalist discourse was thus partly a counterdiscourse to colonial concepts that saw the Turks and the other former Ottoman populations as "unable to stand alone in the modern world." Importantly, Kemalism does not, as we shall see, fully reject the terms of modernity. Rather, it asserts them in part to secure both Turkish national rights and its own legitimacy as the governing power. Seeing nationalism as the universal, emancipatory discourse of the time, Kemal asserted, "[t]oday all nations of the world recognize only one sovereignty: national sovereignty" (*SD* 2: 1920, 11; see also *SD* 1: 1923e; *SD* 2: 1930a), and he undertook to constitute and legitimize the national struggle in unsurprisingly highly nationalist terms. The language of national sovereignty had defined the terms of the national struggle from its inception.

But Mustafa Kemal interpreted the identity of the nation in particular ways. The Turkish nation, he said, was not prepared to submit to the will of foreign occupiers because it "is a masterful nation, if it is one, not a slave nation as they imagined" (*SD* 2: 1919, 3). For Kemal, the Turkish nation "possessed," as he understood or defined it, "certain special qualities and distinct manners"—qualities that made it unique relative to other nations—necessary for it "to realize its sovereignty and to securely maintain it" (*SD* 1: 1923e, 310–11). In his terms, it was a "noble" being (*SD* 4: 1926, 574) with "high interests" (*SD* 2: 1929a, 253–54). It had its own "will" (*SD* 1: 1920, 60; *SD* 1: 1923a, 307)—indeed, a "high national will" (*SD* 1: 1920, 60)—its own "purpose" (*SD* 1: 1923a, 307–8), and its own "path" (*SD* 2: 1925c, 219), "the right path" (*SD* 2: 1929a, 254), on which it would "march unhesitatingly" (*SD* 4: 1926, 574). The nation was and could be an agent of its own history. National sovereignty was a force of its own in Kemalist discourse: it is "such a light that, in front of it chains melt, crowns and thrones burn and perish" (*SD* 2: 1924a, 179).

Furthermore, Kemal consistently stressed the authority of the nation over individual wills. He emphasized the need for all members of the nation to be "loyal" to the nation and to "conform," in the spirit of unity and solidarity, to its "enormous" "will and purpose." His opening remarks to the Fourth Assembly of the first GNA session, he declared, "The fate of those who do not conform to the nation's will and purpose is disappointment and extinction. Gentlemen, let us bow with all due respect and submission before this enormous will" (*SD* 1: 1923e, 310). Thus, he was at times to describe himself in such humble terms as "an insignificant individual," as he did while assuming the presidency of the GNA in 1923 (*SD* 1: 1923b, 326). Much later in his life, when discussing matters of history and politics with the foreign minister of Romania, he stated that "if a man thinks of himself rather than [of] the happiness of his country and nation, his value is of secondary grade" (*SD* 2: 1937, 281). Insofar as one's value depends on one's subordinating one's individuality to the solidarity of the nation, one's self-worth is to be determined greatly by one's "capacity for serving the national ideal" (*SD* 1: 1931a, 368) and for practicing "national politics" (Atatürk 1960, 74).

This discourse was effective for Kemal's various legitimation purposes, but it had other objectives as well. Specifically, Kemal used the nationalist discourse to gain ideological leverage over opponents in the GNA. To this end, he identified his RPP's ideals with the nation's and sought to mobilize people around them as one and the same. In January 1925, in a speech on the liberation and prosperity (*saadet*) of the nation, Kemal declared "our aims" to be "the implementation of *our ideals* for the nation" (*SD* 5: 1925a, 209, emphasis added)—not "the nation's ideals," but "our ideals." This kind of statement, while the Kemalists were engaged in consolidating power for themselves, was a far cry from the customary calls heard earlier of the need to "mobilize the nation as a whole in a unified and solidary way to secure real prosperity that is common and general" (*SD* 2: 1923g, 60), as Kemal offered to secure the support of skeptical journalists in Istanbul at an earlier date. The language of general unity and solidarity often concealed the particularity of the Kemalist plans.

This language also concealed the exclusivist account of Turkish national identity, which can be seen in Kemal's understanding of the relationship between the Turkish nation and other nations and in his attempt to imbue the collectivity of the nation with "special" characteristics vis-à-vis other nations. As much as Mustafa Kemal took nationalism to be the motif of the age for all peoples, he believed that there were inequalities between the nations of civilization. His view of the potential structure of these inequalities shifted. At times, he believed that the Turkish nation would be equal—in terms of prosperity and prestige—with the most advanced nations, as stated in the 1931 RPP program: the Turkish nation "marches alongside modern nations and in harmony with them on its path toward progress and development and its international contacts and relations" (RPP 1931, Section 2, Article 1, Paragraph B). At other times, he declared that the aim of the Kemalist project was to surpass all other nations. This was possible because "the nation" possessed "special" qualities. He defined these qualities in different terms, suggesting at times that they were related to shared social factors, but at other times that they were products of an ethnic or racial identity.

Kemal's statements in this regard are extremely important, for they illustrate two faces of Turkish nationalism: one that posits membership in the nation as a membership that transcends particular ethnic or religious identities, and one that posits it as an ethnic, or even racial, trait. The former has been a formally codified ideal of Turkish politics since the founding of the republic. The ideal stipulates that Turkish identity is nonrestrictive in ethnic terms, that all persons of different ethnic backgrounds should consider themselves to be "Turks." Article 88 of the 1924 Constitution states this "civic national" position very clearly: "The people of Turkey regardless of their religion and race are, in terms of their citizenship, to be Turkish." Kemal gave voice to this view in his public statements as well. In a 1925 speech to the Ankara Law Faculty, he stated that "our form of government [has] changed the nature of the common tie among the members of the nation for the maintenance of the existence of the nation that persisted for centuries, that is instead of religious and sectarian ties, has assembled the members through the bond of Turkish nationality" (SD 2: 1925b, 237). The implication was that all those of different local identities could consider themselves Turkish nationals.

Additional assertions by Atatürk and other chief ideologues, however, yield a slightly different conclusion—namely, that the inclusive definition of national membership was not the only definition articulated within Kemal's or Kemalist official discourse. The evidence suggests a view of the nation with distinctly exclusive connotations. In speeches and public statements (which also included legitimation and mobilizational rhetoric), for example, Kemal invested the concept of the Turkish nation with meanings associated with ethnonational and racialist discourses of the time. Our claim is not that Kemal was a *racist* as the term is understood in present-day discourse. Such a charge involves extremely complex interpretive issues that extend beyond the scope of our analysis. Suffice it to say that there are different racialist and racist discourses wherein the concept *race* may take on different meanings with different political implications. Even if the evidence does not evince a definitive conclusion about the specific and explicit role of race in Kemalist discourse, it suggests nonetheless that Kemalist nationalism had a "second face," one whose criteria for national membership were less inclusive, and one that was embedded in the power dynamics of the nationalist arrow. In short, by employing ethnic and racial concepts to describe the special qualities of the Turkish nation, Mustafa Kemal loaded the Kemalist conception of nation with ethnically restrictive meanings along with the more open ones.

Kemal employed three terms interchangeably when trying to capture what he considered the "special qualities" (*SD* 1: 1923e, 310) of Turkey's national character: *kültür, kavim* and *ırk*. We translate these terms, respectively, as "culture," "ethnicity," and "race." Of the three terms, the most difficult to translate directly is *kavim* because it has a meaning in Turkish somewhere between *millet,* which means nation (and had religious connotations in prenationalist discourses), and *ırk,* which means "race." *Kavim,* which Kemal used more often than *ırk,* contains within it hues of "culture" as well. Neither the mixing of these terms nor their use to instill national pride was uncommon in nationalist discourses of Kemal's time, including and especially those in Europe. Nationalists commonly viewed the terms *ethnicity* and *race* as coterminous with *culture* and *nation.*

A common function of these terms within the Turkish nationalist discourse was to combat the perceptions of others about the nation, such as the derogatory racialist discourses common within Western characterizations of the Turk. As such, to a certain extent, Kemal's use of these various concepts should be seen as what might be called "defensive" responses to such depictions. Similarly, the discourse also had a related, domestic aim: to debunk, or at least to displace, various political cultural concepts held by the people themselves that were contrary to nationalist aims and aspirations. All three of the crucial terms—*culture, ethnicity,* and *race*—were purposefully counterposed to alternative ideological concepts, especially the transnational grouping of the politically powerful Muslim concept of *ümmet,* which means the "(Muslim) community of believers." At this level, the conceptual battle reflected a real political one. For the Kemalists, *ümmet* was an opposing term, and *ümmetçilik* (*ümmet*ism) was an opposing movement. Its implications and political imperatives were Muslim transnational, whereas the Kemalists' were Turkish-Muslim national, referencing what they considered the specific experience and qualities of the Turkish nation. They sought to raise the consciousness of the Turks as a nation, something distinct and more primary for their purposes than the community of Muslim believers. In this regard, especially after 1928, their emphasis was unfailingly consistent. From the 1931 RPP program: the party "finds it essential to preserve the special character of the Turkish social whole and of its singular, independent identity" (RPP 1931, Section 2, Article 1, Paragraph B).

Kemal employed the ethnoracialist discourse in contexts that shared a common feature: they were contexts in which he praised Turkish national characteristics, either to cheer the Turks on as they strove toward modern civilization, to congratulate them for the achievements therein, or to point out how they differed from those nations with whom they competed. These uses transformed the politics of legitimation and mobilization into a congratulatory politics of national enthusiasm. "Congratulatory" because Kemal exerted a great deal of rhetorical energy in praising his audiences, and "enthusiasm" because it seems that this, in the end, is what he hoped to generate. He wanted not simply to cultivate merely the identity of a Turk (dryly described as "national-identity building"). He wanted people to experience this identity with pride, good feeling, and a great sense of potential achievement.

Some examples help to illustrate these conceptual tendencies:

(*a*) Employing *kavim* (ethnicity), he stated that "The Turkish society of today, today's children of the Turkish *kavim* who have a claim on having been the founders of the most profound civilizations of the past, have found the clearest and soundest path" (*SD* 2: 1930a, 255).

(*b*) Employing *ırk* (race), Kemal declared in a speech to the Assembly in 1922: "Gentlemen, the people of Turkey are a social whole that are unified racially, or religiously and culturally, filled with feelings of mutual respect and sacrifice for one another and whose destiny and interests are common. In this social collectivity it is among the fundamental points of our internal politics to observe in this society racial rights (*hukuk-u ırkiyeye*), social rights, and local conditions" (*SD* 1: 1922a, 221).

(*c*) In his 1932 speech on Keriman Halis, the winner of the Miss World contest, Kemal joined "the Turkish nation" in congratulating "our Turkish daughter" for having had the world's referees recognize her beauty. Using the term *ırk,* he went on to say that her beauty did not "belong to her person." It was, rather, a manifestation of the innate beauty of "her race": "The Turkish race is the most beautiful race in the world." He punctuated this speech with a call to all the Turkish youth to retain their "high culture" and "high virtue," illustrating how the terms *race* and *culture* were bound up together when he actively showered the nation with praise (*SD* 3: 1932, 92–93). This way of thinking relates to his view that the Turkish nation could "surpass" and not simply progress "alongside" other nations of contemporary civilization. The nation enjoyed a superior status in Kemal's mind. Its potential was not limited to catching up to the most advanced nations of the world. It included going beyond them.

(*d*) In an arousing 1933 speech commemorating the tenth anniversary of the republic, he declared, "We shall take our national culture above the level of contemporary civilization" (*SD* 2: 1933, 275).

(*e*) In 1926, in a context not unlike that in which he lauded the achievements of Miss World, Kemal raised the questions of race and the position of the "Turkish race" vis-à-vis the rest of the world in a discussion with athletes. He said that sport is more important than perhaps the athletes could appreciate "[b]ecause it [sport] is an issue of race. It's a matter of improving and purifying the race. It is a question of selection of the race, and even is somewhat a question of civility" (*SD* 2: 1926, 244). He refrained from too much detail on this point, stating that his praise was intended to show the practical value of athletics for creating an army that would "defend the high honor" of the country (*SD* 2: 1926, 244) (more on this later); but he went on to describe a view of the "Turkish race's" position vis-à-vis other nations that was distinctly hierarchical:

> Gentlemen, there have remained in the Turkish race the ominous, negative, meaningless traces of the past. I have explained the historical reasons for this many times on other occasions. I will not repeat. However, you behold that, at the time when our present generation inherited the grandest Turkish nation that

has been in histories the master of worlds, we had found this grand nation somewhat weak, a little sickly, a bit puny. Gentlemen, I want robust, bold children. You are the men who have undertaken the measures and responsibility of raising these. (*SD* 2: 1926, 245)

This view of the "master" potential of the Turkish nation is clearly at odds with a view of equality among nations. Indeed, in conceptual form alone, it bears resemblance to hierarchicalist and supremacist views prevalent also in Western imperialist discourse of the time, only reversing the terms of emphases: the imperial nations are not the superior human collectivities, the Turks are.

Discernable in these characteristics is a tendency in Kemal's spoken discourse to use terms of an ethnoracialist nationalism alongside terms of a civil or civic nationalism. The effect is that the latter take on hues of the former. For Kemal, the Turkish "nation" is not only defined by social norms of culture and ethos, but also by ethnoracial characteristics. Its position vis-à-vis others is not only one of integrity and equality; it is one of superiority and potential magisterial advantage. The egalitarian aspects of the national discourse were weakened by their association with ethnoracialist and inegalitarian tendencies. If what was meant by "Turkish national" was not only a "common tie regardless of race" but also a member of a "masterful ethnic or racial group," it would have been difficult to be a good civic national Turk if one lacked the right ethnic or racial characteristics.

It is true that some of these assertions may be read to imply that the Turkish nation would, in the company of other nations, reach the highest levels of contemporary civilization. But this interpretation would fail to account for other statements, such as Kemal's speech to an audience in Diyarbakır in 1937 in which he visualized the Turks marching ahead of other nations. The speech is interesting as well because it was given in a location with a large Kurdish population. One of Kemal's purposes in the speech was to legitimize Turkey's claim to sovereignty in the area. What is significant for our purposes is Kemal's congratulatory rhetoric, which accords the "nation" an exemplary status vis-à-vis other nations of the world:

I've visited the centers and surroundings of the 11 provinces of the country. I've seen the Turks, with all its fathers, mothers, and children, of all these centers and surroundings. I've rejoiced a lot. I've witnessed foundations of high civilization: a human society that possesses high understandings with minerals, technicians, [and] workers that is Turk from top to bottom. We have traversed such areas of this country [where we have seen] there the women who grabbed the ploughshare much more than the men, and who, with their hoe in one hand, were working to enrich the fecund earth of the Turk[s], who love the land and who are tied to it with the heart. All these people give the surplus of their own lot lovingly, without hesitation, and with great sacrifice to the state treasury so that the Turkish Republic becomes rich, strong, and magnificent. It is not possible for an intelligent person who has traveled, visited, and studied all that we have seen and expressed in this short account not to feel himself within *a mighty and noble being that diffuses grandeur to the whole world.* Leaving aside unconscious beings who do not feel in the same way, real humanity would unhesitatingly accept that the Turkish Republic and its present day owners, Turks, are an *exemplar for the civilization and humanity of the world.* More than that, the Turks are a *sublime being* who are preparing to perform again, but this time in a much more sublime way, the cultural duties [*kültürel vazifeleri*] that they have fulfilled for humanity in the very old periods of history. (*SD* 4: 1937, 591, emphasis added)

It was a recurring theme for Kemal that the Turks, humanity's exemplar nation, had been eclipsed in history and were now preparing to rise once again. They were proudly gearing up once again to "diffuse grandeur to the whole world." The language evokes hierarchical images of unparalleled superiority in the relationship between the Turks and the rest of humanity. It is language very similar to that found in *Nutuk,* where Kemal suggested that "[a]mong the nations of the Orient it is known that the Turkish element was in the front and was the strongest" (Atatürk 1960, 72–74).

Indeed, Kemal may have had in mind Kurdish claims to autonomy in the region designated as Kurdistan by the Treaty of Sèvres when he made his comments in Diyarbakır. It was certainly with such intent that he made a 1923 speech to the people of Adana in which he directly challenged Armenian territorial claims. One of the effects of his hierarchical view of the relationship between the Turkish nation and other nations can be seen in his following comments:

The Armenians have no right whatsoever in this beautiful country. Your country is yours, it belongs to the Turks [*Memleketiniz sizindir, Türklerindir*]. This country was Turkish in history; therefore, it is Turkish and it shall live on as Turkish to eternity. . . . Armenians and so forth have no rights whatsoever here. These bountiful lands are deeply and genuinely the homeland of the Turk. (*SD* 2: 1923b, 126)

There is little doubt that one of Kemal's purposes in these texts was to inspire national cohesion and action. As analysts of ideology, we must note as well that the meanings evident in Kemal's discourse had the effect of constituting and investing the Kemalist nationalist project with particular understandings as opposed to others. Kemal believed that the Turkish nation enjoyed a position of prestige and advantage over others in world history. This view implied, among other things, that the Turks could legitimately see themselves in a position of racial and ethnic superiority and advantage over others (including their neighbors) in the present. Even without the language of race and ethnicity, this view enabled Turks to see themselves as a nation with an elevated status over others. There was no subtlety in the delivery of this point when the party ideologue and former justice minister Mahmut Esat Bozkurt stated in 1930 that there was only one place for those who were not "genuine Turks":

Because this party [the RPP], by the works it accomplished heretofore, restored to the Turkish nation its position that is essentially the master [*Çünkü bu fırka buğüne kadar yaptıkları ile esasen efendi olan Türk Milletine mevkiini iade etti*]. My idea, my opinion is that, harken ye friend and foe [*dost da, düşman da*], the master of this country is the Turk. Those who are not genuine Turks can have only one right in the Turkish fatherland, and that is to be a servant [*hizmetçi*], to be a slave [*köle*]. We are in the most free country of the world. They call this Turkey. (Bozkurt 1930, 3)

Bozkurt's pronouncements demand that all citizens freely embrace Turkish nationality, thus securing "the most free country of the world." Yet explicit themes of master and slave weaken, if not undercut entirely, implied themes of egalitarian citizenship and liberty. The discourse reinforces a master-servant understanding of relationships between those who are Turks and those, "friend or foe," who are not. The latter must know who "the master of this country is"—"the genuine Turks," who are the only ones who rightly possess authority in "this country." The others possess "the right" to serve and to be a slave, a willing slave, but "a slave" nonetheless, one who recognizes who the "master of this country" is. For Bozkurt, the language of rights and freedom had meaning only within a hierarchical understanding of Turk/non-Turk relations. Bozkurt here pronounced the hegemonic authority of the Turkish nation over all space and relationships within Turkey. Indeed, this was the meaning of "Turkey" for him: the place where the Turkish nation is a masterful authority over all within it.

It is this kind of imagination that lies behind the Kemalist "Turkish Historical Thesis," which maintained that the original Turks of Central Asia had through their migration given birth to all the world's great civilizations (from the Hittite and Sumerian to the Chinese and European). This thesis was promulgated as part of Kemalist official history by the Society for Turkish History, founded in 1932. The Kemalists had been hard at work creating a "national history" for several years. In a statement in 1930, Kemal announced that "the principle of nationality that is modern has spread internationally. We too shall take great care to keep our Turkishness. Turks are noble in civilization. We are working to prove scientifically that we are an old nation residing in the environs of Izmir [on the southwestern Aegean Coast of Anatolia] before the Greek" (*SD* 3: 1930, 89). While opening the Third Great Congress of the RPP the following year, Kemal underscored the importance of national history to national identity: "If the memory of deeds performed for the nation and by the nation is not kept above all other memories, it would not be possible to appreciate the notion of national history" (*SD* 1: 1931a, 368). The party's program of that year reiterated the point: "Our party places extraordinary importance on our citizens' knowing the profound history of the Turk. This knowledge is a sacred treasure that nourishes the Turk's ability and might, his feeling of self-reliance, and his indestructible resistance against all currents that would harm the national being" (RPP 1931, Section 5).

This "nationalist historical" imagination articulated by the party also lay behind various episodes in the Kemalists' language-reform policies. These episodes include the founding, in early 1932, of the Society for the Study of the Turkish Language, which revived old Central Asian languages to replace parts of the Ottoman language that were adopted from Persian or Arabic roots rather than from Turkish, and the society's promulgation of the "Sun Language Theory" in 1935. This theory maintained that all the world's languages had developed through the Turkish of the tribes of Central Asia. Rather than requiring the revival of old Central Asian terms, the theory eased the project of the Turkish language revivalists: insofar as all world languages had original Turkish roots, any term in any

RETHINKING KEMALISM'S "SIX ARROWS"

language could be used to replace Ottoman terms that were deemed to be of impure origins. The 1935 RPP program included an index ("Progamının Sözlüğü") for words used within the program that were part of the reform efforts. Some contemporary terms of wide usage today, such as *eğitim* for "education," may be found in this index. But so, too, may other, more curious, purified Turkish national substitutes, such as *endüstri* and *endüstriel* for "industry" and "industrial" (to replace *sanayi* and *sanayi erbabı*), *nomal* for "normal" (to replace *tabii*), and *sosyal* for "social" (to replace *içtimai*).[1] The ruling party thus claimed the Turk to be the background master of the languages of other nations, as well as over the country and its residents.

Courses in the Sun Language Theory were made compulsory by Ankara University in the 1930s, and the national language institute has been an arena in which Turkey's cultural wars have been played out ever since. It is true, as Erik Zürcher notes, that "the language reform movement lost much of its *élan* after the death of Kemal" (1993, 198). But the political imagination that conceived of this thesis remained vital—in terms of promoting both Turkish national sovereignty in contested areas and the rightness of the Kemalist project. It is not accidental that the bas-reliefs and the statues found at Kemal's mausoleum in Ankara, constructed by the state between 1944 and 1953, resemble closely the architecture of the Hittites. Underlying these national history theses and the social and architectural polices shaped by them is Mustafa Kemal's belief in rekindling the past "greatness" of the exemplary Turkish nation: "It was," after all, to his mind, "the Turkish nation who first taught agriculture and crafts to all humanity. Today, true scientists do not harbor any doubt anymore that the Turkish nation has been the educator of the world" (*SD* 2: 1931a, 264–65).

Kemal thus believed himself to be the latest leader of what, on one interesting occasion, he termed "Turkdom" or "Turkishness" (Türklük): "I have no doubt whatsoever that the great forgotten civilized quality of Turkdom, upon its further development hereafter, shall rise in the future horizon of high civilization like a new sun" (*SD* 2: 1933, 276). To consider oneself a member of this social collectivity and to accept the national identity that the Kemalists described in their nationalist arrow, Kemal believed, ought to bring one "happiness." Hence, his 1925 declaration to an audience at Bursa: "Respected people of Bursa, I would like to express heartily and definitely that the path we are following to-

---

1. The full index is reproduced in Parla 1992b, 100–105.

gether is true. This path will enable us to attain happiness" (*SD* 2: 1925c, 218). Hence, also, the famous saying that one finds printed in textbooks, carved below Atatürk's busts, posted in newspapers and upon the walls throughout Turkey, and articulated in the 1933 speech for perhaps the first time: "How happy is one who says, 'I'm a Turk' [*Ne mutlu Türküm diyene*]" (*SD* 2: 1933, 276). The saying joins the goal of happiness with the Kemalist concept of being a Turk. Within this ideological frame, the Turk will be a slave to others no more; she or he will be a master once again. To wit, it is crucial to note that the saying is not "How happy is one who says, 'I'm a Turkish citizen.'" The concept of a "Turk" in Kemalism not only stops short of conveying civic national meanings, but also has other, more exclusive, supremacy-oriented ethnoracialist elements as well.

POPULISM

The idea that the Turks constitute a "nation" closely relates to the idea that they constitute a "people." Kemalist discourse often employs the two interchangeably, such that the idea of popular rule overlaps with the idea of national sovereignty. In a 1922 discussion on conditions for peace in domestic and foreign affairs, for example, Kemal sought to legitimize the new Ankara regime by claiming that "our form of government is entirely a democratic government. And, in our language this government is called 'People's government'" (*SD* 3: 1922a, 51). As we shall see, this form of government would come to be called a republic, not a democracy, but Kemal's understanding is clear enough: the people rule in Ankara. Popular sovereignty thus meant something akin to national sovereignty, rather than the Ottoman sultan's sovereignty or foreign control.

There is more to the meaning of *people,* however. Kemalism's "peopleist" arrow does not simply overlap with "nationalism." In the Kemalist view of the "people," we find a particular depiction of relations between social groups and individuals within the nation. Understanding this aspect of Kemalist populism is crucial to understanding Kemalist politics because Kemal initially named his political party the People's Party so that it would both be and be seen as the representative of the "people," where this was to be understood as a particular kind of social grouping. The party was also so denominated in order to construct it as the rightful inheritor of the torch of national freedom and the voice of Turkey's "general," "popular" will.

The most important element of the Kemalist "peopleism" is its solidarist core—namely, that the interests of all members of society are not and should not be considered to be in conflict. As Kemal stated on numerous public occasions and as the RPP documents repeated almost verbatim again and again, the "interests and happiness of the people" are "common and general" (*SD* 2: 1923g, 60). All those "individuals," for instance, who accepted Kemalism's principle of legal equality and did not claim special privileges were rightfully considered of "the people," according to the RPP 1923 statutes. Conversely, all political organizations based "not [on] national aims but [on] personal interests" were seen by the RPP as illegitimate and "harmful" to Turkey's social and political fabric (*SD* 2: 1923g, 60). Herein lies the ideological fulcrum for policies designed to exclude from the political sphere of "national politics" those parties or social movements that the regime considered divisive.

Especially significant in this regard is Kemal's rejection of class-based conceptions of the "people" and of Turkish society itself. Like his view of nationalism, this rejection had two sometimes contradictory, but nonetheless salient aspects, each of which must be understood if we are to grasp Kemalism's essentially solidaristic corporatist character.

The first aspect of Kemal's stated view on "the people" was his claim that the Turkish nation was composed of classes that were *not* in conflict. The second was his claim that the Turkish nation was not composed of any classes at all. If one is searching for contradictions within Kemalism, some may be found here. If not, what one finds is an emphasis on the latter aspect in Mustafa Kemal's thought and RPP documents, with the former sometimes emerging as a poorly articulated rendition of the latter. The question of emphasis is important because, ultimately, Kemal and the RPP used their view of "the people" to justify their sole position as rulers in the state—that is, to enforce and reinforce their position as the representatives of all interests in society over and against those they considered to be representatives of the interests of particular sectors and classes. From a legitimation perspective, both aspects of Kemal's view amounted to the declaration by the Kemalist leadership that Turkish society was (and would be) no place for a socialism because economic classes either did not exist or, if they did, were not in conflict with each other. The Kemalist party offered the solidaristic corporatist alternative, preferring to say that the classes did not in fact exist and that the people consisted of occupational groups. Turks were farmers, herdsmen, landowners, artisans, small merchants, workers, laborers, free professionals, industrialists, businessmen, and merchants (all their terms, see Texts 1 and 3 given in chapter 4). Grouping according to profession or occupational categories, as opposed to either wealth or wage status, is a quintessential corporatist characterization of society.

Evidence of the presentation of the first aspect of "the people"—that classes were not in conflict in Turkey—can be found in a 1923 excerpt from Kemal's speech to journalists, quoted also in chapter 4: "In my view, our nation does not possess various classes that would follow very different interests from one another and because of this be in a state of struggle with one another. The present classes are in the nature of being necessarily complementary of each other" (*SD* 2: 1923h, 82). There is no denial of the existence of classes in this statement, only a denial of their relationship as antagonistic.

Evidence for the more prominent, second aspect—that no classes existed in Turkey—can be found in both Kemal's utterances and the chief RPP documents, which reiterated Kemal's statements almost verbatim. The basic point found therein is that Kemalist populists did not consider "the people of the Republic of Turkey" as "composed of fully separate classes." This conceptualization can be found in Kemalist documents as early as 1923. Noteworthy in Texts 1, 3, 4, 6, and 9 in chapter 4 is that this claim is almost always accompanied by the alternative corporatist conceptualizations of the constitutive groups of society, including "occupations" (Text 1, *SD* 2: 1923f, 97–98), "department[s] of the division of labor" (*SD* 1: 1935, 380–83), "major occupational groups," and "practitioners of various activities from the point of view of the division of labor for social life" (Text 3, RPP 1931, Section 2, Article 2). The people of Turkey do not reside in classes, these documents asseverated. They reside in different functional units of society, organized harmoniously along with and according to the role that these units play in the occupational division of labor. The occupational groups have interests that are "compatible" (Text 1, *SD* 2: 1923f, 98) and not "mutually contradictory." They coexist and operate in "harmony," not in conflict. In short, their workings "provide or secure social order and solidarity rather than class struggle" (RPP 1931, Section 2, Article 2, Paragraph A). The people exist to enjoy relationships and interactions of "tranquility," not antagonism. This is a "truth" that "should be plainly known by all citizens," said Kemal (Text 6, *SD* 1: 1935, 383).

This kind of populist discourse ensured the RPP's claim to represent all members of society and to buttress the party's assumed role of "protecting" the "interests" of these occupational groups: "The work of each of these [groups]," said one RPP organ, "is requisite for the life and happiness of one another and of the general body social" (Text 3, RPP 1931, Section 2, Article 2). Conversely, the party assumed the role of "preventing" all class-based ideological expressions and movements. The 1943 party text spoke of this inherited role in no uncertain terms:

> Organizing classes, allowing class struggle that would bring into relief the contradiction between their interests would serve nothing but wasting the energy of the society for naught and spoiling the tranquility of enterprise and employers. One should not consider the Turkish nation as consisting of various classes, but view it as a coming together of occupational groups, and should never give way to the formation of classes that would exploit one another.
>
> In order to secure the Turkish nation's rapid advancement in civilization as well as to prevent classes that would exploit others contrary to the manner which populism requires, it is necessary in the economic field to utilize all means that individuals and legal entities possess and the power of the State both at the same time and in a harmonious way. (Text 9, RPP 1943b, Section 1, Article 1, Paragraphs C and D)

The ideological thrust here differs little from the thrust behind Kemal's expressed view of 1923. His long description of the constituent groups of the nation (in Text 1, an excerpt from Mustafa Kemal's 1923 "Speech with the People in Balıkesir") includes an explicit rejection of class-based parties: "Well known are the consequences that we witnessed thanks to political parties that have been formed as if there existed in our country separate classes. Whereas when we say People's Party, not only parts but the whole of the nation is included" (*SD* 2: 1923f, 97).

This description of the groups concluded with Kemal linking nationalism and peopleism by declaring that *"It is thus I see our nation.* Therefore, it is not possible to separate into classes practitioners of various occupations because their interests are compatible with one another, and all of them comprise the people" (Text 1, *SD* 2: 1923f, 97–98, emphasis added). Hence, the 1943 RPP document reasserted the Kemalist nationalist-populist understanding when it declared that "It has been clearly shown to everybody that there can be found a way of not giving way to the formation of classes and occurrence of class struggle although the principle of individual property is preserved" (RPP 1943b, Section 4). The Kemalists had found their way to preserve the core component of capitalism (private property) while also promoting a view of "society" that was "unified" in its interests. Analytically speaking, neither the liberal statement "society is composed of individuals" nor the socialist statement "society is the arena of class conflict" appeared in the thematic emphases of populism. Rather, Kemalism at this time exhibited the prototypical Third Way emphases of solidaristic corporatism, evident in Turkey from the moment the republic was founded. The "nationalist-populist republic" was to be a Kemalist corporatist republic.

These populist emphases, of course, effectively shaped RPP policies, especially those designed to ensure solidaristic and unitary-based economic and political organizations by eliminating or manipulating liberal or class-based movements—hence, for example, the elimination of the leadership of the Communist Party and establishment of an "official" Communist Party. Class conceptions and class-based movements were divisive threats to the social order consistent with the RPP's solidarist corporatist views. To this end, it found useful the Italian labor code, with its ideologically fascist prohibition of class-based politics. All corporatist ideologies seek harmony between labor and capital, not tension or struggle. The RPP declared its interest in this goal in Article 5 of its 1931 program (Text 4) in which it declared itself committed to the goal of "establishing harmony between labor and capital." Such a goal would require that unharmonious interests be repressed, while cooperative ones be incorporated. In the view of the party, all interests should be brought into the process of active harmonization because class-based ideas "exploit others" (Text 9, RPP 1943b, Section 3), whereas the Kemalist corporatist view protected the interests of the "landowners" as well as the "herdsmen." It ensured the interests that were "general." In *Nutuk,* Mustafa Kemal spoke of the RPP's role as the official organ of Kemalist corporatist populism. It was to be "based on the principle of *halkçılık* [populism]" (718). In the official discourse, its "point of departure" was conceptualized as securing "the sublime and vital interests of the nation" (*SD* 2: 1924b, 190), the *"general* well-being and prosperity" of the nation (*SD* 1: 1927a, 352, emphasis added), considering "without bias" "the private *and general* interests of the citizens positioned in each department of the division of labor" (*SD* 1: 1935, 383, emphasis added). The party will ensure "tranquility," "solidarity," and "order," as it "protects" and "cares for" the interests of all.

The RPP leadership described and justified these policies in both nationalist and populist terms simultaneously, such that the meanings of each arrow overlapped and reinforced the terms of the others, both implicitly and explicitly. Consider the language of Kemal's statement of 1927, made while opening the Second Great Congress of the RPP, in which he argued that the RPP was the rightful heir to the Erzurum and Sivas Congresses because "the general objective [from Erzurum and Sivas] concerning the country and the nation—which consists of providing the general well-being and prosperity—has been followed without any change in its essential nature" (*SD* 1: 1927a, 352). By speaking of "the nation's" "general objective" and "general well-being," Kemal evinced language central to both the nationalist and populist arrows. The language of the larger interest of the people overlapped with the nationalist discourse, indeed with the achievements of the nation in its recent struggle. What is significant is that Kemal traced this Kemalist interpretation of the people back to the organizational and institutional structures of the "national struggle": he created a direct link between the national struggle and the RPP's "general" aims. Thus, the linkage between the populism and nationalism arrows was a significant component—in ideological terms—of the Kemalist internal legitimation strategy. Kemal consciously forged and actively enforced the relationship between (its) populism and (its) nationalism. Given the ideological contestation within the early national movement, one must not lose sight of the strategic legitimation advantage the Kemalists obtained by doing so. By forging this organizational, institutional, and conceptual continuity between the RPP and the nationalist movement, or between populism and nationalism, they ideologically prepared the ground for a specific kind of nationalist politics, that of corporatism.

Nor must one ignore how the rhetorical-masking operation typical of corporatist ideological discourse is at work here, beginning with the claim that Turkey had no significant class developments or class divisions in the 1920s. Kemalism's outlook to the contrary, not only did a class structure exist, but the national struggle could be interpreted, at least partly and fruitfully, as a class alliance. A full analysis of this kind is beyond the scope of our concerns here. Suffice it to point out that, in our view, the Turkish national movement may be compellingly interpreted as an alliance of several classes: bureaucratic actors (military, civilian, intellectual); a petit bourgeoisie; an Anatolian, "national," commercial bourgeoisie; an incipient and subordinate metropolitan industrial bourgeoisie who sought protection and monopolistic favors from the state and the state's party; a set of capitalist big landowners and feudalistic landed interests; a numerically and organizationally weak urban working class; and a sizeable landless peasantry.[2] This alliance fought against a minority and comprador metropolitan commercial bourgeoisie in addition to the apparatuses of European political and military domination. The alliance splintered as the Kemalist faction eliminated competing elites from the victorious classes and attempted to organize the remainder, the inchoate working class included, in a solidaristic corporatist manner. Their claim that no classes existed is thus suspect. More accurate was their claim that no acute class polarization between labor and capital existed, but in this instance their actions spoke louder than their words, for the "nonexistence" of classes did not prevent the Kemalists from adopting preemptive measures—such as importing the corporatist fascistic labor legislation from Italy—against a class-conscious proletariat. The properly so-called ideological rhetoric of "no classes" was not so much a description of the situation as much as it was a corporatist ideological denial of potentially antagonistic class relations that was meant to mask, or to occlude, certain realities as part of the Kemalist (third) way of capturing political and economic power. A fuller discussion of this matter awaits a discussion of the statist, or etatist, arrow. At this point, we may say that with their populist arrow the Kemalists sought to annihilate obviously visible disagreements about the nature of the people's (and the nation's) interests. Their parallel denials of extant fundamental disagreements over both matters of nation and populism enabled them to deny others a space and say in the people's or nation's political realm. Thus, the denial of class struggle enfolded within their obfuscation of relations of domination within the state more generally.

Some would suggest that the Kemalists "constructed" a vision of the people that ensured their hegemonic rule. We do not disagree that this was part of the project, but the term *construction* fails (even if it is intended otherwise) to capture the "misconstruction" evident in their vision. The RPP consciously engaged in making new beliefs for legitimation purposes in order to obfuscate the reality of conflict and power relations both in the economic and political spheres.

REPUBLICANISM

Classical republican political thought, from Aristotle and Cicero to the Italian Renaissance thought of Nicolo Machiavelli, depicts the general political ideals of

2. See Keyder 1979, 3–44, 1987, and Parla and Öncü 1990 for historical sociological considerations of the class context.

republicanism in very specific terms. As the theorist Margaret Canovan has put it, "The term is defined by contrast with monarchy. Whereas a traditional king enjoys personal authority over his subjects and rules his realm as his personal possessions, government in a republic is in principle the common business (res publica) of the citizens, conducted by them for the common good" (1987, 433–34). Republicanism evokes some of the most profound political achievements in human political history: the creation of governments by human beings so that they can rule themselves freely. It emphasizes the importance of citizenship and the value of "civic virtue," defined as the capacity of human beings to act politically to secure their own individual interests as well as common interests. Hence, classical republican theorists envisioned government to be truly public— of the people and by the people, not only for the people. The twentieth-century theorist Hannah Arendt, whose name is often invoked in contemporary republican theory, captured the spirit of republican governance when she cited the "men of the eighteenth century revolutions" who "turned" to the Athenian examples of equal rule by law (isonomy) and to the Roman practice of the citizen rule to constitute "a form of government, a republic, where the rule of law, resting on the power of the people, would put an end to the rule of man over man, which they thought was a 'government fit for slaves' " (1986, 62). Kemalism, as the solidaristic and partly fascistic corporatist successor to Ottoman reign, exemplified some aspects of classical republican governance, but it also was clearly at odds with others. Our discussion here focuses on the meaning of *republicanism* within the discourse of the six arrows. Insofar as understanding Kemalist republicanism requires thinking not only about understandings of the term itself, but also about understandings of the very mechanisms of governance (such as leadership, political parties, citizens' role, army, youth, etc.), our interpretation of the kind of "republic" the Kemalists founded continues throughout the book.

For Kemal and the RPP, the republic was the broadest institutional agent of their transformation. The meaning of republicanism, therefore, cannot be comprehended apart from the meanings of the other arrows, especially nationalism and populism because these two arrows express antimonarchical interest in elevating the position of popular organs of governance over and against the organs of arbitrary government by the Ottoman sultanic regime. "Such a government," Kemal said of the former, "is the people's government based on national sovereignty. It is a Republic" (Atatürk 1962, 438). Note the juxtaposition of concepts

related to populism ("the people's government"), nationalism ("national sovereignty"), and republicanism. The 1927 statutes said that a republic was the
"only form of state" that could continually elevate the "position of prestige and
prosperity of the Turkish nation" (RPP 1927, Article 2). Echoing themes of
the men of the eighteenth-century revolutions, the statutes enthusiastically
proclaimed that it is the republic that "closes the door to all kinds of domination
[of the people/nation]." As the 1947 RPP program would summarize, a "Republican regime" was created that "abolishes all obsolete institutions" and "expresses in the best way the sovereignty of the national will" (RPP 1947,
Introduction).

The republicanist arrow thus expresses the particular Kemalist understanding of populist and nationalist governance. Kemalism imbued republicanism
with *its* understanding of nationalism, saying, for example, that the republic "personifies the properties of virtue, integrity, and rightness of the great nation" (*SD*
1: 1927b, 354). It embodied the nation's "special qualities" and thus was to be used
consistently with manifesting those special qualities once again. In his 1933 anniversary speech, Mustafa Kemal declared: "In a short time we have accomplished much and great deeds. The greatest of these deeds is the Republic of
Turkey, whose foundation is Turkish heroism and the high Turkish culture" (*SD* 2:
1933, 275). "Republicanism" here has a personal and personifiable character, a
"national character," such that it—meaning the RPP-controlled state—would
"find" and "learn" the "inclinations and needs" of the nation (*SD* 4: 1927b, 584).
In the official ideology, one finds *republic,* where one might expect to find the
terms *people* or *nation:* "The future children of the Republic shall be much more
prosperous and happier than ourselves" (*SD* 4: 1927b, 584). Like the nation, the
republic is also something special: it is a "sacred Republic," the RPP said, the work
of which is "based on high principles" and "loyalty" (*SD* 3: 1926, 80). The republic's work is the nation's work, the institutional manifestation of all that the nation
can and will do. It is thus, like the nation's sublime quality, to be protected at all
costs, especially from socially divisive currents and movements.

One consequence of the RPP's equation between the nation, the people, and
the republic (as the people's work) is that the ideological character of the republic may be understood by examining the party documents as much as by examining the formal constitutions and laws of the state. In the single-party period, the
party's formal documents were not mere partisan declarations. They were the official views of the state and thus defined the real character of the Kemalist res

publica. The Kemalists considered the statutes of 1923 and 1927, for instance, to be the determinative declarations of their purposes and thus the purposes of governance more broadly. Similarly, the separate pamphlets issued after 1931 as "programs" functioned both as party programs and as official statements of governance. They were, moreover, intended to be understood in these ways. The language of their opening clauses was that of state proclamation. Consider, for example the definition of the "fatherland" and the "nation" in the 1931 program:

> 1. The fatherland is the homeland within the political boundaries of today, in which the Turkish nation lives with its old and sublime history and its works that maintain their presence in the depths of its lands.
>
> The fatherland is a whole that does not accept any division under any constraint or condition.
>
> 2. The Nation is a political and social whole that is formed by citizens who are connected with one another by the unity of language, culture, and ideal. (RPP 1931, Section 1, Articles 1 and 2)

Both paragraphs proclaim governing-policy attitudes as much as they define the RPP's "particular political platform." The RPP identified the party institutions as the institutions of the state. The 1931 program goes on to describe the "basic organization of the state," its public law, its form of education, and so on (all of which we examine later). Even major statements regarding the institutionalization of power are found in these texts. In a passage whose significance we further analyze in part 2 of this work, the paragraph on the "basic organization of the state," for example, posits that the "form of administration [*idare*]" is based on the "principle of unity of powers" between various branches of government. This form constitutes an important alteration in the tendency toward separate legislative and executive powers, as was the case in the 1924 Constitution. But "the Party is of the opinion that the most suitable form of state is this"—that is, one that is based on unity of powers (RPP 1931, Section 1, Article 3). It further clarified its stance in the 1935 program, stating that the legislative and executive powers are unified in the Assembly, which uses its legislative power directly and delegates executive power to the president and the Council of Ministers formed by him (RPP 1935). This stance extended the tension between the party documents and the constitutional principles, clearly indicating that the place to find the evolving understanding of republicanism was in the party's public statements. Kemalist governance thus blurred the classical republicanist distinction between "the state," which, in principle, is the property of "the people," and "the political party," which is, in principle, the property of a portion of it. For the RPP, the state was the party's state, which it would use to govern the people.

This is not to say that the classical republicanist features of Kemalism are to be ignored. They should not be, but they should be interpreted in classically corporatist terms consistent with Kemalism's central ideology. (Republicanism may, though need not, take corporatist forms.) The 1935 program mentions, importantly, the "independence of the Judiciary," and elaborates on the 1931 solidarist pledge to "protect the rights of individual and social freedom, community, and property, which are given to the Turkish citizens by the Constitution, saying that these rights are limited by the boundaries of the state's existence and authority." In classical republicanist terms as well, this program goes on to state that "the interest of individual and legal entities shall not be contrary to the public interest" and that "laws shall be enacted according to this principle." But the historical evidence is clear enough: the interest of the state was to be determined by the party alone, which in turn determined the corporatist character of rights, freedom, and authority. Kemal himself was explicit on the relation between the party and the state. In a speech to party members in Izmir in 1931, he said plainly, "If our laws are not fit, we amend those laws and enact new laws. If we deem it necessary and obligatory in the last resort, we never hesitate in marching toward our target on this path, rising above everything" (*SD* 2: 1931a, 264). The party will rise above everything, especially particular interests and even the republic's Constitution. This is not the language of a classical republican leader. It is the language of exclusionary political practice that followed the Kemalist consolidation of power. After consolidation, it was only apt for the party to declare that it "believes that Republic is the form of state that best and in the surest way represents and implements the idea of national sovereignty. The Party, with this unshakable conviction, defends the Republic by all means against danger" (RPP 1931, Section 2, Article 1, Paragraph A). It was *their* regime, their republic. Dangers to them and, as would be the case for many years, to their transformation were to be considered dangers to the republic itself.

THE KEMALIST TRANSFORMATION:
TRANSFORMATIONISM, LAICISM, STATISM

> The new Turkey has no relation whatsoever with the old Turkey. The Ottoman Government has passed into history. Now a new Turkey has been born. (*SD* 3: 1922a, 51)

> The Republic, that has neither the principle of nor inclination to numb with half measures any event or problem of our social structure, has experienced the first stages of the radical improvements it has attempted and has entered the phase of reaping the benefits that shall increase everyday. (*SD* 1: 1926, 344)

> A country in ruins on the brink of the abyss . . . bloody skirmishes with all kinds of enemies . . . years of war . . . and then the new fatherland, the new society, the new state [continual applause] and in order to achieve these uninterrupted transformations that are recognized with respect from within and abroad . . . here is a short expression of the Turkish general transformation. (*SD* 1: 1935, 380)

Probably no term in the Kemalist frame conveys more the desire on the part of the leadership to reconfigure anew the post-Ottoman, Turkish governing structures and symbols than *transformationism* or *inkılâpçılık,* whose meanings are closely related to laicism (*laiklik)* and statism (or etatism: *devletçilik*). Not uncoincidentally, the latter two arrows have been objects of criticism and alteration in the past seventy-five years. Kemalist laicism, which expressed an interest in expelling Islam from certain spheres of governance and social life while maintaining it in others, has remained to some extent, but in an altered form as state actors have found it increasingly useful on the Kemalist pattern to use and manipulate Islam for various instrumental purposes. Statism is the single arrow to have eroded significantly after 1947, when the less-statist economic factions captured the state and, while still seeking rents meted out by the state, resisted the previous high levels of state interference and supervision. In this chapter, we develop the conceptual net of these arrows in the context of interpreting the transformationist arrow more generally, first by indicating its contrast with ordinary Western liberal and socialist understandings of *revolution,* with which it is often associated, and then by unpacking in greater detail its meanings along with those of its laicist and statist components. The former analysis is important, for the Kemalist transformation, given its class and "above-class" character, committed itself to certain forms of political and cultural change, but not to a fundamental transformation or to an uprooting of the social, political, and economic structure of the ancien régime. If one is to call their transformation a *revolution* one should at least be clear on this content and on the fact that, in the eyes of the Kemalist leadership, a large transformation was desirable, whereas a revolution—understood as *radical* transformation—was not.

REVOLUTION?

Scholarly and nonscholarly observers alike frequently translate the term *inkılâpçılık* into English as "revolutionism." Even the widely used *Modern Turkish-English* dictionary published by Redhouse publishers of Istanbul, which has been publishing authoritative Turkish dictionaries since the late nineteenth century, defines *inkılâpçılık* as "(nonviolent) revolutionism." This translation is consistent with many other contemporary lexiconigraphical sources as well as with very many ordinary understandings of the English meaning of this particular Kemalist arrow, but it raises serious problems in understanding the ideological substance of Kemalism's transformationist ends. The Kemalists explicitly defined their project as a "transformation" in contrast to a "revolution." Mustafa Kemal himself was wary of using the concept *revolution* because he believed that it may have signaled an association between Kemalism and communist movements in the Soviet context that he was eager to avoid. That said, it is true that, like those ordinarily considered "revolutionaries," the Kemalists surely thought that their program of transformation would bring about progress and rapid improvement in the lives of Turks. Their transformation was in some ways massive and drastic, even forceful, which are basic elements in any revolution. Nonetheless, from an ideological perspective, we must take heed of the words of the Kemalists themselves. Their view was that their achievements were distinct from other kinds of large-scale change.

To be sure, there is no single, essential understanding of revolution, but in the ordinary understandings of Western parlance that are often used to evaluate Kemalism, the term *revolution* is most frequently associated with revolutions in the liberal and Marxian senses. In liberal terms, one tends to think of revolutions, for example, as efforts to reconstitute political and social institutions in order to secure individual rights of liberty and political equality. In the Marxian sense, by contrast, revolution occurs when the class relations characteristic of capitalism are brought to an end by a class-conscious, universal movement of the proletariat.[3] In both discourses, the term *revolution* connotes something much different today than it did in its Greco-classical sense. According to Aristotle, a revolution occurs not when a new order of things comes into existence, but rather when the order of the world returns to a beginning point. This meaning derives from the root of *revolution,* which is "to revolve." A revolution was said to occur when history returned to a previous order.

The late-seventeenth-century liberal theorist John Locke employed the term in its Aristotelian sense as well, but also imbued it with a different, "progressive" historical meaning. A revolution in the Lockean liberal sense was not to be a simple return. For Locke, a revolution occurs when power, having been abused by a political sovereign, returns to the people after a "long train of abuses, prevarications and artifices." The people then may "rouse themselves, and endeavor to put the rule into such hands which may secure to them the ends for which government was at first erected" (1988, 225). Power, having thus returned to the people, is then reconstituted in institutions that will secure the people's rights "anew," "providing for their safety anew, by a new legislative" (226). In this more modern sense of the term, revolutions aim not only to return to the people something that has been taken away or lost through abusive behavior (such as rights, liberties, well-being, etc.), but also to improve conditions, to work for human betterment and an ethically informed expansion of human opportunity. In this sense, revolutions are said to be progressive. Revolutionaries seek not to return, but to advance and to develop humanity, or a small portion of it, in ways that are new relative to the ways of the past.

---

3. Our discussion of these concepts of revolution is not intended to endorse uncritically the liberal or Marxian views thereof; rather, we seek to show how Kemalism offers a corporatist conception of revolution, not a liberal or Marxian or socialist one, as has too often been assumed. We are aware of important rethinking about both the conception and the character of social change as induced within liberal and Marxian discourses, especially in the context of their non-European forms and application, specifically in their association with colonialism and empire. See important studies on these themes in the context of India, such as Mehta 1999, Prakash 1995 and 2000.

One early spokesperson for the progressive dimensions of liberal thought was John Stuart Mill. According to Mill, the distinguishing characteristic of "modernity" is that human beings are "no longer born to their place in life, and chained down by an inexorable bond to the place they are born to, but are free to employ their faculties, and such favorable chances as offer to achieve the lot which may appear to them most desirable" (1995, 134). Giving voice to the progressive aims of modern, philosophically liberal thought, Mill also gave clarity to the meaning of the term *liberty* when he defined "the appropriate region of human liberty" as follows:

> It comprises, first, the inward domain of consciousness, demanding liberty of conscience in the most comprehensive sense, liberty of thought and feeling, absolute freedom of opinion and sentiment on all subjects, practical or speculative, scientific, moral or theological. The liberty of expressing and publishing opinions may seem to fall under a different principle, since it belongs to that part of the conduct of an individual which concerns other people, but, being almost of as much importance as the liberty of thought itself and resting in great part on the same reasons, is practically inseparable from it. Secondly, the principle requires liberty of tastes and pursuits, of framing the plan of our life to suit our own character, of doing as we like, subject to such consequences as may follow, without impediment from our fellow creatures, so long as what we do does not harm them, even though they should think our conduct foolish, perverse, or wrong. Thirdly, from this liberty of each follows the liberty, within the same limits of combination among individuals; freedom to unite for any purpose not involving harm to others: the persons combining being supposed to be of full age and not forced or deceived. (1988, 15–16)

As we shall see, this notion of liberty was far from the minds of the solidaristic corporatist Kemalists, who rejected Western philosophical and ideological liberalism as a basis for or goal of social transformation. With our interest in ideological classification, we might note here that Mill is understood as an advocate of liberalism precisely because he sought to delineate the conditions for individual freedom. "No society," he wrote, "in which these liberties are not, on the whole, respected, is free, whatever may be its form of government; and none is completely free in which they do not exist absolute and unqualified" (1988, 71). A revolution in the liberal sense requires expanding the domain of individual opportunity significantly.

By contrast, a Marxian revolution takes place when a united movement of human beings overthrows capitalism in order to end the kinds of oppression that occur when one class owns all the forces of production in a society and another class, the majority of human beings, owns only its power to labor, which it must sell to the owners for a wage. Like the liberals, Karl Marx theorized conditions necessary for an expansion of human opportunity. Unlike them, he did not think in terms of "individual freedom and rights." He thought that although these categories constituted a historical advance over other ways of thinking about the human being historically (such as "subject" or "slave"), they were insufficient to capture the relational and historical characteristics of the human being. According to Marx, human beings are not best conceived as "individuals" but as species beings, whose particular forms of activity and consciousness participate in the historical activities and forms of consciousness of the species as a whole. Capitalism, with its ideology of egoistic and liberal individualism, conceals the human being's essential relationality, so Marx distinguished between what he called political emancipation—emancipation as the liberals might understand it—and what he called real, human emancipation. He argued that political emancipation is indeed a great step forward, but it is not human emancipation.[4]

Real human emancipation will occur when the class-oppressive and alienating relations typical of capitalism are historically transcended in a revolution that will destroy the conditions for class oppression—namely, the institutional complex of what Marx called "bourgeois property." Thus, Marx and Frederich Engels analyzed history and theorized revolution in terms of class categories, understood as the relationship between human beings and their economic position under capitalism. Their analytical focus was based in neither individual nor corporate social units of analysis. It was class oriented. The *Communist Manifesto* began with the observation that "the history of all hitherto existing society is the history of class struggles." A revolution by the proletariat, then, would end such history and initiate a new period of classless relations, where economic relations would be organized "from each according to their ability to each according to their need," and human relations would be progressive relations of absolute human equality.

4. For these concepts and emphases, see Marx 1994, especially 1–102.

If the proletariat during its contest with the bourgeoisie is compelled, by the force of circumstances, to organize itself as a class, if, by means of a revolution, it makes itself the ruling class, and, as such, sweeps away by force the old conditions of production, then it will, along with these conditions, have swept away the conditions for the existence of class antagonisms and of classes generally, and will thereby have abolished its own supremacy as a class.

In place of the old bourgeois society, with its classes and class antagonisms, we shall have an association, in which the free development of each is a condition for the free development of all. (Marx 1994, 176)

Like the concept of a liberal revolution, this concept of revolution was far from the Kemalists' minds. Marx, Engels, and, later, Lenin anticipated that such a socialist revolution would occur following the global spread of capitalism, whose dynamics would intensify the miserable conditions of existence for the majority of human beings. The Marxian variant of a revolution is, in this sense, internationalist in scope. It shares this feature with liberal ideologies as well. For the liberals, no one is at liberty until all are at liberty. For the Marxists, no one is free until all are free and equal.

Both the liberal and Marxist understandings of revolution therefore share an interest in human betterment, but the terms and categories in which this interest is understood differ. Moreover, as modern concepts of revolution, both advocate a fundamental alteration in the power relationships between human beings and their authorities in the direction of greater human freedom or greater equality or both. This fundamental alteration is captured in a variety of terms, such as *old* and *new* or others that mark a progressive transition from one kind of society to another. For the liberal, the transition is one toward greater individual freedom of conscience, taste, pursuit, feeling, thought, publication, and so on. For the Marxist, it is brought about by the end of oppressive class relations such that all humanity may develop their humanity as species beings. To our minds, these are the assumptions—though not the only ones—that are frequently packed into contemporary understandings of the term *revolution*. But these two classical modern senses of revolution are also often mistakenly imposed upon the Kemalist transformation.

So what, then, is the precise Kemalist understanding of the transformationist arrow? And what is the relationship between revolution and transformation as the Kemalists understood it?

TRANSFORMATIONISM

The original term *inkilâpçılık* was replaced in the 1935 RPP program with a Turk-ified form of the arrow *devrimcilik*, a term that is indeed more easily translatable as "revolution." Understanding the original as such, however, obscures the distinc-tions between revolution and transformationism as they were elaborated by Mustafa Kemal. In November 1925, in a famous speech at the opening ceremony of the Ankara Law Faculty, he described the "great achievements" of the trans-formation as "much more than and much more sublime than any one revolu-tion" (*SD* 2: 1925b, 236–37), insisting that the meaning of the term *inkilâpçılık* differed from ordinary understandings of the term *revolution*. "What is the Turk-ish transformation?" he reflected in January of that year. "This transformation, other than the meaning of *revolution* that the word implies at first sight, expresses a much greater change than the latter. The present form of our state has become the most progressive form that has eliminated the old forms that have persisted for centuries" (*SD* 2: 1925b, 237). Similarly, one of the regime's ideologues, Ahmed Ağaoğlu, argued in an essay entitled "İhtilal mı, İnkilâp mı?" (A revolu-tion or a transformation?) that the Kemalist transformationism was not a revolu-tion. Part of the reason why was that, in Kemalist discourse, the Kemalist transformation pursued a break from certain institutions and patterns of gover-nance and understanding without the undesirable, destabilizing overhauls im-plicit in revolution as it was understood at the time. *Transformation* was a positive term, *revolution* a negative one. The latter had associations with Bolshevism espe-cially, and as early as 1922 Mustafa Kemal had asseverated that "It must not be forgotten that this form of administration is not a Bolshevik system. Because we are neither Bolsheviks nor communists. We cannot be one or the other. Because we are patriotic and we respect our religion" (*SD* 3: 1922a, 51).

Not only, then, is the distinction between transformation and revolution one that the founders made; it also comports with the character of the regime's ideo-logical and practical achievements. The central Kemalist transformationist inter-est was nationalist, populist, and corporatist. It was not to produce conditions that would promote individuality in Mill's sense; nor was it meant to propel a class-based, mass movement to overthrow capitalist relations. From what we have seen thus far, the Kemalists' central conceptual frame was that of an organ-ically conceived people or nation, directed by the national leadership. They posited a conception of a cooperative society made up of occupational groups, not individuals, and they denied the existence of classes with conflicting interests. And, as we shall see in their understanding of statism, they promoted capital accumulation for purposes of profit and reinvestment. They were thus not, in this sense, anticapitalist. They themselves said as much: they were not interested in the betterment of individuals or classes; rather, they were interested in the betterment of a metaphysicalized mass nation through the elimination of what they considered "old" and outdated Ottoman political structures and certain sociocultural ways of life. Thus, much of what we have already said about nationalism, populism, and republicanism must be understood as part and parcel of the Kemalist transformationist aims. The metaphysicalized nation and its corresponding term *the people* constituted their conceptual ideals, and the corporatist republic was their central political aspiration.

Note that in his 1925 remarks Kemal drew attention to the establishment of a nationalist republic in place of the old multinational Ottoman sultanate. This republican development itself was seen as central to the transformation, and it is one reason why it has been called a "revolution": a new state was born in place of the old one. Kemal stressed this shift as early as 1922: "The new Turkey has no relation whatsoever to the old Turkey. The Ottoman government has passed into history. Now a new Turkey has been born. It's not that the nation has changed. The same Turkish element constitutes this nation, but the form of administration has changed" (*SD* 3: 1922a, 52). The 1925 statement is also significant in that it drew attention to the accomplishments of the regime in its first year of existence, the most important of which were its laicization policies. By January of that year, the caliphate had been abolished, education unified, and sartorial reforms enacted. There were also developments in the economic sphere of the transformation, with the establishment of the Turkish Business Bank (İş Bankası). The regime at this time had neither established institutions to protect the various aspects of liberty in the liberal sense nor expressed any intention to abolish capitalist class relations. Indeed, suspicions were growing that Kemal and the RPP were planning to pursue a significantly antiliberal, authoritarian path of reform rather than enhancing individual liberties. (The new civil code was not in place until 1926.) This was suggested by the manner in which the republic was proclaimed, by dynamics within the Assembly itself (which we discuss later), and by the use of the Independence Tribunals to limit expression and publication in events surrounding the abolition of the caliphate. Moreover, the regime denied the existence of class antagonisms and forcefully eliminated movements organized along such alternative ideological lines.

Kemal's statement of 1925 is thus significant in that he perceived a transformation to have occurred by that time, well before many of the policies usually associated with the transformation—policies that lasted well into the 1930s—had taken shape. Why is it the case, one may ask, that a transformation was perceptible by Kemal in 1925? This question may be answered by noting that Kemal used *transformation* in an accumulative or aggregate fashion. It became the general term for those policies that altered the political, social, cultural, and economic dynamics from the Ottoman period. Each and every policy that the Kemalists viewed as a success in this regard became part and parcel of their transformationist aims.

What was the common ideological thread that linked all of these policies? The essential Kemalist transformationist goal was first and foremost *to create a sense of fundamental change* among the members of the nation by attaching the meaning of all its new policies to this term *inkılâp*. The terms in which Kemalism even today identifies its policies for change, whether they constitute fundamental changes in relations of power and domination or not, are *progress, civilization,* and *modernity*. This was the "transformationist" spirit to be imbued in the consciousness of the nation: "The country shall soon become contemporary, civilized, and modernist. For us this is a matter of life and death. . . . We shall go forward crushing those who want to stand in our way of progress. We are not to stop in the valley of renovation. The world is progressing with an enormous movement. Can we remain outside of this harmony?" (*SD* 3: 1923a, 71–72). The RPP reflected the transformationist spirit: "The People's Party is the manifestation and organification in all the towns of a transformationist spirit that founded the Turkish Republic without paying heed to falsehoods whatsoever. The People's Party is a determined party that has undertaken to inject Turkey into the civilized world and to elevate it therein" (*SD* 2: 1924b, 189). There was, then, no "Turkish revolution" in 1923 in the ordinary liberal or Marxist senses of the term, or in either ideological or practicopolitcal senses. Rather, there was a "Turkish transformation," both in theory and practice. *İnkılâp* was meant to be a transformation by those who carried it out and was intentionally identified with specific "civilizing," republicanist, laicist, and (after the depression of 1929–30) statist changes in political, legal, cultural, educational, and economic spheres. That the Kemalists considered these changes progressive and civilizing does not mean either (*a*) that they considered the changes revolutionary or (*b*) that the changes were revolutionary in noncorporatist ideological terms.

LAICISM

Laicism stood for several central transformationist objectives: the expulsion of religion from certain spheres of governance and social life; the reconstitution of education according to the presuppositions and aims of the positive sciences; and the establishment of uniform, nonreligious laws of a centralized administration that would serve all citizens of the Turkish Republic. Laicism also guaranteed, in principle, freedom of religious conscience as long as this freedom did not conflict with the tenets and political purposes of laicism. All of these goals were central to the Kemalist understanding of what they called a "contemporary," "civilized," or "modern" state. The justice minister at the time of the promulgation of the Turkish civil code, Mahmut Esat (Bozkurt), made the case for a uniform civil code on the pattern of European states by stressing the determination of the regime to comply with the requirements of states of the current "civilization": "The principal distinguishing characteristic of states that belong to the civilization of the present century," he stated, "is their considering religion and the world separate" ("Preamble," the Turkish civil code).[5]

The party ideologues repeated this goal in successive party documents, beginning in the RPP statutes of 1927. Here are the major statements from 1927 and 1931, which express several of the central understandings of the laicist arrow.

> The Party considers it among its most important principles: by rescuing matters of belief and conscience from politics and from various conflicts of politics to realize all political, social, [and] economic laws, organizations, and needs of the nation according to the principles and forms that the positive and experimental sciences and technologies have granted and secured to contemporary civilization, that is, to completely separate from one another religion and the world in the affairs of the state and nation. (RPP 1927, Article 3)

5. Entire translated text, "The Rationale for the Draft Bill (of the Turkish Civil Code)," may be found in Davison 1998, 167–73.

The Party has accepted as a principle that in the administration of the State all laws, regulations, and procedures should be made and applied according to the principles and forms that the sciences and technologies have secured for contemporary civilization according to the needs of the [contemporary] world. Because the view of religion is a matter of conscience, the Party sees it as the main cause of our nation's success in contemporary progress to keep separate religious ideas from affairs of the state and the world and from politics. (RPP 1931, Section 2, Paragraph D)

Several themes outlined previously warrant analysis and detailed elaboration.

First, we might note that the meaning of the phrase "positive sciences" is very particular in the Kemalist discourse. In its use in this context, positivism refers to the modern ideological doctrine and mid-nineteenth-century movement founded in France by Auguste Comte (1798–1857). The central idea of positivism is that knowledge should be based on the observation of general, lawlike cause-and-effect relations in nature and society. Such knowledge allows human beings to predict, manipulate, and order those relations so as to produce outcomes according to their designs and wishes. This is why Comte's motto was "Order and Progress": order would be achieved by carefully identifying and arranging relevant causal variables to produce desired outcomes; and progress would be achieved by the application of knowledge to the solution of problems in the natural and human arenas, such as in the cure of diseases or the development of new agricultural techniques and societal institutions. Central to the positivist approach to the world is its rejection of alternative ways of knowing and organizing human society, such as the abstract meanings of patriarchal authorities or the purported utterances of divine oracles. Thinking of himself as a kind of prophet of the scientific age, Comte maintained that the positive stage of history—that is, the stage of history where all sociopolitical institutions would be organized according to the principles and understandings of modern scientific knowledge—would supercede other stages of human civilization in which the organizing principles of society were based on either "theological" or "metaphysical" precepts. "It is reserved for our century," he wrote, "to take in the whole scope of science" (Comte 1975, 46).

Comte had a significant impact in a variety of domains in politics and academia. Schools of contemporary sociology and political science that seek to explain causal relations in human society consider Comte their founding father. In practical ideological politics, effective positivist movements occurred in Europe and Latin America as well as in Western-oriented intellectual circles in the Muslim world. A discernible intellectual lineage can also be traced between some of Comte's followers in Paris and some influential figures in the early Turkish nationalist movements who were exiled during the last years of the nineteenth century. These exiles' ideas worked their way into the ideological framework of the CUP, whose motto "Union and Progress" not uncoincidentally was directly influenced by Comtean positivism. These ideas were not entirely new in the Ottoman context, however. They were part of the Ottoman *tanzimat*ist trend that promoted administrative reforms based on the techniques of Western science.[6]

The most famous of the CUP ideologues, Ziya Gökalp, was deeply influenced ideologically by another famous positivist, Emile Durkheim. Gökalp held the first chair of sociology at Istanbul University (after 1912), and although he was not the first person in the late Ottoman context to argue that Turkey needed to import the positive sciences in order to accomplish its economic developmentalist goals, no other ideologue stated that nationalist aim more succinctly than he did when he said that "a modern nation was one that thinks in terms of the positive sciences" (Gökalp 1959, 279). The Kemalists absorbed this goal to some degree within their laicist aspirations. In speeches, party documents, school texts, and so on, they made positivism a central tenet of their transformationist aims. Kemal himself enthusiastically declared that "the torch that the Turkish nation is holding in its hand and its head marching on the path of progress and civilization is positive science" (*SD* 2: 1933, 274). One of his more famous maxims, inscribed on the Ministry of Education building in Ankara, is "Science, the truest guide to life." The Turks, the Turkish positivists firmly believed, urgently needed to learn to think scientifically for the "nation's success in contemporary progress." Science was the gateway to progress in contemporary civilization.

In partly accepting the positivist notion that scientific ideas must *replace* theological ones, the Kemalists staked a claim in an active debate of their day. The debate had philosophical as well as the more commonly known political dimensions to it. Many non-Kemalist nationalists disagreed that scientific advancement required separating religion and politics, not to mention subordinating all education as such to the positive sciences. Consistent with Islamic reformist

---

6. See, e.g., Mardin 1962 and 1989, 136–80.

discussions of the era,[7] they believed Islam could be maintained as a cultural institution of value while Turkey's scientific and economic development proceeded. Scientific and Islamic cultural development are not antithetical pursuits. Positivism got it wrong, or, alternatively, it was dependent on European/Christian presuppositions about the need to separate affairs of religion from those of the temporal world. Islam, it is argued, makes no such separation, considering all life, including the life of the mind, to be the domain of God. If Islam itself makes no necessary distinction between rational reflection and belief, then religion and scientific understanding—conceived within the totality of God's creatorship—cannot be incompatible.

Borrowing from the logic of positivism, the Kemalists rejected this view and those who believed it, arguing that theology precedes science historically and is neither necessary for nor compatible with "modern" scientific knowledge. Therefore, in the context of the present inquiry, scientific reason ought to replace theological belief as human beings employ their own faculties—freed from the constraints of religion—in order to know their world. Those who thought otherwise perpetuated historically "regressive" and "obscurantist" (*irtica*) views. Those who followed the path of positive science were the only proper rulers for so-called properly modern states.

Not particularly concerned with the historical genesis of positivism in the "Christian West," the Kemalists accepted in part its universal, culturally neutral claims that scientific knowledge is not dependent upon a priori doctrines or philosophical beliefs, but is rather received through experimentation. The Kemalists thus dropped God from the nationalist school curriculum—though not from all state school curricula—believing, like Ziya Gökalp, that "a modern nation thinks in terms of the positive sciences." Science does not look particularly European or Christian, or Muslim for that matter, to those who subscribe to the positivist doctrine. Rather, it looks, in principle, like it can belong to all, regardless of particular historical location or cultural identity, and can therefore benefit all. In the conceptual dimensions of the Kemalist transformation, positive science thus became one aspect of what it meant to achieve human progress: to support scientific research for the benefit of the nation that the Kemalists had thrust on

7. The classic position in this regard is that of Jamal ad-Din al-Afghani; see Keddie 1983. In the Turkish context, the leading figure is Said Nursi; see Mardin 1989. For positions from contemporaneous Arab Muslim milieus, see Abu-Rabi' 1996.

the path to contemporary civilization. Although this view was at the core of Turkish national thought before the Kemalists came along, they made it a center-piece of their laicist aims. Religion, they maintained, must be separated from sci-entific and all other worldly pursuits. We return to this theme in our discussion of national education at the end of this section. Let us for now, however, continue to reflect here on the elements of the 1927 and 1931 party statements regarding laicism.

There is a nuance in the phrasing of the separation between religion and the world that also warrants attention. The 1927 statutes refer to separating com-pletely "religion" and "the world" in the affairs of state and nation. The 1931 document narrows this goal slightly. It specifies that "religious ideas," not "reli-gion" more generally, are those things that must be maintained as separate from the political, social, and economic laws, organizations, and needs of the nation. This is an important specification; neither document indicates explicitly or im-plicitly, for example, that "religious" personnel or institutions must be com-pletely separated from the state.

To our minds, this is an important and, indeed, informed clarification on the part of the Kemalists because the regime did not entirely separate religious insti-tutions, personnel, or practices from the state. Rather, as we noted earlier, the regime maintained integrated, institutional relations of interpretation, subordi-nation, and control over Islam through the office of the Directorate of Religious Affairs. The aim of laicism, therefore, was to remove religion as a rationale from certain spheres of governance without fully separating its institutions and per-sonnel from the state—that is, from other spheres of governance concerning the administration of faith. This lack of a full separation should not occlude the fact that the Kemalists undertook to establish a greater separation between politics and religion than had been established previously in Ottoman or Turkish gover-nance. This is one reason that the separation was seen as central to the transfor-mation. The abolition of the caliphate, the adoption of the Swiss civil code, and the near total elimination of an Islamic school system ("near total" because the Unity of Education Law made a stipulation for "separate *mektep*s" [small schools for Islamic study]) were, in the Turkish context, significant steps in laicizing the politics of Turkey.

Part of the reason for maintaining the administration of Islam was that the Kemalists knew that some of their opponents would use religion against them. The RPP ideologues gave expression to these political power dimensions of their laicist aims in the language of the programs excerpted earlier. The 1927 statutes emphasize the need to separate completely "religion and the world" so that "matters of belief and conscience" would be "rescued from politics and from various conflicts of politics" (RPP 1927, General Principles, Article 3). The Kemalists knew they were participating in a political battle regarding religion. Their view was that "religion," as conceived by their opponents, was getting in the way of the tranquility needed to carry out the Kemalist transformation. Unity and harmony in affairs "of the world" were central to the laicist reforms, and the Kemalists considered the existing religious leadership and institutions both divisive and impractical. In *Nutuk,* Kemal described the idea of a caliphate as absurd given the multiple national affiliations of various Muslim societies. In the preamble to the new Turkish civil code, Minister of Justice Mahmut Esat derided religious laws (*"fikih* rules") as "coincidental, change dependent, and mutually contradictory." It was necessary, he argued, "to rescue republican Turkish justice from this chaos, deprivation, and very primitive situation" by creating "quickly and legislat[ing] a new Turkish civil code that is fitting to the requirements of our transformation and of the civilization of the present century." The only alternative for states that are interested in respecting religious conscience is "to make separate laws for subjects belonging to various religions," a move that, ultimately, "is totally opposed to the political, social, economic, and national unity that is a fundamental condition in states of the present century."

The use of the term *primitive* to designate religious laws indicates Kemalism's positivist assumptions that theocentric governance was backward. Laws in modern states, the Kemalists claimed, cannot be based on religious codes. Echoing what should by now be the familiar themes of Kemalist laicism, the justice minister defended the adoption of the new, nonreligious civil code by stating:

Laws that derive their principles from religions unite the communities in which they are being implemented with the primitive ages from which they have descended and constitute one of the major factors and reasons impeding progress. It should not be doubted that our laws that receive their inspiration from the immutable judgment of religion and are still linked to divine law are the most powerful factor tying the Turkish nation's destiny to the stipulations and rules of the Middle Ages, even during the present century. The Turkish Republic's remaining deprived of a codified civil code that is the regulator of national social life, a code that should be inspired only by that life, is irreconcilable with the meaning and the conception required by the Turkish revolution. ("Preamble," Turkish civil code)

By 1931, the RPP had secured harmony and "tranquility" in part through policies designed to eliminate opposition forces that were considered to be throwbacks to a previous century.

As the 1927 document also shows, the Kemalist view at that time was that religion needed to be "rescued" from political conflict. This view was in part reflective of the context; the Constitution still declared Islam to be the religion of state, ensured the application of Islamic law, and required that officials declare their oaths "by God." These articles were not removed until 1928, the year when the RPP completed its consolidation of power. The language of the 1931 party program concerning laicism reflects this new situation. Rather than stressing first and foremost the need to rescue religion, the document now implied that the existing institutional relations should be kept the way they were. It began with a statement about the need to apply "the principles and forms that the sciences and technologies have secured for contemporary civilization." It concluded, however, with the implication that the battle had been won, saying that because "religion is a matter of conscience," "success in contemporary progress" required "keeping [as] separate" religious ideas from "affairs of the state, the world, and politics." The promises regarding matters of conscience should be seen in part as another move within a debate over the proper role of Islam in governance. This dimension of the meaning of laicism is extremely clear also in Mahmut Esat's preamble to the Turkish civil code of 1926, wherein he stressed the themes of unity in direct relation to the need to "allocate" religion to a matter of "conscience":

> The distinguishing characteristic of states that belong to the civilization of the present century is their considering religion and the world separate. The opposite of this results in the domination of the conscience of someone who does not agree with the accepted religious foundations of the state. The understanding of states of the present century cannot accept this. Religion is to be revered and would be immune as long as it remains a matter of conscience from the point of view of the state. Intrusions of religion into laws and articles and stipulations have always during history resulted in serving the arbitrary will and de-

sire of rulers, the mighty, and oppressors. In separating religion from the world
[in civil codes], the state of the present century saves humanity from these
bloodstained afflictions of history and allocates religion to the conscience as
the real and eternal throne for it. Especially in states that contain subjects belonging to various religions, in order to acquire the ability of carrying out a single law in all of the community, this severing relations with religion is a requisite
for the sovereignty of the nation. This is because if the laws will be based on religion it becomes necessary for the state that is faced with the necessity of accepting freedom of conscience to make separate laws for its subjects belonging
to various religions. This situation is totally opposed to the political, social, economic, and national unity that is a fundamental condition in states of the present century.[8]

One indication here is that the regime had no qualms with Islam as a matter of
conscience, as long as Islam subordinated itself to the contemporary interests of
the nation. An often neglected component of the interpretation of *laiklik* is the
extent to which Kemal and the Kemalists promised to *secure* religion in what
Mahmut Esat referred to as its "real and eternal throne"—that is, as a matter of
conscience. There is no expressed interest here, or in any other official document
from the period, to eliminate religion from the sphere of private morality or individual conscience. The Kemalists were not atheists, and their laicism was not, in
principle, thoroughly antireligious. They had no argument with religion as an individual or social norm. Indeed, in this way, the Kemalist doctrine of laicism
bears some, albeit slight, relation to liberalism, which preserves the freedom of
religious belief and expression in what it construes as the "private" sphere.

Similarly, the Kemalist conflict with an Islamic strata was only partial: they
opposed those who opposed the Kemalist interpretation of Islam's place in the
state (whom the Kemalists defeated in the struggle for power) and promoted
those who supported that interpretation in the state's Directorate of Religious

8. The population in Turkey was in a general sense nearly all Muslim, and there were important
differences in rituals and practices across the different Muslim groups, both Sunni and Alevi, and
within Sunni Sufi orders. This diversity on matters of religion also includes the Kemalist position,
which sought to reinterpret Islam in order to elevate national identity as the common bond for all
Turks, which is not to say that various Muslims as Muslims were necessarily opposed to laicization,
whether they were opposed to Kemalism or not.

Affairs. It was to be the state and its official class of religiously esteemed personnel that oversaw the institutions and personnel of Islam in such a way as to secure its version of "freedom of conscience." Kemalism's laicist arrow thus expresses a partially anticlerical, lay interest in securing Islam's exclusion from certain spheres of governance and life *and* in ensuring a version of its vitality in other spheres. Hence, it is difficult to describe the laicist politics or intentions as secular, insofar as the latter is commonly understood as nonreligious or even antireligious in its anglophone meanings.[9]

The classic statement to this effect appears in *Nutuk,* where Mustafa Kemal described the rationale for the abolition of the caliphate. He stated, "The faith of Islam should be *purified and raised* from the political situation in which it has been put for centuries" (Atatürk 1962, 684, emphasis added). This comment is strategically very important in the context of the political battles of the time, but it is symbolically very significant as well, for it is consistent with Kemalism's nonsecularist and nonatheist understandings and practices. The idea of "purifying Islam" links strongly with the idea of "rescuing" it from politics, seen in the party's documents. Kemal's view was that the pinnacle policy in the laicization process—the abolition of the leadership position in Islam—had the purpose of rescuing, not abandoning, the tradition by disentangling it from its previous position of political importance, "the political situation in which it has been put for centuries," not from politics as such. Part of this purification process had to do, again, with the Kemalist understanding of the needs of the modern state, but part of the explicit intention also had to do with protecting religion in certain senses within the "consciences" of the nation. Kemalism did not exhibit an interest in establishing either atheistic governance or a governance entirely disinterested in religion. Rather, it offered a limited laicism that rejected one form of Islamic institutionalization, a highly integrated one, in favor of another; the new form was still integrated. To many of Kemal's and the RPP's opponents, the policies that cut the regime's previous ties to Islam made the regime appear entirely antireligious. A participant in a Sufi order whose institutions were closed or a teacher in the *medrese* system could hardly think that the regime had a supportive position on Islam. But the view of Kemalism's theopolitical opponents or the actual effects of particular policies should not occlude the fact that Kemalism as a laicist ideology was *not* a thoroughgoing "antireligious and anticlerical belief,"

9. For an elaboration on this particular point, see Davison 2003.

and, we believe, the Kemalists themselves did not uniformly see themselves as antireligious as such. In fact, regardless of what Mustafa Kemal did or did not believe, his significant statement in *Nutuk* suggests that he distinguished between "pure" Islam and an impure Islam tainted by its excessive entanglement in political affairs. That Mustafa Kemal supported any form of Islam might strike some readers as surprising, for he has been depicted as a consistently radical secularist activist intent on eliminating religion from life. But his own public historical record does not accord with such a view.

Interestingly, prior to 1924, it was not unusual to hear Mustafa Kemal praising Islam and claiming that, along with science, it had an important role to play in the development of Turkey's national consciousness. Indeed, until 1924, he acted more like the leader of an Ottoman-Islamic loyalist movement than of a Kemalist-laicizing one. His speeches during the early phase of the national struggle were peppered with praise for the sultan and for Islam. The following statement shows how, in one of the movement's most precarious moments, when their declarations of loyalty to the sultan were under suspicion, Kemal beseechingly rededicated himself and the movement to a "sacred fight" on behalf of the Ottoman regime. The statement was made on April 27, 1920, four days after the opening of the Turkish GNA:

> Our Majestic Master, there are traitors who are continually trying to seduce the people and to present our national defense as a rebellion against your blessed imperial office. They want to have the nation murder each other and to leave the way open to enemy conquests. Whereas, both those who kill and those who are killed are all yours. All are your equally loyal children. We cannot abandon our national defense until the flags of the enemy are withdrawn from the roofs of our fathers' hearths. We are bound to continue our sacred fight, unless the feet of alien men retreat from the soils of our homeland and as long as foreign soldiers linger around the temples of Istanbul all parts of which are gorgeous and venerable proof of our great Khans' religion and divine love. God is one with your children, who are toiling for the honor and independence of the Caliph-Khan who defends the homeland of his ancestors. (*SD* 4: 1920, 321)

The statement seriously calls into question Kemal's secularist (qua nonreligious or antireligious)—and indeed laicist—commitments, and it helps to remove some of the surprise that one may experience when today's apparently non-

Kemalist Islamists stake a claim to carrying his mantle. The phrase that we translate as "sacred fight" is the religiopolitical concept *mücahede* (from *cahid*). It comes from within the cluster of Islamic political concepts and reveals that Kemal's ideological discourse at the time was quite different than the doctrine many describe as "Kemalism" today. Such terms hardly evince an attitude of hostility toward religion as such or even toward the ancien régime. To be clear, our point is not that Kemal's discourse at the time lacked symbolic references to what would become the transformationist goals of the regime. Rather, it is that the transformation did not begin from clearly atheist or even secularist (qua nonreligious) foundations. Kemal's early Ottomanist-Islamic loyalties coupled Islam and scientific progress. In the early 1920s, Kemal could easily have been seen as a supporter of Islamic reform, especially if we consider his public statements, such as a lengthy speech to the people of Izmir at the end of January 1923, in which he declared: "Our religion is a most reasonable and most natural religion, and it is precisely for this reason that it has been the last religion. In order for a religion to be natural, it should conform to reason, technology, science, and logic. Our religion is totally compatible with these" (*SD* 2: 1923i, 90). Similarly, in a talk with *lise* (lycée) students the same year, Kemal spoke of bringing "reason, logic, and the Shariah" together (*SD* 2: 1923m, 154).

Historians are quick to point out that Kemal's intentions in promoting Islam may have been solely strategic. After all, they argue, Kemal was trying to maintain power in a highly diverse movement under highly fluid political conditions. The language of Islamic reform should be seen as part of an early legitimation strategy to ensure Kemalist hegemony so that the reforms could be implemented at a later point without resistance. This view is consistent with the interpretation that Kemal's actions and statements were designed not to reveal his true intentions until his and his party's positions were secure, able to advance the interests of the regime and to prevent their opponents from doing the same.

It is very likely that there is a calculated dimension to Kemal's statements. Indeed, we do not deny that he was a very clever political actor. Nonetheless, there is an ideological dimension to the public statements that cannot be considered simply strategic if we are to grasp the full thrust and significance of the meaning of the laicist reforms to those who participated in them. The record is very clear that Mustafa Kemal expressed his sincere commitments to religion both before and after the reforms. Some documents show Kemal tracing the ancestral history of Central Asian Turks as far back as Noah (*SD* 1: 1922b, 270). These texts, which are very difficult to translate from Ottoman Turkish into English, are permeated with references to the greatness of God, Muhammad, and, of course, the Turkish nation. Mustafa Kemal knew his religious history and employed it for mobilizational purposes. As he did, he invested the movement with certain religiopolitical meanings. In front of a very receptive Assembly audience in 1922, for example, he hinted at the modernization of Islam by a committee formed in the Ministry of Shariah Affairs:

> I examined with all due significance the annual work of our Ministry of Shariah Affairs. I found the results admirable. I thank and congratulate [them]. In fact, there is no need to express any view about the progress of Shariah affairs. Because this matter is already determined by the Koranic dogmas. However, I shall not proceed before I mention a point that comes to mind: Gentlemen, the sacred pulpits of the mosques are the most sublime, most inspirational sources of the people's spiritual, moral nourishment. Therefore it is one of the most important duties of the illustrious Ministry of Shariah to provide the people with the possibility of divining the spirituality of the valuable sermons that shall enlighten and guide the people from the pulpits and *mescit*s. (*SD* 1: 1922a, 231)

This statement indicates that religion was not simply to be respected as a matter of individual conscience; it was to be institutionally supported and promoted by the official religious organs of the fledgling state. At this point, the documents tell us, Kemal received applause. He then continued, using language symbolic of his purification aspirations: "By addressing the spirit and the brain (*demağ*) from the pulpits in a language that can be understood by the people, the body of Muslims gets rejuvenated, their brains purified, their faith strengthened" (*SD* 1: 1922a, 231–32).

It is true that after 1924 the Ministry of Shariah Affairs was nonexistent and that after 1927 Kemal stressed nationalism and positivism as opposed to religion. Still, one should note that the goals of religious sermonizing continued to be met by the new Directorate of Religious Affairs, which replaced the Ministry of Shariah Affairs, and whose head was to be "appointed by the President . . . on the recommendation of the Prime Minister," to whose office it was to be "attached" (Law on the Abolition of the Ministry of Shariah and Foundations and the Ministry of General Staff, Article 4). It is significant that in the next line of the 1923 speech in Izmir, Kemal endeavored to portray the upcoming policies to unify the educational system as consistent with "religious commands," thus perhaps strategically anticipating and rejecting objections by religious authorities who formed part of the antilaicist and anti-Kemalist opposition, but also simultaneously investing these laicist reforms with religiously conceived meaning. He argued that those who claimed authority to represent Islam were themselves in conflict with the egalitarian essence of Islam. He thus sought to undercut the religious authority of his more religiopolitical opponents by arguing for laicist policies on partly religiously conceived grounds. Neither the strategic nor the symbolic dimensions should be ignored:

> In the social life of Islam, nobody has the right to maintain its existence as a special class. Those who presume such a right for themselves cannot be considered as having acted in compliance with religious commands. There is no clergy [ruhbanlık] in us here; all of us are equals, and we are equally bound to learn the rules of our religion. Each individual needs a place where he can learn his religion, religious affairs and faith. And that place is the school [mektep]. . . . Our nation's, our country's, institutions of learning should be one. All children of the country, women, and men should emerge from practitioners of high professions and specializations; we should also possess high institutions that will also raise elite and true, honorable ulema who shall acquire the scientific and technical capacity to study, investigate, and inculcate the philosophical truths of religion. (SD 2: 1923i, 90)

These schools would function under the Directorate of Religious Affairs, which, as Şerif Mardin has shown, elevated "lower level religious personnel" to new positions of authority within the new state structure (1994, 165). The Law on the Abolition of the Ministry of Shariah, which created the directorate, endowed it with the following functions: "the dispatch of all cases concerning the Exalted Islamic Faith that relate to beliefs [itikadât] and rituals [ibadat]"; "the administration of all mosques . . . and of dervish houses within the boundaries of the territories of the Republic of Turkey"; and "the appointment and dismissal of all imams, hatibs [orators], vaizs [preachers], şeyhs [leaders of dervish houses], muezzins [callers to prayer], kayyims [sextons], and all other employees of a religious character" (Article 5). The law also stipulated that "the Directorate-General of Religious Affairs is the proper place of legal recourse for the müftülük [jurisconsults] of Islamic law" (Article 5).

Kemalist laicism is not, in sum, ideologically antireligious, thoroughly anti-clerical, or fully antireligiopolitical. It both institutionally and interpretively ra-tionalizes a series of important connections between the state and political power, on the one hand, and matters of religious affairs, on the other. In the founding practice of the state as conceptualized according to the laicist arrow, the degree of connection between the state and Islam were less than they had been in Ottoman governance, but the relation was not cut altogether. It was re-fashioned within the ideological transformationist and nationalist goals of the Kemalist program. Just as Kemal had his "purist" interpretation of Islam, his regime had its religious authorities—that is, its institutionalized religious author-ities who supported Kemalism's account of Islam and politics. Kemalist laicism was clericalist in this sense: it sought to support and, indeed, to create official re-ligious personnel to staff the state's religious institutions and to meet the reli-gious "needs" of the nation. As late as February 1923, as Kemal was preparing the grounds for the restriction of the role and function of the caliphate in the new Assembly, he was asked by a reporter whether or not in the policies of the "new" Turkey there would be any inclination "contrary to religion." Here is Kemal's response:

> Never mind/Let alone [seeing] our politics [as] contradictory to religion, we even feel that this [policy] is inadequate in terms of religion. . . . I mean to say that the Turkish nation should be more religious; that is, it should be more reli-gious in its whole plainness. I believe in this in the same way that I believe in my religion, truth itself. [Our religion] contains nothing that is contrary to con-sciousness, nothing that impedes progress. (*SD* 3: 1923b, 70)

Laicism, Kemal suggests, is not antithetical to religion. This was clearly the view of its principle architect.

As the historical record suggests, antilaicists nonetheless understood many of the policies associated with laicism as antithetical to Islam. To be sure, insofar as the Kemalists partially removed religious theory and practice from its presti-gious institutional and symbolic position in governance, closed the very active in-stitutions of folk Islam, and thus restricted the activities of the persons in those institutions, they dealt a heavy blow to traditional outlook and practice. To un-derstand the traditionalist, antilaicist view of Kemalism as an attack on Islam, one needs to see Islam not only as a "religion" (to be separated from and superceded in affairs of politics and education), but, according to Şerif Mardin, as a "rich store of symbols and ways of thinking about society" (1989, 156). Kemalism clearly rejects this holistic outlook. Its discourse is permeated with the idea that those who opposed laicist changes were "backward," "reactionary," and "obscurantist."

In the 1923 interview quoted here, Kemal continued the last line regarding progress with the following statement: "Whereas within this Asian nation that has given Turkey its independence there is another more confused and artificial religion that consists of superstitious beliefs. But these ignoramuses, these misers, shall receive enlightenment when the time comes. If they cannot attain light, it means that they have destroyed and condemned themselves" (*SD* 3: 1923b, 70). The language here expresses not only a difference of opinion, if you will, but a disgust and distaste for those who might emerge as antilaicists: they are "confused," "destroyed" "ignoramuses" who "shall get" what "they need." They oppose "true salvation and liberation" for the nation, and the nation thus rejects them. On the decision, for example, to abolish the caliphate, Kemal stated:

> The decisions made by the Assembly in the past days are matters that have already been wished for by the nation in a natural and true way. There is no reason for considering these as being extraordinary. The nation was desiring these with its manner of attitude and in a natural way. And no other inclination could have been expected from a nation that has decided for true salvation and liberation. (*SD* 3: 1924b, 74)

Kemal portrayed opponents of his policies as inciters of fear and anxiety for their own interests, and he reminded them in very harsh terms that their goals would not be implemented:

> There was groundless fear, there was anxiety; the scene seen by all upon the proclamation of the Republic and [upon] the abolition of the institutions made redundant by the requirements of the former have caused a relief in the hearts of those fearful and anxious persons.
> From now on only one thing can come to mind. And that is that some base politicians and egotistical self-seekers may reawaken that fear and fancy for satisfying their ambitions and interests. I assure you and assure you with all my

being that such [people] shall not be able to escape from being a target for the Turkish nation's merciless annihilation the moment they insinuate their presence in any form, manner, and occasion.

From now on, Turkey is far above being a stage for games of religion and Shariah. If there are such players, let them search for a stage elsewhere. (*SD* 3: 1924a, 75–76)

We examine Kemal's coercive leadership strategy and response to opposition more generally later. Here, we note the initial development of standards that would be employed through the history of the republic: those who would contest the laicist institutions would be considered not simply anti-Kemalist, but antirepublican and antinationalist as well. Guarding laicism became tantamount to guarding the Kemalist republic. Indeed, the Kemalists became adept at blurring these distinctions to their advantage, so that even those anti-Kemalists who were not necessarily opponents of the regime's laicization policies found themselves face to face with charges similar to those made against the antilaicist, so-called religiopolitical reactionaries.

The PRP was among the first to learn this lesson. It was closed by an Independence Tribunal in 1925 on grounds that it had abetted "reactionarism," even though the leadership of the party was in no significant way antilaicist. It was interested, by its own party declaration, in a politics of "liberalism" and "democracy" (Article 2; qtd. in Tunçay 1992, 371). Later that decade, underscoring the regime's concern over maintaining the state's laicist foundations, Mustafa Kemal told the organizer of the FRP, Fethi Bey, "as long as I am President, . . .you can be assured, Sir, that within the principles of a laicist Republic no political activity of your party will encounter any obstacle." Not accidentally, the FRP's party program declared the name of its party to be the "Free, Layik, Republican Party" (qtd. in Tunçay 1992, 398). RPP authoritarianism was such that when challenged on a variety of grounds, it frequently considered all objections as if they had emerged from religiopolitical sources and promised to protect its laicist politics with all its determination. The language in which it characterized its antilaicist opponents and those opponents who may have been more anti-Kemalist than antilaicist, but who nonetheless were targets of the same rhetorical strategy, became a central dimension of the laicist discourse. These assumptions were part of the ideological frame of the Kemalist laicist arrow. Freedom of religious conscience—and indeed of political conscience to a certain extent—was effective, therefore, only if one accepted the new laicist principles of the regime. The language of protecting the conscience of the citizens of the new Turkish Republic was weighted quite heavily with Kemalist power considerations. A precondition of enjoying that protection was that one accept the Kemalist "laicist republic," its interpretation of Islam, its place in Turkey's new institutions, and, hence, its definition of progress within contemporary civilization.

One final dimension of the meaning of laicism must be addressed: the legitimation strategy pursued externally—vis-à-vis Western states especially—by declaring laicism to be the manifestation of the European ideal of "separating" religion and state. This dimension has at least two aspects, an explicitly political one and a rhetorical one.

An example of the political dimension may be found in the paragraph where Justice Minister Mahmut Esat described the separation of religion from the state as a prerequisite for sovereignty in the twentieth century. He elaborated further on this issue in a speech he gave on the fifteenth anniversary of the adoption of the civil code. In that speech, he discussed how the adoption of the new code was linked to discussions at Lausanne, including the status of the capitulations treaties that the Ottoman Empire had signed with foreign governments beginning in the sixteenth century. These treaties allowed foreigners in the Ottoman Empire to be subject to their home legal systems rather than to local Ottoman courts. Mahmut Esat suggested that as a condition for their acceptance of Turkey's sovereignty, the foreign powers insisted on a new civil code in Turkey that did not "impose" Muslim religious laws on "subjects who belong to other religions":

> They were saying that "that the laws should be *layik*" is a requirement of the idea of a modern state. As for yours [they said], they are taken from religious foundations. We cannot give up our subjects to the principles of the Muslim religion. . . . You cannot impose these on your subjects who belong to other religions. The twentieth century cannot accept this kind of understanding. (Bozkurt 1944b, 9–10)

The former justice minister thus situated Turkey's adoption of the civil code in the context of meeting preconditions for Turkey's independence. He suggested, essentially, that a central pillar of the laicist project was undertaken in order to achieve recognition for Turkey's sovereignty:

> What would be the character of this organ of justice to which foreigners as well should bow [*baş eğmek*]? What possible form would it take?
>
> We may say this in one word: *layik*.
>
> We know that this is the important attribute that distinguished modern states from those of the past. (1944b, 9–10)

The description of subjects "bowing" to laws promulgated by a regime suggests a peculiar view of "citizenship," which we explore in chapter 6. Here we wish to note how, in addition to the components of the laicist arrow we have already discussed, laicism also had for the Kemalists a meaning directly linked to their interest in legitimizing their new nation-state in the eyes of the European powers. On Mahmut Esat Bozkurt's account, the foreigners were not prepared to recognize a regime based solely on Islamic law, at least not in the Turkish setting where their own nationals or coreligionists resided as well.

The second dimension of this external legitimation strategy, that of rhetorical effect, is evident in Bozkurt's language as well. This effect is produced when language and ideals that external political actors would like to hear are incorporated into the domestic legitimation ideology in order to secure external legitimation (recognition, favor, etc.). The Kemalists said in effect that real modern states followed the model of the Westerners and undertook the project of persuading their own population that the norms for living in the contemporary world were to be found in the West. Their justifications had the effect of securing support from external actors in part because the latter found aspects of their own ideals—certain Western understandings, practices, styles, and modes of thought—confirmed by the new regime. It is no accident that many contemporaneous Western scholars and policymakers promoted Kemal as the exemplary alchemist of modernity or that they refused to see an ideological dimension to Kemalism. To them, it looked like truth in practice. One reason behind the nearly universal approval of Kemalism in the West was that the Kemalists consistently held the West as the great model of civilization to be emulated.

Indeed, the term *laiklik* is itself expressive of this strategy. It is a Turkish adaptation of the French term *laicisme,* intended to articulate the Kemalist self-conscious affiliation with the solidarist ideology of the French Third Republic. The term stands for governance in worldly matters by the lay class instead of by the religiously esteemed class. It resonates with the anglophone concept of secularism and thus, as a formal term for Kemalist practices, suggests a close correspondence between so-called Western and Kemalist practices—one reason why *laiklik* is consistently translated as "secularism," not, more properly, as "laicism." The concept of Turkey as a modern, secular state founded by Atatürk has enabled decades of international political alliances between Turkey and the West despite the fact that Turkey's "secularism" was not intended to achieve institutional or interpretative secularization of political or public life and has not achieved it. Even compared to the laicism of the French Third Republic, there are important differences. As Alfred Stepan has noted, "France in 1905 never assumed this degree of management of religion" (2001, 245). By employing the French-derived concept *laicism,* the Kemalists wanted to create the impression that their state was not governed according to religion or by a religious class. And it must be said that in this regard, despite Kemalism's official Sunni Islamic religious policies and institutions, they succeeded. To this day, professional scholarly and journalist observers of Turkish history analyze laicism as if it were secularism—as if, that is, the regime had fully separated religion and politics.

A clear component of this political and rhetorical legitimation strategy was connected to the regime's interest in integrating Turkey into the Western capitalist political economies to promote national economic growth and industrial and scientific development. The various emphases on training and education in the positive sciences within the laicist discourse were crucial components of this strategy. A laicized state and a laicized system of education went hand in hand with the imperatives of national economic development.

The laicist-positivist goals of national education also provided the bridge between the laicist and the etatist arrows of Kemalist ideology. The one would generate the knowledge, the other the production for economic development. Both would be carried out not for the sake of any particular class, but for the sake of the nation as a whole and for the republic, to which all would be forever loyal. The laicist arrow's central role in providing the terms for this new outlook and attachment to Kemalism as "progressive," "modern," "civilized"—not "superstitious" or "obscurantist"—is too often overlooked. While opening the very important Izmir Economic Conference in 1923, Kemal stressed the primacy of the "economic program" of the new regime vis-à-vis "our education program":

> Friends, in my mind, all the principles, all the programs of our new state, should emanate from the economic program because, as I have said a moment ago, everything is inherent in this. Therefore, we should so train and educate our children and give them science and knowledge that they should be useful, effective, active, and practical organs in the world of commerce, agriculture, and crafts and in all fields of activity thereof. Therefore, our education program, all things to be imparted [to the children] in both primary and secondary education, must conform to this perspective. (*SD* 2: 1923j, 111)

The ideologically key language in this statement is "train and educate." In the Kemalist perspective, the new national education system assumed a twofold role in relation to the national transformation. On the one hand, it was to train people in the positive sciences in order to advance the economic developmentalist goals of the regime "in contemporary civilization," and, on the other, it was to educate the populace to be loyal Kemalist supporters. In the latter role, "education" essentially meant to be good Kemalist citizens, capable of participating in the new republic and of resisting what Kemalism's documents describe as "all superstitions, alien, and foreign ideas."

This is the language that Kemalism attached to its laicist-transformationist educational policies. "Superstitious," "alien," and "foreign" were the categories for ideas that were at odds with Kemalist priorities. These categories show up frequently in the documents concerning national education, side by side with the concept of "training" people in terms of the new sciences. The section of the 1931 party program entitled "National Training and Education" poignantly illuminates the political objectives of the new educational system in this regard. It begins with the party declaring that "the cornerstone [*temel taşı*] of our educational policy is the elimination of ignorance." In striking language, the program declares that "to raise strong republican, nationalist, and laicist citizens for all stages of education is a matter of obligatory diligence. The quality of respecting and making [citizens] respect the Turkish nation, the Turkish Grand National Assembly, and the State of Turkey is inculcated as a duty" (RPP 1931, Section 5,

Paragraph B). We translate the next three paragraphs as they appear in the party program (the outline letters correspond to the Turkish alphabet):

> (C) To give importance to bodily development as much as intellectual development and to especially elevate the national character to the high degrees to the extent inspired by our profound history is a great aim.
> (Ç) The plan pursued in education and instruction is to make knowledge an apparatus that secures for the citizen success in material life.
> (D) Education should be superior, national, and patriotic, and distant from all kinds of superstition and foreign ideas. (RPP 1931, Section 5)

We understand these three paragraphs as elaboration on the meaning of "strong, republican, nationalist, and laicist citizens," mentioned earlier, as well as of "all kinds of superstition and foreign ideas." By "strong," the document suggests the Kemalists meant a "high degree" of both bodily and intellectual strength characteristic of the "national character," capable of defending the republic both physically and mentally. The document counterpoises a "superior, national, and patriotic" character in its children to one that is cultivated by "all kinds of superstition and foreign ideas." The children should be well nourished both physically and intellectually, and thus be ensconced entirely within solidaristic corporatist-nationalist aims as defined by the Kemalists. They should not be exposed to ideas that threaten or undercut the Kemalist laicist project. The "foreign" ideas are often assumed to be those the Kemalists associated with religious reaction. But this assumption only replicates the loose and problematic usage of this term within Kemalist laicist discourse. By "superstition," to be sure, the Kemalists meant those ideas contrary to their own interpretation of Islam; "foreign" ideas must have included those of liberalism and socialism, especially the latter, because the Kemalists viewed both as harmful to the solidarist corporatist order. The 1935 program added "alien" to "superstitious" and "foreign." Clearly, as nationalists, they were not interested in cultivating supra- or nonnational ideas. The fact that they believed their highest priority was to "make [children] respect the Turkish nation, the TGNA, and the State of Turkey" means that they consciously ruled out the inculcation of alternative values. Their educational aims were neither liberal nor socialist. For this to be the case, there would need to have been some emphasis on respecting the liberties and full equality of human beings, references that are not found in these documents.

The "laicist" dimension of the nationalist education system is also visible in these mission-defining paragraphs. "Knowledge," the 1931 program says, should lead to "success in material life." The implicit reference is to the project of promoting education in positivist sciences and technology in the new school system. In fact, the opening line of the 1935 program changes the cornerstone of the educational policy from the elimination of ignorance (*cehlin izalesi*) to the elimination of "lack of science" (*bilimsizlik*). "Scientific" knowledge was to advance "our nation on the path of contemporary civilization," according to the 1935 program's definition of laicism (RPP 1935, Section 2, Article 1, Paragraph D). By this, the party meant material advancement—that is, the kind produced by the technological fruits of the positive sciences. This understanding of the role that scientific knowledge plays in economic development appears throughout Kemalist discourse. Kemal repeatedly tied plans to achieve economic prosperity (*refah*) directly to the aims of national education regarding science. A classic example can be found in his discussion with the representatives of Istanbul in 1927: "The development of the homeland and the prosperity of the nation requires greater effort and work. It is a sublime point of view to work for the true tranquillity and happiness of our social body by cultivating and educating emotions and beliefs of conscience by science and technology" (*SD* 2: 1927, 247). The cultivation of such "emotions and beliefs of conscience" was to be undertaken by the new national schools, which would simultaneously "inculcate [children] as a duty" to "make them respect the Turkish nation, the TGNA, and the State of Turkey."

It is important to see both goals working hand in hand in the new schools. Some scholars have made the mistake of thinking of positivism as the single reigning doctrine in the new national schools system, suggesting that, for example, as Özbudun and Kazancıgil state, "if it is possible to reduce Kemalism to a single dimension, it would not be wrong to single out rationalism, since it was a rationalist and positivist mentality that underlined all of Atatürk's speeches, thought, actions, and reforms" (1981, 4). We think, however, that the record is quite clear that positivism was only a part of the program and that the commitments to rationalism expressed therein were diluted heavily by the extreme emphasis on cultivating feelings and consciences loyal to Kemalist aims. The party programs consistently suggest that education was to be a "school for national values" as well as for scientific ones; these national values consisted of those duties and understandings that would create feelings of loyalty to the Kemalist regime.

The Kemalists consciously institutionalized their ideology as hegemonic at all levels of education (RPP 1935, Article 42, Paragraphs A-F), including the university system (Article 42, Paragraph F) and in the party's People's Houses (Article 48). Indeed, one section of the 1931 program emphasizes the cultivation of national citizens: "(F) Our Party places extraordinary importance in our citizens knowing the profound history of the Turk. This knowledge is a sacred treasure that nourishes the Turk's ability and might, his feeling of self-reliance, and his indestructible resistance against all currents that would harm the national being" (RPP 1931, Section 5, Article 1, Paragraph F). The 1935 program elaborates in even stronger language:

> The Turkish Youth shall be tied to a national organization that shall assemble it around a clean morality, a sublime love of the fatherland, and the transformation. To the whole of the Turkish youth physical training shall be given that will nourish their enthusiasm and health, their belief in their person and the nation; and the youth shall be brought up with a mentality that make the youth prepared to consider as the most superior duty to protect the homeland with all due maturity and to give up all their being for the sake of this duty. So that this fundamental training yields complete results, on the one hand, the high potential of success of the Turkish nation shall be developed such as thinking, making decisions, and taking initiative, and, on the other hand, the youth shall be made to work under the influence of tight discipline, which is the singular instrument of success in the achievement of all difficult tasks. (RPP 1931, Section 5, Article 50)

Positivism was to be the nourishment for the laicist mind; national history for the "strong republican, nationalist" citizen. All other ideas were labeled as "superstitious, alien, and foreign" and were to be consciously excluded lest they disturb the "assembling," "training," "developing," "making," and "disciplining" nationalization of the youth. Indeed, it would be quite apt to say that nationalism would provide the "moral" content in education, and science would provide the technical. A "strong, republicanist, national, and laicist" training and education would, again in the terms of the 1931 program, "prevent them [youth] from becoming faulty persons in life" and cultivate in them "clean morality, a sublime love of the fatherland and the transformation" (RPP 1931, Section 5, Article 50). There were other articles and stipulations in these documents—regarding, for example, lan-

guage, arts, music, and so on—but the ones given here offer the evident political
ideological emphases.

In addition to the themes of science, nationalism, and resistance to non-
Kemalist ideas, we find one more very important theme emphasized throughout
these laicist documents. This theme relates to the Kemalist understanding of history and the passage of time. We have seen that, like modern "revolutionaries,"
the Kemalists believed history could be made anew, that they could create a nation, nation-state, and loyal citizens almost from ground zero, drawing upon
myths and ideals that were, in their own understanding, insufficiently active in the
contemporary Turkish historical context. Their view of history stressed a rapid
and radical break between the past and the present, a movement to a new location
in historical time. They rejected the ideas—characteristic of conservativism, for
example—of historical continuity and the view of social change in which one
historical stage develops or grows out of the womb of another. The Kemalists
wanted to achieve a dramatic exit from one historical dynamic to another, to pass
quickly from what they considered an uncivilized period to a civilized one, to relegate backwardness to the dustbin of history and to become, as a nation, contemporary (*asrî*).

In this regard, Kemalism bears some resemblance both to liberal conceptions of an emancipatory movement from "uncivilized," authoritarian pasts and
to Marxist views of history as the successive transcendence of historically different modes of production. That is, to a certain extent, Kemalism resonates with
liberal and Marxist sensibilities of social change. But liberalism extensively—and
controversially—theorizes the presence of particular identities (individuated,
law-abiding citizens) and of relationships (state and society) as essential conditions for liberal governance, and Marxism explains—again, controversially—
capitalism's growth out of feudalism and what it sees as communism's historical
evolution out of capitalism. The Kemalist conception of change, by contrast,
pays very little attention to the historical or sociological conditions for change.
The Kemalists announced the passage of the old and considered it as having
passed. They stipulated the character of the loyal citizen and built an educational
and training structure to produce it. This view of rapid, manufactured sociopolitical change—that change comes from a rapid restructuring of personal and social identities out of either nothing or irrelevant prior bases—bears some
resemblance, in analytical terms, to the conception of social change found in
fascistic ideologies. Urgency and quick results based on "high ideals" are valued

over deliberative, incremental steps resulting from inquiry. Kemalism's conception of change emphasizes the rapid production of the new rather than the lethargic reproduction of the old. Turkey as a whole was not to lose time in its pursuit. It was to advance quickly, to march unhesitatingly, to get with the flow of the civilized world. Through the creation of myths and new, sublime ideals, Kemalism sought to create a new kind of nation out of ashes and to achieve this result quickly through instant declaration: Turks needed to rid themselves quickly of the "lax mentality" of the Orient and to join the movement of the contemporary century. In an extremely famous speech, given in 1933, Mustafa Kemal put it this way:

> For this purpose the criterion of time as we see it should be thought of not according to the lax mentality of the past centuries, but according to our century's notion of speed and movement. . . . The Turkish nation is industrious. The Turkish nation is intelligent. [This is] because the Turkish nation has known how to overcome difficulties through unity and togetherness. And because the torch that the Turkish nation is holding in its hand and its head marching on the path of progress and civilization is positive science. (*SD* 2: 1933, 275)

Through a Kemalist-forged unity and togetherness, the Turkish nation, marching forth through history, would use science to make great advances. This is the core of the laicist arrow. Religion needed to be separated from certain affairs of the world for "the advancement of our nation on the path of contemporary civilization" (*SD* 1: 1935, 380). The RPP would "inject" Turkey into a new stage of history, elevate it on the road of progress, enable it to enter the movement of the contemporary century. The declared goals of laicism thus interacted with the declared goals of the final arrow, statism, precisely on matters of time and advancement. In the definition of its statist (*devletçi*) arrow in the 1931 program, the RPP stood for quick economic advancement under the direction of the state:

> Although it considers as basic individual work and activity, it is one of our important principles to have our nation attain prosperity and our county a high level of development in the shortest time possible, to engage the State actively in those affairs—especially in the economic field—that are necessitated by the general and high interests. (RPP 1931, Section 2, Paragraph Ç)

All too often the laicist reforms are currently seen as independent of the economic objectives of the regime, but many of the former were precisely aimed at the latter.

STATISM

The first arrow to erode after 1947, etatism or statism (*devletçilik*) was also the final arrow to be promoted. It became part of the Kemalist economic program in response to deteriorating conditions for capital accumulation in the late 1920s (brought about in part by the drought of 1927–29 and the global depression). The Kemalist economic program had been highly state oriented before the declaration of statism as a formal strategy. Its economic policies were defined in the main according to the views of what was called the New Turkish Economic School, which took shape during the 1923 Izmir Congress. According to this school, economic policy should encourage private capital accumulation while maintaining strict control over the economy and major industries therein. The aim was to find a way between liberal capitalism and socialism in order to promote prosperity and advancement within the capitalist global economy. The state established ownership in certain sectors (e.g., rails, tobacco, alcohol, sugar, matches, explosives) and supported its own entrepreneurial class, or national commercial bourgeoisie, whose assets were seen as essential to further capital accumulation and development.[10] In his opening speech to the Izmir conference, Kemal laid the groundwork for a strong role for the state in economic affairs, arguing that the regime needed to take into consideration "the very strong organization of the economy that is present in the whole world." "Today's state," he declared, "is an economic state," and "the real elevation shall be advancement in the economic field" (*SD* 2: 1923j, 111).

The seizure of assets from the Greeks and other minorities following the war for independence—what Kemal once referred to as "rescuing our commerce from the hands of foreigners"—was intended "to enrich the merchant class of our people" (*SD* 2: 1923k, 136).[11] Similarly, the regime passed the Law on

10. See, for example, Keyder 1987.

11. It is a myth that the regime sought to "create a bourgeoisie." When asseverated by the ideologues, this utterance meant three things: (*a*) to help the national commercial bourgeoisie expropriate and replace Levantine and minority mercantile groups; (*b*) to help a very subordinate

Encouragement of Industry in 1927 to help a very subordinate industrial bourgeoisie develop through state franchises and credits. The regime also strongly supported agricultural production in the rural sector, hoping in part to ensure political support. From very early on, Kemal offered lavish and high praise for the role of agricultural producers in the Turkish economy. He told the Assembly in 1922 that the "peasants" were the "the owners and masters," the "real producers" of Turkey (*SD* 1: 1922a, 225).

The depression hit the agricultural sector hard in 1930, and the state's response was *devletçilik*, "to engage the state in those affairs—especially in the economic field—that are necessitated by the general and high interests" (RPP 1931, Section 2, Paragraph Ç). Within the frame of this arrow, the state founded the Agricultural Bank in 1932, the Sumerbank in 1933, and the Etibank in 1935. These banks joined the Turkish Business Bank (founded in 1924) as the regime's organs for managing the economy. The 1935 RPP program amended the description of the etatist principle with the following two paragraphs, further authorizing the state to appropriate private enterprises in order to achieve the ambiguously defined "general and high interests of the nation."

> The relation of the state with economic matters is to encourage private enterprise and to regulate and control, too, current activities as much as to undertake direct [state] enterprises.
>
> The determination of which economic activities shall be directly undertaken by the state is dependent on the general and high interests of the nation. If the work which the state decides to undertake directly upon this necessity is in the hands of a private enterprise, its appropriation [by the state] requires the enactment of a special law in each case. The form of compensation by the state of the loss to be incurred by the private enterprise shall be indicated in this law. In the estimation of this loss, probabilities of future earnings are not taken into consideration. (RPP 1935, Section 2, Paragraph Ç)

To say that etatism meant only greater state involvement in the economic affairs—with the intention to support and "encourage private enterprise"—is, however, insufficient to capture additional ideological meanings this arrow had

---

industrial bourgeoisie develop through state franchises and credits; and (*c*) to rationalize the bureaucrats' entrance into commerce and industry through political perquisites.

for the Kemalists. For example, we should note how the meanings constitutive of the nationalism arrow—such as the desire to lift Turkey into and sometimes above contemporary civilization—were written into the names of the Sumerbank and Etibank. Sumerbank received its name from the ancient Sumerians, one of the earlier civilizations of ancient Babylon. "Eti" means Hittite, the name of another ancient civilization that resided in parts of Asia Minor. In naming the economic organs for the advancement of Turkey in contemporary civilization after the earliest human (and pre-Islamic) civilizations, the Kemalists hoped to build a bridge in the popular mind between the renowned greatness and creativity of the earlier Anatolian civilizations and the Turks. These names thus reflected the central premise of the Turkish historical thesis—namely, that the Turks were the progenitors of all civilization. *Devletçilik* was the economic wing of Kemalist nationalist policy, designed to raise Turkey rapidly to a level of civilization consistent with the nation's ancient greatness. It was another aspect of their general national mobilization efforts.

Furthermore, Kemalism's understandings of capital and capital-labor relations—a central component of any modern political ideology—may be found in the RPP official programs, within the definitions of the regime's economic objectives regarding balance of payments, taxes, customs, trade, import-export, national resources, price controls, and so on. In general, as we have seen, the regime stood for harmony and solidarity in all spheres of national policy. "The work of each occupational group," the 1931 program stated (in a passage analyzed earlier), "is requisite for the life and happiness of one another and of the general body social. The objective that our party aims at attaining with this principle is to provide or secure social order and solidarity instead of class struggle and to establish harmony of interests" (RPP 1931, Section 2, Article 2). *Harmony, tranquility,* and *unity* became in many ways the buzzwords for this regime whenever confronting conflict, be it in political matters such as territorial control or in economic matters. The Kemalist elaboration on etatism in their party programs thus promised to protect and encourage capital, on the one hand, and to guarantee "the lives" and "rights" of "nationalistic workers," on the other.

Regarding capital specifically, the etatist party was committed to encouraging and protecting private capitalist accumulation outside the sphere of strict state control. The 1931 program stated this goal without ambiguity: "In the development of the country, all commercial activities are important. All capital owners who work normally and who rely on technology are entitled to encouragement and protection" (RPP 1931, Section 3, Paragraph 6). The 1935 program repeated this goal almost verbatim: "All commercial activities are important in the country's development. Those capital owners who work normally and who rely on technology shall be protected and encouraged" (RPP 1935, Section 3, Paragraph 16). The reference to "working normally" may have many meanings. The most likely relates to what the Kemalists defined as "normal capital," meaning capital whose source "is national work and savings," as opposed to "active" or productive capital, not the result of rent, savings, or assets (see RPP 1931, Section 3, Paragraph 1).

These statements express the determination of the state to delineate a realm for private accumulation not fully influenced by restrictive, statist economics: "Unless there is definite necessity," Kemal announced at the newly convened Fifth Assembly in 1937, "markets should not be interfered with; however, no market is entirely free either." Etatism meant, at least in part, support for capitalist relations under the tutelage of the state. Insofar as the market supported the nation's goals, the state would support the market. Kemal referred to the bourgeoisie in the same 1937 speech, for example, as the "trusted merchants": "Let me, at this juncture, express the Republic's view of merchants: the merchant is the man whose hand and intelligence is trusted and who should deserve that trust for the purpose of valuing the labor and production of the nation" (*SD* 1: 1937a, 396).

The regime, then, supported relations of capital accumulation in the sense that it valued a role for private capital in building the national economy. Some observers, most notably the national "left" in Turkey, but also scholars such as Alan Richards and John Waterbury, have mistaken etatism for socialism (see Richards and Waterbury 1996). Although this corporate etatism resembled and indeed paved a path for many other examples of so-called state socialism, it did not constitute the foundations for a socialist state. It defined normal capital as the result of "national *work* and savings" (emphasis added) rather than of "national labor." There was no emphasis in the Kemalist ideology on the labor theory of value, characteristic of more socialist-oriented political economic thought, just as there was no emphasis on establishing a classless, egalitarian sociopolitical order. The emphasis was on production for the nation by merchants and by other occupational groups.

The ideology similarly lacked a universalist concern for the condition of the laborer, both in terms of labor's exploited status and in terms of the relation between laborers at home and those in other contexts, Soviet or not. The discourse of the laborer paralleled the discourse of the merchant: just as the Kemalists trusted merchants who worked for the development of the nation, they also expressed "concern" for "nationalistic [*milliyetçi*] Turkish workers and laborers" (RPP 1935, Section 3, Paragraph 14). The 1931 program expressed the now familiar emphasis on harmonizing interests: "We shall take into account the lives, the rights, and the interests of the nationalistic Turkish workers and laborers. Establishment of harmony between labor and capital and enactment of stipulations adequate to the need by a labor law are considered among the important affairs of the Party" (RPP 1931, Section 3, Paragraph 5). "Take into account" contrasts sharply with the promises to "encourage" and "protect" capital. The priority here was to ensure "harmony" between "nationalist Turkish workers and laborers . . . and capital" to the extent required by economic objectives. This is truly a *nationalistic* labor policy, designed in part to preempt alternative dispositions of laborers. It was institutionalized in the regime's 1936 Labor Law, copied directly from the Italian fascistic corporatist labor law. Although the 1936 Labor Law guaranteed some industry safeguards and access to insurance, it prohibited all activities that were seen by the regime as class based, such as forming trade unions and holding strikes. The law was passed in the Assembly in 1935. More important, the restrictions placed on labor were articulated first in the RPP's 1935 program. The following excerpt from that party document gives voice to the full spectrum of corporatist themes we have identified in Kemalism thus far:

> No economic enterprise can be contrary to the public interest as it cannot be against the harmony between national and all other private activities. This harmony in the unity of work between employers and the employees, too, is fundamental.
>
> Mutual relations between the workers and employees shall be regulated by the labor law.
>
> Labor disputes shall be settled by our arbitration, and if that proves not possible, by the judgment of the instruments of arbitration to be formed by the state.
>
> Strikes and lockouts shall be prohibited.
>
> We are concerned with the life and rights of the nationalistic Turkish workers within these basic rules. (RPP 1935, Section 3, Paragraph 14)

The idea of etatism was, in short, to create a "national economics" (RPP 1931, Article 13) parallel to and part of "national politics," one that emphasized capital accumulation and work for national economic development. The regime both protected local capital and encouraged the formation of a class of national merchants. Its long-term goal was neither a classless society nor a liberal-capitalist one, but rather development that satisfied the "high interests" of the nation.

TOWARD PROSPERITY

Kemalism emphasized national economic development as part of its primary objective to make the nation "prosperous and happy." "We shall become rich, prosperous, and happy," Kemal promised farmers in Adana (*SD* 2: 1923a, 122), and, upon his selection as president in 1923, he pledged that "The future children of the Republic shall be much more prosperous and happier than ourselves"(*SD* 1: 1923b, 326). Of course, equating economic development and prosperity with happiness or well-being is nothing unique to corporatist ideologies of the twentieth century. Ideologues of hegemonic global liberal capitalism have either identified or rationalized a close connection between the accumulation of wealth and property, on the one hand, and individual fulfillment and social well-being, on the other. Kemal understood very well the appeal of this link in the context of emerging global capitalism, and he frequently reinforced it from very early on. To a crowd gathered in front of the municipality in Kastamonu in the summer of 1925, he emphasized advancements in agricultural mechanization, cheaper goods, and Western sartorial styles, saying: "We shall go far. We can't go back. We must go forward. Civilization is such a strong flame that those who are detached from it [*bigâne olanları*] are burnt and destroyed. We will find, protect, and make known our deserved, special place in the family of civilization in which we find ourselves. Prosperity, happiness, and humanity is in this" (*SD* 2: 1925d, 207). The rhetoric of advancement and prosperity was almost as central to Kemalist ideology as was the language of science and technology. "The real elevation shall be advancement in the economic field" (*SD* 1: 1935, 381), he told the Assembly. The "ideal" is a "most advanced and prosperous Turkey," he said to that body in his later years. Economic development is the "skeleton" of a Turkey that is "free, independent, always stronger, always more prosperous" (*SD* 1: 1937a, 398). Achieving material and economic prosperity would thus constitute a successful transformation. Speaking in monetary terms to the people in Balıkesir, Kemal promised, "we shall see to it that many millionaires, even billionaires, grow up in our country" (*SD* 2: 1923f, 98).

To be sure, the emphasis on economic prosperity is not unique to Kemalism or corporatism. It is a component of liberal and Marxist ideologies, with which Kemalism has been equated, as well. But the Kemalists explicitly rejected the qualitative human ends of these alternative conceptions of society and legitimate power. They considered it rational to support capitalism, founded on "private enterprise," but they explicitly rejected the liberal rationale of economic liberty and standard liberal guarantees such as the right for individuals to associate for political purposes, including political-economic purposes. The Kemalist etatist arrow was the economic prong of the corporatist agenda, with relevant shades of more rightist governance designed actively to prevent and preempt class politics of any kind. Etatism was a rationale to promote and enhance the role of the state in capitalist accumulation, while simultaneously disciplining a nationalist workforce.[12]

For the Kemalists, this was the "rational" way. "We shall give importance to rationalism," the party said in a discussion of price controls, trusts, and cartels. "Trusts and cartels that will unify prices shall not be permitted to the detriment of consumers. Those trusts and cartels that are to be established with the aim of rationalization are exempt" (RPP 1935, Section 3, Article 15). The "rational" mode referred to here is the mode of finding the most profitable way to integrate the state with the economy while also encouraging capital accumulation. From the Kemalist perspective, etatism enabled the regime to do what was "necessary" in the "economic field" to build its national future. "Rationality" here therefore refers to the reason of the economically active state under corporatist inspiration. To show this, we have only to refer once again to Kemal's 1937 speech, wherein he discussed "economic life"—that is "the activities of agriculture, commerce, industry, and all public works" that "form a totality, intimately connected with one another" (Text 8, *SD* 1: 1937a, 394). In that speech, one of his last on the occasion of the opening of the Assembly, Kemal felt compelled to "remind" his audience that

---

12. There were within the regime differences of opinion over the desired duration of the etatist polices. Some viewed etatism as a temporary patchwork given the economic downturn (the Bayar faction); others viewed it as an important balancing mechanism for a developing state (the İnönü faction); and finally, others viewed it as precisely the (third) way to achieve the regime's ends (Kadro movement).

in the machine of political existence that gives a nation independent identity and value, the mechanisms of the state, the idea, and economic life are so inter-related and so interdependent with and on one another that if these apparatuses are not operated in full harmony and in reciprocal accord, the motive force of the government machine will have been wasted and the full yield expected of it cannot be realized. (*SD* 1: 1937a, 401–2)

What was rational, therefore, was to use the "government machine" to operate the "apparatuses" such that they work "in full harmony" so that nothing would be "wasted" and expectations would be fully "realized." This is the statist perspective that informed the transformationist goals of the regime, and this perspective lies at the core of Kemalist ideology. We have more to say about the Kemalist understanding of politics ahead. But let us now review and evaluate the transformationist arrow, its relationship to other revolutionary political thought and practice at the time, and why the Kemalists saw it as, in some ways, more "radical" than revolutionism in the liberal or Marxist senses.

PRELIMINARY EVALUATION OF THE TRANSFORMATION

In this chapter, we have endeavored to clarify both the substance of the transformation from within the Kemalist ideological frame and the reasons why its practitioners saw it as a "radical" and "progressive" step in the "advancement" of the nation. We have argued that central to the transformation was the Kemalist laicist interest in promoting nationalism, positivist science, technology, and certain aspects of Western culture, while demoting and controlling Islam in particular political, legal, social, and cultural spheres—all related to the republicanist goal of replacing the empire with a nationalist state. We have also shown how the etatist economic objectives related both to the earlier state-centric economic ideology and to the overarching goals of economic development and prosperity were central to the transformation's "progressivist" ideological frame. Laicism and etatism summarized the political, cultural, and economic means for elevating the Turkish nation to a position of prosperity, prominence, and superiority within the field of "contemporary civilization." The Kemalists believed they had the recipe for Turkey's arrival in the twentieth century, and they used the "mechanisms" of the new republic to implement that recipe as well as to make others believe in it. Indeed, in the party's eye, the goals were to be enshrined for all time. Its

1935 program declared that "The Party shall found a museum of transformation. We consider this an influential instrument in inculcating in the people the idea and feelings of transformation" (RPP 1935, Article 49).

We have also argued that all of the RPP's goals were intimately tied to legitimation considerations, both inside and outside of Turkey. Mustafa Kemal's early exaltations of religion are exemplary in this regard. His mobilizational rhetoric gave the national movement a clear religiopolitical identity, but the discourse was as much a part of a domestic legitimation strategy as were his subsequent vitriolic and vituperative condemnations of his opponents, whom he would accuse of pursuing similar religiopolitical aims against his own regime. Indeed, the ideology of transformation was deeply colored by the power politics of legitimation, the central aim of which was establishing the "rightness" of the RPP's single-party rule. Mustafa Kemal emphasized these considerations in his speech during the opening ceremony of the Ankara Law Faculty in 1925, in which he described the "grand achievements" of the Turkish transformation as "much more than and much more sublime than any one revolution." The speech is interesting in that it dates the beginning of the transformation as 1919, the year Mustafa Kemal took the helm of the nationalist movement, not 1923, which is usually taken to be the date of the founding of the "new form of government." But mostly it is important because it underscores the Kemalist distinction between transformation and revolution.

> [This form of government] has changed the form and nature of the common ties among the members of the nation for the maintenance of the existence of the nation that persisted for centuries; that is, instead of religious and sectarian ties, [it] has assembled the members through the bond of Turkish nationality.
>
> The nation has established the principle as an unchanging truth that the climate and instrument that shall be the raison d'etre and *raison de pouvoir* [power] in the field of international general struggle can be found only in contemporary civilization. In short, Gentleman, the nation, as a natural and necessary requirement of the changes and transformations I have enumerated, has considered as the source of life a worldly mentality of administration that holds essential that its general governance and all its laws should be inspired only by worldly needs and, with the change and advancement of needs, should continuously change and progress.
>
> ... These changes that our great nation created in the course of its life within six years are among the most enormous transformations that are much

more than and much more sublime than any one revolution [*ihtilâl*]. (*SD* 2: 1925b, 237)

İnkılâp is not *ihtilâl.* Transformation is not revolution, not in the Kemalist frame according to its grand orator and chief ideologue. Executing a shift in ties from "religion or sect" to nation and entering the "international general struggle" of contemporary civilization by living and governing according to "worldly needs" constitute changes that are "much more than and much more sublime than any one revolution."

In the second paragraph of the excerpt, Kemal used very interesting language to describe the party's allegiance to contemporary civilization. The "climate" and "instrument," he said, "for the raison d'etre and the *raison de pouvoir* [*sebebi hayat* and *sebebi kuvvet*] . . . can be found only in contemporary civilization." In other words, Kemal was telling his Law Faculty audience that contemporary civilization is both a context and a tool for the life and power of the nation as it participates in what he called "the field of international struggle." If Turkey was to advance and compete, the dynamics of the struggle within contemporary civilization had to penetrate the local life. Kemal posited this point as "an unchanging truth." More generally, the idea is that particular external dynamics dictate the necessities for internal ones. As the next sentence in the statement shows, he meant to emphasize the laicist foundations of the republic's transformation—that is, that the source of life (raison d'être) should be "a worldly mentality of administration" and that the source of governance (*raison de pouvoir*) "should be inspired only by worldly needs." The speech followed the abolition of the caliphate and the construction of the new national educational system. The "worldly" administrative outlook is the mentality *"necessary"* for "governing": "the principles in this [party program] are the major guidelines that illuminate us in administration and politics. But one should never equate these principles with the dogmas of the books that are thought to be descended from heaven. We have received our inspirations not from heavens or from any void, but directly from life" (*SD* 1: 1937a, 405). Meeting worldly needs meant being governed not by religious theory and practice, but by science, all of this to achieve success as Turkey struggled internationally for advancement and prosperity.

The Kemalist ideology thus constructed at least three dualities, two explicit and one implicit. The explicit ones are between religion and nationalism (a duality that has been overemphasized given Kemalism's institutionalized pure Islam) and between religious theory and science. The implicit duality, one that has serious implications for the status of Kemalism as a *worldly* ideology, is between the worldly needs and worldly ideas in general. Kemalism speaks only of meeting specific worldly needs. It has little to say about worldly "theory" or worldly ideas. By this, we mean that it does not elaborate a concern with experience-based, theoretical development outside of science or nationalism. These are Kemalism's worldly emphases; otherwise, it is basically silent about worldly ideas as such. It is even difficult to consider the content of the six arrows as "ideas" in this sense of "worldly theory," for their meanings were fixed by declarative fiat in the ruling party's political programs. The arrows were not, from the party's perspective, theoretical frameworks to be elaborated and evaluated differently as Turkey's experience within them unfolded. Kemalism's nationalism is not, for example, a worldly idea in the sense of an outcome of empirical engagement and consideration of the complex historical and sociological realities in Turkey. (It is not unique in this regard, to be sure.) Nationalism appears to be worldly within the discourse because Kemal said people should think in particular national and scientific terms rather than in terms "descendant from the heavens," but there is much more outside of religion than nationalism, positivism, or corporatism. Alternatives were considered superstitious, foreign, or alien and deemed a threat to the Kemalist project. There were reasons for this denial, as we further explore later. Nonetheless, the implications of restricting the meaning of worldly administration as it meets the worldly needs of economic and scientific development of particular kinds must be noted. Insofar as Kemalism, in the developmental stages of the republic, excluded other forms of worldly considerations from the "mode of life and power in the state," it established a distinctly antitheoretical and, in this sense, anti-intellectual bent toward alternative ways of conceptualizing political activity—what might be called other forms of worldly political and political ideological engagement, other ways of thinking about and relating to the world. It excluded an expansive engagement with worldly ideas. It viewed the world as something to be shaped by a class of administrators schooled in nationalism and positive sciences. Central to the Kemalists' doctrine was social engineering, which would establish the "right kind" of politics, education, and economy to bring about "prosperity and happiness." Thus, the crucial question emerges regarding whether or not Kemalism sufficiently addressed other worldly needs, such as for human worldly ideas and worldly theory.

We have stressed that Kemal and the RPP pursued a strategy of rhetorical effect, hoping to acquire legitimacy in the eyes of outsiders whose cultural attributes they held as a standard, to some extent, to be emulated by the Turkish nation. Given the ideology of transformation, the Kemalist estimation seems to have been quite correct. Kemalism's central transformationist emphases on laicist, national economic development were very much in sync with views of modernization that dominated Western social science and policy discourses in the twentieth century (Davison 1998). To outside observers, Turkey seemed to be coming of age under Kemalism. Kemalism became a model of development largely because it articulated the enduring dominant ideals of national prosperity, material success, scientific research and advancement, and economic development under capitalism, ideals that in and of themselves did not require democracy, full political equality, relative economic equality, or extensive education in worldly ideas and theories.

Some of Kemalism's self-representations suggest that it was a democratizing, even if not a democratic, ideology. Kemal suggested a link between democracy and populism, for example, stating that the word for *democracy* in "our language" is "people's government." Analyzing the assumptions about politics behind this suggestion is our task in the next chapter, so a full evaluation of this apparent democratizing commitment awaits further documentary and ideological analysis. Here we may note that although the populist arrow exhibits some resonance with democratic sensibilities, the word *democracy* seldom arises elsewhere in the documents of the single-party period. Nor are other principles associated with modern democratic political objectives to be found, such as political liberty, relative economic equality, social justice, and toleration. These themes are central to democratic perspectives of varying ideological orientations, but they are not pronounced in the central texts defining the six arrows. It is a mistake, then, to conclude even preliminarily, as some observers have, that Kemalism's transformation stressed modernist, democratic political and theoretical goals *or* that it may be interpreted as in support of either fully democratic, modern politics. The emphases in the six arrows were on eliminating old imperial, strongly religious governance and socialization, and on replacing them with institutions founded on nationalist and economic developmentalist goals. Thus, the hegemonic ideology's "modernist" reputation is surely derived more from its constant declarations that it was bringing Turkey into the "contemporary" era rather than from any substantive, political commitments to full-fledged democratization.

The fact that more democratic, Western regimes have found Kemalism's central transformationist emphases by themselves to be sufficient bases for economic and political cooperation with Turkey in the "field of international struggle" is not sufficient grounds for affirming democratic ideological commitments on the part of Turkey's founders. The history of the twentieth century is ripe with examples of gainful interaction between countries of the hierarchically superior first world and countries of the so-called second or third worlds on the basis of "economic development" alone. As long as the latter pursued various strategies of rhetorical effect, liberal and corporatist regimes and even liberal and fascistic regimes have forged profitable economic and political relations. The absence of concerns for self-government in one or more of the countries where democracy is only said to be a cherished value has not been an obstacle to all sorts of cooperative relationships. In the pre–World War II European context of Kemalism's emergence, the liberal capitalist West coexisted with European fascism until the latter revealed its anti-Semitic, belligerent, expansionist, and intolerant faces. During the Cold War, often out of calculated geostrategic advantage, liberal capitalist regimes were more than prepared to accept ideologically rightist regimes if the latter were able to convince their external observers of their deep commitment to progress through capitalist accumulation, science, and technology, or through "shared values." (In some cases, no doubt, even less was required.) In authoritarian Muslim political milieus at the time of this writing, the key language to be used is "democratic reform."

The rhetorical effect strategy can be particularly successful for authoritarian regimes that claim to be initiating a longer-term transition to democracy for peoples who are said to have little experience in self-government—or, in the case of Kemalism, that claim to be "civilizing" those they considered uncivilized. The Orientalist ideological language of civilizational advancement implies some sort of defect in an existing sociopolitical, cultural, and ethical structure. Mustafa Kemal reproduced this sentiment when he said that he wanted to lift his nation to the level of contemporary civilization. In saying that, he implied that the Turks needed to be lifted. As he promised to elevate the nation, he simultaneously devalued it by implying that it needed elevation from some diminished, current state. This reproduction of Orientalist sentiments has proved over time to be a very successful legitimation strategy, for it has clearly helped mobilize external support for Kemalist political organs and lasting adulation for Atatürk as a great modernizer. Few Europeans during the early state period thought of Turkey as either sufficiently "modern" or "civilized." From their point of view, Kemalism looked extremely revolutionary because it reproduced European prejudice within its transformationist objectives. Here was a movement whose leader wore a bow tie and a frock jacket and told his people that they were insufficiently civilized were they not to do the same. Western powers thus endorsed Kemalism's transformationist project not only because it supported the aims of capitalist developmentalism—because it was not revolutionary in that sense—but also because Kemalism sought to inculcate the Turks with certain cultural modes of life found in Western societies. Kemalism reinforced dominant Western views that the Turks needed to alter their ways of life and power in order to join the ranks of contemporary civilization. Lost in the mix of all the appreciation for Kemalism in the West, however, was a failure to consider the full extent of Kemalism's corporatist commitments and that its goals were not entirely those that they were taken to be. Kemalism did not mimic "the West" in ideological terms. If the West was the benchmark, then it was the nationalist-corporatist-laicist West in which Kemalism participated, not the democratizing West of the other two dominant political ideological traditions of the era, liberalism and Marxism (problematic though they may appear to be in contemporary social theoretical terms).

Although Kemalism shares with liberalism an interest in antimonarchical republican governance, it emphasizes solidarity and national achievement rather than political liberty and individual and social development. Liberalism's concern to disestablish religion in order to ensure freedom of religious belief and practice also differs from Kemalist laicism. Kemalism offers and institutionally controls its own interpretation of Islam, one that formally guarantees freedom of religious conscience, but it also supports policies that limit freedom of religious thought and expression as well as freedom of political thought and expression more widely. In comparison with Marxism, Kemalism does not exhibit an interest in abolishing capitalist relations or in establishing an egalitarian social order, even though Kemalist ideology allows for a larger role for the state in political economy than does liberal capitalism. The visible hand of a state in the political economy does not make a socialist state; the Kemalist ideology guarantees protection for those accumulating capital and encourages market relations characteristic of capitalism as a means toward expediting national economic development.

The cultural reforms and adoption of the new civil code with increased rights for women have suggested to many that Kemalism contains a partial, if not a full, interest in political liberalization in the sense of constituting moves against patriarchal relations of domination. We believe that policies with such intent and motivation do constitute an emancipatory attack on patriarchy and arbitrary male activity in general. However, although the language in the ideological documents suggests that partial liberalization may have been an outcome of the reforms, it may not have been their primary intent. Kemal was, as we show in part 2, the archpatriarch. It is difficult to discern any explicit interest on his part in attacking the relations of authority characteristic of patriarchy. It was not a goal close to Kemal's mind, even as his regime advanced some liberties for women. We would say that the reforms that amounted to a lessening of the patriarchal chains were only *partly* liberalizing. After all, the ideological emphasis in Kemalism is solidarist and cooperative, not individualist and participatory. The stress is on harmonious relations between the occupational groups of the solidaristic whole, not on individual development and unpredictable social growth. Moreover, sartorial requirements for men were issued in all social spheres and for women in state and public institutions. If there had been a greater stated interest in securing liberty in the broadest sense for everyone—male or female—we might interpret the cultural reforms differently. But the language, calendar, and sartorial reforms and even the adoption of last names were all part of an ideologically explicit and conscious strategy of cultural reform to make Turks "civilized"—to transform them in *that* sense—not to make them politically freer. Goals of freedom, equality, even justice, simply put, were and are not the explicit emphases of Kemalist ideology.

Kemalism espouses the idea that history is progressive, but its measure of progress is not democratic norm and institutional development. It is, rather, the technical goals of scientific research within an overarching and particularist-nationalist-corporatist worldview. Here we find some overlap between the emphases of Kemalist transformationist and economic developmentalist ideals found in both liberalism and Marxism. All three traditions endorse the activation of human technical rationality for the purposes of societal improvement. The entire Kemalist program, however, excludes other democratizing ends such as the development of democratic political rationality and its institutional bases. These qualitative ends are differently conceptualized in various forms of liberal and democratic-socialist theory, but they are evident as primary ends. Such is not the case with corporatism in general or with Kemalist corporatism in particular. Our position in this regard requires further development in the next chapter. Here, however, we note that Kemalism's progressiveness stemmed from its stress on making "the nation" contemporary, progressive, and prosperous in the context of positivist scientific development. The transformationist policies of the regime were to the Kemalists "a monument of leaping forward" (*SD* 1: 1931b, 367) toward the ideal of future prosperity (*refah*): "Prosperity, happiness, and humanity is in this" (*SD* 2: 1925d, 207)—*in this,* not in accompanying democratic norm and institutional development. Prosperity brought about through the Kemalist transformation is what happiness is all about.

We question whether or not this view is adequately considered "revolutionary" in political theoretical terms, and we think our judgment is supported, though for different reasons, by Kemalism's own distinction between transformation and revolution. In the same utterance in which Mustafa Kemal underscored that distinction, he also described Kemalism as democratic, but even he quickly qualified the claim. "It must not be forgotten that this form of administration is not a Bolshevik system . . . we are patriotic and we respect our religion. In sum, our government is entirely a democratic government. And in our language this government is called 'People's Government' " (*SD* 3: 1922a, 51).

Kemalist populism was a form of nationalist, laicist, solidaristic corporatism, not of liberal or radical democracy, even as it participated in some "progressive" tendencies of the modern age by promising, in its own corporatist terms, national economic liberation. In the 1922 interview, Kemal was effectively saying, "Fear not Western capitalism. We are neither internationalists ['we are patriotic'] nor atheists ['we respect our religion']. We seek only prosperity, and to that end we shall eagerly comply with and participate in the institutional requirements of civilization." Kemal knew that, in context, the Kemalist transformation was distinct from a revolution; observers of Kemalism would only be giving him his due by acknowledging this point.

The Larger View of Politics and Society

6

THE KEMALIST MODEL
OF POLITICS

Leadership

Great Turkish Nation! For fifteen years, you have heard many words of mine that promised success in the acts we have undertaken. I am happy and proud that in none of these words have I fallen into error in a way that would shake the nation's trust in me. (*SD* 2: 1933, 275–76)

If our actions and work of nine years is to be considered with a logical chain, the general direction that we followed from the first day till today appears as an entity that never swerves from a line drawn of the first decision and its aimed-at objective. (Atatürk 1960, 14–15)

There is no doubt that the highest measure of these joys shall be felt with the most profound sensitivity by the Turkish nation. Because the Turkish nation loves and appreciates every beautiful thing, every civilized thing, every sublime thing. But it is absolutely certain that, if there is anything that it worships above all, that is heroism. These words of mine shall no doubt produce high and effective echoes in the ears of today's vigilant Turkish youth. I demand nothing less from Turkish children in whose sublime qualities I place significance. (*SD* 3: 1931, 91)

Although Kemalism is defined in popular and scholarly consciousness in terms of its six arrows, there are other deeper and even more politically and culturally important dimensions of the hegemonic ideology that require analysis. Central to any ideology is its conception of politics, power relations, processes of governance, and the proper, legitimate role of political office holders and institutions. We turn now to examine these dimensions of Kemalism. In this section, we examine the concept of leadership in Mustafa Kemal's political discourse and his conception of his own role therein. We contest the dominant view of Kemal as a "reluctant" charismatic leader and argue that patterned elements of Kemal's understanding of himself as leader of the Turkish transformation and of leadership more generally demonstrate his self-conscious attempt to create a relationship with members of the Turkish nation typical of the classical, charismatic leader, which we describe in detail. Our central point is that Kemal consciously formulated a set of institutionally effective beliefs about his leadership in such a way as to ensure that his status would forever occupy a central focal point in Turkish politics. It is well known that Kemal and his followers, including subsequent generations of state leaders, have exploited the memory of his daring, heroic feats on the battlefield and in the early years of the national struggle in order to promote various agendas consistent with the solidaristic corporatist ideological setting. As our documentary analysis shows, one need not look to his acts on the battlefield alone to understand the sources of this charismatic relationship. They reside in his own understandings of his role as leader of the great Turkish nation.

In a classically charismatic fashion, Kemal represented himself as the embodiment of the new, unquestionable truths of civilization and, consequently, developed a social and psychological relationship of dependence between himself as a humble, but extraordinary leader and "his" great nation, whose will he claimed to serve. He created both intense sentiments of national pride and enthusiasm for "the nation," one the one hand, and equally strong feelings about his own indispensable role as the nation's hero, on the other, to the point that he equated the nation's goals with his own and vice versa. To induce others to follow him, he threatened those who strayed from these goals, rejecting the value of their opinions or castigating them as mindless seducers and dangerous traitors to the nation's—meaning his—cause. As such, he created in form and substance a "political" arena whose central function was to reproduce his Kemalist corporatist truths. This style of leadership thus fortified the essential solidarist kernel with a partly fascistic model of the extraordinary, charismatic leader. Or, put in other terms and despite some of the "political" rhetoric to the contrary, the Kemalist conception of leadership effectively eliminated politics—understood as the practices of collective deliberation and consensus formation—from Turkish political culture at the time of the republic's founding. By using definitively antipolitical rhetorical techniques to establish unquestionable hierarchical relations between himself as the valued leader and the nation that he viewed as essentially valueless in his absence, Mustafa Kemal prioritized the implementation of his great truths over the construction of self-governing institutions and dynamic ideational outlooks to suit them. By embedding his own truths and his own charisma in both the public consciousness of the new nation and the private psyches of his followers, he thus produced psychological constraints on deliberation and questioning as an essential part of Kemalist ideology, purposefully laying the bases for his own cult of hero worship, which continues to dominate individual and public life in Turkey today. The conception of leadership found in Mustafa Kemal Atatürk's discourse, therefore, reinforced the highly antidemocratic tendencies of the ideology that bears his name. It established an antipolitics of tranquil obedience to the great leader to accompany the anticonflictual social premises of solidarist corporatism.

In this discussion, we also depart from one of our methodological habits at work in the first part of the book. We look less at the party documents and more at Kemal's public speeches and statements, providing a rigorous ideological examination of Kemal's *Nutuk*—the six-day, 36.5-hour speech of 1927—as well as shorter speeches and public statements presented in various modes and formats throughout his career.

Nutuk has been read by generations of Kemalists and their observers, but it has not been analyzed, we think, as a central text of Kemalism's corporatist ideological intent. Kemal presented *Nutuk* to the RPP's Second Great General Assembly between October 15 and October 20 in 1927. It is indeed his most complete, prepared, and integrated work. In it, he renders his account of the Turkish struggle for independence and the early years of the transformation. It contains statements on diplomacy, domestic and foreign affairs, political developments, crucial events in the military struggle, relations between Istanbul and Ankara, and so on. It also contains Atatürk's judgments and observations about a wide range of political personalities and their ideas. In this way, it is a portrait of the period's political elite and, more important for our purposes, a glimpse at Mustafa Kemal's own political character and personality. It depicts his views of others involved in the struggle and of the conflicts in which he was involved along the way to establishing the single-party regime and the hegemony of his vision for Turkey. *Nutuk* was delivered at a crucial point in the early history of the republic—the Law for the Establishment of Tranquility was in effect, and political rivals had been cleared from the scene—and ends with a discussion of the events of 1925. Kemal's other speeches and public statements not only are more spontaneous, but also provide access to Kemal's ideas throughout his entire political life. An examination of their ideological content thus provides insight including and beyond themes taken up in *Nutuk* and helps to explain Kemalism's deeper content as well as its ongoing efficacy. Following a brief description of the characteristics of charismatic authority, we present original translations of the main passages of *Nutuk* and of the public speeches on which our subsequent interpretation is based.

"CHARISMATIC LEADERSHIP" AND KEMALISM

A general call for strong leadership had already become prevalent in the prefascist European intellectual climate since the 1890s, a phenomenon that in part led the sociological theorist Max Weber to theorize charismatic forms of leadership and authority. According to Weber's insightful analyses, the concept has biblical origins and describes a relationship between leaders and followers in which the former's actions are viewed as fulfillment of a mission contained in some eternal truths, access to which the followers themselves lack. A charismatic person has authority over others by virtue of the fact that he or she either possesses or is recognized as possessing a special relation to these truths. The prophets of the monotheistic traditions are the classical, theopolitical examples of charismatic leaders, although Weber describes this form of authority in other historical contexts, including those of the Chinese monarch and Native American tribal chief. Either way, proof of charisma must be established through some great deed, some demonstration of the leader's "strength in life": "If he wants to be a prophet," Weber writes, "he must perform miracles; if he wants to be a war lord, he must perform heroic deeds. Above all, however, his divine mission must 'prove' itself in that those who faithfully surrender to him must fare well" (1968, 22–23). The charismatic leader thus, by definition, embodies the ultimate "oughts" of life in word and deed—the ways in which humans beings in a given society believe they ought to live and behave if they are to live up to the standards they take to be true. He or she sets an example for others who, on this model of leadership, are said to possess no real or acknowledged access to special truths. Not all followers of the leader, though, need be of equal status. The charismatic leader often enjoys the assistance of a group of followers whose higher status vis-à-vis the rest of society is established by their proximity to the leader.

Authority on this model is not—nor should it be—dictated by tradition or formalized in established laws. The charismatic leader may threaten both traditional patterns of custom and governance, on the one hand, and formal democratic rule, on the other. Both may constitute constraints for the charismatic leader, who must enjoy the greatest amount of latitude to adjust human affairs according to truths that only she or he initially comprehends. The collected wisdom of human experience may be a constraint because traditional rule depends on relatively stable and widely shared understandings and judgments that dictate the needs of a society. Formal democracy may be a constraint because it requires rule by law, which operates under the assumption that all should be equal, free, and held accountable to the same, commonly accepted, fixed, and established standards ("laws"). By contrast, the charismatic leader's supposed extraordinariness enables the leader to suspend traditions or to cross commonly accepted lines because she or he possesses access to higher truths. Neither the wisdom of old traditions nor the ordinary opinions of equal citizens, as such, check the power of the great leader. Charismatic authority, then, by definition, may be quite hostile to the ideals of classical republicanism (rule by law) and populism (sovereignty resides with the people).

An exception to a full incompatibility between charismatic leadership and democracy is when a given charismatic leader acts in ways required to implement democratic truths into a context that lacks them—when, that is, charismatic leadership is employed, in either democratic or antidemocratic forms, to make the transition to democracy possible because the ideals requisite for democracy to take hold are absent in a given social order. Indeed, this is the basis for the tutelary democratic thesis in the case of Kemalism: insofar as its dominant theme is that Kemalism was a tutelary democratic ideology—meaning that Kemal's intention was to create the conditions for democracy through necessary authoritarian measures—Mustafa Kemal is portrayed as a "reluctant" charismatic leader, if one at all (see the introduction). On this account, the assumption is that because the nation was not ready for democracy, Kemal played the role of the transitional charismatic leader, embodying the truths of civilization necessary for bringing the slumbering nation into a democratic future. We think otherwise. Consider the following evidence.

EVIDENCE

TEXT 10

But we did not at first totally display and express these sentiments and thoughts of ours that directed our course of action to the very end. Elaborating on future prospects would have given the perceived nature of an illusion to the real and material struggle that we had undertaken; also, in the face of the immediate impact of the external danger, it would have suddenly instigated the resistance of those affected thereby, who would have become apprehensive of the probable changes adverse to their traditions, intellectual capacities, and psychological states. (Atatürk 1960, 14–15)

TEXT 11

The practical and secure path for success was to implement each phase at the most opportune moment [literally, "when its time came"]. This was the sound way for the development and advancement of the nation. However, this practical and secure method of success has sometimes been the reason for and explanation of certain essential and secondary conflicts, indignations [vexations], and even separations between some of the gentlemen who were known to be my close associates with regard to convictions. Some of the fellow travelers who started the national struggle have come to the point of resisting and opposing me as they have reached the limits of their own ideas and psychologies in the course of the progress of the national life leading up to the present Republic and its Republican laws. I will indicate these points one by one in due course in order for you to become enlightened and also to facilitate enlightenment of the public opinion.

If it is possible to summarize these last words of mine, I can say that I was bound to put into force step by step this great capacity for progress that I sensed in the nation's conscience and future, all the while carrying it in my conscience like a national secret [millî sır]. (Atatürk 1960, 15–16)

TEXT 12

I notified the armies and the nation of this state of affairs. Since this date, we continued our duty of conscience without any official title and power, relying on the nation's affection/compassion and brave generosity and by taking inspiration and strength from its endless/inexhaustible guiding light and might. (Atatürk 1960, 47–48)

TEXT 13

Whatever happens, it is required of those who are to become leaders/guides [*pişüva*] that they decide at the very beginning of the undertaking not to abandon the objective and to continue to make sacrifices for the sake of the objective until they breathe their last breath on the last spot where they are able to take their last stand. It is obviously preferable that those who do not feel this force in their hearts should not even start to act because in that case they would have seduced both themselves and the nation.

Furthermore, the duty in question is not capable of being performed under disguise by donning a uniform in an official position. A dose of this style may well have been permissible; but the times are not conducive even to that. It is necessary to come forward publicly and to cry out in the name of the rights of the nation, and it is necessary to make the whole nation participate in that way. (Atatürk 1960, 44)

TEXT 14

There is no doubt about my being expelled from office and being condemned to all sorts of detrimental consequences. To collaborate with me openly means to accept immediately partaking in such consequences. Besides, no claim is made here that the man demanded by the situation we described should definitely be my own person. However, it has been perhaps indispensable that a son of this county should have come forward to the scene. It is even possible to think of another associate other than myself. It should only be so that that associate accept to act in a manner that is required of him by the present situation. . . .

At our meeting [they] stated that I should continue to lead the mission and that they will assist and actively support me. . . . I said that success requires an essential formal condition carrying out my orders as the supreme commander just like as it has been since I resigned from office and military service. The meeting was concluded upon the full approval and affirmation of this point. (Atatürk 1960, 44–45)

TEXT 15

Above all, I should have definitely participated in the Congress and directed it. Because I was convinced of the necessity of activating the national will without delay and making sure that the nation starts to take measures in the form of real and armed action by itself. In order to make the Congress appreciate and confirm these fundamental points, I deemed it very necessary that I should work by illuminating, guiding, and personally directing it. In fact, this is what happened. I confess that I had no confidence in the ability of any representative council to have the principles and decisions of the Erzurum Congress that I have previously explained. As a matter of fact, time and events have confirmed me. Furthermore, I must express openly that I was not convinced that any collective body was able to realize/deliver the following ends: to achieve the convening of the Sivas General Congress, the decision for which I had already secured in Amasya and notified the whole nation thereof with available means; and to represent the whole nation and the country with only a single council, and then to try to find means of defending with the same care and sensitivity and rescuing not only the eastern provinces but all parts of the fatherland. For, had I had such a conviction I would have found a way of not resigning and waiting for the results of the work of those who had undertaken enterprises and activities until the day I took the initiative. I would not have found it necessary to rebel against the government, the sultan, and the caliph. (Atatürk 1960, 69)

TEXT 16

Can any society in history be shown to have succeeded in this way? Second, Gentlemen, could the situation and the duty at hand be left to any representative council that probably might have consisted of random persons who had no connection with or relationship to the administration of the nation, the country, politics, and the armed forces and who lacked any demonstrated ability or experience in these respects, for instance such pitiful people like a Nakşibendi sheikh from Erzincan or a tribal chief [aşiret reisi] from Mutki? And in case it was left to such a council, would we have not committed the error of seducing the nation and ourselves when we were saying that we shall rescue the country and the nation? Even if it could be said that a council of this nature could have been supported behind the scenes, could this approach be considered safe? There is absolutely no doubt anymore about the fact that the whole world today, if not then, sees these things I say as one of those undeniable truths. Still, I consider it a duty for the sake of social and political morality of the future generation to corroborate what I say here with certain remembrances and documents of the past. (Atatürk 1960, 70–71)

TEXT 17

Gentlemen, had I given in to the opinions and apprehensions expressed by some of the associates, great liabilities would have resulted in two respects.

First, it would have meant admitting error and weakness in my opinions, my decisions, and in all my identity, which would be an irreparable mistake from the viewpoint of the duty I had in my conscience undertaken. Gentlemen, history has incontestably proved that for success in great matters, the presence of a chief [*reis*] whose ability and might are unshakable is indispensable. In a time when all the high functionaries of the state are desperate and inept, when the whole nation, without a head, is engulfed in darkness, is it possible to proceed in a sound, thorough, and especially violent way, and eventually to arrive at the very difficult target, by consultations in a chaotic situation in which a thousand and one persons who call themselves patriots behave and opine in a thousand and one ways? (Atatürk 1960, 70–71)

TEXT 18

In civilized states that are seriously administered on the basis of national sovereignty, the accepted and enforced principle is that the political group that best represents the general aspirations of the nation and that possesses the highest power and authority to execute the interests and the requirements that these aspirations entail, should undertake the governing of state affairs and entrust this responsibility to its highest leader.

As a matter of fact, a government that does not meet its conditions cannot continue to fulfill its duty. It is of course incorrect to form a weak government from among those members of the group who are significant but not first rate and to have that government conduct affairs according to the instructions and advices [*sic*] of the first-rate leaders of the party. (Atatürk 1960, 221–22)

TEXT 19

I should have been able to give orders unconditionally; therefore, the powers of the Grand National Assembly should be relegated to my person. This was indispensable for success. That's why I insisted. . . . According to this article, the orders I was going to give were to be laws.

. . . At this moment, the army is without a commander [according to the decision of the Assembly]. If I am continuing to command the army, I'm doing this illegally. According to the vote that obtained in the Assembly [which did not renew his command], I would have liked to relinquish immediately the command, and I notified the government that my [term as] commander in chief has ended. But I was under the obligation of not giving an opportunity to an irreparable evil. Our army, which was facing the enemy, could not have been left without a head, therefore I didn't relinquish, I couldn't relinquish, and I wouldn't relinquish [the powers of commander in chief]. (Atatürk 1962, 611, 614, 662)

TEXT 20

Gentlemen, if you will, I will express it openly; it is I who has worked to have each of you elected with extraordinary powers, and to form an Assembly that possesses extraordinary powers [*salâhiyeti fevkalâdeye malik bir Meclis*], and to have this Assembly acquire a nature that controls the destiny of the country. I engaged in debates with my closest friends in order to succeed in this. I placed my life, my being, all my honor and prestige on the brink of peril. Therefore this is my creation. I have the duty of not deprecating but exalting my creation. (Atatürk 1962, 655)

TEXT 21

The decision of the Assembly constitutes an important point in our history of transformation because, in taking this decision, the Assembly has demonstrated that it has come to confess the sickness that afflicted it and to realize the agony felt by the nation because of this. (Atatürk 1962, 728)

TEXT 22

We participated in the new elections by announcing our known principles. Those people who wanted to become deputies upon accepting our views were first informing me that they were in agreement with the principles and shared our points of view. I was going to designate the candidates and duly announce them on behalf of our party.

I had favored this above method because I knew that there were too many who in the forthcoming elections would try to become deputies with various objectives by seducing the nation. My public statements and guidances [*sic*] were received in all parts of the country with full sincerity and trust.

The whole nation totally adapted the principles I announced, and it became clear that it was not possible to be elected by the nation to the deputyship of those who would oppose the principles and even my person. (Atatürk 1962, 728–29)

TEXT 23

İsmet Pasha answered my telegraph. I'm presenting this reply in full because it is a valuable document that shows the degree of İsmet Pasha's agony, which, at the same time, is evidence of his purity, and sincerity, and his humbleness.

Gazi,

You come to my aid like Hızır in all my difficult times. Imagine the agony I underwent for the past four or five days. You are a man who has done great deeds and has had great deeds done. My devotion to you has been doubled. I kiss your eyes, my beloved brother, my dearest Chief [*aziz Şefim*]. (Atatürk 1962, 788)

TEXT 24

I did not consider it proper to give an opportunity to the ignorant and the reactionaries to poison the whole nation by including these matters in the program before their time had come. [This was] because I was definitely certain that these matters will become resolvable at the opportune time and that the nation will eventually be pleased with it. . . . There were those who found the program I announced inadequate and short for a political party. They said that the People's Party had no program. Actually the program we announced under the name of the principles was not the kind of book that was familiar to those who objected to it. But it was thorough and practical. We, too, could have written a book by gilding inapplicable ideas and certain theoretical details. We didn't do so. *With a view to the material and spiritual renovation and development of the nation, we preferred to give precedence to actions and deeds over words and theory.* (Atatürk 1962, 718–19, emphasis in original)

TEXT 25

Gentleman, as you see, in taking the decision to proclaim the Republic, I never thought it requisite and necessary to invite all of my associates in Ankara and negotiate and debate with them. Because I had no doubt about their being basically and naturally in agreement with me. (Atatürk 1962, 803)

TEXT 26

I advised the people that they should not be deceived by the words of their bad shepherds, but unfortunately my advice then was not effective, and it produced the sad result that you know. Be assured that there is no event that aggrieves me more than affliction of innocent people who have no fault. . . .

The Republic is for freedom of thought. We respect every idea on condition that it be sincere and legitimate. Every opinion is respectable to us. But it is necessary that our opponents be equitable. . . .

Not a fragile and precarious stability and law and order, but a tranquillity in a measure that obtains in those countries considered as most advanced shall be attained. We shall certainly attain a position in this respect where we will not envy France or England. The country shall soon become contemporary, civilized, and modernist. . . .

For us this is a matter of life and death. Fruition of all our sacrifice depends on this. Turkey will become or not become an honest administration, equipped with a new idea. I have much contact with the people. You wouldn't know how much that pure mass is for renovation. In our deeds, obstacles shall never come from this dense stratum. The people want to be prosperous, independent, and rich; it's very hard to be poor while seeing the prosperity of neighbors. Those who are nourishing reactionary ideas think that they can rely on a class. This is definitely an illusion, a delusion. We shall go forward crushing those who want to stand in our way of progress. We are not to stop in the valley of renovation. The world is progressing with an enormous movement. Can we remain outside of this harmony? (*SD* 3: 1923a, 71–72)

TEXT 27

I see you before me as a single conscience and a single heart. To this heart I touch with a pleasure of conscience. This contact grants me a very high degree of happiness. Friends, I was for a long time very convinced that the respected people of Bursa were of this high capacity. But unfortunately several [literally, three to five] fools wanted to get in the way of this mass and to cover this intelligence and ability. Whereas that it is impossible to cover truth is manifested by your ovation today. . . .

Friends! There have been times when *sheikhulislam*s were changed in order to have this nation wear the fez. *Fetva*s were issued. How fortunate it is that our nation today needs none of such senseless meaningless illogical means. It shows no need for such guidance. Whereas our guidance is nothing and cannot be but the inspiration we take from our nation. Respected people of Bursa, I would like to express heartily and definitely that the path we are following together is true. This path will enable us to attain happiness. There is no reason to hesitate. That the path we are following is really sound is again obvious from your comport [hal], your glory, and your sublime behavior. You have been aggrieved. Friends, the path we follow does not mean just any line of action drawn by just any one from among us. It means the main road that is determined as the end product of all ideas. Therefore, it is sound. Friends, in any part of our country, the same feeling is manifest. But the first actual expression of this feeling is occurring today in Bursa. (SD 2: 1925c, 219)

TEXT 28

Gazi says: Shepherds know nothing but the sun, clouds, and stars. Peasants of the earth, too, know only these. Because the yield is subject to the weather. The Turk consecrates only nature.

[reporter says something about mysteries of god in Göethe]

Gazi says: I cannot accept this mystery; the person who's entitled to be consecrated is only he who is the chief [reis] of the human community. . . . You are asking about fortune. The essence of fortune is to take up action after thinking about and giving consideration to only those matters that can be put into practice. A person who is a commander must show great determination not to miss opportunities. At the same time, he should pursue things that are fitting to reason [akıl]. Phenomena change: they lack constancy and definiteness. Furthermore, these vicissitudes are convenient for those persons who undertake action. . . .

You have previously mentioned the question of ambition. As a matter of fact, no great work can be accomplished without it. But that [ambition] should in any case have as its objective a service for the nation. He who is a chief should first act according to the ideal of the nation and, after grasping the psychology of the nation, be subject to that nation's inclination. I, too, before our salvation from the Sultan's was complete, I immediately invited the Assembly to review elections, and, giving up the matter of presidency, I even accepted pardon. Sovereignty wholly belongs to the nation. That is, to the deputies elected. I do not interfere in the matters of administration to the extent that you think I do.

Here is one of the ministers before you. If you wish, you can personally ask him whether I interfere with his duty. I'm ready this very day to withdraw from the presidency and even from the command of the army and to go into seclusion for my own studies.

The correspondent asks: I asked him if he would give up the presidency of the party as well.

He replied: No . . . I would never, because in my opinion this party is representing the true political ideas of the country. (*SD* 3: 1930, 85–86)

TEXT 29

Nations should not know sorrow and grief. The duty of chiefs is to show their nations the way of taking in life with joy and enthusiasm.

I had delved into books in [my] time. I had wanted to understand what the philosophers said about life. Some of them were seeing everything as black. They were saying, "Since we are naught and shall arrive at zero, there can be found no joy and happiness during the transient life in the world."

I read other books; these were written by wiser men. They were saying, "Since the end is tantamount to zero, let us be joyful and rejoicing at least while we live."

In accord with my own character, I prefer the second viewpoint of life, but with the following reservations:

Unfortunate are those men who see the being of all humanity in their persons. It's obvious that such a man shall be annihilated as an individual. The thing that is necessary for any person to be content and happy while he lives is to work not for himself but for those who will come after him. A reasonable man can act only in this way. All pleasure and happiness in life can be found only in working for the honor, being, happiness of the future generations.

A human being, in acting this way, should not even think to the effect of asking, "Will those who shall come after me discern that I had worked with such a spirit?" Furthermore, those who are the happiest are those who are of the character to prefer that their services will remain unknown by all the coming generations.

Everybody has his own idea of pleasure. Some want to cultivate their garden, to raise beautiful flowers. And some others take pleasure in bringing up people.

Does the man who raises flowers in his garden expect anything from the flowers? The man who brings up man should, too, act with the same feelings that are felt by the man who raises flowers. It is only such kind of men who think and work in this way who can be useful to their country and their country's future. If a man thinks of himself rather than [of] the happiness of his country and nation, his value is of a secondary grade. Those men who primarily value themselves and who identify the nation and the country to which they belong with their own person, cannot be considered to have served their nation's happiness. It is only those who can think of the generations that come after them who can provide their nations with the possibilities of living and progressing. It is an illusion to think that progress and movement stops when their own selves cease to exist.

On this occasion I shall say this to our respected guest: I say exactly what I think to those whom I love. At the same time I'm not a man who is able to carry in his heart a secret that is unnecessary. Because I am a man of the people. I should always say what I think before the people. If I have an error, the people negates me. But, up to today, I have never seen in this open conversation the people to negate me. (*SD* 2: 1937, 280–81)

TEXT 30

Like our friends and all members of the nation, if my effort had been anterior to our national cause, if there is powerful execution and success in this effort, don't attribute this to my person. Attribute it only and only to the moral person of the whole nation. I'm proud of being an insignificant individual in the sublime moral person of this nation. Gentlemen, the nation in its totality, like a moral person and in the form of a unified mass, manifested itself, and by maintaining the lofty unity, it eliminated those who where its enemies. (*SD* 2: 1923c, 115)

TEXT 31

[I]f I have performed any service for my nation, if I have taken initiative in any enterprise, the real source of this service and enterprise derives from you, my dear nation, to which I will from here onward dedicate with respect and love my body and my life for its happiness and well-being.

Gentlemen, there may be present persons in a nation who think of doing nice things, but such persons cannot become anything on their own unless they be the agent, expression, representative of a general feeling. I have done nothing but closely penetrate my nation's thoughts and feelings, and express the ability and the need I saw in my dear nation. I'm proud of my grasp of its ability and feelings. To have seen that quality in my nation that brought about today's victories, that is what my whole happiness is. . . .

. . . too many persons who have acquired glory and reputation in history do not possess virtue from the national point of view. For instance, think of Napoleon, who indeed possessed military prowess, but went all the way to Moscow and wore out the French army dragging it over fires and ruins. His actions were for satisfying less the real and national interest of the French nation than his personal aims of world conquest. (*SD* 2: 1923d, 161)

TEXT 32

We read with friends who love you very much the telegram that informs that you reunited with one of the parts of the country and the whole that I love very much. The love bestowed by the residents of Balıkesir to the Great Chief of the Congress of the great Whole, with which they united with great desire, was highly received by us as if it were directed to all of us, that is our great Whole.

What I wish is this: speak to all the Balıkesirians of the things we wish to do for the Whole, for the country selflessly and forsaking ourselves. (*SD* 6: 1932a, 393, uppercase *W*s in original)

TEXT 33

It is obvious that the secret political maneuvering was directed against the being of the nation rather than my person. I'm moved very much. I know how much my noble Nation loves me. This public ovation is another proof that confirms the high degree of love and affection for me, and especially of the loyalty to our shared ideal; I am thankful, I am happy. If they kill me, I am sure that my citizens will take my revenge. If I die, I am satisfied that our noble nation will never deviate from the path we have walked together; I'm at ease with this. (*SD* 4: 1926, 574)

TEXT 34

You have gone out of the way for me. I'm embarrassed by this. To see me does not only mean to see my face. If you understand and feel my ideas and my feelings, that is enough. Before coming here from Ankara, I heard that they have said about me that "He's ill, his hand and foot are giving out, he's certain to die." Well, I'm in front of you, I'm in health, my hand and foot are functioning. You see with your own eyes that I'm in full health. I have never been healthier. My strength is in place. Tonight you are before me a mass, a symbol of the nation. While addressing you, I'm convinced that I will have my voice heard by the whole nation. Hear and make it heard. The man who has dedicated and devoted his health, his life, for your interests is in good health and is going to work for you. He lives for you. My power is [derives from] my love for you and your love for me. This nation, this country, upon its new regime, will be a most reasonable presence in the world. I will not die before I see this with my own eyes. (*SD* 2: 1929b, 254)

TEXT 35

Condemned to be damned are those efforts directed at violating the social order of the Turkish nation. The Turkish nation is not a collectivity that cannot understand or will tolerate the secret and dirty aims in the incoherent ravings of those corrupt, base, brainless ones who are without fatherland and nationality and who want to work against the high interests of the nation and the country.

It [the Turkish nation] sees the right path as it always has. Those who want to lead it astray are condemned to be crushed and annihilated. In this, the peasant, the worker, and especially our heroic army are all heartily united. Let no one doubt this. (*SD* 2: 1929a, 253–54)

TEXT 36

You announce a brand new program to the nation. This program is [nothing but] the points I have promised the nation. Celal Bayar and his associates promised me and the nation that they shall implement what I have promised the nation. I shall, together with the nation, see to it that Celal Bayar's and his associate's program is implemented point by point. Let me explain better: I, Atatürk, the President of Turkey, and the Turkish nation are overseeing Prime Minister Celal Bayar's and his government's program. And we want to see its actual results. (*SD* 3: 1937, 101–2)

TEXT 37

Youth speaking: "Our great Gazi, you are history itself, and we too in having been before such a living history have become historical persons. In the future, our progeny thinking of this fortunate lot of ours and of your greatness shall say about you: Was he a human being like us, did he walk and talk like us, did his eyes see like ours, did his ears hear like ours?"

Atatürk speaking: "I think that I possess no superiority over any individual of the nation. If more initiative has been seen in me, this is an enterprise that has emanated less from me than the sum of the nation. Were it not for you, had the inclinations of your conscience not constituted a point of support for me, none of my initiatives could come about." (*SD* 2: 1923e, 158–59)

THREE RHETORICAL STRATEGIES

"Objectively" speaking—speaking, that is, outside the charismatic relation—the relationship between leader and follower is, most basically, a diadic, two-term

power relation with the extraordinary leader on one side and the collectivity following him on the other. In Kemal's case, the two-term relation is between leader
and "the nation." He himself confirms this objective dimension when he describes the collectivity in singular terms as a "mass" (e.g., Text 34). From his perspective, the followers are one: the nation appears "like a moral person and in the
form of a unified mass" (Text 30), with "a single conscience and a single heart"
(Text 27).

"Subjectively" speaking—speaking, that is, from within the point of view of
the relationship itself—the relation between leader and follower is much more
complex. In order to complete and to ensure the charismatic tie, this two-term element must be collapsed. The leader must not be seen as a dominator who is exercising raw power over the collectivity. The leader must be seen as acting on
behalf of the highest interests of the followers, who, in turn, must recognize the
leader as embodying their truths, their "oughts" of life. Within this relation, the
leader seeks to cultivate a bond between himself or herself and the collectivity
that ensures that his or her actions are seen as the actions of the collectivity. The
leader must be perceived and understood as acting for and within the collectivity,
not over it, and the members of the collectivity must feel and think that they are
being led, not dominated.

Kemal's discourse exhibits three essential, charismatic power dynamics. The
first is a false humility wherein he poses as the humble servant of the nation, not
as its Great Leader. In this context, he rhetorically plays down his role as the
knower of the truth and transfers responsibility for understanding the truth to
the "nation." This dimension follows naturally from the nationalist arrow and the
particular truth of national sovereignty expressed by it. If all power comes from
the nation, it would be inconsistent for him to be the power—or, more important, to be perceived as exercising power for his own interests, on his own behalf,
or on the behalf of a particular sector of the population: "He who is a chief
should first act according to the ideal of the nation and, after grasping the psychology of the nation, be subject to that nation's inclination. . . . Sovereignty
wholly belongs to the nation" (Text 28). As such, Kemal is "proud of being an insignificant individual in the sublime moral person of this nation" (Text 30). Even
though he is the one who discovers and knows the truth, the truth does not belong to him. It belongs to the nation. It is their truth, not his, even though he is
the one with special access to it. His role, he humbly declares, is "nothing but [to]
penetrate closely my nation's thoughts and feelings, and express the ability and

the need I saw in my dear nation" (Text 31). Even if "the nation's thoughts and feelings" are ultimately his own, he cannot reveal them to be so. He must be seen as a servant of the nation, not its master. "[I]f I have performed any service for my nation, if I have taken initiative in any enterprise, the real source of this service and enterprise reverts to you [derives from you], to my dear nation" (Text 31). One "cannot become anything on [one's] own, unless they be the agent, expression, representative of a general feeling. . . . To have seen that quality in my nation which brought about today's victories, that is what my whole happiness is" (Text 31).

In this first element of the charismatic relation between leader and mass, the leader rhetorically shifts the powers of agency from his "humble" being to that of the "great" nation. Consistent with his continuous practice of heaping praise upon members of the nation, Kemal made[1] the nation *the* collective actor and thus diminished the appearance of his own ambition. His humble proclamations reinforced the nation's agency. To appear humble before them is to continue to elevate their status in their own eyes and to insinuate that they are the agents of existing political practice. To appear humble is to ensure that they see his actions as theirs and, therefore, to create the perception that his actions are legitimate in their eyes, for his actions are theirs. It is to construct the recognition of his unique access to their will. To appear humble is, in fine, to fortify the perception that his extraordinary insight is right and good for them.

Proclaimed humility builds the charismatic link; it does not weaken it or eliminate it because success counts when the people accept the leader's will as their own. The charismatic leader cannot be seen as imposing his own will on them. He must be seen as fulfilling the nation's will, leading it, serving its highest interests. A discourse of false humility that conceals the extent of domination at work suits this strategic end. The leader is successful when the members of the nation accept his will as their own, without his saying or demanding this explicitly. He gains their resolve while masking his own resolve to do so. For Mustafa Kemal, the key was to establish his indispensable, humble "value" in the eyes of those who must value him: "If a man thinks of himself rather than the happiness of his country and nation, his value is of a secondary grade. Those men who prima-

---

1. Our discussion here shifts between past and present tense. We use the past tense when offering Mustafa Kemal's utterances and the present tense when making analytical observations about them.

rily value themselves and who identify the nation and the country to which they belong with their own person, cannot be considered to have served their nation's happiness" (Text 29).

Despite the fact that the charismatic leader stands alone in his extraordinariness, he demands that his nation's success not be attributed "to his person." "Attribute it only and only"—an idiom expressing his insistence on thinking exactly as he says—"to the moral person of the whole nation. I'm proud of being an insignificant individual in the sublime moral person of this nation" (Text 30).

It is precisely on this basis that Kemal rejected and his partisan followers to this day reject the idea that he was a dictator or that he was at all committed to leading according to traditional models of authority. Kemal fostered this interpretation as early as 1923.

> Friends! There is no King, no dictator in the Turkish state and in the people of Turkey who founded the state of Turkey. There is no King and there won't be any. Because it cannot be. . . . The whole world should know that there is no power, no office anymore at the head of this nation. There is only one power. It is national sovereignty. There is only one office. And that is the heart, the conscience and the being of the nation. (*SD* 1: 1923e, 311)

The rejection of any hint of dictatorship depends on the idea that there is no relation of domination between the humble leader and the nation. The only relevant power is the power of the nation. The offices of the (nation's) state exercise no illegitimate power over the nation; they emerge—democratically, this view goes—from the power of the nation, that single entity with a "heart and conscience." Kemal's "guidance" is not his; it "cannot be but the inspiration we take from our nation" (Text 28). The discourse of humility ensures that followers will follow without believing or knowing they are being led. In 1923, Kemal stated: "I am not a dictator. They say that I am powerful; yes, this is correct. There is nothing whatsoever that I desire and cannot do. Because it is not my way to act forcefully and unjustly. In my mind a dictator is one who makes others submit to his own will. I wish to rule by winning hearts, not by breaking hearts" (*SD* 3: 1935, 100). Kemal is seeking to "rule," not simply to serve, and he does this, according to his own description, not by hurting, but by nurturing, not by "breaking hearts," but by "winning hearts." His claim—apparent in many of the representative texts given at the beginning of this chapter—was that he was no dictator because those who were ruled by him knew that he ruled them with love, not with hatred.

Love dovetails with the will to establish the charismatic linkage, which is a relation in which the loving "leader" "rules" those who love him in return. This is the second element of Kemal's rhetorical style that enabled his charismatic tie: Kemal described his bond as humble ruler and his followers in emotive terms of love and affection. Love here reinforces the false humility. Their joint effect—that of love and humility—remains only implicit; nevertheless, by winning hearts, the ruler-leader also wins wills. Love helps to create the will to follow. By cultivating a relationship in which the bond is understood as one of love and deep affection, Kemal thus ensures that his collectivity sees him as their humble leader, not as an aggressive dictator. Such was the purpose and the effect of his very well-known statement concerning his health in 1929, when there were suspicions of his imminent demise.

TEXT 34

You have gone out of the way for me. I'm embarrassed by this. To see me does not only mean to see my face. If you understand and feel my ideas and my feelings, that is enough. Before coming here from Ankara I heard that they have said about me that "He's ill, his hand and foot are giving out, he's certain to die." Well, I'm in front of you, I'm in health, my hand and foot are functioning. You see with your own eyes that I'm in full health. I have never been healthier. My strength is in place. Tonight you are before me a mass, a symbol of the nation. While addressing you, I'm convinced that I will have my voice heard by the whole nation. Hear and make it heard. The man who has dedicated and devoted his health, his life, for your interests is in good health and is going to work for you. He lives for you. My power is my love for you and your love for me. This nation, this country, upon its new regime, will be a most reasonable presence in the world. I will not die before I see this with my own eyes.

The statement contains many of the themes we have examined thus far. Kemal infuses himself into the hearts and minds of the nation; he lifts the nation and humbles himself—simultaneously lifting himself as a result of their high and healthy recognition of him. *Then* the charismatic leader requests explicitly that his extraordinariness be transmitted through the nation by those who love him. Love, as such, should spread.

Moreover, Kemal uses the language of love explicitly and the idea of love implicitly to buttress the follower's unquestioned will to follow. He does not say "think about it" or "consider what I am saying." He says, "love me as I love you. Activate your emotive powers for me as I do for you." Love, like action for Kemal, stands in distinct contrast to reflection. The language of love and affection bonds Kemal to his audience like a father to his children. The nation should not think or question their leader. The hierarchy between them is legitimate in part because it is founded on his professed care for them and their corresponding recognition that he cares for them. This is Kemal's own understanding, his construction of the source of his "power." He claims that his power comes from love. Kemal thus exemplifies par excellence the charismatic leader's aspiration to be seen acting entirely on the nation's behalf.

He stood before audience after audience and impressed upon them that he was moved by their love and affection for him. He, in turn, dedicated his love and affection to them. For Atatürk, the bond symbolized their trust in him to do what was right for them. Their public displays of affection—such as ovations and ritual acts of deference—proved their love for him; no other form or mechanism to establish his legitimacy seemed necessary. And rather than reject their love with humility, he accepted it because their love symbolized both their greatness and his success in making them love him. "To this heart that I touch with a pleasure of conscience," he said in Bursa, "this contact grants me a very high degree of happiness. Friends, I was for a long time very convinced that the respected people of Bursa were of this high capacity" (Text 27). This was his great nation loving him, making him great, even as he posed humbly before them. When opponents rejected him, he could always fall back on the nation's love for him as his pillar of support, as in the case of his statement after an assassination plot was uncovered:

TEXT 33

It is obvious that the secret political maneuvering was directed against the being of the nation rather than my person. I'm moved very much. I know how much my noble Nation loves me. This public ovation is another proof that confirms the high degree of love and affection for me, and especially of the loyalty to our shared ideal; I am thankful, I am happy. If they kill me, I am sure that my citizens will take my revenge. If I die, I am satisfied that our noble nation will never deviate from the path we have walked together; I'm at ease with this.

The leader is certain that he has successfully paved his true path. The people of the nation have come to know, as he put it in the 1925 speech at Bursa, that "the path we are following together is true. This path will enable us to attain happiness. There is no reason to hesitate" (Text 27). Even through the 1930s, Kemal continued to adopt the humble stance. To the people of Balıkesir in 1932, as to other audiences throughout his tenure as chief, he said, "The love bestowed by the residents of Balıkesir upon the Great Chief of the Congress of the great Whole, with which they united with great desire, was highly received by us as if it were directed to all of us, that is our great whole. What I wish is this: speak to all the Balıkesirians of the things we wish to do for the whole, for the country selflessly and forsaking ourselves" (Text 32). The leader works for a great, single "Whole"; the bond between them is selfless love.

The third element of Kemal's rhetorical style in this charismatic relation is the conditionality of his love, expressed in often vituperative diatribes against those who did not love him, who did not recognize his position as humble leader, who did not see that his only ostensible interest was to serve his nation, or who did not accept his logic as such. Those who did not love him, he said, opposed him. The *political* significance of the language of love in Kemal's discourse is thus revealed in his equation of the lack of love with "opposition."

Those who loved were not simply lovers: they were "supporters" in political terms. Those who did not love were opponents. They "play the role of instigators in the opposition currents," he said in *Nutuk*. In the liberation struggle, they were the "pessimists," "helpless and fearful human beings," "who give hope to the enemy" (Atatürk 1962, 637, 639). "Those who are preparing to oppose us are forgetting the high interests of the nation" (501). Throughout his public speeches and statements, Kemal constructed opponents in terms that contrast sharply with his own professed humility: he charged them with being "fools," the ambitious ones harboring "secret and dirty aims," the ones who threatened the national interests with "incoherent ravings" that led the nation "astray" (Text 35), who "violate[d] the social order" by tearing holes in the national body, who divided the nation and thus threatened to force a deviation from the true path that Kemal had established for it. They were not simply wrong. They were outside of the requirements of history. Unlike the nation, the opponents were "unfortunate" and "pitiful" (Text 16). To the audience at Bursa in the 1925 speech quoted above, he noted that "unfortunately several fools wanted to get in the way of this mass and cover this intelligence and ability" (Text 27). The fools were "base, brainless ones who are without fatherland *and nationality*" (emphasis added)—including "those who are nourishing reactionary ideas think[ing] they can rely on a class" (Text 26). Here, importantly, the concept "reactionary" is linked with class-based critics, not the religious right. The solidaristic corporatist charismatic leader would countenance no antisolidarist ambitions. Loyalty to Kemal constituted support for Kemalism, not only for his person. There existed an intimate linkage between the broader ideological objectives of Kemalism and the charismatic leader's ambitions, concealed as they were in a pseudohumble disposition.

A glowing example of such connections can be found in another talk from the 1926 discovery of the assassination attempt:

There is no doubt this despicable attempt has been directed less against my person than our sacred Republic and the high principles on which it is based. It is for this reason that upon expressions of the public I was convinced once again of how entrenched the overwhelming loyalty to the Republic and to our principles has become. Those who imagine that our principles—inspired by the spirit of the nation and our Republic, whose foundation has been established in the conscience, mind, and consciousness of the great Turkish nation and our great army made up of the nation's heroic children—can be harmed by removing a body are the unfortunate ones with very weak brains. Those unfortunate ones can have no lot other than to be subjected to the treatment they deserve in the Republic's paw of justice and might. My humble body will certainly become a [piece of] earth some day, but the Turkish Republic will endure to eternity. And the Turkish nation, with principles that guarantee its security and happiness will continue to unhesitatingly march on the way of civilization. (*SD* 3: 1926, 80)

Kemal equates his own identity first with that of the republic, then with that of the nation, and *then* with that of justice. Aim at him, and you aim at the others. Those who "resist and oppose" (Text 10) him, oppose the republic, oppose the nation, and oppose justice. As such, it is legitimate to "crush them." Violence against members of the nation is legitimate if the "despicable" dare to cross Kemal. The charismatic leader tolerates little opposition. His way—and the way that his followers would later employ—is to destroy those who cross him, his republic, and his truths because opponents degrade the nation, whereas he lifts it up. They seek to misdirect the nation on a path of their own selfish making, whereas he leads it on the straight and true path. They are "bad shepherds" (Text 26)—with "perplexed and ignorant brains" (Atatürk 1962, 690)—who lead the nation "astray." They are "condemned to be damned." As the good shepherd, he beckons his followers to join him in opposing those who oppose him and hence their own directions, hence their/his order, their/his path.

TEXT 35

Condemned to be damned are those efforts directed at violating the social order of the Turkish nation. The Turkish nation is not a collectivity that cannot understand or will tolerate the secret and dirty aims in the incoherent ravings of those corrupt, base brainless ones who are without fatherland and nationality and who want to work against the high interests of the nation and the country.

It [the Turkish nation] sees the right path as it always has. Those who want to lead it astray are condemned to be crushed and annihilated. In this, the peasant, the worker, and especially our heroic army are all heartily united. Let no one doubt this.

Kemal's love was always conditional on the mass's showing its love for him by joining him in opposing those who opposed him, those who had other ideas, those who he said could hardly have any ideas at all. His is the only relevant mind. He castigates the others by declaring their brains to be "weak." His is the active mind, their's the organs of "seducers." He is the brain for the headless mass that is the heart. They need to recognize him as the brain that knows what the body should do. Of course, he does not say this explicitly at all times. He says the nation knew the truth and it loved him, not the "damned." The implication is: "they are brainless, and I am the one with the brains."

Kemal expressed particularly vituperative views of those who challenged his authority from within the antilaicist conservative Muslim opposition, but the record is clear that he was also nervous about criticisms that emanated from other nationalist spheres as well. Both layers of recrimination are somewhat evident in his explanation for why he could not transfer power to a "representative council" during the national struggle:

TEXT 16

Could the situation and the duty at hand be left to any representative council that probably might have consisted of random persons who had no connection with or relationship to the administration of the nation, the country, politics, and the armed forces and who lacked any demonstrated ability or experience in these respects, for instance such pitiful people like a Nakşibendi sheikh from Erzincan or a tribal chief [*aşiret reisi*] from Mutki? And in case it was left to such a council, would we have not committed the error of seducing the nation and ourselves when we were saying that we shall rescue the country and the nation?

Here, the charismatic leader eliminates the possibility of turning decision-making power over to other members of the collectivity, especially those whose goals are not apparently in tune with the laws of history. Such a procedure would not have been "safe" (Text 16) because they are fools who might steer the nation astray.

The passage clearly intimates the place of the conservative religious deputies in Kemal's mind. To Kemal, these "pitiful" opponents thought in terms of "religious clichés" and were on the wrong side of history and reason. He was determined to have them see the light. In *Nutuk,* he proudly recalled a day in the early history of the Assembly when, upon overhearing some words of praise for the sultan-caliph and the Ottoman regime, he took the podium to declare the Ottomans to be usurpers of the sovereignty of the Turkish nation. He then stated, "If those who have gathered here, the Assembly and all, see the problem as it should naturally be seen, that would be proper to my mind. If they don't, the truth will anyway be duly expressed. But probably some heads will roll" (Atatürk 1962, 691). Evident here is the overlap between the charismatic leader's claim to truth and his authoritarian discourse on politics. The literal translation of the phrase used for "heads will roll" is "heads will be chopped off." The point Kemal was making was, roughly paraphrased, that "those of you who support the sultanate and caliphate, and hence oppose their abolition, should not resist or oppose us. You should see the truth in what we say. And, if you don't, we will express and implement it anyway, at your expense if necessary."

Coercive demands reside, then, side by side with Kemal's discourse on love. Kemal threatens those with different ideological positions. What he calls "reason" resides with him and his path alone: "A person who is commander . . .

should pursue things that are fitting to reason (*akıl*)" (Text 28). Indeed, contestation itself signifies foolishness, a charge that his adversaries knew they would be colored with if they objected. Kemal declared one member of the Assembly who expressed an interest in restoring the Ottoman state to be "a reactionary in the eyes of the government and of the nation" (*SD* 2: 1923f, 96). Others knew the power of such public denunciations. Kemal recalled once in *Nutuk* when, after his denunciations of the *hoca*s (persons of religious background), one *hoca* apologized, explaining that he and his associates had been considering the question from another point of view and that they had "now been enlightened" by his explanation. By force of his discourse of threat and condemnation, he cows them into a position of willing submission. This was, after all, their only "safe" option. To express themselves or to act otherwise is to risk expulsion and derision. Success for him, then, requires in his mind that his echo be heard throughout the nation. His words are to be the words of the nation; his mind, the nation's mind. His head, the nation's head.

It is important to note that the discourse of "reactionarism" that Kemal used to condemn the outlooks of religiously driven opponents partly occludes the extent of his own more general political reactionarism and the ways in which he used a discourse of threat, insult, and derision to have all opposition—not only the antilaicists—willingly submit to his will. He did not reserve his condemnations for the antilaicist opposition alone. A hegemonic ideology dominates all subject to it, not only those who are identified from within as its enemies. Kemal sought to have the entire nation submit willfully to the Kemalist truths.

THE LEADER AND OPPOSITION

Several examples drawn from *Nutuk* serve to illustrate this more general dynamic. In one, Kemal discussed some editorials published in two Istanbul newspapers, *Vatan* and *Tanin,* in 1924. The editorials offered very strong, but measured and discerning criticisms of what might be termed Kemal's arbitrary style of rule. (The concept *arbitrary* makes sense only from a vantage point outside the charismatic connection.) The editorial writers voiced concerns, for example, about Kemal's tendency to personalize and monopolize power in his hands and in the hands of the protective regime that had sprung up around him. Among other things, the newspaper critiques show that the political context was not entirely sterile. They also illustrate power politics between Istanbul and Ankara, of which Kemal was quite aware. Kemal tried to use this material to his own advantage, but, in our view, his response reveals his essential "leadership" style of arbitrary categorization, unreflective denunciation, and threat.

> In the 5 Teşrinisani copy of the *Vatan* newspaper, in its editorial, those who criticized the government and those who assume opposition are being praised and eulogized while adherents of the government are being blamed. The editor in chief says that, "Against those potential critics who haven't yet uttered even a word of opposition new words of threat are being whispered into ears everyday. Whomever you encounter from the governmental faction, you can definitely hear the words that are contained in that day's secret order"; and continues to give some examples to verify his words: "They resort to all kinds of means to silence from the very beginning those personages who do not blindly obey orders who see the truth and express it" and "Arbitrary will [it seems] is going to maintain its nature of being a determinate factor [in our country's political life] beyond the natural order of things and requirements for stability."
>
> Gentlemen [Efendiler], what was the author trying to announce to the nation by the phrases "daily secret order" and "arbitrary will"? Who was giving the secret order and who enforced his arbitrary will? The author who used these vague expressions in the end advises us that, "the most delicate and important duty of the president of the republic is like an umpire to summon both sides and to listen to them objectively." He demands that this duty should be performed immediately and he threatens [*tehdit ediyor*] because "tomorrow may be too late."
>
> The same author commenting the next day on my new year's speech says that: "A monopolistic political system that often tries to eliminate those citizens of the most independent mind of a critical bent, creates an informal situation that annihilates [the prospects] of development and progress." By this sentence the author issues a very unjust and unfair calumny about the system we are pursuing and was impressing upon us again our duty by saying, "it is necessary that this ill-boding course be stopped at a certain point and a new one be initiated." (Atatürk 1963, 874–75)

Kemal does not even consider the elements of the editorial writer's critique as "criticisms." He calls them "demands" in the form of a "threat" and turns the editor's fundamental charge that government is undermining "development and progress"—two terms about which one presumes Kemal might have argued on principle—into "calumny." Indeed, he describes the "demand" for greater neutrality and liberty as "vague," suggesting that these terms, too, are not points open to consideration in his mind. The editor's fault lies not in an erroneous analysis of the political situation as such; Kemal does not object to the criticism on principled analytical grounds. He says that the editor's error lies in his "praising" and "blaming" the wrong parties. Kemal's entire disposition to this critical voice is dismissive: he unreflectively denounces those who disagree with his truths. Note that we are not now discussing his response to the antilaicist traditionalists—the so-called permanent obscurantists of the republican era. We are discussing his response to critics who speak the same progressive language he does, but who associate progressivism with less authoritarian politics. Kemal constructs their political criticism as insult and threat, however, and in doing so suggests that their concerns possess no merit. They are not even worth engaging. Indeed, clever actor that he is, Kemal uses the exchange to buttress his absolutist self-conception.

Rather than engage the concerns addressed to his regime, he turns them to his advantage by constructing the author's intent as hostile to "the nation": "What was the author trying to announce to the nation?" Kemal asks. A "threat," he concludes. The politics of praise and blame quickly slide into threat. Praise and blame the right parties, and you are a supportive, loving, and dedicated member of the nation. Praise and blame the wrong ones, and you are an opponent filled with "unjust and unfair calumny," a "threat" to the nation. The critic is a traitor whose views damage the nation. The republic's "paw of justice" awaits these opponents as well. This is the ideological core of the leader's posture toward those who disagree.

In using the terms *blame* and *calumny* and in construing the suggestion "tomorrow may be too late" as a "threat," Kemal in effect brings his critics into his own antipolitical framework for understanding opposition. Rather than engaging the critics respectfully as equals, he adopts the view that they should know better than to question the path that "the nation" is following; they should be following him like others do. From a strategic vantage point, the discourse is quite impressive: Kemal assumes that all criticism is intended to undercut his plan or position. Any debate or deliberation over differences of opinion carries a harmful intent. He then projects that intent onto his critics and returns the threat that he constructed. He retaliates against a threat that he projected onto the "enemies [of the nation]." He is simply astonished that someone would tell "us"—read "me"—or the nation how to rule.

Of course, his threat in this case is not directly confrontational. As charismatic leader, he counts on the nontextualized dynamics of power and authority to clarify the force of his point. He counts on the recognition of his created role as the Leader, the Chief, and the agent for the nation's development and progress. Those who know where he stands (and where they do!) will assist in silencing the critics through a variety of measures, including ostensibly coercive ones, such as conviction under the Law for the Establishment of Tranquility and subtle pressures of social conformity and enthusiastic support in the official media organs. The charismatic leader is successful when he captivates his followers to his purposes. In short, Kemal knows that he is held in high esteem. In order to discourage more criticism, it is enough for him to say that criticisms voiced in the press are worthless. The implication of his language and tone is that he may not "crush" you as he does others, but he will humiliate you publicly. This is in part what Kemal's rehearsals of the "history" of the liberation struggle in *Nutuk* are intended to accomplish: Editors beware. Your principled criticism will be neglected and your honor destroyed.

The tendency to dismiss and eliminate principled discussion over fundamental political issues, classifying such issues in ways that purge them of any possible relevance to the nation's goals, is one of Atatürk's most entrenched legacies in Turkish political culture, though it is, of course, neither limited to the Turkish context nor specific to Kemal himself. This antideliberative and hence antipolitical disposition is significant especially in the sense that Atatürk's leadership style has been taken as being revolutionary and as having changed Turkey's political course by laying the grounds for modern politics, where *modern* is understood as committed to developing functioning institutions for collective, democratized (if not democratic) decision making. *Modern* here refers to democratic respect for the participatory capacities and potentials of all citizens.[2] It refers to what is assumed to be the case in the tutelary democratic leadership style and political example set by Atatürk.

We suggest, however, that his leadership behavior was more antimodern, an-

---

2. *Modern* is a category that has been worked and reworked tremendously in contemporary political theory. As we stated earlier, our interest is in showing that Kemalism defies rather than exemplifies the democratizing principles associated with it.

tidemocratic, and dismissive than tutelary democratic. He may have given the impression of a genuine interest in political modernization, but his language and discourse of "leadership" suggest that his intent was much less progressive. In *Nutuk,* he proudly set an antipolitical example that leaders may dismiss their opponents by classifying, rejecting, and humiliating them. We have more to say about this later. Here, sticking with the documents themselves, we note that for Kemal, it was legitimate to resist argument, debate, and contestation, which, from a democratic perspective, are indispensable to *politics* in any collectivity. A democratic leader, tutelary or not, must demonstrate some willingness to subject his or her own ideas to revision and alteration in light of the ideas of others, who are in principle his or her equals. Kemal, who promoted himself as charismatic leader and enjoyed his promotion by others as such, never saw any reason to engage in discussion. There was no need to listen to the ideas of others who were unequal in status. Indeed, he called the ideas of his toughest critics "artificial": "The artificial ideas that are being presented as the public opinion can at most be considered as private ideas. They are taken into consideration if they are seen as worthwhile and beneficial. But they cannot be considered as principles that should be observed in general governance" (*SD* 5: 1925b, 210–11). He represented the general, his critics the particular. The general was that of the nation, the particular that of weak and limited brains. The former had to be listened to and institutionalized; the latter had to be dismissed and excluded.

In one of Kemal's most interesting public speeches, he asserted that multiparty political competition was not necessary, in part because his own party, the RPP, was capable of being "sensitive and vigilant" by acting *"as if* there were many parties facing" it (*SD* 2: 1930b, 257, emphasis added). Kemal uttered this remark shortly after the second legal opposition party of the single-party period, the FRP, dissolved itself under pressure. The statement suggests to our minds that Kemal showed no interest in pursuing the practices of competitive party politics.

> We are bound to work with ever-imposing activity everyday as if there were many parties facing us, to disseminate our ideas to the masses of the people, and to take them all the way to the villages. It is necessary to be at every moment in a position of being able to account for our movement before history and before the world. By being this sensitive and vigilant in our project and activities,

we shall have eliminated the drawbacks of an oppositionless party. (*SD* 2: 1930b, 257)

It is difficult to espy any tutelary democratic intent in such statements. Kemal explicitly rejects any need for an opposition as the party "disseminates" its/his ideas. He confidently states that there is no need for another party.

Our intent here is not to idealize Kemal's opponents. Their politics exhibited many shortcomings as well, including the racist statement contained in a passage that Kemal cited in order to counter more criticisms of his style. The passage nonetheless indicates this consistent sentiment regarding the unaccountable power relations between the leader and others in the new republic:

The editor in chief of *Tanin* in his leading article of 4 Teşrinisani 1924 entitled "Army and Politics," expresses the following opinions, "the form of government is republic. But there is no use in just changing the name of government. What really needs to be changed is the spirit and principles of the matter. With the exception of the United States, there are about twenty countries in the Americas which all bear the name of republic. Even Haiti, which consisted only of Negroes, was a republic. But in that region the difference between a republic and an absolute government is very little. Instead of a hereditary ruler, we see an autocrat who has usurped the presidency. That's it! The despot who bears the name of president governs as he wills it. Like an absolute monarch, he doesn't recognize any law other than his own pleasure and whims."

The editor in chief of *Tanin* has the following to say, with the exception of Chile, about these American republics: "None of them today is entitled to bear the name of a real republic. Because they are not based on democracy . . . [ellipses in original]; It is because of military chiefs that these absolute governments prevail under the name of republic."

I should like to dwell upon this for a minute. Gentlemen, this article is being written upon and on the occasion of the resignation of those commanders who were also deputies. But it is being written at such a time when the inspectors of our armies, abandoning their troops, have come to the Assembly in order to topple the government [i.e., the council of ministers that he had formed], and this author, with the purpose of proving the legitimacy of their desire to get into power, has written a long article of many columns just yesterday. The author, who gives examples to the effect that republic can be the same as absolute government and who says that the reason for that is not grounding it in democracy, is the same person who states that "the democraticness of the party in government is only on its lips." The person who says that this is so "because of military chiefs" is a person who knows that Turkey's President too is one of the military chiefs. It is this person. (Atatürk 1962, 874–75, 877–78)

Kemal again immediately takes the criticism of the government—the full details of which remain unclear in the text—first as a threat to his regime ("the party in government") and then as a personal offense. This person who criticizes the fusion of the military with politics as antidemocratic, Kemal says, is one "who knows that Turkey's President too is one of one of the military chiefs." Significantly, this is one of the few times the word *democracy* appears in *Nutuk,* and, presented with the opportunity to reassert and exhibit democratic behavior, Kemal opts instead for his classic antipolitical posture. In a controlled and measured countercritique, he implies—again, with all of the force and authority of his charisma behind him—that the writer of the editorial has demeaned Kemal with his criticism. He immediately attributes bad faith to the critic: "This person knows that I am a chief and says such things!" Kemal does not deign to engage the critique. To do so would be to level the playing field, which, in turn would be to descend to the level of those who insult the president and the republic. Far be it for the charismatic leader to engage his detractors. He need only view them as hurlers of insults and then project that demeaning attitude back onto them in order to subdue them and eliminate the relevance of their voices. Such ambitious detractors aim "to create negative and harmful influences." They are threats and must be dismissed.

Such statements by Kemal demonstrate a fundamental trait of charismatic leadership. The leader, in his dismissal of those who break through the charismatic link, shows that he lacks inner respect not only for others' ideas, but for their persons as such. The leader holds only himself in esteem and respects only his own truths. He displays no respect for his opponents' ideas, and he shows that he is prepared to humiliate them in order to ensure that they do not threaten his creation—his nation and his ties with the nation. Revealed in Kemal's denunciations of his political critics is his self-understanding that he stands above all in terms of respect and status. Indeed, it is questionable whether he respects those who follow him as well. He loves them, but they are not his equals. He says they are brainless without him, *and* they comply with whatever he wishes. From the perspective of the charismatic leader, all others are limited, lesser creatures. He need only say this, however, directly to those who oppose him, and when he does, he calculates that doing so will shore up his position in the eyes of others. He is polite with those who are politically weak, those whom he has captivated and subdued by the charismatic relation. But he is harsh with those who display political "strength"—that is, those who resolve to contest the authority dynamics. His harshness with them, in their company or not, is intended to solidify further his love with the others. Love for the weak, who need his help; invective for those who challenge. Hence, Kemal's anger toward those who criticized him, his sub-chief (İsmet Pasha), or his government and who betrayed, or appeared to betray, him and the nation: "Gentlemen, our face has always been clean and pure, and it will always remain so. Those whose faces are ugly and whose consciences are full with ugliness are those who dare to present as ugly our patriotic, conscientious, and honest actions because of their own petty and ugly ambitions" (Atatürk 1962, 881–82).

The charismatic leader does not say, "Perhaps I have been mistaken." He says, "You are ugly and unpatriotic." He assigns categories, bad faith, bad intent, and bad character to his opponents. A very harsh example of Kemal's charismatic antipolitical rejectionist discourse outside of *Nutuk* is his speech of 1925 on "national liberation and prosperity." In this speech, Kemal elides his person with the nation and the party, simultaneously speaking at every level against "base politicians" who seek to "seduce/distract the nation" from its march toward civilization.

We do not deign to attract transient favors by seducing the nation concerning matters that our mind does not comprehend or that we do not feel within our power and ability. We hate to make false promises to the nation like base politicians. While marching for the cause of the country and the nation, we are pleased with and thankful to those who warn us with goodwill when they see our ideational and actual faults and inadequacies. But we cannot attribute goodwill to those who try to misconstrue and misinterpret our aims and impede the implementation of our ideas for the nation and the country. If not really traitors, such are absolutely heedless and for this reason are instruments of treason, evil, and malice. (*SD* 5: 1925a, 209)

The leadership accepts "warnings" by those of "goodwill" who "see our ideational and actual faults and inadequacies," but it cannot attribute such will to those who impede the nation's path. They are treasonous, evil, malicious seducers, not loyal, good, and beneficent leaders who possess the nation's mind and feel its power and ability. The leadership, moreover, tells the truth. It does not misrepresent itself like its opponents, who heedlessly conceal their real intentions to "disrupt the cause of the country and nation," who purposefully misinterpret the leadership's goals.

INSTITUTIONALIZATION OF CHARISMATIC DOMINATION

An intimate link existed between the model of charismatic leadership set by Mustafa Kemal and many of the policies established to maintain single-party rule during the foundational period of the state. Kemal and Kemalism's antipolitical disposition underlay the imagination for many of the institutions of the single-party period that ensured the Kemalists' sole grasp of power. How can there be more than one legal party or political movement if there is only one truth? To Kemal, the law should conform to the existing needs of the nation—namely, that his hegemonic party enjoy the reins of government in an uncontested and unfettered way. The legal apparatus that ensured the RPP's single rule was thus constituted by the notion that there exists one truth and that it alone should be backed by power. A good example is the Law for the Establishment of Tranquility because it expresses in its name Kemal's desire to eliminate opposition and establish the "tranquil" conditions for the RPP to implement Kemalism's agenda. A brief examination of its application and the RPP's treatment of the short-lived opposition parties illustrates this relation between the ideological rejection of legitimate opposition and the institutions that guarded the RPP's single rule.

Both in theory and practice, early Kemalism posited that order was necessary for progress, "not a fragile and precarious stability and law and order, but a tranquility in a measure that obtains in those countries considered as most advanced" (Text 26). The Law for the Establishment of Tranquility created Independence Tribunals, whose task was to eliminate or silence treasonous, evil, "harmful political organizations" from the political scene and thus to engineer tranquility by shutting down opposition and debate. Order would enable the regime to build unity and solidarity around its goals. "Unity" here further implies unison around Kemal's ideas for the corporatist ideal. The nation was not to speak in many discordant voices. It was to speak with one voice, and that voice would pronounce the truths of the Great Leader.

Of course, Kemal did not demand "unison" explicitly, but it *is* what he desired. He claimed that the Law for Tranquility was necessary in order to protect the state and to create the conditions for his policies to take hold, but his intent was to create unison around those policies by abolishing the voices of opposition. In his view, the measures taken to do so were both within the letter of the law and, more important, consistent with Kemalism's higher civilizing mission, such as its "civil and social development" of the nation. As he maintained, "We never used the extraordinary but legal measures taken in any way as an instrument for rising above the law; on the contrary, we applied them to establish tranquility and order in the country; we used them to assure the life and independence of the state. We utilized these measures for the civil and social development of the nation" (Atatürk 1962, 894). He also stated: "We accomplished [these transformationist goals] during the time when the Law for the Establishment of Tranquility was in force. If it had not been in force, we were going to do it anyway. If, however, it is suggested that the existence of the Law facilitated this, this would certainly be true" (895). In light of the latter statement, it is interesting that Kemal offered any legalistic defense for the law whatsoever in the former statement. The law was used initially to crush "religious reactionarism," but consistent with the general antioppositional tendencies of Kemal's antipolitical discourse, it had the effect of silencing opposition within the Assembly and from urban journalistic circles, too, especially when the opposition party, the PRP, was closed down on charges of abetting the struggles in the periphery. For legitimation purposes in the political center, it was thus important that Kemal defend these actions as legal.

Kemal's views on the opposition in the center slightly varied as the context shifted, but his antipolitical disposition remained consistent. On his own account, in a little-known interview in 1924, he said he initially permitted the formation of the PRP because it represented the same goals as his own party. After several ethnic and religious uprisings in Anatolia, however, he claimed that the PRP represented the same goals as the rebels. At first, that is, the PRP was unnecessary because it was redundant. The message there was that politics between like-minded groups was superfluous and unnecessary. Later, he rejected the

PRP's presence in the Assembly because it was a threat. The message there was that political debate between opposing views would be "harmful." On both occasions, Kemal refused to engage politically. He clung to his own truths, unwilling to countenance the political presence of those who accept and reproduce them. In the 1924 interview, Kemal clarified precisely how he felt initially about the opposition party. Although he did not deny its procedural legality, he suggested that it was redundant, that the "details" they raised could be addressed among the members of the existing party ("the experts," as he phrased it):

The questioner asks: Does the Gazi accept the PRP as a real new political party? If not, why?

Kemal answers: Formation of a new political party in Turkey is subject to some legal procedures; since the new party has fulfilled this formality, it can be considered to have been formed.

The questioner: [How does] the Gazi find the program of the PRP? What are [his] ideas especially about [this party's] ideas about the right of veto and the power of abolition [of the Assembly] and about its insinuations and allusions concerning freedom of religion, protection of National Sovereignty, and the existence of absolute rule?

Kemal: In the program of the PRP, one doesn't see any essential principle and idea *that is worth discussion beyond the principle of the present party.* Some points that can be seen as pertaining to details are nothing but matters than can be examined daily anew and discussed by the experts leading to new conclusions. The power to veto and the power to abolish have been clarified and established by the special articles of the Constitution.

To be respectful of religious ideas and beliefs is a natural and general convention ever since. There is no reason to think otherwise.

Our national sovereignty is certainly not in jeopardy. The whole nation is the conscious and loyal guard of it. The insinuations and allusions to the presence of absolute rule are to my mind inexplicable. The RPP and all of its leaders and members are people who have not hesitated to stake their lives and who will never abstain from staking their lives together with the nation till today in order to destroy all kinds of absolutism in Turkey and to provide the country and nation with complete freedom; therefore, alleged absolute rule most certainly does not exist. The insinuations and allusions suggested with this purpose have no value whatsoever in the eyes of the nation. (*SD* 3: 1924c, 77–78)

Kemal's point here is full of complicated aspects that can be understood when viewed through corporatist and charismatic lenses. On the one hand, he asserts that the RPP exists to "destroy all kinds of absolutism." On the other, he rationalizes a closed political system. The message Kemal wishes to convey to his interviewer is something like the following: "Turkey has arrived. The RPP will 'provide the county and nation with complete freedom' according to the RPP's ideals (its solidarist corporatist agenda). Therefore, there is no need whatsoever to share power. An opposition party is unnecessary. The opposition claims to represent respect for faith, but we already do. They claim to represent progress, but we already do. Why are they necessary?" Kemal cannot grasp the need either to share power or to establish a forum for political debate. What he sees is a threat, so he devotes himself to the idea, at least initially, that the creation of another party would be redundant. In public statements such as these, the charismatic leader reinforces the idea that he alone (along with his party) is the real revolutionary. Those who claim that their voice must be added to political considerations suggest that his rule is insufficient, rather than, as he sees it, more than sufficient—an emanation of historical truth itself.

The interviewer then asked Kemal what influence Kemal believed that the critical journalists had over the majority of people. In response, Kemal issued another veiled threat:

> There is no need to explain in the Gazi's language the fact that most of the papers in Istanbul are criticizing the RPP and its government and favor the opposition. The reasons that would explain this situation can be easily divined by those who have closely observed and understood Ankara and Istanbul.
>
> The influence that is exerted over the majority of people by some papers that propagate special [but concealed] aims is not in favor of those papers as is the case in all countries. (*SD* 3: 1924c, 77–78)

In other words, "what they say is not viewed favorably here in Ankara."

After 1925, the PRP became less a redundancy and more a threat, which was owing less to its programs than to its existence. In the context of rebellion in the periphery, Kemal denied his potential rivals in the center any exposure in a legitimate public forum and classified the PRP as an "abettor of reactionarism," determining that it represented in the Assembly broadly the same tendencies that the rebels in the periphery represented. In *Nutuk,* he claimed that "the party formed by Rauf Bey" now lacked genuine republican and progressive credentials, in part because of its declared support for "religious ideas and doctrines."[3] Kemal portrayed the PRP as political reactionaries carrying "the banner of superstition," who threatened the state and the transformation itself (Atatürk 1962, 889–91). Kemal's regime later claimed that his enemies in the party participated in the Izmir assassination attempt, and so, using "the crushing paw of the Republic" (Atatürk 1962, 894), it purged many members, including Rauf Bey. It is important to distinguish Kemal's criticisms of the PRP from his opposition to the antilaicist traditionalists, but it is also important to see how both critiques had essentially the same end—namely, the rhetorical delegitimation of all opposition. This view undergirded the state's institutional repression in the name of "tranquility" (progress, the people, the nation, and so on). Ideologically speaking, the need for tranquility made it necessary to purge any and all rivals who threatened the policies of the charismatic leader's transformation. They were potential distracters—"seducers"—who undercut, though in different ways, the authority of Kemal's truths.

This is why even though Kemal offered a legal defense for actions carried out under the Law for the Establishment of Tranquility, his emphasis throughout *Nutuk* regarding the need for such activities was not legality, but the RPP's progressive, civilizing mission—the relevant "truths"—embedded in its solidaristic corporatist ideology. In his legal justification, it is significant that he used the term *kanun,* meaning codified laws, in this case those promulgated by the regime. He did not say that "our actions were lawful" in the sense of being legitimate. In fact, he said that, law or no law, "we were going to do what we did anyway." The charismatic leader is not concerned with law as such. He is more committed to the ultimate rightness of the regime's activities. In this respect, Kemal's second comment about the regime's relation to the Law on Tranquility is more significant than the first.

Kemal's ability to make "either-or/both" assertions—that is, "we were following the law" and "the law didn't matter"—was founded on his self-conscious

3. Rauf Bey (Rauf Orbay, 1881–1964), a member of the internal RPP opposition to existing leadership, was a former Ottoman officer and parliamentarian who resigned his position shortly after a conflict with Kemal over the Lausanne negotiations. He founded the PRP in 1924. After its closure, he was accused of participating in the Izmir assassination attempt and fled the country until 1936. He returned to public service as the ambassador to London in the early 1940s.

charismatic leadership style. His statements were more than simple words; they were actions consciously undertaken to establish a specific ideological point. He alerted his audience that he was lawful *and* that he would have acted without the law, conveying his extraordinariness vis-à-vis common standards. Following the law alone was not, for Kemal, "extraordinary." What was extraordinary was his plan for the nation, a plan that was simple, but one that easily seduced minds did not understand. The standards that one must follow are thus not the laws of the state. They are the suprahistorical truths of civilization. Actions under the Law for the Establishment of Tranquility were undertaken to "assure the life and independence of the state . . . for the civil and social development of the nation." That is, repressive activities by the state were designed to create the stable and tranquil conditions for the implementation of Kemalism's corporatist agenda, the truth of which superstitious or traitorous minds were unable to grasp.

Note the integration of the corporatist scientistic ideals with the idea of political tranquility in Kemal's speech to an audience in Istanbul in 1927: "The development of the homeland and the prosperity of the nation require greater effort and work. It is a sublime point of view to work for the true tranquility and happiness of our social body by cultivating and educating emotions and beliefs of consciences by science and technology" (*SD* 2: 1927, 247). Kemal thus defined the contours of political tranquility according to the corporatist-laicist ideological agenda. Indeed, he made laicism the criterion for opening the system to the second legal opposition party, the FRP, in 1930. "We agree on principles of 'laic republic,' Kemal told the founder of the FRP and his old friend Fethi Bey "of whose human and political morality I am sure." "As long as I remain the president, I shall justly and neutrally perform the high and legal duties that the presidency entrusts in me concerning the parties, be they in government or not. You can be assured, sir, that within the principles of a laicist Republic no political activity or your party will encounter any obstacle" (*SD* 4: 1930, 598). The FRP was disbanded shortly after it was created, however. "Political activity" thus had a very brief existence under Kemal's rule. Kemal once again erected "obstacles" (his term) to politics.

It is significant, though, that some of those dominated by Kemal—people such as Rauf Bey and Fethi Bey—had once believed that they could, in fact, be active and participate in a competitive party system. Their view that there existed some space for the exercise of their independent political will in the Assembly raises the possibility that our interpretation of the power dynamics of Kemal's rule overreaches itself. We see, however, no grounds for weakening our critique. Empirical evidence of restrictions on expression abounds. Nevertheless, we must address this issue. Our interpretation requires making a distinction within the arena of "those dominated" in order to explain why some believed that there may have existed some "free" spaces from which a challenge to Kemal and the RPP could be mounted.

LOYAL SUBCHIEFS

Kemal's distrust and domination of others must be qualified to some extent. He was distrustful of everyone except those most obedient to his will and closely associated with him. This distinction effectively exists in the documents we have analyzed thus far. It may be espied as well in a set of concepts he employed to distinguish those whom he would allow to hold major positions of power in the state from those he would not: there are the "first rate," "the significant," and the rest. In *Nutuk*, he declared that "It is of course incorrect to form a weak government from among those members of the group who are significant but not first rate" (Text 18). Thus, Kemal packed the councils with "the first rate," meaning those most trustworthy and loyal to his truths. The texts given at the opening of this chapter suggest that both his closest associates and his opponents were aware of this distinction in their ranks.

Mustafa Kemal's representation in *Nutuk* of İsmet İnönü's view of him is a prime example of the "first-rate" characteristic defined within the charismatic relationship of authority. It shows both İsmet Pasha's loyalist disposition and Kemal's proud acknowledgment of it. The political dynamics that set the context for this particularly illuminating depiction were exchanges that took place between İsmet Pasha and the Ankara regime during negotiations over the Treaty of Lausanne. For several days after the signing, İsmet Pasha had received no correspondence from anyone in Ankara. In *Nutuk*, Kemal explained that this oversight was owing to the negligence of the Council of Ministers and the political opposition of its head, Rauf Bey (later, the founder of the PRP—needless to say, Rauf Bey was not "first rate" in Kemal's eyes). Kemal sought to reduce İsmet Pasha's anxiety by acknowledging his "purity, sincerity, and humbleness":

TEXT 23

İsmet Pasha answered my telegraph. I'm presenting this reply in full because it is a valuable document that shows the degree of İsmet Pasha's agony, which, at the same time, is evidence of his purity, and sincerity, and his humbleness.

Gazi,

You come to my aid like Hızır in all my difficult times. Imagine the agony I underwent for the past four or five days. You are a man who has done great deeds and has had great deeds done. My devotion to you has been doubled. I kiss your eyes my beloved brother, my dearest Chief [*aziz Şefim*].

The idiomatic term *hızır* carries religiopolitical prophetic connotations, meaning a "godsend," but in human form. A *hızır* is a human agent of great fortune, promise, and deed. İsmet Pasha tells Kemal that he is a man, but nearly a divinely ordained man. And so İsmet Pasha speaks as Kemal hoped the entire nation would: he elevates Kemal to the rank of the extraordinary (he "come[s] to my aid like Hızır in all my difficult times").

Kemal quoted these words in *Nutuk* in order to send several strong signals. First, he signals to the nation as a whole that he wants the people to believe that he is a great man who has done great deeds, who gets great deeds done, who saves them from agony, and to whom they must now devote themselves. Second, he signals to all aspiring Kemalist elites exactly what he wants them to believe of him. He wants those who seek to rise in power to acknowledge his power. The "subchiefs," as they have come to be called, ought humbly to recognize his greatness. They must know that even though they have power *by being* close to him, they are nonetheless subordinate to him as well. Kemal is proud of İsmet Pasha for displaying the correct posture of the Kemalist subchief—proximate but still subordinate to the leader.

This relation is expressed in the idiom "I kiss your eyes," which indicates a very intense relation of intimacy, but also de facto subordination. Kissing the eyes of another is possible only with the other's permission. In one very brief moment, the kiss, there appears to be a temporary footing of equality, but a subordinate may gain that moment only on the condition that the superior grants it. Once granted, the subordinate has no other choice because the subordinate is in no position to reject what has been granted (or to give permission in the first place). The subordinate must acquiesce. Thus, in accepting the permission, the subordinate accepts the leader's superiority. The kiss thus exalts the leader and temporarily raises the subordinate's status. It is simultaneously an expression (1) of the power of the leader to grant others access to him, (2) of a subordinate's proximity, and (3) of the subordinate's unequal status. The kiss thus does not make the two politically equal; it reinforces the superiority of the kissed.

This relation enables the superior to claim all the achievements of the subordinate as partly his own. Such was Kemal's claim when he interpreted İsmet Pasha's performance as a military commander as proof that his own decision was sound: "Because the soundness of my decision of assigning these duties to him was proven by the competence and zealous effort İsmet Pasha had demonstrated as Chief of General Staff and then again as the actual Commander of the Front, I am fully at ease before the nation, the army, and history" (Atatürk 1960, 44). The "soundness of my decision" to elevate the status of some commanders must be known by all. Such statements are complexly constituted by both political and psychological authority dynamics. They illustrate Kemal's narcissism, which had him interpreting every success as his own.

Whether in the Assembly or in the world at large, Mustafa Kemal, Turkey's charismatic leader, makes little room for the role of others. He is always the hero whose subchiefs' accomplishments are not independent of his own. It is not İsmet Pasha who has been successful; it is Kemal because it is Kemal's will that has been implemented. Just as there will be no clash of opinions in politics, there is no clash of wills among the leadership either because the achievements of his subchiefs are an extension of his will; they are proof of his achievements. It must be remembered that İsmet İnönü, Kemal's successor as head of the RPP, was one of the main members of the elite who approved Kemal's enormous authority. Kemal saw no reason to grant even him equality, however. Indeed, Kemal expressed his appreciation for him, in part, to keep him down. To act otherwise might have been irrational, for it would have subjected Kemal to challenges to his entire discourse as a willing (absolute) charismatic leader, challenges that the charismatic-leader dynamic is meant to prevent. Those like İnönü who accepted Kemal's will embedded themselves in the paternalism of the charismatic-authority relation. This dynamic represents another severely entrenched pattern among political elites that has existed since the early days of the republic.

To this day, politicians all across the political spectrum scurry to represent themselves as Atatürk's preferred descendant, especially during political campaigns. Atatürk's image and pithy maxims are everywhere at these times, as the politicians try to exploit the internalized hegemonic cult of the hero for their electoral purposes. They do this precisely to capitalize on the charismatic-authority relationship. In their pursuit of such power, however, they simultaneously perpetuate, often unwittingly, the embedded infantilism of the ideal charismatic relation, subordinating their wills to his. Exalting Atatürk's ego is a way of exalting oneself subjectively, but it is effectively a self-abnegation because Atatürk, as all know, has no equal. In this persisting power relation, no independent roles emerge, no autonomous personality development occurs, and, hence, no political exchange between equal citizens takes place. Under Kemalism, Turkish political life seems permanently committed to apolitical, infantilist relations of hierarchical subordination.

Certainly, given the risks of challenging Kemal's authority, this disposition within İnönü's context is quite understandable. Were one to disturb the desired charismatic relation, one would certainly have been retired from public service very quickly. The case of Rauf Bey stands as a well-known example. Indeed, immediately after discussing his lengthy exchanges with Rauf Bey, Kemal related in *Nutuk* another quick vignette relevant to his view of the mounting opposition. This vignette—an exchange with Ali Fuat Pasha (Ali Fuat Cebesoy, 1876–1924)—illustrates the second aspect of the understandings between Kemal and those most closely associated with him. Subordinates knew full well that Kemal demanded their wills in exchange for his love.

> With Ali Fuat Pasha, too, there took place a short exchange of opinions. Fuat Pasha directed such a question to me: "Who are your present apostles; could you inform us?"
>
> I said I could not answer anything from this question.
>
> Pasha explained his meaning. And then I, in turn, made the following statement:
>
> I have no apostles. Whoever serves the country and the nation and demonstrates competence and capacity to serve, they are the apostles. (Atatürk 1962, 794)

Kemal does not reject the category of the apostle. He retains it against the implicit charge that he has elevated some over others. Exactly why he retains it is not entirely clear from the text. In one reading, Kemal may be the astute revolutionary deploying traditional terms like an apostle in a new and innovative way, hoping to undercut their traditionalist connotations and use them for his progressive goals. In another, he may be assenting indirectly to the idea that there are some who are more favored than others. The review of his discourse to this point, especially his view of his relation to the nation as the charismatic loving leader, suggests the latter interpretation. Kemal seems to enjoy the authority relations implied by traditional terms of discourse.

One should take careful note as well that Kemal implicitly agrees that he is the best judge of those who served the nation best. He does not say, "there are no apostles," or "those who seek to serve the nation must be judged by the Assembly." Rather, he says, "these are the apostles." The charismatic leader is always the judge, even in this case, where his Hızır role has been unmasked by others. His readiness to judge others is evident as well in his direct reply to an opponent of İsmet Pasha, Refet Pasha, when the latter criticized İsmet Pasha's assuming the role of chief of general staff or commander in chief. Kemal says, essentially, that he alone can be trusted to make all the right decisions: "[Refet Pasha] objected. He said that he could not consent to İsmet Pasha's position that implied his being commander in chief. I said that the duty was very important and delicate, and that it would be proper to have trust in my knowledge [*vukuf*] and impartiality about all associates. I also added that it was not appropriate for him to put forth such a claim himself" (Atatürk 1962, 440). Kemal thus responds to Refet as he did to Ali Fuat, by trying to undercut Refet's confidence in opposing his (Kemal's) decisions. Again, the subtext is clear: Kemal knows who is competent and who is not, so others should "trust" him and his "knowledge." The term *vukuf* connotes knowledge that commands respect, which, being the kind of wisdom or knowing one has on one's own, does not require others' input. Kemal thus indirectly conveys to them that it is not appropriate for them to question him.

This leads to the third dimension of the relationship between Kemal and those closely associated with him. This dimension highlights the category of "question" explicitly, though it is not about the ability or liberty of others to question Kemal. Rather, it is about his liberty to question them. In his 1930 discussion about the founding of the PRP, Kemal had the following exchange with Talat Bey over the election procedure:

Talat Bey:
    Sir, wouldn't it have been better if you had conducted the forthcoming elections all by yourself; and then we were to make a division of parties within the Assembly.

Gazi:

No this is not an honest thing; it is necessary that the people should first express their political color, vote and resolve cleanly and in a manner understandable by the nation. The manly, the honest way to act is this. Fethi Beyefendi [his excellency], is one of those friends who can act only in this way, and he did act in this way.

Talat Bey, the way you have just commanded has been experimented with in old organizations. The results it produced have subjected the nation to griefs and agonies. From now on we, as experienced people who have seen these events and results, cannot implement such things that have been tantamount to sophistry. The Turkish society of today, today's children of the Turkish race (*kavim*) who have a claim on having been the founders of the most profound civilizations of the past, have found the clearest and the soundest [*salim*] path.

Fethi Bey:

Our opposition shall take place within the limits of politeness, dignity, purity, and it will never lose its seriousness.

Gazi replies:

I foresee that he [Fethi Bey] will struggle a lot with the chiefs [*reisler*] of the RPP. But I shall observe with pleasure these struggles that will serve to strengthen the Republican principles, and I can already say that, even at nights when we have the strongest quarrels, I shall unite you at my table, and thence I will again ask you each separately: What did you say? Why did you say it? What was your answer? What was it based on?

I confess at this moment that that shall be a high pleasure for me. (*SD* 2: 1930a, 255)

Always the supreme judge, Kemal here sets himself up to be the grand inquisitor. On the one hand, his disposition appears noble: he is going to ensure that the struggles between the RPP and the FRP are consistent with solidaristic corporatist republican principles. On the other, he shows himself to lack respect for the capacities of others to fulfill their duties without his intervention. He will put the people to the test: "What did you say? Why did you say it? What was your answer? What was it based on?" They will be forced by him to defend themselves to him. Even after Fethi Bey assures Kemal that the new opposition will be "serious," Kemal says, "yes, but I will interrogate you nonetheless." Everything must pass his test. As such, he once again makes it known to his closest associates that they are not his equals. Because he has established the course of the republic, they must answer to him. Hence, they must know his will and be sure that they implement it. Even members of the opposition must assure the charismatic leader of their faithfulness to the goals of the ruling party! Obviously there is little ground for real opposition here. (In the background, of course, he is also playing İsmet Pasha and the other RPP chiefs off their rival elites, represented here by Fethi Bey. This is a way to keep his own subchiefs in line as well.)

Kemal's stated role throughout the single-party era is made extremely clear in a statement on the program of the new government in 1937. Kemal addressed his remarks to the new prime minister, Celal Bayar, who had served many nationalist causes in the prestate and single-party period and was among the future leaders of the Democrat Party, a trusted opposition party founded in 1946. Kemal's statement back in 1937 illustrates the continuity of his narcissistic attitude regarding the politics of the period of his rule:

> You announce a brand-new program to the nation. This program is nothing but the points I have promised the nation. Celal Bayar and his associates promised me and the nation that they shall implement what I have promised the nation. I shall, together with the nation, see to it that Celal Bayar's and his associate's program is implemented point by point. Let me explain better: I, Atatürk, the President of Turkey, and the Turkish nation are overseeing Prime Minister Celal Bayar's and his government's program. And we want to see its actual results. (*SD* 3: 1937, 101–2)

The language is fully self-serving. The government program is "nothing but" the fulfillment of Kemal's promises. The RPP elite has "promised" to implement Kemal's will, and Kemal will "oversee" them to make sure of it. Kemal's tendency to elevate himself above all others and the corresponding tendency of others to elevate him reflect the absolute hold over power and destiny that he claims and that others, to differing degrees and with different interests, grant. Put in more formal terms: the power dynamics reflect Kemal's charismatic absolutism. He will question, and others will defend themselves. He will speak, and others will listen. Those whom he swayed saw him as the incarnate representation of their goals.

Conversely, those whom he did not sway with his charisma were cowed with threat and innuendo. A discourse of fear resided on the other side of his discourse of love. While he was creating a relationship of love with those who obeyed him, he was also securing that relationship by threatening to pounce upon those who withdrew their love. Kemal made sure that those who did not support him knew that they would be considered traitors and condemned to an uncomfortable life of lonely detachment from the nation. Subject to innumerable declarations of love and hateful accusations against those who did not love, Kemal's audience internalized an awareness of the fate of those who opposed him.

It is in this awareness that one element of domination between the charismatic leader and his followers can be seen very clearly. Not only will a follower lose the love of the leader were she or he to be disloyal (or said to be so), she or he will lose the love of the others who love the leader. Love as a pillar of obligation to the leader (and, consequently, to the nation, society, people, and the republic) develops an atmosphere of emotional conformity, one in which the "high" public interest is equated with feeling a deep emotional bond with the goals of the leader, the nation, and so on. This conformity in turn shapes the expectation that all will continue to conform (by marching, cheering, waving, kissing, smiling, bowing, etc.), and thus plays a coercive role in shaping both political attitudes and values over the long run. That is to say, the charismatic leader is not satisfied simply by securing obedience based on the recognition that she or he is extraordinary (and that all others are not). She or he must also create an awareness of the rewards and punishments for withdrawing that recognition. "The fate of those who do not conform to the nation's will and purpose is disappointment and extinction. Gentlemen, let us bow with all due respect and submission before this enormous will" (*SD* 1: 1923a, 307—9). Were followers to ask themselves (consciously or not), "What if we were not to love the leader?" the answer would be, "We will suffer." Even to this day, to question the relation is not only to face political costs and legal action, but to place social ties, personal comfort, and one's status within the nation at risk. To withdraw one's love is thus to enter into a more ambiguous relationship with others.

Kemal produced this sensibility about himself and about the stakes of avowing or disavowing one's relationship to him. He made sure that those who loved him understood the fear of not doing so. Were they to withdraw their love, Kemalists would punish them by withdrawing the nation's love. The consequent atomization testifies to the authoritarian and partly totalitarian character of any discourse of charismatic authority, and it illuminates the political power embedded in Kemalism's doctrine of leadership. By "authoritarian" here, we mean the form of rule based on cultivating fear between the rulers and the ruled, such that the ruled do not challenge the rulers' authority. Under authoritarian rule, association for the purposes of politics is allowed as long as it does not challenge the authorities. By "totalitarian" here, we mean the use of various coercive tactics to penetrate much further into the psyches of a population in order to discourage all forms of political activity. In highly violent totalitarian contexts, this penetration occurs through terror and threat. In nonviolent totalitarian contexts, it may occur through ideological indoctrination and socialization of various forms. The point is that in totalitarianism a population is atomized in political terms. Politics itself is given up willingly or coercively, for it becomes either habitually discouraged or too risky.[4]

Kemal's doctrine of leadership exhibits authoritarian characteristics, for it was partly based on fear cultivated by the charismatic chief himself and was partly totalitarian insofar as, in some senses and to some degrees—because this is a very delicate matter—it demanded that followers of the new regime give up political activity of certain kinds or else suffer serious personal and social consequences. Where lack of love for the leader is interpreted as lack of national resolve, *questioning* Kemal—and, hence, questioning the nation's guiding truths—becomes very difficult. (Believing, of course, is the most secure option, at least in the short run.) Charismatic relations of power inherently cannot tolerate serious questioning of the leader on the part of the followers. All questioning is interpreted suspiciously. The immediate response to those who do not love the leader is vilification for having potentially contravened the laws of history.

Kemal and the Kemalist discourse that has perpetuated his charismatic stature have been immensely successful in Turkey. Kemal himself relished the early signs of this stature. We draw an example of his joy from 1923 to show that he was engaged this early in perpetuating the impression of his own extraordinariness. The example involves an exchange with the youth in Afyonkarahisar:

TEXT 37

Youth speaking: "Our great Gazi, you are history itself, and we too in having been before such a living history have become historical persons. In the future, our progeny thinking of this fortunate lot of ours and of your greatness shall

---

4. These understandings are adopted in part from Hannah Arendt's work on the concepts (Arendt 1958).

say about you: Was he a human being like us, did he walk and talk like us, did his eyes see like ours, did his ears hear like ours?"

Atatürk speaking: "I think that I possess no superiority over any individual of the nation. If more initiative has been seen in me, this is an enterprise that has emanated less from me than [from] the sum of the nation. Were it not for you, had the inclinations of your conscience not constituted a point of support for me, none of my initiatives could come about."

"You are history," say the youth at Afyonkarahisar, expressing beautifully the subordinate end of the charismatic power relation. Kemal's response suggests that he knows he has succeeded. He does not reject the category of being "history itself" or of having superhuman qualities. Although he tries to affirm a footing of equality with the youth, in the end, he still claims the "initiatives" to be "my initiatives." Their position is reduced to the now familiar position of a "support," as the collective conscience of the nation that he has constructed to represent. His quasi-deification is complete. He feels it and his audience now knows it. "Were it not for [us] . . . none of [his] initiatives could have come about." He needed "us" for his success, and "we" gave ourselves to him. He exhibits no regrets, no sense of reluctance for having been raised to the level of superior greatness, for *our* perception of him as extraordinary. He says, "You are truthful: I am moved by your sincerity."

RECONSIDERING THE LESSONS IN *NUTUK*:
THE "NATIONAL SECRET" AND THE DECLARATION
OF THE REPUBLIC

Kemal's style of charismatic domination forces, we think, a reinterpretation of the very character of the national movement and the foundation of republic as he described it in *Nutuk*. His narrative therein is most often interpreted to support the nonideological, pragmatic understanding of Kemalism's alleged tutelary democratic model. A reexamination of *Nutuk* at this point shows that his characterizations of his actions were themselves constituted by self-conscious charismatic intentions, specifically by his sense of his own extraordinariness and his claim that he alone possessed the nation's truths. In several places in the speech, he "confessed" and "admitted" his need to aggrandize powers for himself because he lacked full confidence in shared decision-making arenas. He also expressed the belief that others would either be in agreement with him or that history would prove him right. Either way, he described how he lacked any confidence in consultative decision-making practices. Moreover, he explained that although he could not trust others to participate in making decisions, he was sure that they would trust him. In other words, charismatic assumptions were evident in Kemal's self-conception as the sole person capable of leading Turkey out of "darkness," along the "logical" "stages" of development en route to the "original target" that only he knew. *Nutuk,* in this light, turns out to be more than Kemal's own account of the struggle. It turns out to be precisely what he had tagged it: a lesson in "social and political morality" (Text 16); a lesson about who was right and who was wrong at Turkey's founding; a lesson about whose path should be emulated and whose path avoided; a lesson, in short, of Kemal's infallibility as the unparalleled father of the Turks.

According to Kemal's account of the events of the war for independence, he made a crucial decision not to explain his actions to others before those actions were concluded, but rather to conceal his plans by "carrying" the "nation's future" in his "conscience" like a "national secret." Note the equation between his conscience and the nation's. "I was bound to put into force step by step this great capacity for progress that I sensed in the nation's conscience and future, all the while carrying it in my conscience like a national secret" (Text 11). His preference for deeds over words (Text 24) and his view that one should "give consideration to only those matters that can be put into practice" (Text 28) may have earned him a reputation for pragmatism in the eyes of most of his interpreters, but it is now possible to see that the reason for acting without explanation derives significantly from his charismatic intentions, informed by the corporatist and transformationist goals of the six arrows.

Kemal suggested in *Nutuk* that he could not explain his policies in advance in part because the "ignorant reactionaries" who could not comprehend their status as "undeniable truths" (Text 16) would oppose them; also, he had no desire to create a "chaotic" situation in which "a thousand and one" different persons— both those resistant to his path and those closely associated with it—expressed "a thousand and one" opinions. Either consequence would have destabilized the "logical chain" (Atatürk 1960, 14) of events by stirring and creating doubt where there should be none. The ignorant reactionaries would not have seen the reality of the struggle for what it was, and others would force a reappraisal of Kemal's actions that would be ridiculous. The "whole nation" was "without a head[,] engulfed in darkness," and what was needed, Kemal said, was quick and decisive action by a "mighty," "unshakable" leader:

TEXT 10

But we did not at first totally display and express these sentiments and thoughts of ours that directed our course of action to the very end. Elaborating on future prospects would have given the perceived nature of an illusion to the real and material struggle that we had undertaken; also, in the face of the immediate impact of the external danger, it would have suddenly instigated the resistance of those affected thereby, who would have become apprehensive of the probable changes adverse to their traditions, intellectual capacities, and psychological states.

TEXT 24

I did not consider it proper to give an opportunity to the ignorant and the reactionaries to poison the whole nation by including these matters in the program before their time had come. Because I was definitely certain that these matters will become resolvable at the opportune time and that the nation will eventually be pleased with it.

TEXT 17

Gentlemen, had I given in to the opinions and apprehensions expressed by some of the associates, great liabilities would have resulted in two respects. First, it would have meant admitting error and weakness in my opinions, my decisions, and in all my identity, which would be an irreparable mistake from the viewpoint of the duty I had in my conscience undertaken. Gentlemen, history has incontestably proved that for success in great matters, the presence of a chief [reis] whose ability and might are unshakable is indispensable. In a time when all the high functionaries of the state are desperate and inept, when the whole nation, without a head, is engulfed in darkness, is it possible to proceed in a sound, thorough, and especially violent way, and eventually to arrive at the very difficult target, by consultations in a chaotic situation in which a thousand and one persons who call themselves patriots behave and opine in a thousand and one ways?

Kemal is the infallible guardian who alone understands how "to proceed in a sound, thorough, and especially violent way, and eventually to arrive at the very difficult target." He appropriates the concepts *sound, safe, practical,* and similar positive terms to describe his capabilities, whereas chaos, harm, danger, and doom lie with "a thousand and one persons." This construction is self-serving: it is intended to underscore his possession of extraordinary insight into what is right and good, both ideologically and practically.

His highly revered "pragmatism" cannot be understood outside this conceptual frame, the essential purpose of which is to show the truth of the political ideological aims of Kemalist corporatism: that he alone knows what is good, safe, practical, and so on for the headless nation. He is not trying simply to demonstrate his ability to shift plans according to shifting circumstances. His use of various terms of "practicality" is intended to establish his path's truth-bearing status. Thus, when he asserts that "the practical and secure path for success was to implement each phase at the most opportune moment," "secure" connotes those means that he alone knows to be without "danger" or "chaos." "Practical" means that deeds will speak as evidence of the rightness of his ideas. The use of "phase" signals the existence of a larger plan, not simply a pragmatic accommodation of adjustable plans to changing circumstances. He does not simply want to be followed: he wants to be recognized as the one person with access to the truths of history. This was central to his conception of what it meant "to lead" and to be "a leader," and this view, as we have argued, is hardly nonideologically pragmatic or absent ideological motivation.

Of course, his logic in the third quote (Text 17) is somewhat circular. He states that had he listened to others, he would have admitted error or weakness. This would be a mistake from the perspective of his duty, which was to be always right. The Turkish word for "unshakeable" is *lâyetezelzel,* the inner connotation of which is "infallible." Kemal interprets the national struggle and transformation as his mission and his duty from the start, a duty that he defined for himself and by himself—and kept to himself. The more fundamental dynamic indicated by "secret," then, is Kemal's personalistic style of drawing power from himself and keeping it for himself. He perceives Turkey's transformation to be his historical mission, the dynamics of which only he understands and can guarantee, and the responsibility for which he alone has to assume. He holds the national secret in his heart, protected from others because "to pronounce the situation as it was would have resulted in losing the objective totally" (Atatürk 1962, 437–38). With the aim fixed and held by him, the struggle will be his personal—and thus his nation's—achievement.

It is true that at times in *Nutuk* he was self-deprecating: "No claim is made here," he stated, "that the man demanded by the situation we described should definitely be my own person" (Text 14). It was "even possible to think" that "another associate besides myself" could be "the man demanded by the situation," an "indispensable son of this country." He is humble in these statements, but the question of sincerity arises once again. In *Nutuk*, there is no second colleague, no decision-making partner whose autonomy, "ability, and might" he respects. In fact, Kemal implies that it is highly unlikely that there exists such a person, and he reiterates the idea that whoever occupies the leadership role must act according to the higher truths of history, which only he understands. This imaginary alternative leader, he said, must "accept and act in a manner that is required of him by the present situation" (Text 14). This person can lead only by knowing what is required of him, and the only way to know that is by having the access to truths that Kemal believed only he possessed.

His humble statements are part of his falsely humble posture and are intended rhetorically to reinforce both his own standing and his own truth that charismatic leadership by a select one is indispensable for the nation's success. No one can meet the conditions of the situation that Kemal has stipulated without actually being Kemal himself:

TEXT 15

I was convinced of the necessity of activating the national will without delay and [of] making sure that the nation starts to take measures in the form of real and armed action by itself. In order to make the Congress appreciate and confirm these fundamental points, I deemed it very necessary that I should work by illuminating, guiding [*irşat*, with connotations of "showing the right way"] and personally directing it. In fact, this is what happened. I confess that I had no confidence in the ability of any representative council to have the principles and decisions of the Erzurum Congress that I have previously explained implemented. As a matter of fact, time and events have confirmed me. Furthermore, I must express openly that I was not convinced that any collective body was able to realize/deliver the [goals of the national movement].

Well after the events in question, he "confesses" that he had "no confidence" in others to "decide" on "principled" grounds. He is not simply pointing out others' limitations here; he is saying that he viewed others as inept in relation to "principles" of the national struggle. Whether or not he would have stood aside had there been other extraordinary persons is very difficult to say. The historical record suggests that he eliminated potential rivals rather than share power with them. He believed he alone had to lead the nation.

The concept he used to define his role is *chief,* our translation of the Turkish word *reis,* which may also be translated as "head" or "president." We choose *chief* because this term more accurately captures Kemal's meaning and self-understanding as unshakeable "leader" or "head" of the collectivity. "[H]istory has incontestably proved that for success in great matters, the presence of a chief [*reis*] whose ability and might are unshakable is indispensable," whose historic role is to "guide" the masses and to "oversee" the institutional processes so that the historical target may be achieved. The Kemalists themselves dubbed this a "chief system," patterned along the lines of the French idea of chefs and sous chefs (in Turkish, *şefler* and *alt şefler*). This was their parlance (see, for example, İsmet Pasha's note to Kemal, Text 23).

We choose to use the Kemalist term for "chief" also because we are reluctant to describe the charismatic-authority leader in terms more appropriate to constitutional forms of authority—that is, those forms of authority that seek to describe and delimit the powers of office holders according to popularly mandated law. To translate *reis* as "president" would imply that Kemal either was or understood himself as a constitutionally supported holder of an office capable of acting owing to a collective mandate conferred upon him. In fact, however, Kemal understood his power as unlimited and himself as the sole judge of national politics. Indeed, "superior leader" and "final judge" might better capture Kemal's meaning of the powers he held as *reis.* He did not see himself as a constitutional president. He saw himself as a charismatic president.

Kemal's use of *reis* is very consistent with its use in aspects of popular discourse of the time. *Reis* means "head" or "chief" in the Ottoman-Islamic idiom, and it was a very congenial term for Kemal, who wanted to be viewed as more than a president, but without the overtones of being an arbitrary autocrat. *Reis* connotes a person who is respected and honored for his wisdom and judgment, a person who represents what is right and true. "I completely comprehend and realize in my heart and my conscience what weighty and serious duties are demanded of me by the presidency of the republic that personifies the properties of *virtue, integrity, and rightness* of a great nation" (*SD* 1: 1927b, 353, emphasis added). Kemal's task, as he saw it, was to represent the new ideals of Kemalist corporatism as "right and true" and to have the people agree to them. That is the role of the chief, one who, when "asked if he would give up the presidency of the party," would reply: "No . . . I would never, because in my opinion this party is representing the true political ideas of the country" (Text 28). The Kemalist president must represent the nation's truth.

To be sure, Kemal claimed that the nation's path was what "science, reason, and logic" demanded, but, importantly, he never claimed that this is what popular mandate required. His justification was charismatic-national positivism, not legal-constitutional populism. The language of rationality and truth was intended to buttress his charismatic grasp of the truths of contemporary civilization, not his constitutionalism or respect for the rational faculties of others in the decision-making process. Hence, "He who is chief [*reis*] should first act according to the ideal of the nation and, after grasping the psychology of the nation, be subject to the nation's inclination." This statement, made in an interview in 1930 (Text 28), was not entirely sincere either because in his mind he was the sole fitting "agent" of the nation's "general feeling" and will, not merely its interpreter. "The results that have been achieved by the Republic in a short time in realizing the ways of prosperity and development of the nation [have been achieved] by finding and learning the nation's needs" (*SD* 4: 1927b, 584). The learning here was not from the nation in its history, as it were, but for the nation from the truths of history. In this sense, he was the minder as well as finder of the national will.

Interestingly, he distinguished himself in this regard from Napoleon, who, in his mind, represented military prowess, but not national virtue:

TEXT 31

Too many persons who have acquired glory and reputation in history do not possess virtue from the national point of view. Think of Napoleon, who indeed possessed military prowess, but went all the way to Moscow and wore out the French army dragging it over fires and ruins. His actions were satisfying less the real and national interest of the French nation than his personal aims of world conquest.

Beyond the critique of deviating from the national interest in favor of personal aims, there is a more important, more subtle point in this comment. Kemal suggests that for the great leaders of nations to be recognized as great leaders, they must gain from their nation the recognition that their deeds embody the nation's "virtue." The people will watch the leader's deeds and must see their truths embodied in those deeds. This observation expresses more than an ideologically nationalist outlook; it expresses attention to specific kinds of perceptions in the field of political power that are of importance to the charismatic leader.

Identifying charismatic manipulation in Kemal's discourse is thus not always very easy, for he was a gifted charismatic dominator. Take, for example, comments he made while visiting with the Romanian foreign minister in which he explicitly described the "duty of chiefs," using the literal Turkish equivalent term for "chief," *şef*. His first remarks in this context are effusively self-effacing. The duty of chiefs, he said, is "to show their nations the way of taking in life with joy and enthusiasm," by which he means life in this world, as opposed to life after death: "Let us be joyful and rejoicing at least while we live." A "reasonable man," he said, "works not for himself but for those who will come after him." This is "necessary" to be "content and happy." "Those who are the happiest are those who are of the character to prefer that their services will remain unknown by all the coming generations." Words of true humility.

TEXT 29

Those men who primarily value themselves and who identify the nation and the country to which they belong with their own person, cannot be considered to have served their nation's happiness. It is only those who can think of the generations that come after them who can provide their nations with the possibilities of living and progressing.

But Kemal cannot utter these words without drawing attention to himself. He goes on to make it known that his ability to utter them comes from his being recognized, in his mind, by the nation as its agent, and, as such, he intimates himself as the great leader of his nation. "It is an illusion to think that progress and movement stop when their own selves [i.e., that of the chiefs] cease to exist. On this occasion I shall say this to our respected guest. I say exactly what I think to those whom I love." Selfless utterances come from his heart, he tells Mr. Antonescu. "At the same time I am not a man who is able to carry in his heart a secret that is unnecessary. Because I am a man of the people." And what does this mean? That he views himself equal with others? No. That he takes their views into account when he makes decisions for the nation? No. To Kemal it means: "I should always say what I think before the people. If I have an error, the people negate me. But, up to today, I have never seen in this open conversation the people to negate me."

We know that those who negated Kemal were not treated with the utmost respect; what is important here is that in his own mind he is the embodiment of the virtue of the people. His pseudohumility in statements in which he criticizes those who put their "own person into everything"[5] is intended to reinforce his own ability to do so without being seen as doing so. Kemal's humility in his discourse on the duty of chiefs is not humility for its own sake. It is humility for his sake, which on the surface is for the truths that reinforce his charismatic position. As "president," he was more than an executive empowered by ordinary legality. He was "Atatürk," the heroic savior of the Turks. In the party alone, he became the RPP's "eternal chief," the party's "unchangeable *genel başkanı.*" The titles and honors reinforce his infallibility, his indubitability, his unquestionability, his singularity, his unmatched patriotism and devotion. This is how Kemal wanted us to think of him, and it was this status that enabled him to assert so confidently in *Nutuk* his conception of his personal role in the national struggle.

This role is evident in his account of the decisive moment in the transition from Ottoman to republican rule—namely, the decision in 1923 to proclaim the republic. At a dinner with close associates, he announced that "we shall proclaim the Republic tomorrow" (Atatürk 1962, 803). This decision was considered an insult by some influential deputies who were not in Ankara, but in *Nutuk* Kemal explained that they were not consulted because he was certain that they would have agreed with him: "Gentleman, as you see, in taking the decision to proclaim the Republic, I never thought it requisite and necessary to invite all of my associates in Ankara and negotiate and debate with them. Because I had no doubt about their being basically and naturally in agreement with me" (Text 25).

5. Other words he had for Napoleon appear in a 1923 interview. A questioner stated to Kemal, "I didn't bring you anything but my congratulations for your brilliant historical victory. If only I had brought you a work on Napoleon." Kemal responded by asking, "Why should you have done so? Napoleon does not interest me more than any other military man." The questioner conveyed Atatürk's reported "affection for Napoleon." Atatürk then said, "Where did this strange rumor come from? I made studies on Napoleon and his strategy. But I conducted the same studies on all others too. To compare Sakarya War with Austerlich War cannot be considered a compliment. I do not love/admire Napoleon at all. Because Napoleon used to put his own person into everything. His struggle was not for a certain cause; it was for his own person. And because of this he met the disaster that is unavoidable for these kind of men" (*SD* 5: 1923, 97).

Kemal's basic view is not simply that he can make the decision without consultation because he is certain that the others are in agreement, but that he can do so because they will see that he is right—"in agreement with me."

Kemal's account of both the national secret and the declaration of the republic are then part of a broader dynamic at work in *Nutuk*. He is not simply "facilitat[ing] the study of our transformation" by "indicating and establishing the general direction of events." He is both building his legacy and indicating how the specifics that are "protected and recorded in the minutes of the Assembly in the files of the Ministry and the archives of the press" (Atatürk 1962, 483, 114–15) should be interpreted. He intends the speech to create the impression among future students of the struggle that all of the *national* institutional initiatives bear his personal mark. His aim is clearly to infuse the institutions with his own personal identity so as to be remembered as their true and sole founder. Both the personal and impersonal-institutional dynamics thus appear side by side in order to reinforce the charismatic leader's heroic deeds. It is this dynamic that informs Kemal's use of the term *reis:* it conveys an institutional position that he has fully infused with his personal identity.

Similarly, in *Nutuk*, when he described the need to "remove the personal quality" during the implementation of some policies—that they should be undertaken in a fashion that is "impersonal and in the name of the council" in order to "secure and represent national unity and solidarity" (Atatürk 1960, 30)—he made it clear that he was at the helm from the beginning. The organization of the movement would not have been possible without his indispensable, personal contributions. In his 1927 speech marking the opening of the Second Great RPP Congress, he similarly noted his role in presiding over the congresses of the national movement at Erzurum and Sivas, and, as he did, he effectively claimed sole responsibility for leading the movement itself (*SD* 1: 1927a, 352–53). His acknowledgment that the decisions of the council would, without the impersonal name of the council, be seen as "absolutely personal" is an effort to conceal what he did not want others to believe (the "absolutely" is important), even if it was accurate about his role. This is not to say that he wanted people to believe that he was an absolutist. To the contrary, he wanted them to believe that what he did for them was best for them, even if they could not know it themselves. He was concerned with the appearance of legitimate methods insofar as they buttress his role as the leader of the nation's general feeling and will.

In the final analysis, "the nation" and all its achievements, especially the new

Kemalist republic, are quintessential depersonalized expressions of his person. The discourse as a whole suggests that this understanding is intentional, in the sense that Kemal intends to be associated with the institutions as their unparalleled founder. Whether or not he always and explicitly claims institutional ownership, it is his aim to cultivate a conceptual relationship between the institutions and his own person based on the heroic acts he undertook to create them. The link is most clear in the "humble" statements he made following the 1926 assassination attempt. (See Texts 33 and 34; he uses the word *humble* to describe his "body" in the famous 1926 statement.) There, he suggests that by taking aim at him, the plotters had taken aim at "our sacred republic and [at] the high principles on which it is based" (*SD* 3: 1926, 80). Only to clarify the connection to his person, he depersonalizes what was clearly a partly personal attack. "It is obvious that the secret political maneuvering was directed against the being of the nation rather than my person" (Text 33).

The obviousness is "obvious" to Kemal because it is his intention to make the connection obvious. The mixture of the national and the personal is intentional, designed to underscore the affective politics of emotional attachment between the charismatic leader and his followers. He wants what he calls "my noble nation" that "loves me" to feel the pain and the threat of the assassin's attack, and he is pleased to utter, "This public ovation is another proof that confirms the high degree of love and affection for me, and especially of the loyalty to our shared ideal; I am thankful, I am happy" (Text 33). Crucially, he further anticipates political action by "his" citizens to take "revenge." "If they kill me, I am sure that my citizens will take my revenge." The state, in his mind, is his; hence, it cannot be the case that the attack was simply against the Turkish state. It was against his state, and his citizens—his noble nation—must take his revenge by crushing those not loyal to his principles or to him. He thus uses the assassination as an opportunity to reinforce his identification with all that has been done by the nationalist movement. Ultimately, for Kemal, all important decisions in the days of struggle and founding were his work, all powers accrued to him, rightly possessed by him. "I should have been able to give orders unconditionally; therefore, the powers of the Grand National Assembly should be relegated to my person. This was indispensable for success. That's why I insisted" (Text 19).

He declared his absolutist intentions forthrightly in *Nutuk* because, by 1927, he could express "openly" his real view of the relationship between the state and its leader:

TEXT 20

Gentlemen, if you will, I will express it openly; it is I who has worked to have each of you elected with extraordinary powers, and to form an Assembly that possesses extraordinary powers (*salahiyeti fevkalade malik bir Meclis*), and to have this Assembly acquire a nature that controls the destiny of the country. I engaged in debates with my closest friends in order to succeed in this. I placed my life, my being, all my honor and prestige on the brink of peril. Therefore this is my creation. I have the duty of not deprecating but exalting my creation.

This latter statement looks like a moment of openness, but he is forthright because he is confident. He can honestly tell them that the Assembly is his creation. The point here is all too clear: "You owe all that you undertake, even your existence, to me, and, I expect your undivided loyalty in return. I am the creator, your raison d'être; you are the created. Your institutions, your status, your power, your success, your position are my work."

Kemal's charismatic assumptions and antiparticipatory style, therefore, had the effect of creating a new kind of hierarchical and patriarchal absolutism in Turkish politics, even as the idea of the republic killed the idea of "Ottoman absolutism." Although Kemal's own discourse skillfully obfuscates his own charismatic interests as well as the difference between absolutism of the past and charismatic absolutism in the present, analysis suggests a closer relationship and continuities. "We take advantage of all kinds of means from one and only one point of view. And that is this: To promote the Turkish nation in the civilized world to the position to which it is entitled and to strengthen daily the Turkish Republic, ever strengthening it on its unshakable foundations . . . and for this purpose; to kill the idea of absolutism . . ." (Atatürk 1962, 897, ellipses in the original). This discourse promotes the idea that Kemalism ended absolutism in Turkish politics, but the rhetorical style and intent of Kemal's broader statements and reflections on the struggle suggest otherwise. They suggest that the Turks had a great leader, that no one else was qualified to undertake the salvation of the nation or the founding of the republic, and that the nation should be eternally

grateful. To see it in the former manner is to defy the national truth that itself was
first located in the inner thoughts of Mustafa Kemal.

MESSAGE TO THE YOUTH

Kemal closed *Nutuk* with a grand charismatic utterance: his "Message to the
Youth"—an explicit attempt to reach beyond the walls of the Assembly to future
generations. The message prominently adorns one wall in Kemal's mausoleum
and countless other public sites in Turkey. Turkish youth memorize it at an early
age. It is widely sold in book and gift stores and distributed and broadcast on national holidays in the media. It carries his "point of view" for "our children yet to
be born" and his clarion call that they remain totally loyal to him and to the Kemalist state. Kemal introduced the message by addressing the "esteemed gentlemen" in the Assembly:

> Muhterem Efendiler, my long and detailed statement that has occupied you for
> days is after all the story of a bygone period. I will consider myself fortunate if
> in telling it to you I have been able to show clearly certain points that may invite
> attention and vigilance for my nation and for our children yet to be born.
>
> Gentlemen, in my speech, I have tried to express how a great nation whose
> national life was assumed to have come to an end gained its independence and
> how it founded a national and modern [*asrî*] state based on the very recent prin-
> ciples of science and technology.
>
> *The point of view at which we have arrived today is the emergence from national disasters
> that have been experienced for centuries, and it is also the price of the blood that irrigated every
> corner of this cherished country.*
>
> *I'm entrusting this product to the Turkish youth.* (Atatürk 1962, 897–98, emphasis
> in original)

The story that he has told about the national struggle, its significant (or insignificant) moments and actors, is something that must be remembered with
vigilance exactly as it has been told. Kemal does not call for future generations to
study and understand more of the struggle than he could have covered. He says
that these days are past, and here is how they should be remembered. The story is
"after all, the story of a bygone period." It is less important to examine the past
than to look ahead. In effect, then, he asks his audiences to accept and maintain

his account—"the point of view"—as *the* account of the Turkish national struggle. It is the story of a "great nation" that has a state based on "science and technology"; it is the "point of view" born of "disaster" and "bloody" struggle. He is imparting the story of the nation's birth and its most prized achievements, and he is entrusting their protection to the youth. Anticipating future generations, he links their projects with his while providing them with a way of viewing their own existence:

> *Ey* [Hey! Attention! Look!] *Turkish youth! Your very first duty is to protect and defend eternally the Turkish independence and the Turkish Republic.*
>
> *The sole foundation of your being and future is this. This foundation is your most valuable treasure. Even in the future, you will have enemies, internal and external, who will want to deprive you of this treasure. If one day you find yourself forced into the position of defending the independence and the republic, in order to take up duty at once, you should not think about the contingencies and constraints of the situation in which you find yourself.*
>
> *These contingencies and constraints may manifest themselves in very inconvenient ways. The enemies who will have designs against your independence and republic, might be the representatives of a victory never seen before in the world. By force and intrigue, all the fortresses of the dear country may have been captured, all the shipyards penetrated, all the armies dispersed, and every corner of the country actually taken over.*
>
> *Even sadder and graver than all these conditions, within the country, those who are in power might be inept or astray or even traitorous. Furthermore those in power might unite their personal interests with the political aims of the invaders. The nation might be desolate and exhausted in destitution.*
>
> *Harken, children of the Turkish future. So, even under such conditions and situations your duty is: to rescue the Turkish independence and the republic. The power you need is present in the noble blood in your veins!* (1963, 897–98, emphasis in original)

Kemal asks the future generations to defend the republic against enemies and imparts to them these specific ways of understanding their political existence. That is, he provides not only a "story of a bygone period," but specific terms for understanding that history and for undertaking their defense of the state: they must be wary of "traitors" who will lead them "astray."

The message is an effort to maintain unity around the rightness of Kemalism. Outside of the charismatic relation, it is a relatively empty, almost paranoid, patriotic message. Inside it, however, it inspires a constant alertness on the part of Kemal's youth that they should always be prepared to face the dangers of ene-

206 THE LARGER VIEW OF POLITICS AND SOCIETY

mies of and traitors to the nation. With language such as "enemies" and "force" and "intrigue," Kemal seeks to inspire vigilant obedience both to his project and to the history of it that he has presented in *Nutuk*. He uses the omnipresent possibility of the traitorous enemy to motivate the youth to defend their "treasure"—that is, his creation. Some will try to lead the nation astray for "personal" or "political" gain. This is not only what *may* happen, but how they should understand those who question their/his path when challenges are raised. These "traitors" will have "personal" and "political" motivations. Their disloyalty will be evident from their refusal to respect the state as he, Kemal, has conceived it, the specifics of the Kemalist project as he has conceived them, and, no doubt, his status and stature as the great leader. "The enemies" will try to "seduce the nation" by interpreting the story and its goals differently. The youth must be prepared to defend the nation's work. If confronted with seducers, they must rise up to preserve all that the great Turkish nation has achieved. "Rescue the Turkish independence and the republic. The power you need is present in the noble blood in your veins!" This well-known message does not nuance the blood versus sociological bases of membership in the nation. You either have the blood and feel its nobility, or you don't. The Kemalist youth should know this message and teach it to their children so that they, too, may follow Kemal's example by being alert to enemies and rooting out any and all opposition in and to his republic. As proof of Kemal's success, the message remains a classic in Turkey's public psyche. Many see it as the most important speech in Turkish political culture. Most have not read *Nutuk* in full, but they know the leader's message to them by heart.

The final statement, that "the power you need is present in the noble blood in your veins," transcends the ideological framework of solidaristic corporatism and leans quite clearly in the direction of the other subspecies of corporatism—fascistic corporatism. We take up this issue in detail in chapter 8. Here, we must note that Kemal's organic reference to the blood of the collectivity as noble vis-à-vis enemies (whose blood, it seems, may be different) is classically fascistic. It constitutes an invitation to the youth to exercise their (his) will in violent ways against those perceived to threaten the realm of Kemalist political and moral concern. The value of independence and the republic exceeds the value of all else—"the sole foundation of your being and future is this"—and the youth must be prepared to battle those who act on the basis of views to the contrary.

In this sense, Kemal's message to the youth contains several disquieting implications. Among them is Kemal's insinuation that all of the important work of independence and statecraft has already been accomplished, and that all that remains to be done for the youth is dutifully to protect and defend what exists. His message is not a call to develop their own projects, to create their own messages, or to extend or revise the founding project in fruitful ways. The emphasis is not even incrementally progressive in political terms. His words, his truths, should be the last words and truths for the nation. His work should be the last historical project of the Turkish epoch. Kemal's message to the youth is a call for alertness against the ever-present enemy of the Kemalist republic, against "threats" to the "world" that Kemal has built. It instills constant paranoia against the possibility that the country will be "actually taken over." It is a warning placed before his audience to "remind" them of their highest obligations. The message thus parallels his fear-laced and suspicion-inspiring discursive practices in the Assembly. Each speech was intended to secure and ensure absolute loyalty to his truths, his will, his nation, his state, and the Kemalist project that bore his name. The implied cognitive orientation of the message to the youth is thus extremely conservative despite its insistence on national progress. The strong implication is that there is no need to go any further in public-political terms. Kemal does not even gesture in the direction of politically encouraging advice for future generations in Turkey. The key words in the political vocabulary of the youth should be *protect, defend, rescue,* and *duty.*

This emphasis is indeed quite consistent with Kemal's understanding of the integrity of other human beings' wishes. Just as he expects his contemporaries' wills to submit to his, he makes it known that he expects future Turks also to carry out his will. Their energies should be devoted to preserving the result of his energies. The youth, then, will be his youth; indeed, *their* youth, their upbringing in their formative years, will be shaped and constituted to follow his lead. They shall forever be his offspring—"the *children,*" not the adults, "of the Turkish future" (emphasis added). Beyond demanding vigilance in protecting the state, the message to the youth thus erects barriers to the historical development of the youth. The actual history of the future must comply with the leader's historical design. The youth must not betray the leader by deviating from his path, neither in terms of thought—how they understand their historical identity and obligations—nor in terms of practice—how and for what purposes they live.

Kemal thus puts a mortgage on the development of the youth as he freezes and stifles the so-called project of modernity. The corporatist vision shall have confident guardians who will see their understandings and modes of correct social, political, and cultural practice as unquestionably right and true for the nation. They shall unhesitatingly use all means to implement, preserve, and promote these ways of thinking and feeling about the nation and its course as the fulfillment of their charge set down for them by Atatürk. As they think and walk in his path, their certainty—his certainty, inherited by them—shall fortify them. It shall also protect them from considerable engagement either with alternatives or with the limits and constraints placed on their political existence by the Kemalist outlook.

7

THE KEMALIST MODEL
OF POLITICS

Institutions

As part of the republican discourse of the earliest period, Kemal once stated that the "sublime National Assembly concentrated the high national will" (*SD* 1: 1920, 60–61), which emphasized that "the Turkish state is governed not by a constitutional monarchy, but directly by" an assembly and "shall be to eternity" (*SD* 3: 1922b, 53). Such statements support a view of Kemal as a protodemocratic leader. But what were, in more precise terms, his views of the new republic, the Assembly, political parties, the military, and the other central governing institutions and practices of the period? Party documents and important statements made by Kemal himself show how, during the single-party period, the Assembly and various other institutional spaces and processes became nothing but institutional vehicles for the concentration of Kemal's and the RPP's will, arenas shaped for their specific ideological and practical purposes. The result was an institutional environment of limited participation, informed by a discourse at odds with democracy rather than compatible with or conducive to it. In this chapter, we describe and analyze Kemal's characterization of the role of political institutions and practices, including the party, the Assembly, the army, citizenship, and elections. Kemal's understandings of each inform a conception of politics and the state that we further explore in the next chapter.

THE PARTY (AND PARTIES)

Just as Mustafa Kemal viewed himself as the sole responsible leader at the helm of the movement, he consistently promoted the party as the sole organizational heir of the national struggle. The party was the institutional manifestation of the same personal power dynamics as his leadership. In the same speech in which he noted his role in presiding over the Congresses of the national movement at Erzurum and Sivas, Kemal dubbed the First RPP Congress of 1927 "really the second Great Congress after Sivas" (*SD* 1: 1927a, 352). Both gatherings represented "the aims and feelings of the whole nation." For Kemal, then, the RPP, like him, was the unparalleled carrier of the truth, which paid no "heed to any falsehoods." It was a "sacred" "manifestation and organification" of the founding "transformist spirit":

> Friends; the People's Party is a sacred association that embodies the whole nation in its cadres, that created force and might, expelled eternal enemies, extinguished internal enemies, provided freedom and sovereignty for the people, in that sinister tumult in which the country and the nation were deprived of all kinds of support and thrown into disaster. The People's Party is the manifestation and organification in all the towns of a transformist spirit that founded the Turkish Republic without paying heed to any falsehoods whatsoever. The People's Party is a determined party that has undertaken to inject Turkey into the civilized world and to elevate it within. . . . The point of departure of our Party is the sublime and vital interest of the nation. (*SD* 2: 1924b, 189)

Party documents stress a similar continuity between the party and the national movement. We quoted some of these statements at length in previous chapters. Here we note continuities in the 1947 program, which looked back at the party's history as a singular trajectory for single-party rule: "The Republican People's Party has been born of the transformation into a political party of the Association for Defense of Rights of Anatolia and Rumelia that conducted the National Liberation War under the leadership of Kemal Atatürk and secured National Sovereignty" (RPP 1947, Introduction).

It was truly Kemal's party, in several senses. From the start, he "imagined" it as a party that would reject the antisolidarist and anticorporatist versions of class-divisive politics. In an early statement that illustrates one of Kemal's positions on the status of classes in Turkish society, he claimed: "I shall enlighten those who are worrying about my forming a party. I am imagining forming such a party that this party possesses a program aiming at securing the prosperity and the happiness of all the classes of the nation. Circumstances of our nation suit this" (*SD* 2:

1923n, 50). Kemal uses "enlighten" here in the sense of showing doubters that he can and will form a party that aims to raise the nation's level of prosperity without being a class-based party.

The RPP's interest in representing the "whole nation" must be thus understood in terms of its solidarist and corporatist commitments. In its view, the "general" interest was the interest of a society conceived in occupational group terms, wherein groups related in harmony fulfill their part in the greater social whole. It was a party for all classes (if they indeed existed), rather than a party for some classes. Kemal reiterated this point as a kind of reminder in a speech to the Izmir Party Congress:

> As you well know, political parties are formed for limited purposes. For instance, merchants of Izmir may create a party that would satisfy any of their own interests. Or there may be a party that consists only of farmers. Whereas, our party is not an organization that pursues such a limited objective. On the contrary, it is a formation that aims at securing in an equal way the interests of people of all classes without injuring others. This is proven by our attitude and action. It shall continue to be so. There is no need to look for a counterpart of this organization in other countries. (*SD* 2: 1931a, 263–64)

One of the party's roles was thus to ensure unity around corporatist goals. In a 1925 speech, Kemal drew the link between the RPP and the Association for the Defense of Rights, and he underscored its solidaristic corporatist credentials in front of the nation and against those who would resist:

> A nation, a social collectivity, cannot take even a single step with the effort and work of an individual. The People's Party, of which I'm the proud president, is not a party that conducts ordinary street politics as is the case in other countries. I will respectfully repeat that the People's Party, like the Association for Defense of Rights, carries the duty of enlightening the whole nation and serving the whole nation. Those who attribute base politicking to the party are ungrateful people. The country needs a solidary unity. It is treason to divide the nation by ordinary politicking. Our party, with its clean proceedings, shall make its pure aims known to the world with new means every day.
>
> [on record:] In addressing the Gazi, Dr. Şemsettin Bey, President of the Turkish Hearth, says:

You are not just one person, you are a whole nation, your person, your party, is the person and the party of the whole nation. Long life to you.

Upon this statement Gazi Mustafa Kemal Hazretleri has uttered the following:

I shall say just one thing to the words of our young friend. The cadres of the People's Party comprise all the individuals of the nation. Those who cannot think this truth are the unfortunate ones who have not yet made their brains accustomed to this thinking. (*SD* 2: 1925a, 224)

Hence, one of the functions of the RPP from the earliest days was to mobilize the masses in a unified and solidaristic way, eliminating those who threatened this conception of society. From the Kemalist perspective, there could be no more legitimate political organization: it was a party for "the whole nation," not for factional "limited objectives." To allow other parties to participate would be to cause "pain" and harm for the nation. Kemal explained:

This nation was very often pained by political parties. Let me put to you that in other countries parties have been formed and are being formed on the basis of economic objectivity to be sure. Because there are various classes in those countries. In return for a political party that is formed to protect the interests of a class, another party is formed with the purpose of protecting the interests of another class. This is very natural. Well known are the consequences that we witnessed thanks to political parties that have been formed as if there existed in our country separate classes. Whereas when we say People's Party, not only a part but the whole of the nation is included. Let us first review our people . . . [see Text 1 and analysis in chapter 4] . . . thus I see our nation. Therefore, it is not necessary to separate into classes practitioners of various occupations because their interests are compatible with one another, and all of them comprise the people.

The People's Party shall be a school for giving political education to our people. Some of my friends, who love me very much, and who are concerned with my life, have recommended that I should not form such a political party. In fact, it is in my interest to withdraw into my corner and rest at the fulfillment of the national duty. In order to do that, it is necessary to have trust in the continuation of the results achieved to date as they are established. But in this respect I cannot yet be without worries. I recommend that none of you too should be without worries. (*SD* 2: 1923f, 97–98)

And so the party was formed to teach the people and the world of the rightness of its cause. It was entrusted by the charismatic leader with this mission and, it seems, would not have been formed had the leader had any doubts or worries.

Unsurprisingly, Kemal claimed to have formed the party "personally," and also unsurprisingly, the party documents, especially after 1927, promoted his eternal charismatic position. In 1930, in a communique to Fethi Bey, who was then ambassador to Paris, he described the RPP as the party "that I had personally formed [*bizzat teşkil ettiğim*]" (*SD* 4: 1930, 598). And, in *Nutuk,* Kemal noted with great pride how he had been entrusted to lead the party by the logic of power and politics in "civilized states":

> In civilized states that are seriously administered on the basis of national sover-
> eignty, the accepted and enforced principle is that the political group that best
> represents the general aspirations of the nation and that possesses the highest
> power and authority to execute the interests and the requirements that these as-
> pirations entail should undertake the governing of state affairs and entrust this
> responsibility to its highest leader. (Atatürk 1960, 221)

Kemal used his position as leader of the party to promote himself as the "highest leader" in the nation. In turn, the members of the party promoted him as such.

The party documents illustrate how the RPP, consistent with its claim to represent the entire body, assumed powers to legislate for the entire body as well. Its official position was that it established rule by law and was governed by those laws:

> [The People's Party's] aim is to guide the exercise of national sovereignty by the
> people and for the people and to elevate Turkey to the level of a modern [*asri*]
> state and to work to establish the guardianship of law (*kanunun velâyeti*) above all
> other forces. (RPP 1923, Article 1; reiterated in RPP 1927, Article 4)

The more effective position, however, articulated by its general president to the Izmir Congress in 1931, was that the laws that the party followed were its laws, and if the leadership found those laws to be obstacles, then it would change the laws: "If our laws are not fit, we amend those laws and enact new laws. If we deem it necessary and obligatory in the last resort, we never hesitate in marching toward our target on this path, rising above everything" (*SD* 2: 1931a, 264).[1] In its own conception, the party was not simply an association for the aggregation of interests. It was an association with power to change the Constitution and to lay down the law: "The Party, in giving rights and duties to the citizens, does not discriminate between man and woman" (RPP 1935, Section 1, Article 4, Paragraph B). The party gives and the citizens receive, in this case suffrage rights. In its own conception, the party was the effective state; all power flowed from *it*.

In addition, the party had overt symbolic political value to Kemal. He used it to deflect criticism of his absolutist tendencies by rhetorically concealing his grip on the state, on the nation, and, indeed, on the party itself. Where he could not sway his audience charismatically, he could always point to the existence of his political association to counter criticisms of his absolutism. In the context of his 1924 interview about the program of the PRP, he stated:

> The insinuations and allusions to the presence of absolute rule are to my mind inexplicable. The RPP and all of its leaders and members are people who have not hesitated to stake their lives and who will never abstain from staking their lives together with the nation till today in order to destroy radically all kinds of absolutism in Turkey and to provide the country and the nation with complete freedom; therefore the alleged rule most certainly does not exist. The insinuations and allusions suggested with this purpose have no value whatsoever in the eyes of the nation. (*SD* 3: 1924c, 78)

Of course, Kemal does not really address the criticism directly here. He assumes that because there is one functioning political association made up of devoted nationalists dedicated to overcoming Ottoman absolutism, there cannot be any absolutist power dynamics. Either he did not believe that he should stoop to answer the charge directly, or he did not grasp the requirements for political freedom, which he and his closest associates curtailed as a matter of practice on the assumption that their party secured the general interest. Notwithstanding the very shallow discourse on political freedom, we note that Kemal appeared to believe genuinely that hard work by the party could ensure the best possible world

1. Kemal made this statement in the context of describing how, having "won the war," Turkey now had to "win" the economic war. He stated: "It was the Turkish nation who first taught agriculture and crafts to all humanity. . . . [T]he Turkish nation has been the educator of the world." For an analysis of these statements, see the discussion of the nationalist arrow in chapter 5.

for the Turks. With "vigilance," the party will capably and proudly "eliminate the drawbacks" of being unopposed. Without any sense of reluctance or misgiving regarding the limits of single-party rule, Kemal told an audience in Trabzon in 1930:

> We are bound to work with ever-increasing activity everyday as if there were many parties facing us, to disseminate our ideas to the masses of the people, and to take them all the way to the villages. It is necessary to be at every moment in a position of being able to account for our movement before history and before the world. By being this sensitive and vigilant in our project and activities, we shall have eliminated the drawbacks of an oppositionless party. (*SD* 2: 1930b, 257)

The drawback here is not a matter of principle; it is a matter of practicality to be overcome by "being sensitive and vigilant." This statement raises the question: Is there *any* tutelary democratic intent here? Any interest in stimulating politics based on political equality and respect for alternative positions concerning the goals of the new republic? Is Kemal interested in stimulating multiparty politics? Our answer is no. In such utterances, he creates the belief that a single party can govern itself entirely under his guiding light by simulating democratic practices, not stimulating them. Rather than multiparty experimentation, the expressed interest is in convincing the masses that alternatives are unnecessary.

PARTY, POLITICAL CULTURE, AND FREEDOM

The party documents propagated a view of culture consistent with the Kemalist emphasis on ethnonational, monolithitic cultural homogeneity; a set of political-cultural ideals stressing Kemal's extraordinariness; and the eternal role of Kemalism as the foundation for all solidaristic corporatist ideals in contemporary Turkish political culture.

Party membership, for example, required that one "accept Turkish culture" (RPP 1923, Article 3: "Every Turk and every individual who comes from abroad and accepts Turkish citizenship and culture can enter the People's Party"). More profoundly, the 1927 statutes accepted as a basic principle "the spread of the Turkish language and Turkish culture with the conviction that the strongest tie among the citizens is unity of language, unity of sentiment, unity of idea" (RPP

1927, Article 5). There is an implicit recognition here that such unity did not exist within Turkey's borders and that it had to be created. This is the partly corporatist aspiration to homogenize society in terms of its most basic values.

The ideational logic at work behind these claims was Kemalism's uniform application of a principle of generality and its pursuit of "unity of idea" in the realms of both state and society. The ideal of a uniform political culture created as an outcome of Kemalist institutional reforms went hand in hand with a uniform culture created as an outcome of the cultural reforms. Legal homogenization was, for example, one of the goals of the legislation of a new civil code adapted from the Swiss civil code. As the minister of justice at the time explained, the new code would eliminate what he referred to as a "medieval" structure of "coincidental, change-dependent, and mutually contradictory" rules. Such reforms were "fitting to the requirements of our transformation and of the civilization of the present century."[2] Similarly, the Kemalist political cultural ideal was one that spoke in unison, felt in unison, and thought in unison. As Kemal put it in *Nutuk*, "Be it in the West or in the East, the internal organization of a state will certainly be unsound and frail if it combines conflicting elements that possess very different natures, cultures, and aspirations" (Atatürk 1962, 435). To the leadership of the party, Kemalist ideas and Kemalist policies would be most conducive to uniformity, order, and homogeneity in the legal, constitutional, social, and cultural spheres.

Importantly, and perhaps understandably, the unity applied within the party as well. As leader, Kemal demanded the same relations inside the party that he demanded outside of it. He wanted the party to enjoy what he believed he enjoyed—namely, "the nation's love and trust" (*SD* 1: 1931a, 368–69). To that end, he conceived of relations within the party in familial and familiar terms:

> Friends, we are all members of a great Party family with high ideals, who are connected to each other with sincere friendship. The requirement of the common ideal and mutual sincerity is to have the general march on the sound path by illuminations and guiding each other.
>
> The more this principle of our Party's members goes up the more the soli-

---

2. See "Appendix: The Rationale for the Draft Bill (of the Turkish Civil Code)," in Davison 1998, 197–204.

darity in our Party and the more the capacity for the national ideal develops and increases. There is only utility/usefulness in guiding each other and illuminating the people. No harm ever comes from this, but that the contrary will produce much harm has been proven by experience. (*SD* 1: 1931a, 368–69)

Harm is avoided and the national ideals secured when the members of the "party family" are themselves organized in relations of solidarity and unity. The harmful path is the path of contestation; the secure and safe and sound path is that of solidaristic unity.

Kemal's role as the charismatic agent of this unity was reflected in the position he was ultimately and infinitely accorded as the "eternal chief" of the RPP. He thus effectively occupied two positions of stately power, as president and as "founder of the revolutionary party" (RPP 1927, Article 6). The principles to govern the party bore his name ("Kemalism"), and the party declared, as constitutions and educational curricula would later, that "these principles cannot be changed in any way" (RPP 1927, Article 7). Interestingly, Kemal's fixed position in the leadership as "eternal chief" was not initially envisioned in the party stipulations. According to Article 5 of the 1923 statutes, the "General President of the People's Party is [to be] elected by the Great Congress from among those currently members of the [Assembly]" (RPP 1923). The president's term was to last until the next general elections, although the general president could be reelected with no set term limit. The articles could be "changed and abolished" only by the assent of two-thirds of the Great Congress. By 1927, after Kemal was at the helm, Article 7 of the party program stated that "general principles cannot be changed in any way" (RPP 1927). This stipulation includes the preceding article, Article 6, which named Kemal as "the General President of the RPP." In the words of the article, he "is the Esteemed Gazi Mustafa Kemal, who is founder of the Party." Kemal thus secured tenure for life and became "the eternal chief."

The underlying philosophical dynamic of "fixing general principles" and outlooks (of the youth, nation, the party, etc.) reflects one of Kemal's most fundamental political objectives: to control developments over time and, indeed, to control time itself. Kemalism makes various claims on the entire life and history of the Turks and posits itself, as we have seen in Kemal's "Message to the Youth," as the continual reference point for "eternity." It seems to suggest that, beyond developments in the positivist sciences, no additional creative thought or alteration is necessary. Alternative political and cultural reference points outside its dictated truths are ruled out forever because they are alternatives. This is especially true of those ideas that Kemalism consigns to "class" politics and those that it classifies as emanating from the past. Any perspectives that hint of—or are said to hint of—division or of Ottoman values are seen only as obstacles to the Turkish nation's present march toward civilization. In Kemalism, present fractious tendencies and the past are always the impeding Others—impediments to "development" and "progress" to be subordinated and overcome in the progressive march forward. Kemal and Kemalist documents paint only one relevant present and only one relevant past for the future generations of the republic— namely, *their* present, the founding period of the state. Kemalism is to be "the past" of relevance for the new generations. When they look backward in history, they will see the great achievements of Kemalism and seek to reproduce them in their own time.

It was ultimately on this basis that, to Kemal and the RPP, other parties were insufficiently progressive ("reactionary") or without direction ("ignorant"). It was also ultimately on this basis that Kemalists after Kemal have followed their great leader's footsteps and defended the party as the only party of "freedom" and a "model" of political organization to the world. This is precisely how the RPP spun itself in its twentieth-anniversary document and how it continues to be spun in popular and academic interpretive arenas. The 1943 document stated: "With the regime it created, our Party has shown to all the world [original word also connotes "universe"] that the principle of 'freedom' that is fundamental to democracy can be maintained without the existence of parties that are based on class interests and without the necessity of struggle among them" (RPP 1943b, Section 2, Article 2). Similarly, the 1947 program uttered its loyalty to Kemalism in the same sentence that it called itself "advanced and democratic" and stated its commitment to "freedom":

> Our party has founded the republican regime, which expresses in the best way the sovereignty of national will, and by abolishing all obsolete institutions that were impeding our nation's development, prepared the conditions that made the Turkish nation an advanced and democratic community.
>
> The main principles in this program are the expressions of the path of "Kemalism" to which the party is always loyal. This path requires taking inspi-

ration from the realities of the country and relying on the principles of freedom, unity, order, and progress. (RPP 1947, Introduction)

The single hegemonic party provided not only the general interest, but freedom
itself, and as such, in its own eyes it was truly a model to behold.

Freedom, the first document implies, is curtailed when multiple parties contest the public sphere. This is the corporatist viewpoint that freedom can be
found only in an atmosphere of harmony among groups, a harmony enforced by
the practical exclusion of ideas and groups seen as divisive. Solidaristic corporatist regimes do not eliminate freedom; they guarantee it, but freedom comes
with a deep mistrust for *political* manifestations that "threaten" the order and
tranquility of the social whole. Freedom is stressed side by side with "unity" and
"order" but is constrained by "solidarity." For the RPP, freedom meant freedom
within the solidary, unified, corporate life of a corporatist society, wherein all
parts of "the Turkish social whole" (RPP 1931, Section 2, Article 1, Paragraph B)
act with responsibility, vigilance, and duty to secure the "general," collective, and
"public" interest.

The RPP therefore did not seek to secure "individual freedom" in liberal
democratic terms, as hosts of interpreters have suggested. Kemalist freedom
means liberty within the Kemalist view of an abstract, unified, national-social
whole. The liberal view (which also contains constraints, although of different
kinds) is that the state exists to preserve liberty through powers theoretically
given to it by free, sovereign individuals. The Kemalist solidaristic corporatist
view is that the state gives and delimits freedom according to the general needs
that it defines and whose limits it prescribes: Article 4 of the 1931 program stated
that, in public law, the party would protect "the rights of individual and social
freedom, equality, community, and property that are given to the Turkish citizens
by the Constitution" (RPP 1931, Section 1). According to the 1935 program,
rights "are limited by the boundary of the state's existence and authority. The interest of the individual and legal entities shall not be contrary to the public interest. Laws shall be enacted according to this principle" (RPP 1935, Section 1,
Article 4, Paragraph A). Similarly, "all press is free on condition that they not attack *the creed* of the administration and the government" (*SD* 3: 1930, 89, emphasis added). One is "free" only to be a Kemalist, to act according to ideals it
stipulates, ideals summarized in the six arrows and further delineated by the cult

of charismatic personalism, because in Kemalist Turkey today the laws punish persons for derogating the memory of Kemal as well as for attacking the laicist, corporatist foundations of the republic.

From the perspective of corporatism, "individual freedom" is simply too risky politically, whereas "social freedom" may be defined according to what are described as the needs of society. Corporatism sees individual freedom as egoism that threatens social order and that thus undermines the goal of functional harmony to be induced from above by the regime. What are to liberal and postliberal concepts of radical democratic politics the fertile grounds for robust pluralist association[3] are to corporatism (at least in this context) a threat to the harmonizing objective of tranquility. Kemalist corporatism is illustrative. The party said that "These rights are limited by the boundaries of the state's . . . authority" (RPP 1935, Section 1, Paragraph 4A). Securing such limits requires both obvious forms of legal constraints on individual liberty and less obvious forms of ideological domination within milieus of political and cultural socialization. The Kemalists tried both (Law for Tranquility, People's Houses, etc.). The 1943 anniversary document downplays the significance of the coercive bases that are required for corporatism, just as interpreters of Kemalism have downplayed its rightest tendencies by portraying it as a democratizing ideology.

Kemal and the Kemalists understood that they could portray themselves successfully as a party of freedom very early in their project. The twentieth-anniversary document is again illustrative. It declared that the party not only had proved itself to be a protector of "freedom," but also had shown that a single party can govern without being engaged in external conflict. It is a historically remarkable statement in terms of Turkey's external legitimation, aimed to secure support abroad for the single-party hegemony at home: "Although governed by a single party, [our party] has put before the eyes of the world that it is possible to form a regime and to conduct a politics that does not pursue imperialistic aims and especially preparation for war" (RPP 1943b, Section 2, Article 3). The party is saying that it has shown that there can be single-party governance without belligerent disruptions to global stability. This view clearly underlies Turkey's reception as a model in the West. The party, in its own frame, found a way to capture power, to eliminate and remain vigilant against its rivals, to secure tranquility and order, but not to threaten global security. It was clearly posing itself as functional

---

3. See, for example, Mouffe 1995.

for global capitalism, as the next statement in the document strongly suggests: "It has been clearly shown to everybody that there can be found a way of not giving way to the formation of classes and occurrence of class struggle although the principle of individual property is preserved" (RPP 1943b, Section 2, Article 3). This statement echoes Mustafa Kemal's earlier declaration that Kemalism is not Bolshevism. It is nonbelligerent, nationalist, laicist corporatism.

The institutional reality of the RPP's protection of individual property requires analysis that is beyond the scope of our work. It is significant for ideological analytical purposes, though, to understand that the party, not only Mustafa Kemal, promoted itself precisely in terms that would be welcomed by the forces of global capital. The party also saw itself as an "example" to "men of science and politics of the nations of the West and of the East." Its "innovations" stemmed from "the superior ability that the Turkish nation has always shown in founding states and creating chiefs":

> We do not doubt that these innovations [*yenilikler*] that our Party has brought to the world have influenced and will influence even more in the future the thinking of the men of science and politics of the nations of the West and the East. The general impact of the Turkish State regime on the family of nations is not a new phenomenon in history. There is no doubt that the public law doctrine of the monarchies formed in Europe in the fifteenth and sixteenth centuries was considerably influenced by the public law doctrine of the empires founded by the Turkish nation. This includes the Ottoman Empire's public law doctrine, which was very progressive in its times. We are sure that in the twentieth century, too, the state and regime doctrine of Turkey shall again be seen as a model [*örnek*] for many of the nations of the world either explicitly or implicitly. It should be considered as an attractive subject for men of science to start studying these influences, basing their studies on actualities [awkward in original]. This special character of the Turkish regime stems from the superior ability that the Turkish nation has always shown in founding states and creating chiefs [*şef(ler)*]. (RPP 1943b, Section 2, Article 5)

Here Kemal's historic voice and influence comes through very clearly: praise for anything Turkish, and anything praiseworthy is Turkish. Praise for Europe because it has been impacted by Turks. Even praise for monarchies and rule by chiefs! Any means necessary to elevate "the Turkish nation." No one, the party leadership maintained, should doubt the *general* contributions of the Turks to the history of the world, given their "superior ability." This was the RPP's view of its own achievements as the "organification" of Kemalism, as the manifestation of the will of Mustafa Kemal Atatürk, its eternal leader.

THE ASSEMBLY

In *Nutuk*, Kemal noted that he was not interested in working within "the old" form and nature of the Assembly. "On the contrary," he stated, "I thought of forming a permanent assembly of a totally different nature and power and to go through the stages of the transformation that I had conceived with it" (Atatürk 1960, 291). In short, in his understanding, the Assembly was to be, like the party, his creation as well. He conceived of it as a compliant, oppositionless, "enduring" body that would carry out the transformation's objectives.

Kemal asserted in *Nutuk* that he tried, at first, to convey his goal for regime transformation by using the term *meclisi müessisan,* which literally means "founding assembly." The term also carries connotations of "constituent assembly." He presumably wished to convey the idea that the Assembly would be the body to found the new state. Assuming, however, that members of the early nationalist congresses would not understand this term ("the people's" understanding being limited), he then abandoned that term in favor of "an assembly with extraordinary powers [*salâhiyeti fevkalâdeye malik bir meclis*]":

> My goal was to ensure that the Assembly that was going to be convened be endowed from the first moment with the power of changing the "regime." But because I could not adequately explain the objective in using this term [*constituent assembly*], I was warned from Erzurum and Sivas that the people were not familiar with this term. Therefore, it was enough to say "an assembly with extraordinary powers." (Atatürk 1960, 421)

Technically speaking, therefore, Kemal did not want the Assembly to have what constitutional jurists call autonomous "constituent powers" of representation. He wanted a parliament that was willing to work with him to implement his (the nation's) will.[4]

---

4. To that end, he engaged in highly clever politics within the Assembly. For example, in the 1921 debates on the draft of the Constitution, which he no doubt wanted to reflect his aims, Kemal

The First Assembly was conventional in this sense, although the Constitution of 1921 concentrated powers in the head of the Council of Ministers. As a result of efforts by members of the Second Group, the 1924 Constitution further separated powers between the legislative and executive arenas, thus increasing the autonomous powers of the Assembly vis-à-vis the executive. This was an important dynamic for those hoping to establish an opposition party, but the political significance of this development soon waned as the RPP became the sole governing party following the closure of the legal opposition in 1924 and the purges of 1926. Consequently, the RPP arenas and documents became more relevant legislatively than the Assembly and state constitutions. By the Third Assembly, and despite the constitutional separation of powers created in the 1924 Constitution, a unified Assembly with extraordinary powers materialized. It was described in the 1931 party program: Article 3 on the "form of administration [*idare*]," which was more fitting word than "government" (*hükümet*), promoted a "form of state that is based on the principles of unity of powers" between the Assembly, the president, and the Council of Ministers. "The Party is of the opinion that the most suitable form of state is this," precisely as Kemal had "thought" of it (RPP 1931). Unity in administration took precedence over representative parliamentary governance in constituent assembly terms. Again, the institutions of the state came to reflect and express Kemal's personalism and Kemalism's solidaristic corporatist needs.

ELECTIONS

Among the party's tasks, as it saw them, was the creation of electoral processes. Kemal and the RPP's professed commitments to limited citizen participation, evident in many texts, constitute another key component of the interpretation of Kemalism as a tutelary democratic ideology and movement. Here again, how-

---

noted that consistent attendance at the Assembly could not be expected because of climatic and mountainous conditions in some parts of the country. As a result, at the first session, he suggested having an election within the Assembly by open vote and that those present should elect from among themselves one-third of the Assembly to serve as an inner, permanent Assembly, and the rest should relegate their mandate to this new body. Clearly, he aimed at steering a more loyal inner Assembly, an "Assembly within the Assembly," the support bases of which would be apparent from the open vote. See Parla 2001.

ever, there are some problems. These professed commitments to "political development" do not withstand critical scrutiny when analyzed in the context of Kemal and Kemalism's other pronouncements about electoral processes. These pronouncements indicate the now familiar Kemalist characterological constraints on participation and a narrow conception of citizenship designed to suit Kemalism's ideological norms. Many of the party's official statements expressed the democratic potential of citizen participation, but this participation was always constrained by the RPP's dual judgments that neither was the country ready for direct democracy, nor was every Turk capable of serving the "high" interests of the party.

As if there had been no previous elections in the Ottoman Turkish context (which there were after 1908), the RPP judged people to be unfit for democracy in terms of their "qualities, prerequisites, and instruments" (RPP 1931, Section 1, Article 4). This is in part what it meant when it determined that "general conditions in our country" were not conducive to direct democracy. Implied in the statements on elections, then, is the RPP's conception of itself as the great educator of the Turkish political body, as the unparalleled (unequal) organ that would bring the nation to political maturity. Left alone, the nation could be seduced by ignorant fools who sought to move the country "backward" through manipulation and dirty tricks. This discourse served to conceal Kemalism's electoral manipulation. More important, it also forever entrenched the idea that elections should be understood as legitimate only insofar as they confirm a range of outcomes desired by the state's leaders. Understanding the Kemalist view of elections is thus fundamental to understanding the persistent tendency in contemporary Turkish electoral politics to view elections as the arena in which the ideas of the Kemalist state are either confirmed or rejected rather than as the public spaces for the autonomous expression of the will of the people.

This is not a view unique to Turkey, but it is no more democratic as a result. In Kemalism, the ideas of the people are always less politically valid than the ideas of their leaders. The people should therefore defer to their leaders rather than seek to hold them accountable. The institutional view that electoral outcomes should conform to the views of Kemalist leadership, not to those of the persons being led, underlies practices associated with manipulating electoral procedures to fit with Kemalist hegemony. The rigging of the first "democratic" elections in 1946 and recent attempts both to tinker with citizens' preferences and to exclude ideas not compatible with Kemalist hegemony are products of the anticonstituent view of elections. Thus, Kemal and the Kemalists, in setting themselves up as the judges of the "qualities" and "prerequisites" fitting for citizen political participation, set a pattern of governance that has frustrated, rather than served, democratic ideals. The party's posture toward democracy and citizenship had the effect of lowering the standards for both. "Democracy" meant confirming the leaders' decisions by casting a vote that only they would allow to be cast, and "citizenship" meant simply confirming options that had already been decided upon by those especially fit to rule.

In Kemal's public statements and in the party programs, the Kemalist interest in holding elections is clear. The programs also described the RPP's view of the kinds of persons who would be most fit to participate, as those in whom the "citizen" "believes" and in whom she or he has "confidence":

It is one of our highest aims to implement direct/first degree elections. However, it is necessary to equip the citizen with the qualities, prerequisites, and instruments with which he can recognize those whom he is going to elect. Until the day that the desirable result is yielded by the endeavors for securing this, we find it more suitable to the real requirements of democracy to let the citizen free to elect those persons whom it knows closely and in whom he has confidence. (RPP 1931, Section 1, Article 4)

The law for the election of deputies shall be renewed. In view of the general conditions of our country, we find it most fitting to the requirement of democracy to let the citizen free to elect as second electors those persons whom he knows close up and whom he believes, and to conduct the election of deputies in this manner. (RPP 1935, Section 1, Article 4, Paragraph C)

The ideological and practical reality was slightly different than these documents suggest, however. Because the party was the only political organification of the people's spirit, it had already judged those who were to be "believed." In fact, other documents suggest that the party's preference was not for the "citizen to be free to elect those persons whom it knows closely and in whom he has confidence." Rather, the citizen, the party declared, was to be "free to elect" those in whom the party and in particular its chief had the most confidence.

We participated in the new elections by announcing our known principles. Those people who wanted to become deputies upon accepting our views were first *informing me that they were in agreement with the principles and shared our points of view. I was going to designate the candidates and duly announce them* on behalf of our party.

I had favored this above method because I knew that there were too many who in the forthcoming elections would try to become deputies with various objectives by seducing the nation. My public statements and guidances were received in all parts of the country with full sincerity and trust.

The whole nation totally adapted the principles I announced, and it became clear that it was not possible to be elected by the nation to the deputyship of those who would oppose the principles and even my person. (Atatürk 1962, 728–29, emphasis added)

Of course, from within the Kemalist perspective, this was raising the standard because there were clearly those who might "try to become deputies with various objectives by seducing the nation." Consequently, from very early on, Kemal's own personal and ideological views dictated the selection of those who would stand for election, frustrating even ordinary party politics, not to mention democratic habituation.

Kemal's description of the ideal candidate was explained by Fahrettin Altay, who received a dictation from Kemal. The text is from the sixth volume of Kemal's *Public Addresses and Statements:*

(1) The candidate even after chosen, shall remain a farmer, shall not abandon his way of life, shall always remain loyal to his profession. During his tenure of deputyship, even during periods of vacation, he shall again remain tied to his profession and professional occupation; in his vacation, he shall live the same way of life in his village.

(2) He shall in any [i.e., all] case[s] be patriotic, shall be against all international currents; he shall always pursue this point of view in his attitude, disposition, speech, and activity in the Assembly, as well as in his contacts with his colleagues.

(3) He shall possess total loyalty to the Republican People's Party and all its principles, needs, actions, and throughout his tenure as a deputy, he shall maintain this disposition; he shall not be bigoted.

(4) In his life in the Assembly his position and attitude and dress shall be like that in his real [true] country. He shall come to the sessions of the Assembly and to everywhere with his brimmed cap and his baggy pants; he shall not

change his daily lifestyle; only on ceremonial days shall he like every one else, wear frock-jacket-redingote [*frak-jaket-redingot*].

(5) He shall be more or less literate in the new alphabet; if he has any deficiency in this respect, he shall during his service in the Assembly study and complete it.

(6) While speaking, he shall be intelligent and possessive of common sense; he shall not be too old.

(7) He should have no ill reputation during the national struggle; he should have no defect and unattractiveness that draws attention in his environment. It is desirable that he should have served in the national struggle and served our Party in the elections and on other occasions; at least he should have not been an opponent; if he's not a registered member of the Party, he should immediately become one.

(8) He shall submit in a petition for deputyship undersigned with his signature and in a manner that would commit himself to these principles. (*SD* 6: 1931, 390–91)

The first requirement fully underscores Kemalism's corporatist outlook. The candidate must "remain loyal to his profession . . . even during periods of vacation"; that is, he or she must be identified thoroughly in and through his or her occupational group setting (as opposed to class, locale, or his or her own individual judgment). The second requirement rules out ideological affiliation with any internationalist currents: the candidate shall "always be patriotic"—that is, a nationalist in all facets of his or her being ("attitude, disposition, speech"). The third stipulates "total" loyalty to the RPP's principles specifically and dictates against bigotry, although the meaning of this term is not fully spelled out. The fourth stipulates dress requirements, noting that ordinary attire is inapplicable only in ceremonial occasions. The fifth stipulates that the candidate shall conform to Kemalism's language policy. The remaining points suggest conformity with the abstractly defined requirements of "intelligence," "common sense," age (shall not be "too old"), "reputation," "defect," "unattractiveness," and loyalty. These criteria, which are no doubt extremely honest about their purpose, provided a great deal of subjective leeway for Kemal and his top associates to handpick the most trustworthy—that is, those whom they believed and in whom they had utmost confidence. These stipulations allowed the leadership to exclude anyone who did not conform with their sense of "attractiveness." Another important and repeated term in the documents is *sincerity*. Kemal picked sincere loyalists, those who disclosed themselves as full Kemalist partisans—as "friends"—because, despite "all the measures we have taken," sometimes "traitors" sneak in.

Kemal's statements on the occasions of elections indicate his wish that the people express their "trust and support" in him and his candidates, and he used his presence to validate the loyalty of his handpicked deputies, calling on the people to fulfill their duties to the "fatherland" by supporting those who supported his principles. The effect was a rampant use of the term *loyalty,* in which all paths of authority led to Kemal. In Istanbul in 1923 (while the city was still under occupation), Kemal stated: "The people [of Istanbul] should demonstrate its loyalty to the fatherland by uniting around the principles I have announced during the past two days. It should serve its own rescue by electing persons who have resolved to become loyal to our principles" (*SD* 3: 1923c, 61). As with other parts of his discourse, his statements were often intended to confirm his and the party's grasp of the nation's truths, the people's confidence in him, and his status as chief.

The citizen's duty in this regard most often preceded his or her role in confirming the party, and Kemal directly associated this confirmation with his or her duty as "citizen." In a 1927 circular typical of those published by Kemal on behalf of the RPP candidates for all electoral districts, Kemal stated:

> My dear citizens,
>
> I am submitting on behalf of the Republican People's Party to your consideration all of the persons *I have designated* as candidates for deputyship in the Turkish Grand National Assembly for all parts of the country. I thought it useful for each citizen to see in its totality the associates *I have deemed fit to work* with in the new period. I shall under my signature separately submit those candidates for deputyship *who I will allot* to each electoral district. (*SD* 4: 1927c, 582, emphasis added)

The deputies, in other words, are his officials. They are not representatives of the citizens at all, for the citizens cannot choose and should not choose their own. He deems, he allots, he designates.

This is a single-party apparatus run by a single person who claims all powers to choose the people's representatives. Whether necessary for its time and conditions or not, this model of politics is not tutelary democratic. It is not conducive to cultivating autonomous citizen practices. The habits created are those wherein citizens cast ballots to confirm the leader's choices. They are *disempowering* mechanisms that (dis)place power into the hands of those at the top, out of the reach of the alleged citizens. In fact, because the "citizens" choose a second tier or "electors," they are disempowered twice. These elections are not elections of the people, for the people. They are of Kemal, for Kemal. It is unsurprising, therefore, that he cast the results of elections in 1927 as a successful confirmation of his ideas:

> My dear citizens,
>
> The result of the elections is in. The candidates I had introduced on behalf of the Republican People's Party were generally and unanimously approved and elected by my dear citizens in all parts of the country. I duly and with a high sense of responsibility comprehend the noble meaning in the enthusiasm of my dear citizens. (*SD* 4: 1927c, 582)

They are his citizens, doing his work for him. Just as he is convinced in the rightness of his and his party's cause, they should be convinced that their votes have a "noble meaning." The use of the concept *citizen* and the meanings with which Kemal invests it are very important here. To be a citizen means to perform "freely" the duties dictated by the chief by voting for his candidates. It is, indeed, the highest duty that any citizen can perform. One will not be encumbered in supporting Kemal.

Considerations in 1931 for another legal opposition party that would be "laicist, republican, nationalist, and sincere" led to interesting moments in Kemal's discussion of the meaning of elections. On one occasion, he said he was quite open to votes "of conscience." Whether this statement was sincere or not shall never be known. Whatever the case, the opposition interpreted Kemal's openness as possible veiled threats against them for abandoning his cause and consequently dissolved itself as a party rather than meet the fate of previous opponents. The 1931 elections thus mirrored the previous dynamics. Importantly, Kemal showed no regret about the loss of the opposition experiment—there being no real need for an opposition—and he continued his practice of shaping the elections to suit his (the nation's) needs. To the nation, he announced: "I submitted to your vote *the names of my friends with whom I can accomplish* the affairs of the nation and of the state and *whom I have seen fit* for candidacy for deputyship in accordance with very strong considerations of conscience" (*SD* 4: 1931, 553, emphasis added). After the elections of 1935, in an announcement to "citizens" from "Kamal Atatürk" (the spelling during the peak of the Turkish-purification reforms), he stated: "You demonstrated once again your *belief and confidence in me* and in *my Party;* you found deserving of your high estimation the friends *I submitted* to you as candidates for deputyship. Our sincere wish is the elevation of the country and the well-being of the citizen" (*SD* 4: 1935, 574, emphasis added).

Elections conceived as a process of ratifying the will of the leadership were truly works "guided by the Party," as the RPP expressed it in a document for its twentieth anniversary. They were intended, along with all other unified institutional organs, to reinforce Kemalist ideals. Note how they also set a pattern for conceiving elections as processes in which the will of the leadership is executed and judged, rather than as arenas for extensive and expansive competition over political ideals. Years of habituation in such electoral practices have frustrated rather than enabled democratic developments in Turkey (and not only there!). The Kemalists did not so much undercut institutions that reproduce enduring hierarchies as formalize them with ostensibly more modern external appearances, despite true advances in the extension of the franchise to persons and groups previously excluded from participating.

We hasten to point out that the manipulation of institutions by the regime in power was not new. It is a matter of historical record that the CUP used the elections of 1913 to create a compliant Parliament that would be subject to its purposes. Parties had been closed, banned, harassed, and so on in the years prior to Kemal's rule. But those regimes have not been crowned in scholarship as exemplars of modern democratizing politics. Our point is not that this kind of behavior is new in the Ottoman-Turkish context with Atatürk's arrival or that it is unique to him. Our claim is that he did not shift the tide, as many have claimed. To the contrary, he deepened antidemocratic tendencies by promoting himself and those objectives that he determined by himself as the sole rightful options available to "the people" (in whom he lacked confidence unless their estimation matched his, in which case his confidence was "high"). His conception of elections thus further inscribed a dynamic of dependency between the "chief" and his "citizens." The former needed the latter to rule, and the latter needed the former to be ruled, but there would be no possibility for the ruled to rule themselves. In this sense, Kemal arguably weakened rather than strengthened any existing democratic sensibilities. The nation, in effect, became dependent upon him.

THE ARMY

Another important duty for citizens was military service. "Defense of the fatherland is the most sacred of national duties," stated Section 8 of the 1931 party program (RPP 1931). The common interpretation of the military's role in Kemalism follows the basic logic of the modernizing and democratizing accounts of Kemalism by suggesting that the Kemalist movement exhibited a consistent determination to separate the military from politics. This would make the relationship between the military and power "modern" in the sense that these spheres of governance would be structurally as well as conceptually differentiated. The modernist reputation of Kemalism with regard to the military's separation from politics, therefore, feeds the tutelary democratic interpretation. By keeping the military out of the halls of political power, Kemalism is said to have put Turkey on the road to civilian governance and, as a result, to have laid a crucial foundation for democratic government: namely, rule by the people. This account is supported by much official documentation, but, again, it is only part of the story.

It is true that according to Kemalist practice the army was not to participate in the daily political affairs of state, but this did not mean that it was nonpolitical in Kemal's conception. In brief, not only was the military elevated and enshrined as the ultimate "owner" of the state because of its heroic status in the "sublime" history of the "great Turkish nation," but it was also celebrated by Atatürk at his most powerful moments as a model to be emulated in all social and cultural domains, blurring rather than distinguishing the lines between politics, the military, and education. As such, Kemal's own model of political and social life expresses deep and profound militarist dimensions, and, although Kemal rejected direct rule by generals during his time, he made such rule possible by entrusting to the army the high duty of guarding the state from all "internal and external" threats and by infusing the army with all desirable characterological traits (in contrast to his comments about the characters and abilities of ordinary Turks). Kemalism therefore did *not* separate the military or militarism from politics.[5] Rather, it forged a new political relation between them in which the "civilian" identity of the regime was infused with militaristic pride and values consistent with Kemalism's goal of cultivating such values in the conscience of the youth.

Here we offer excerpts from central documents and speeches as primary ide-

---

5. On militarism and nationalism in Turkey, see Altınay and Bora 2002.

ological evidence for this alternative interpretation of the civilian-military relationship:

TEXT 38
Defense of the fatherland is the most sacred of national duties. The Party has accepted the principle of applying without exception conscription to all citizens. The Turkish Army is above any and all political considerations and influences. We find it important that the army be equipped with means suitable to the century's [technological] advancements and possess the might to enable it to perform successfully at every moment the high duty that is assigned to it.

We take special care for having always held in a position of respect and honor the army of the Republic and its self-sacrificing and valuable members who guard and protect the national ideal, national existence, and the transformations that are the unshakable foundation of the grand structure of the state. (RPP 1931, Section 8)

TEXT 39
But why should the officers receive salaries on proportion to the salaries of such and such departments [of government], or why should their well-being be only as much as that of others? I think, gentlemen, that the real inclination and the feelings of conscience of the whole nation is [for] the prosperity, the happiness of all officers and upper echelons of command who defend and shall always defend its [the nation's] life, its honor, its independence above all others. I have no doubt whatsoever that those who belong to the other agencies of the state, can see this in its uniqueness with all glory and joy and this doesn't offend the pride and is not offending of anybody; are we going to make comparisons, Gentlemen, while giving moneys? (Kemal in the Assembly, *SD* 1: 1923d, 324)

TEXT 40
Honorable Members! The principle of isolating the army from politics in the general life of the country is an essential point that the Republic has always upheld. On the path that has been followed to date, Republican armies, as the sure and firm guardian of the fatherland, have remained in a position of respectability and strength. Similarly, we observe the truth of the necessity of absolving and raising the religion of Islam to which we are satisfied and happy to belong,

from and above the position of being an instrument of politics as has been the convention for centuries. (Kemal in the Assembly, *SD* 1: 1925a, 330)

TEXT 41

We lived this heartfelt life in the pure hearth of our officers, who are the elite, heroic children of the Turkish nation. . . .

Friends! All of history shows us that nations, when they want to attain their high ideals, they have found their uniformed children in the way of their rising up. Within all history, a sublime exception is seen in our history, the Turkish history. You well know that the Turkish nation, whenever it wanted to rise, it has always seen out in the front of these steps its army consisting of its own heroic children as its guiding leader, its vanguard of the actions that carry the high national ideal to its conclusion.

It is for this reason that the Turkish nation has nourished profound thirst for its heroic children who are ready to march forward sword in hand against danger. And it shall always do so. From here on, too, the heroic military children will always march at the front for the realization of the sublime ideal of the Turkish nation.

The whole Turkish nation sees as the hero of every vital thing in which it has succeeded its own army, the officer corps, the top echelon of command, which command its army, which consists of its very own children. The nation and the army consisting of its heroic children have united with each other to such an extent that, its like is scarce example [*misali ender*] in the world and in history. We can always be proud of this national fortune.

Friends!

In speaking of the army, I'm speaking of the enlightened children of the Turkish nation who are the true owners of this country.

Among these children, no doubt, are included our educators who educate the heroes of the future. Also included are our friends the teachers, who, when necessary, immediately change their robes and sacrifice their heads when required and march with the army. When I mention the officers of our grand army and alongside them the enlightened children of the Turk, I'm speaking of the Turkish youth who are ready in thought, in conscience, and in science to participate in the national heroism together with the former two. You would understand how much I was moved by the view tonight because it represents for me this supreme youth. The happiness that takes hold of my heart and my thoughts are relayed to you by my looks. In concluding my words, I would like to clearly say that, the Turkish nation loves its army very much, it considers it as the guardian of its own ideal. (Statements made by Kemal in Konya, *SD* 2: 1931b, 269–70)

TEXT 42

Beloved Friends!

The Army, the Turkish Army! Here is the glorious name that swells with feelings of trust and pride the chest of the whole nation. During this year, I saw it up close twice in short intervals, in its great numbers. . . . I saw its discipline, its energy, the expert efforts of its officers, the high strategic ability of our great commanders and generals. I felt profound pride, I appreciated it.

Our Army is a steel-like expression of Turkish unity, of Turkish might and ability, of Turkish patriotism.

Our Army is the invincible guarantee of the Turkish lands and the systematic work we have been conducting to realize the ideal of Turkey. . . .

I have no doubt that this special care and support shall be given to making the army, which is a great school of national discipline, also a great school for bringing up at the same time the most requisite personnel for us in our economic, cultural, social wants. (Kemal to the Assembly, *SD* 1: 1937b, 402–3)

TEXT 43

Respected Friends,

We have accelerated our work to the effect of equipping our invincible army with, as I had explained last year as well, weaponry and motorized equipment of the very recent systems. That invincible army of ours doesn't remain with being the defender of the fatherland and the regime, but also is, in its widest and true meaning, a factor of peace and a hearth of training and education. (Kemal to the Assembly, *SD* 1: 1938, 41)

TEXT 44

[To] the heroic Turkish Army whose victories and past starts with the history of humanity, that has always carried alongside victory the brilliant halo of civilization!

Just like you have protected and rescued your country in the most difficult moments of crisis from oppression, disaster, and evils and from enemy invasion, I have no doubt that you shall perform your duty with the same devotion in the enlightened, prosperous period of the Republic today, too, equipped with all modern weaponry and means of military technology.

> I and our great nation have complete belief and trust in your momentary readiness and serviceableness to perform your duty, which consists of protecting the glory and honor of the Turkish fatherland and the community of Turkdom against all kinds of internal and external danger. (Kemal, to mark the fifteenth anniversary of the republic, *SD* 2: 1938, 286)

THE NEW MILITARY-POLITICAL RELATION

Some persisting themes here should be familiar to any professionalist discourse about the military. Several of the quoted texts, for example, emphasize military readiness, the latest technologies to secure that end, and so on. On the important question of the relation between politics, state, society, and the military, the first two texts contain evidence for the most common account of Kemalism's separation between politics and the military. "The Turkish Army is above any and all political considerations and influences." "The principle of isolating the army from politics in the general life of the country is an essential point that the Republic has always upheld." The connection between the military and politics expressed in the documents, however, forces a slight reevaluation of their emphases and ideological content. The party documents and Kemal described an army that was "loyal to the principles of Kemalism." Consequently, in Kemalist discourse, the army is ideologically constituted as the servant and indeed the embodiment of Kemalist goals. It becomes not only a department of the Kemalist state, but an arena that manifests the highest goals of Kemalism and serves as an exemplary vehicle through which Kemalist ideological ends are achieved. In its glorification and exaltation of the values of military life and learning, the hegemonic ideology evinces a militaristic tone and creates a new political and ideological relation between politics and the military, not no relation, as the common account posits. This new relation has several dimensions.

First, the documents clearly show that this army, like the Parliament, was constituted as an organ to defend not only the state, but the Kemalist state and Kemalism's understanding of the nationalist foundations of the state. It was to guard and protect, inter alia, "the transformations" (Text 38). Moreover, ideologically speaking, the documents are shot through with associations between the military and all of the sacred characteristics that Kemal invested in his particular vision of Turkey: nationality, fatherland, culture, state, history, and the prospects for what he called Turkdom, or the grand collectivity of the world and history of the Turks. It "defends" and "protects" the "glory and honor of the Turkish fatherland" (Texts 43 and 44). This is part of the meaning of the famous maxim "Peace at home, peace abroad" that appears in the 1931 RPP program—that is, the effective Constitution. In the context of Kemalist ideology and our analysis to this point, this maxim conveys the regime's objectives for tranquility and order at home, with no threat to external powers abroad. The ruling party ensured that its military would secure *its* order "at home" and not threaten "orders" abroad.

The second aspect of the new Kemalist military-political relation is that the military's place outside of ordinary politics is, in the Kemalist understanding, not separate from politics, but over politics. In a characterization of its duty that Kemal typically reserved only for the most esteemed nationalist institutions, he said that the army has a "high" duty "above any and all political considerations and interests" (Text 38). It is not that he is placing the responsibilities of the military outside of politics. Rather, he is entrusting it with a special role in the new republic: *"above"* politics. "Above" here does not mean separate from politics or the state; nor does it mean that the military is subordinate to civilian rule, as we discuss shortly. It means superordinate to the other institutions, looking over the Kemalist state (as Kemal did) and preserving it as its highest guardian. As Kemal stressed when opening the Assembly in 1923: "The only guardian of the independence of the state, of the life of the nation and the country, is our heroic army. Therefore, it is among the most important principles to regulate and elevate our military organization with special care" (*SD* 1: 1923c, 319). Kemalism's central ideological documents do not diminish the role of the military in politics as much as they "elevate" it to this new, special position.

Consequently, among other things, the army was to be rewarded over all institutions (Text 40). This practice was almost natural to Kemal, for he portrays the military's status, values, "discipline," "energy," "expertise," "high strategic ability," and "its glorious name" (Text 42) as occupying a special place in the "feelings of conscience of the whole nation" (Text 39)—that is, within Kemal's feelings and conscience. The army evoked "pride," and its "supreme youth" brought out "happiness" for him. It is no wonder that he was so proud, for the army was, in his mind, a Kemalist army: "Our Army is a steel-like expression of Turkish unity, of Turkish might and ability, of Turkish patriotism" (Text 42). It "has always carried alongside victory the brilliant halo of civilization." These are Kemalist reference points, and this is Kemal's attempt both to constitute the army in his ideological terms and to cultivate the deepest and most profound respect for the military as an institution in Turkish national life. Consisting of the nation's "heroic military children" (Text 41), the army, according to Kemal, must occupy a special place of "respect and honor." Its name alone "swells with feelings of trust and pride in the chest of the whole nation" (Text 42).

Clearly, the military's status is not diminished in this political discourse. (Nor is the Kemalist military unique in being promoted to such status.)[6] Mustafa Kemal Atatürk declares its value to be special because the army, like all other institutions, is a tool of the transformation and of the tranquility, unity, and order that he deemed necessary to achieve his solidaristic and corporatistic aims. The 1935 document repeated the formulations of the 1931 program (Text 38) and then added two sentences. First, "It is a principle to use, if necessary, for this purpose, all assets, living and inanimate and instruments of force of the country" (RPP 1935, Section 8, Article 72). In this document, the party declares its preparedness to use all means necessary in order to achieve Kemalist objectives. The exaltation of the means of violence is also a threat to potential enemies. And second, "Our Army is the invincible guarantee of the Turkish lands and the systematic work we have been conducting to realize the ideal of Turkey." The army is ours, the RPP is saying. It is a tool of our political objectives.

Still, Kemal's statement declaring the military's "isolation" from politics requires further analysis, for Kemal believed he accomplished the separation, just as he believed he had taken religion out of politics:

> The principle of isolating the army from politics in the general life of the country is an essential point that the Republic has always upheld. . . . Similarly, we observe the truth of the necessity of absolving and raising the religion of Islam to which we are satisfied and happy to belong, from and above the position of being an instrument of politics as has been the convention for centuries. (*SD* 1: 1925a, 330)

The key idea here is isolating the army from "politics in the general life of the country," not from politics in a general sense, for the military, like Islam, became a political tool of the Kemalists in its new political position. Because, as we have seen, Kemal viewed himself and his party as standing above politics, he did not

6. As Şerif Mardin (1983a) points out, the nineteenth-century political history of Europe, France above all, is full of ideas and groups that invite the military to participate in power.

view his use of either the military or religion as "political." His acts were true and right. As Kemal portrayed it, his government could use the military and religion to crack down on and threaten dissenters or to indoctrinate children because he and his party grasped and implemented truth. In the case of religion, it was true or pure Islam. In the case of the military, it was the just and correct use of force and coercion.

The position of the army in Kemal's discourse also parallels his own position vis-à-vis ordinary political life. Like the leader of unparalleled and unquestionable judgment, the military need not consistently involve itself with the ebb and flow of everyday political life because it effectively oversees the entire context of governance. More important, therefore, than looking for the military's direct involvement in politics is noting its direct involvement in the ideological conception and governing-administrative apparatus of the Kemalist state. Although Kemalism may conceptualize the military as remaining out of ordinary politics, it does not suggest that the military must remain outside the governing administration of the state. In Kemalist terms, therefore, it would be unusual were the military not to involve itself on occasion in governance.

The analytical point here is that in his declaration of the military's isolation, Kemal exploits the language of "modern" professionalization and structural differentiation, but does not secure it in crucial symbolic terms. Instead, his discourse on the military ideologically values the military as part of his project and therefore as part of the Kemalist state's defense apparatus. This is why, in the case of religion, his laicism is only a partial laicism: after separating Islam from power, he used it as part of his state apparatus to infuse his ideals of "pure Islam" in the individual consciences of the people. The case of the military is similar. Kemal's isolation of the military is only a partial isolation. The rhetoric of separation was accompanied by a massive ideological effort at integration. The leader integrated the military within the purposes of the hegemonic ideology. The entire combination in turn was forcefully integrated in the "consciences" of the people—the nation would have religion in its conscience and the military in its heart. It is difficult to evaluate any ideology as "modernist," in the sense of structural differentiation or autonomous moral development, if it insinuates particular nationalist, religious, and military values into the consciences of individuals. The ethical-moral sphere is overtaken by various forms of state power.

This is the significance of Kemal's promotion of the military as a place for national education and his identification of the nation with the military. He describes the military as "a great school of national discipline," "a great school for bringing up . . . the most requisite personnel for us in our economic, cultural, and social wants" (Text 42), "a hearth of training and education" (Text 43), and he equates the nation's successes with the achievements of the army: "The whole Turkish nation sees as the hero of *every vital thing in which it has succeeded its army* that consists of its very own children" (Text 41, emphasis added). The military is Kemal's institution for rearing the "nation's children." Kemal describes the army in the most positive terms in his ideological lexicon. Its personnel are heroic and are the "enlightened" children of the state, experts with great "might and ability."

These statements not only glorify military training as a superior form of knowledge, but also contrast radically with how Kemal depicts other ways of being and knowing. The most rational characteristic of "enlightenment" is assigned to the children in the military. It is little wonder that he considers it a branch of educating and socializing the youth. It is the hearth of the Kemalist-centered scientific and technical rationality, lying at the very core of Kemalist developmental goals. Thus, the military is not merely an institution for the defense of the peace at home and abroad; it is an exemplary school for the children. Isolated from politics, it is a model for "training" the youth. "I'm speaking of the Turkish youth," he stresses:

TEXT 41

Among these children, no doubt, are included our educators who educate the heroes of the future. Also included are our friends the teachers, who, when necessary, immediately change their robes and sacrifice their heads when required and march with the army. When I mention the officers of our grand army and alongside them the enlightened children of the Turk, I'm speaking of the Turkish youth who are ready in thought, in conscience, and in science to participate in the national heroism together with the former two.

The theme of a productive and active military intelligentsia is wholly coherent under the terms of Kemalist nationalism, in which the youth become Turkish under Kemal's leadership, in his "grand army," always "marching" along in the path of "national heroism." Having likened the teacher to an army, he now identifies educators and teachers with the army. They are two armies marching forward, educating the youth in science and national ideals. The one will "raise the nation's" prosperity and status within (and over) civilization; the other will raise nationalistic consciences. Both schools teach toward both ends. Kemal constructs an organic link between his laicist scientistic ideals and the rational powers of the heroic children of the nation's army. The effect of this linkage is to eliminate any differentiation between the military, schooling, and the hegemonic ideology. And it is this effect that makes him "happy": "You would understand how much I was moved by the view tonight because it represents for me this supreme youth. The happiness that takes hold of my heart and my thoughts are relayed to you by my looks. In concluding my words, I would like to clearly say that the Turkish nation loves its army very much, it considers it as the guardian of its own ideal" (*SD* 2: 1931b, 270). It is important to understand that Kemal's glorification of the military was not a defensive action on his part. Even at the height of the consolidation of his power, he was enthusiastically elevating the military's status. Texts 42 and 43 are from 1937 and 1938, respectively. In them, "the glorious name [of 'the Turkish Army!'] . . . swells with feelings of trust and pride in the chest of the whole nation."

As a result of these ideological emphases, Kemal's discourse laid the basis for a new relation between civilian and military institutions in which the values of the latter were indispensable for the governing capabilities of the former. A "civilian" in Kemalist discourse is one raised to embody the heroic ideals of the nation of which the army is the great and trusted symbolic and institutional expression. Ideologically and conceptually, Kemal's state was to be constituted by a fundamental "civilian-military" connection. Kemalism did not isolate the military from politics, but rather read the military into the new Kemalist purposes. The glorification of the military infused the hegemonic political ideology, education, and socialization in general. Our point is not that Kemal did not want to isolate the military. He sought its isolation from the everyday "politics" of others, but not from his own charismatic activity as president and not from the governing apparatus. In isolating it rhetorically but reintegrating it ideologically and administratively, he rationalized a *new political relation*—not no political relation—between the state and the military.

We think, furthermore, that it is precisely this new political relation that allowed Kemal's militarism to creep back in institutionally after the single-party period under the continuing hegemony of Kemalism and to remain both an active player in contemporary Turkish politics and a constant reference point for gauging the direction of political currents and particular political possibilities. The military is no passive sideliner: it even does its own polling, has its own intergovernmental contacts, and issues judgments of various kinds through the media to influence the character and possibilities of Turkish politics today. Kemalism's ideological glorification of the military created an institution with immense "respect" in the Turkish society that sees itself as the ultimate guardian of the Kemalist state against both "internal and external danger" (Text 44). Indeed, in this way the record suggests that Kemal articulated the ideological bases for the direct intervention of the army in politics. For him, the army was not to be merely the defender of the state; it was to be the expression of the future potential of the great nation. Its most honored were to be the nation's "heroic children" who would "always march at the front for the realization of the sublime ideal of the Turkish nation." It was to be "the vanguard of the actions that carry the high national ideal to its conclusion." The army, in short, was "the hero of every vital thing in which it has succeeded." The nation "can always be proud of this national fortune" (Text 41).

Again, there is a rather significant blurring of the lines of "isolation." Swept away perhaps by his own words, Kemal collapses the nation and the army, thus giving the army full representative powers (that otherwise only he had claimed) and declaring it to be the "true owner" of the country. The blurring of lines elevates the army to the highest status that Kemal can imagine. In the statement issued to mark the fifteenth anniversary of the state, Kemal reinforced this notion of ownership. The army not only trained and educated, then, it possessed and owned: "Just like you have protected and rescued your country in the most difficult moments of crisis from oppression, disaster, and evils and from enemy invasion, I have no doubt that you shall perform your duty with the same devotion in the enlightened, prosperous period of the Republic today, too, equipped with all modern weaponry and means of military technology" (Text 44). This is the foundation for the whole ideology behind the history of coups d'etat in Turkey. Kemal marked the anniversary with ever-increasing themes of "great prosperity and might," themes of pride, duties, and so on. Then he stated: "I and our great nation have complete belief and trust in your momentary readiness and serviceability to perform your duty, which consists of protecting the glory and honor of the Turkish fatherland and the community of Turkdom against all kinds of internal and external danger" (Text 44).

The themes mirror those we have seen before, especially in his "Message to the Youth." Recall that there he raised the specter of internal and external dangers as well: "The enemies who will have designs against your independence and republic . . . who are in power might be inept or astray or even traitorous. . . . The nation might be desolate and exhausted in destitution. Harken, children of the Turkish future . . . your duty is: to rescue the Turkish independence and the republic. The power you need is present in the noble blood in your veins!" (Atatürk 1962, 897–98). These words have shaped understandings of obligation in Turkey since the founding of the republic. The state inculcates the message to the youth in their early years and then reinforces it as the military's superior role over society during compulsory military service (for males). It marks their consciences indelibly, precisely as Kemal wanted it to, and raises the expectation that Kemal's military (or his youth) will intervene when the Kemalist state is in danger. The official statements elevate and glorify the role of nation-saving action and legitimate violence by the army and youth on behalf of the Kemalist state and its conception of nationalism. Kemal treats both spheres of experience with the same enthusiastic appeals. He moves comfortably from cultivating militarism and a "live and die for the nation" sensibility in the youth to glorifying the military values of discipline, might, and ability that are essential components of that sensibility. These realms of experience are for him organically connected ideologically.

The military has been an institutionalized part of the republic's power structure since its founding. Its role diminished between 1950 and 1960 during the first sustained multiparty experiments, but it has since consistently participated in governance in various direct and indirect ways. The direct forms include the coups of 1960, 1971, and 1980, as well as the influence it possesses within the the the National Security Council, perhaps the most powerful governing institution in the republic today. The council was established in the 1961 Constitution and subsequently strengthened in the 1982 Constitution. Both constitutions were proclaimed under the aegis of military rule. The military has also activated its power in recent years, by participating in creating the circumstances to induce a regime change in 1997 and, more recently, by flexing its muscles with warnings and commentary to those whom it views as threats to the laicist and corporatist bases of the state. The military's honored and special status as superordinate to the events of general political life is recognized by most Turkish political actors, who, having suffered from the coercive restrictions placed on politics by the military during the coups, know full well that the military stands above them, prepared to descend from its heights to defend a form and structure of politics suitable to Kemalist ideals. The military, in short, is the highest power in the state. The conceptual rationale for this position may be found in Kemal's notion of the army as "true owners of the country," not only as its guardians.

8

THE KEMALIST
MODEL OF POLITICS

State and Society

Thus far we have emphasised the explicitly political dimensions of Kemalism. In this chapter, we depart slightly from this focus to explore the Kemalist conceptualization of society itself and its judgments concerning the relation between society and its explicitly political features. Because we have already covered much of the ideological analytical ground, this discussion is briefer. It is extremely important to our study, however, because it is precisely in the Kemalist judgments about society and the relation between society, nation, culture, Kemal, and the state that some of Kemalism's most striking rightist tendencies become starkly apparent. Our discussion here thus takes us into our final evaluation of the consequences and prospects for Turkey under Kemalism.

KEMALISM'S RIGHTIST TENDENCIES

By "rightist tendencies," we mean the corporatist tendencies in specific parts of Kemalism's conception of the state that may be analyzed in terms of the categories "partly fascist" and "partly totalitarian." As we have stated, we view these terms as analytical categories and attempt in this chapter to show how they help to capture certain very specific dimensions of the Kemalist view of the nation and state. Although these matters are very delicate, it is, we think, neglectful in the context of political ideological analysis not to identify them. We use the term *tendencies* because they are leanings, not full-fledged developments. On balance, Kemalism has remained a more solidaristic corporatist ideology than anything else, but certain aspects of it exceed the limits of the solidaristic corporatist perspective.

The distinguishing characteristic of the corporatist state as such is its view that the state must, as Durkheim puts it, "drag" the individual into "the general torrent of social life." Durkheim suggests that the state must break down the distance both between the state and individuals and among individuals with the aim of shaping society as an organic whole. Society consists of mutually interdependent, functionally complementary occupational groups (not simply abstract individuals), and the state must fashion relations to suit that order. It must "penetrate deeply into the individual consciences" and socialize them into the corporatist order. In the solidarist version, the state is viewed as a regulatory and coordinating set of institutions with jurisdiction primarily in the intercorporation domain. The state directs, supervises, and manages relations between occupational associations. Within those relations, solidaristic corporatism charges "individuals" with a responsibility to their occupations and to society. The state protects individual rights to the extent that they serve, rather than undermine, the constructed social order. The key point in contrast to fascistic corporatism is that "individuals" have rights within the relations designed to ensure social solidarity. We discussed this view of rights with regard to the Kemalist understanding of liberty in the previous chapter.

Rather than ensure and protect autonomous spaces for either the individual or the corporations, the fascistic variant, by contrast, assimilates all within the state. It dominates individuals to the point of eliminating their abstract status. Individuals are insignificant entities on their own. Their status and significance is defined by their contributions to the goals of the state, according to the state, and derives solely from the groups to which they belong, the highest of which is the nation itself. The nation serves purposes much higher than those of any insignificant individual. Hence, in the fascist corporatist state, individuals lose rights as individuals, and the state monopolizes and dominates all spheres of life. Regulatory in posture, it does not respect the autonomy of any sphere; it views them all as subject to definition and control by the state.

Although fascism has historically appeared with racism (in Nazism, for example), the fascist state need not be racist. It demands full conformity to a national will, annihilating individual agency, whether that will is conceived in racist terms or not. The key is the fascist antiliberal attack on individuality and anti-Marxist attack on class struggle through the elevation of the power of the organically conceived nation. Thus, fascism views power as something that is exercised by the nation as a whole, and it takes the energetic exercise of collective national power as a symbol of the nation's supreme moral status. Fascism thrives by vitalistic exertions by members of the nation on behalf of collective goals. Such action establishes the superior status and significance of national identity and expresses the alleged strength and greatness of the nation. This motivation for energetic exertion and the interpretation of its significance are usually established by another key component of the fascism, the great leader, whose function is to inspire vitalistic activity on behalf of the nation. The leader expresses the will of the nation, whose members enact it. The "leader principle" is crucial to eliminating the agency status of the individual. In fascism, the great leader who gives voice to the national will is followed unquestioningly; not to do so, of course, would be to indicate individuality, which is ruled out by the fascist state. Nationalist ideologies need not be fascistic, but they can be, depending on how they construe the relation between the individual, the nation, the leader, power, action, and the role of the state in conjunction with other spheres of life.

The relation between fascism and totalitarianism is complex. Fascism may be understood as a subspecies of totalitarianism. Both aim fundamentally to dominate the totality of life by eliminating human freedom to act politically in ways imagined by liberalism. Hannah Arendt describes how totalitarianism attacks the conditions in which legitimate liberal governance is forged—those "living spaces of human freedom" (1958, 466) in which equal and free individuals may act upon their own wills, convictions, and experience of the world and others in order to generate a legitimate consensus for their own self-governance. As such, totalitarianism and fascism are closely connected. But totalitarianism refers to a strategy for eliminating agency and ethicopolitical relationships between free individuals that may accompany ideologies other than fascism. Totalitarianism as a form of governance, that is, may be found in any ideology that essentially eliminates concern for human agency and relationships founded upon it. Arendt uses the phrase "suprahuman laws of History and Nature" (465), for example, to describe the totalitarian ideals of Stalinism and Nazism. Stalinism was totalitarian in part because it sought to unleash laws of "historical necessity" in which some "decadent" classes would necessarily disappear as other, more progressive ones emerged. Its suprahuman requirements were in part articulated in terms of class supremacy and subordination, not fascistic national will and strength. Similarly, Nazism uses *race* as the central ideological term to justify "Aryan" domination. Totalitarian ideologies need not be phrased in terms of fascistic nationalism. They attack the foundations for freely willed and dynamic relationships of equality, respect, and mutual well-being characteristic of democratic life. The totalitarian leadership implements suprahuman imperatives of various kinds without regard to what stands in the way.

Both fascism and totalitarianism are thus closely associated with the use of propaganda (for example, lies and myths) and of terror (for example, combinations of random violence and arrests, torture, guilt by association, and collective punishment), as was the case especially in many of their twentieth-century forms. Terror is employed precisely to eliminate all opposition and to secure mass obedience by making any dissent or organization against the state extremely risky. It thus simultaneously atomizes and depoliticizes relations of society, making extremely dangerous any association to act against the powers that be. In the age of highly effective mass media, however, both totalitarianism and fascism may be perpetuated without violent forms of terror through the use of effective modes of ideological indoctrination and propagandistic socialization.

Evidence in Kemalist discourse suggests that within the overall and predominating solidaristic corporatist framework, there are dosages here and there of partly fascistic and partly totalitarian tendencies. In ideological analytical terms, each of these characteristics should be distinguished from the others. Fascistic and totalitarian ideological tendencies do not dominate Kemalism, but they are present and were active so that fascistic tendencies could form themselves within and out of Kemalism, as the existence of deeply rightist, Kemalist tendencies in the history of the republic shows. Understanding how this has been the case requires a brief summation and closer evaluation of Kemalism's central political judgments on the nation, culture, the leader, the military, the youth, and the state.

ON THE NATION

Even as early Kemalism identified members of society primarily in terms of their location in occupational settings, its original expressions consistently posited either actual or potential superiority of the nation over all other groupings, local and global. "Nationalism" was "the essential prerequisite and means of attaining a high level of humanity [*insan seviyesi*]" (RPP 1943b, Section 1, Article 1, Paragraph B). Kemal judged that the residents of the remaining territories of the Ottoman Empire could and should be shaped ("assembled") according to a common, unifying Turkish national identity. The goal of much of this discourse was to instill pride with a history and project: "[This form of government] has changed the form and nature of the common tie among the members of the nation for the maintenance of the existence of the nation that persisted for centuries; that is, instead of religious and sectarian ties, [it] has assembled the members through the bond of Turkish nationality" (*SD* 2: 1925b, 237). This identity served as the central category of all political thought and as the single reference point for all policymaking through the entire single-party period. "The very first point to be considered in political and social life is the protecting of the special identity and the interest of the nation" (RPP 1943b, Section 1, Article 1, Paragraph B). The point was that both on their own and relative to other nations, the "Turks" should have the utmost and greatest pride in themselves.

The use of an admixture of terms such as *nation, race, ethnicity,* and *culture* in part made a more chauvinistic form of Kemalist nationalism possible (especially from the point of view of those who, for various reasons, may not have considered their primary identity to be "Turk"), and there is evidence of the emergence of these forms in Kemalist discourse, especially in widely known statements such as the "Message to the Youth," in which Kemal vitalized a blood-based conception of national ties. The Turks were depicted in Kemalist discourse as the "teachers of all civilization," and, as Mahmut Esat (Bozkurt) put it, the "master of the country" (1930, 3). Central, then, was Kemal's idea that "We shall take our national culture above the level of contemporary civilization" (*SD* 2: 1933, 275). These uplifting dimensions of the discourse were promulgated widely by the founders of Turkey in various arenas of society. Consider Mustafa Kemal's conception of sports and physical education. In his 1926 discussion with Turkish athletes, he described the importance of sports: "[I]t [sport] is an issue of race. It's a matter of improving and purifying the race. It is a question of selection of the race, and even somewhat of a question of civility" (*SD* 2: 1926, 244). He went on to emphasize the importance of sports for the children of the country and notes the role of the army in defending the honor of the country. The discussion reveals how Kemal moved easily between sports, civilization, the youth, race, the army, making the point that they all must participate in the unified national project, which was the central project of "civilization" in his mind.

Similarly, the regime believed it necessary to instill an identity in the members of the collectivity that would help them "eradicate" an "inferiority complex" vis-à-vis Western civilization. The 1943 anniversary statement declared this national "resurrection" to be one of the RPP's early achievements and connected it directly with the "great war and transformation":

The People's Party demonstrated the necessity and usefulness of the nation's having confidence in itself, and cleared the way for eradicating the "Inferiority Complex" observed in some groups after the Tanzimat as a result of a variety of regimes. The phenomena that the Party took advantage of in this respect are: (1) the Grand and honorable history of the Turkish nation, (2) the works it accomplished through the great war and transformation it conducted after the time the world thought that the Turkish nation could not resurrect, and as such the example it gave to certain nations. (RPP 1943b, Section 1, Paragraph 2)

The next declaration of this paragraph further reflects how eradicating the inferiority complex allowed certain kinds of energy that past habituation had diminished to emerge on behalf of "your nation and your way": "The Party, by propagating the principle of 'have confidence in yourself as you work and be proud of your nation and your way,' has paved the way for the disappearance of bad feelings that diminished all kinds of energy" (RPP 1943b, Section 1, Paragraph 2). The meanings of the popular Turkish expression alluded to here, *övün, güven, çalış*—literally, "be proud, be confident, be industrious"—like the meanings of *kavim* and *ırk*, slide between the positive connotations of each concept and connotations of vainglory and boastfulness. In its more rightist forms, the slogan is intended to inspire proud confidence in social exertion on behalf of the nation.

The "virtues" of "work and industry" in the interest of "national morality" also clearly and explicitly overlapped with the purposes of solidaristic corporatism, specifically with its anticlass politics. The 1943 document continued:

(3) By not accepting class and by putting in its program [the principle that] partaking in social benefits "will be proportional to the degree of ability and work," the Party has considered work and industry in the forefront of virtues, and has accepted as the criterion of national morality being or not being of use to the good of the nation directly or indirectly. In this respect [it] has prepared a spiritual environment that would be useful for the taking root of a work ethic.

(4) By adopting the ideal of the Turkish nation's attaining a high level of civilization within the family of humanity, the Party has endeavored to spread or propagate to the citizens the goal and world view that is required by it, of attaining the level of civilization that shall prevent the kinds of crisis seen in the other countries and shall even constitute an exemplar amongst the family of humanity. (RPP 1943b, Section 1, Paragraphs 3 and 4)

The rhetoric of "the family of humanity" must be situated within the context of Kemalism's intentional exclusion of other ideological possibilities. It considered them "harmful and foreign" worldviews that would distort their nationalist sensibilities. By reinforcing the undesirability of the "foreign" especially, Kemalism hoped to show the world that Turkey could avoid the pitfalls of radicalism. This goal called for "solidarity instead of class struggle" and informed the nationalist as well as populist planks of the transformation that were designed to encourage the industrial class and make the country rich. We have seen how this aim has been defined in the central terms of single-party officialdom. The 1943 anniversary document defines these continuous goals in terms of the "energy" of society as well as of the corporatist goal of "tranquility of the enterprise and the employers":

> (C) Organizing classes, allowing class struggle that would bring into relief the contradiction between their interests would save nothing but wasting the energy of the society for naught and spoiling the tranquility of enterprise and employers.
>
> One should not consider the Turkish nation as consisting of various classes but view it as a coming together of occupational groups and should never give way to the formation of classes that would exploit one another. (RPP 1943b, Paragraph 1, Section C)

Kemalism—note the ideas *are* those of Kemal—thus posits a single, coherent, elevated national identity in order to instill pride, to serve as the sole reference point for policy and other social concerns, and to mobilize people for action and energetic exertion on the nation's behalf.

The state penetrated the individual consciences of members of society and "dragged" these members, to use Durkheim's term, into social life by fixing their public identity as members of the sublime Turkish nation in order to "save" and "resurrect" it. Put another way, the Kemalist state intentionally delved into the realm of political psychology in order to create values and, moreover, to make individuals attach themselves to and exert themselves for the larger purposes of "the nation." The intention here was not fascistic as such. It was societal mobilization for national economic development—work, "prosperity," and "happiness"—whose results were meant to instill pride and joy in the anticipation that the Turkish nation would one day surpass all others. We turn to the ideological implications of these conceptions later, after a review of Kemalism's other central judgments.

ON CULTURE AND LEADER

As we have shown, the party's interest in creating a unified nation relates as well to its conception of society and the legitimate social life of the nation. Specifically, the party judged that the cultural values of society must be "unified," and it knew very well that the unification of culture required alterations to the most fundamental identity characteristics of some members of the nation. It described this alteration in terms of the need "to develop and spread the Turkish language and Turkish culture with the conviction that the strongest tie among the citizens is unity of language, unity of sentiment, unity of idea" (RPP 1927, Article 5).

The language reforms provide a good example. The party experimented with different versions of the national language, sometimes shifting terms from year to year as part of their effort to "purify" Turkish. (Purification, remember, required removing words derived from "foreign" languages and substituting either defunct Turkish words or neologisms based on original Turkish.) The unity of culture thus involved replacing living aspects of the language of social life with more "authentic" national terms. This was one step in the development of a common societal identity—they called it "sentiment"—that would unify the Turks. Kemalism thus expressed a judgment that existing culture must be changed according to attitudes, values, "sentiments, and ideas" promoted by an unrivaled party according to its "unified" vision of society and Turkish national culture.

Kemalism also clearly promoted the principle of the unquestioned leader— a singular creative, unparalleled, flawless and responsible national savior. Kemal described his role in terms of rule "on behalf" of the nation, but he alone was the maker and arbiter of all important decisions, author of all party programs, and judge of all character. He demeaned all those who questioned his form of rule, cleansed the political arena of all dissenters, stirred the nation to revenge attacks on it by internal and external enemies, and vowed to make the Turkish nation rise above all others. The implications for Turkish society of this intentional leadership style were quite profound. Kemal would forever occupy an unchallenged leadership role in political, social, sentimental, and cultural life.

Kemal cultivated his status as great leader, and he did so with extremely deft use of the nationalist mobilization discourse. For example, he maintained that attacks on him were attacks on the collective and needed to be interpreted as threats to society and culture, not just to the state (whether they were or were not). We noted earlier that he believed that his enemies had erred in believing they could destroy the state by killing him. He thus made the implicit link between his own person and the state. "It is obvious that the secret political maneuvering was directed against the being of the nation rather than my person" (*SD* 4: 1926, 574). He also used the politics of assassination both to reinforce the elements of social solidarity in solidaristic corporatism and to convey the supremacy of the collective national identity and what he called its "manly qualities": "The event of assassination that occurred as the last manifestation of those attempts has been cause for grief not because of its relation to *our humble person,* but in that it displays a reactionary mentality that has so regressed as to even conceiving of using as an instrument of attack such a position of high prestige, like the highest representative of the nation—a mentality that is not becoming of the manly qualities of the Turkish nation" (*SD* 4: 1926, 574, emphasis added). The text of this statement indicates that a member of the Assembly then rose to express an opinion that Kemal no doubt wanted to hear:

> Refik Bey (of Konya): Those misers are not the Turkish nation, the great genius.
> Tunalı Hilmi Bey (from Zonguldak): *Not only Turkdom,* but even hell won't admit them! (*SD* 1: 1926, 345, emphasis added)

Both Kemal and the party consciously used his charismatic status not only to achieve all of the Kemalist solidarist and corporatist goals, but also to stress the supreme status of the national grouping—Turkdom and its corresponding identitarian basis, Turkishness—over all individuals, including Kemal.

Insight into Kemal's conception of the means for carrying out the nation's progress may be found further in his view of life itself. In *Nutuk,* he revealed his profound commitment to the militant application of "power and might" in achieving the nation's "spiritual and material" goals. Life itself is a "struggle and battle": "Gentlemen, you know that life means struggle and battle. Success in life is possible only through absolute success and struggle. And this is a matter that depends on power and might, spiritually and materially" (Atatürk 1962, 434). Kemal's theory of power and life is that the Turkish nation has been and will once again be out in front of the struggle. Everything in history comes "from within the waves of this struggle." Indeed, it makes sense that Kemal would describe activity in terms of struggle, for his entire discourse is permeated with the ever-present threat of the anti-Kemalist Other. "Reactionaries," "fools," and "traitors" lurk everywhere. Similarly, because he said that the nation must work hard, he reinforced the idea that it was already hardly working. From Kemal's perspective, the Turk was engaged in an ever-present struggle against the existing milieu (identity, culture, practice) and against the ever-present "bad shepherds" in society who would lead the nation astray. It was thus necessary for the nation to "move," "advance," and even "surpass" itself. The nation's "power and might" must be exerted to overcome the struggle against its existing character.

ON MILITARY AND YOUTH

We place the two watchdog groups military and youth together because of the joint importance Kemal assigned to them. As we saw in chapter 7, his statements on the military and the youth evince remarkable parallels. He pursued a plan to create loyal children and loyal soldiers as well as loyal children who were loyal soldiers. Kemal's goal was the regimentation of society, or, more specifically, of the minds, behavior, and character of the youth. He viewed the military through which nearly all Turkish males would pass as a primary socialization milieu, and he entrusted the country and its safety to both of them as Turkey's true guardians. He thus legitimized their vanguard role within society and over the state. By designating the military as the nation's guardian, Kemal made it the superior group responsible for the welfare of society and the state. The implication is that Parliament or even existing political parties are lesser institutions. They seem, in Kemalist discourse, to be less deserving of respect as arenas representative of society's highest goals.

Kemal's views of the youth expressed in the 1935 party program show this remarkable continuity between raising "citizens" and raising soldiers. The program speaks of the virtue of "tight discipline, which is the singular instrument of [national] success" in the same contexts as "the most superior duty to protect the homeland." It also speaks of "nourishing their [the youth's] enthusiasm and health," while at the same time mentioning the development of "a clean morality, a sublime love of the fatherland, and the transformation":

The Turkish youth shall be tied to a national organization, which shall assemble it around a clean morality, a sublime love of the fatherland and the transformation. To the whole Turkish Youth physical training shall be given. That would nourish their enthusiasm and health, their belief in their person and their nation; and the youth shall be brought up with a mentality that make the youth prepared to consider as the most superior duty to protect the homeland with all due maturity and to give up all their being for the sake of this duty.

So that this training yields results, on the one hand, the high potential of success of the Turkish nation shall be developed such as thinking, decision making, and taking initiative, and, on the other hand, the youth shall be made to work under the influence of tight discipline, which is the singular instrument of success in the achievement of all difficult tasks. (RPP 1935, Section 5, Paragraph 50)

Kemalism views the education of the youth in schools as education for the Kemalist project (see the discussion of laicism in chapter 5). The schools are to repel "foreign" and "superstitious" ideas while training students in nationalist values and positivist methods (Kaplan 1999). Kemalism expresses the judgment that societal and national mobilization requires the cultivation of a militant alertness among the youth and military to defend the nation and state and society from all threats.

ON STATE-SOCIETY RELATIONS

Kemal thus viewed the different parts of society as vehicles for the realization of the Kemalist project. His views of the youth, education, and even the press indicated that they were to be reared by the state and ultimately existed to serve the interests of the state. We have quoted in previous discussion some of Kemal's dismissals of press criticisms. He praised the freedom of press as long as it operated within Kemalists limits, for the Kemalist party was responsible for its existence. "It is certain that the press of the republican period, which is imbued with its own mentality and *morality, is brought up only by the Republic itself*" (*SD* 1: 1925b, 339, emphasis added). The press had to be responsible to the republic, avoid being distracted by "bandits" (*SD* 1: 1925b, 339), and help facilitate the new life of the great and noble nation. In other words, the press needed to express the values and beliefs of the Kemalist republic, not those of foreign or harmful ideas.

The heart of the message is that there is no other legitimate "ism," no other welcome reference point or set of political standards, than Kemalism.

The various arenas of society are crucial for the exercise of power because they are the "heart" and the "body" to Kemal's brain. They comprise that single national grouping that, as he put it in his speech in Eskişehir that we cited previously, "sees the right path as it always has," especially against "those who want to lead it astray." "In this, the peasant, the worker, and especially our heroic army are all heartily united. Let no one doubt this" (*SD* 2: 1929a, 254). From the Kemalist standpoint, society is not simply constituted by its corporate groups: it has a single identity as well. Kemal and party documents referred to it as possessing a "singular, independent identity," not "identities." This is an undivided "Turkish social whole," "with its old and sublime history and its works, which maintain their presence in the depth of its lands" (RPP 1931, Section 2, Article 1, Paragraph B; Section 1, Article 1). It is undivided in the sense that it is a "singular" entity. "Though it marches alongside modern nations and in harmony with them on the path toward progress and development and in its international contacts and relations, the Party finds it essential to reserve the special characters of *the Turkish social whole and its singular, independent identity*" (RPP 1931, Section 1, Article 1, emphasis added). This singular entity lives in its "sacred" "fatherland": the whole "fatherland is the homeland with the political boundaries of today in which the Turkish nation lives" (RPP 1931, Section 1, Article 1). It is a "sacred homeland" (RPP 1935, Section 1, Article 1). Kemalism judges that society and its constituent parts should reflect and perpetuate all aspects of the Kemalist vision as a singular unit. They must be the organs of a nation that thinks, feels, defends, and expresses Kemal's nationalist vision.

Kemal's earliest views of the organization of power in the new Turkish Republic reinforce this vision. Ideally, he claims, power should flow from bottom to top, but this is the new Turkey, and, "in the beginning," the process should be reversed:

Today all nations of the world recognize only one sovereignty: national sovereignty. Were we to look at the other details of the organization, [it will be seen that] we are starting from the village and the neighborhood, from the people of the neighborhood, that is, from the individual. If individuals are not thinking, masses can be moved by anybody in any direction, good or evil. In order to save himself, each individual should personally attend his own destiny. Such a formation that rises from bottom to top, from the foundation to the roof, would certainly be sound. [*But*] *there is no doubt that at the beginning of everything, it is necessary that it be from top to bottom, rather than from bottom to top.* (*SD* 2, 1920: 11–12, emphasis added)

Society is the vehicle; the state—"the top"—is the governing mechanism. The state stands above the nation and all of its affairs. Although only the statist arrow of Kemalism's six arrows explicitly invokes the role of the state in the transformation, Kemalism's other ideological expressions thoroughly assign to the state the role of implementing the goals of the transformation in all spheres of sociopolitical life, including culture and conscience. Kemalism confers upon the state a "special character" in what Kemal called "the machine of political existence." The state is the manifestation of national sovereignty (and thus of Kemal and the RPP's power). The state, then, is the great nation's great unifier; it is the great creator of the same "nature, culture, and aspiration" in all elements. Its role is to direct, unify, harmonize, and administer the life of the nation. Moreover, it unites the various elements within it in repelling those who wish to divide it ("lead it astray"). To the end of unity, order is necessary, and so the state's laws, codes, and acts stress order and tranquility incessantly. As such, Turkey is clearly a solidaristic corporatist state, but Kemal's own discourse, backgrounded by the set of judgments described here, takes it slightly beyond solidarism into fascism as well, at least at the ideological level.

ON THE STATE

It is important to be clear that although fascistic and totalitarian ideological tendencies do not dominate all aspects of Kemalist discourse, they are present and were active in the past such that fascistic movements could form themselves within and out of Kemalism. Ali Fuat Başgil, one of the leading party ideologues and the holder of the chairs of public law at both Istanbul University and the prestigious Faculty of Political Science before it moved to Ankara in 1935, advocated the classical definition of the fascist state. He argued for extending etatism to all spheres of social, cultural, economic, and political life:

Etatism is the system that regulated from above the economic, social, and even moral life and activity and directs these toward a national ideal; that organizes [the nation] with a view to establishing social justice in economic life; that aims to embrace within the comprehensive vision and orderly activity of the state all national forces, activities, and capabilities, especially the economic ones. Everything within the state, nothing against the state, nothing outside of the state. Here is today's formula of etatism. (1935, 3)

Kemalism did not, in practice, reach anything like what Başgil was describing. Still, it did evince several propensities in that direction, both in ideological and practical terms, which indeed have had long-term consequences *ideologically* in the Turkish Republic.[1]

Kemalism's solidaristic identity is most clearly expressed by its determination to create a conception of the people without class conflict-that is, to organize society in harmoniously functioning occupational groups. We have documented this commitment extensively in previous chapters. Kemalism's solidaristic corporatist achievements were precisely those achievements that, in the party's official discourse, made the regime and its ideology an exemplar to the world (see RPP 1943a, Part 1, Section D). In the Kemalist frame, the role of the state, however, extends beyond economic affairs of the world. The state is also the director of other transformation affairs and as such the chief unifier. The theme of unification pervades every sociopolitical dimension of Kemalist discourse. Government is based on "principle of unity of powers" (RPP 1931, Section 1, Article 3; RPP 1935, Section 1, Article 3). Rights and liberties cannot threaten that unity: "The interest of individual and legal entities shall not be contrary to the public interest. Laws shall be enacted according to this principle" (RPP 1935, Section 1, Article 4, Paragraph A). "The Fatherland is a whole that does not accept any division under any constraint" (RPP 1931, Section 1, Article 1); "The Nation is a political and social whole that is formed by citizens who are connected with one another by the unity of language, culture, and ideal" (RPP 1931, Section 1, Article 2). Society is composed of occupational groups forming a "general body social": "Be it in the West or in the East, the internal organization of a state will certainly be unsound and frail if it combines conflicting elements

1. Our focus here is on ideology. For practical manifestations, see certain aspects of the 1935 labor code, the penal code, the 1937 Physical Education Act, the 1938 Associations Law, the 1938 Press Union Law, the 1938 Lawyers' Act, and the 1943 act concerning the reorganization of the Chambers of Industry, Commerce, and Artisanry.

that possess very different natures, cultures, and aspirations" (Atatürk 1962, 435). The inclusion of "aspirations" is indicative of Kemal's intent to deny multiplicity politically, to form and generate singularity and homogeneity, as he launched Turkey in the direction of his arrows. Identities would be shaped and molded according to the new unity. The state was conceived as the assemblage of laws, codes, and other mechanisms of enforcement to create the order necessary to achieve these high, civilized, modern ends.

Kemal described the mutually reinforcing relationship between the state and society in a speech given to the Assembly in 1937. Discussing the state's role in the realm of "physical education," he said that physical education should serve more than the general health of the person so educated. It should serve the purposes of the state as well. While describing the great works of the nation and the role of the Ministry of Health in integrating society, he stated:

> The health and strength of the Turkish citizen, to whom transformation and transformism have given various and vital duties, is our national matter, which will be always dwelt upon carefully . . .
>
> I find it worthy of commendation that the ministry is working with very good grasp of the principle, "Healthy and robust offspring is Turkey's brood stock." (*SD* 1: 1937a, 393)[2]

The health of the citizenry is tied to the citizens' "vital duties" in the Kemalist transformationist project, the nation, and so on. Later in the same speech, reflecting on the role of the state, Kemal also described his regulative guiding outlook on administration.

> I should also remind you on this occasion that, in the machine of political existence that gives a nation independent identity and value, the mechanisms of the state, the idea, and economic life are so interrelated and so interdependent with and on one another that if these apparatuses are not operated in full harmony and in reciprocal accord, the motive force of the government machine will have been wasted, and the full yield expected of it cannot be realized.

2. Kemal then expressed his "total" vision about economy and its elements: "Now friends, I will review our economic life. I should immediately inform you that, I, when economic life is mentioned, I consider activities of agriculture, commerce, industry, and all public works as a totality that it would be incorrect to be thought of as separate from one another."

And it is for this reason that the level of culture of a nation is measured in three fields, with the end product of the results of their activities and successes in the three fields of the state, the idea, and the economy. (*SD* 1: 1937a, 393)

Kemal stressed the interrelated responsibilities of the affairs of the state as that organ that "gives a nation independent identity and value." Its various objectives should be organized harmoniously, without wasted energy. In that way, the state is like a machine and politics a mechanistic process in the "fields of the state, the idea, and the economy." We know what it should produce: the integrated powers of the monoparty regime, Kemalist nationalism, prosperity, and development. Kemal conceptualized politics as a method for achieving those ends and the fulfillment of the Kemalist dream, no more, no less. The state should be operated like a machine in order to change "the level of culture." Kemal was, of course, drawing attention to what he considered his own successes. The year was 1937, and he had established himself as the machine's grand operator. The mechanistic analogy implicitly called on all to continue to act in unity and unison.

The speech also contains parts of a quote we analyzed earlier. After saying that "our Party's principles have become the principles of the state," he said that the sole standard for existence should be the "fatherland," the "nation," and "inferences" (by and for the nation) from "the history of nations." He emphasized that the RPP's guidelines were not to be found in books; they were to be derived "entirely" and "directly" from life—meaning the life of the Turkish nation, "from whose bosom we have emerged."

> The principles in this [party program] are the major guidelines that illuminate us in administration and in politics. But one should not ever equate these principles with the dogmas of the books that are thought to be descended from heaven. We have received our inspirations not from heavens or from any voids but entirely, directly from life.
>
> What shapes our path is the fatherland in which we live, the Turkish nation from whose bosom we emerged, and the inferences we have made from the leaves of the history of nations that record one thousand and one agonies. (*SD* 1: 1937a, 405)

An organic nation, whose offspring "we" are, "shapes our path." The speech continues with Kemal congratulating servants of the whole nation, but note what he said here: the principles of the nation—his principles, really—are better guides than anything written anywhere. The fatherland is our guide for life and action, and the nation is its essential source.

EVALUATION

The Kemalist movement created one chief, one nation (society, people), one state, and one party to secure together the high public interest of the singularly conceptualized, unified nation. Kemalist "political ideology" (the Kemalists' term) legitimated this vision in the consciences of the members of the Turkish nation, especially the preferred special groups such as the youth and military. This ideology envisioned a concentrated power structure to direct conflict-free sociopolitical and cultural change. The power structure was considered, by necessity, hierarchical and closed, with all administrative, political, legal, and military institutions under the direction of the charismatic leader.

From that early period on, Kemalism's nationalist ideological discourse has viewed the members of the nation—the individuals who comprise it—as means to the ends of national economic development. There is no emphasis in the ideology on the intrinsic worth of the individual, a tendency consistent with solidaristic corporatism in general. It is the "effort and work" of the individual that matter, not the individual as such: "A nation, a social collectivity, cannot take even a single step with the effort and work of an individual" (*SD* 2: 1925a, 224). Kemalism, in its partial leaning toward fascistic nationalism, further devalues the individual by constantly reinforcing and glorifying the nation as the single and superior identity for all inhabitants of the "fatherland." The nation's existence depends on constant vigilance, discipline, and training of children and soldiers to fulfill their heroic and vital duties in maintaining the state from all omnipresent dangers:

> There is no doubt that the highest measure of these joys shall be felt with the most profound sensitivity by the Turkish nation. Because the Turkish nation loves and appreciates every beautiful thing, every civilized thing, every sublime thing. But it is absolutely certain that, if there is anything it worships above all, that is heroism. These words of mine shall no doubt produce high and effective echoes in the ears of today's vigilant Turkish youth. I demand nothing less from

Turkish children in whose sublime qualities I place significance. (*SD* 3: 1931, 91–92)

If there had been any accompanying emphasis on the autonomous status of the individual as such, these statements would not have the fascistic tendencies that they do. However, the sole identification of members of the nation as its heroic children makes those who comprise the nation simply the means to its goals. Individual selfhood is irrelevant and inadequate as a building block of the new national life.

Early Kemalism feared the potential disorder created by the spontaneous articulation of vastly different interests. It directed this fear most explicitly against what it viewed as class-divisive politics. But its determination to shape and constrain every member of the nation with beliefs, values, hopes, aims, and aspirations of the nation above all others—in its word, to create "virtues"—constituted a quest to conquer the human conscience and placed enormous constraints on individuality itself, not only on obvious forms of individual political expression and association. The demand for unity and desire to homogenize culture in terms of an overarching, vitalist nationalist identity effectively derogated the status of all other identities. Individual assertion was seen as an inferior form of political expression relative to expression that voiced Kemalism's general interests. The nation must be glorified. Its power is always to be found in the blood that runs through the veins of the youth ("Message to the Youth").

The guiding administrative idea was that all important aspects and processes of life should be shaped from the top. Embedded therein was the presupposition that only one true self existed for the nation and that self should be shaped by the only real knower, Kemal. When Kemal elevated the nation to the status of the single standard against which all should be judged, he inevitably lowered other standards, be they individual conscience or other collectively generated ideals.

In the practical context of Turkish political culture, the consequences of this lowering have been severe. Trust in Kemal's ego or in those who claim to follow his footsteps has displaced any trust individuals may have in themselves and in others. The single self of the nation reinforced by the single great self of the incomparable leader thus eliminates the requisite bases for egalitarian human relationships. It generates a search beyond "the ordinary," which is, as such, deemed inadequate for those elite who endeavor to best embody the honored national characteristics. As a further, explicitly political consequence, various deeply entrenched inequalities perpetuate themselves—not only economic inequality, but also what Rousseau termed "moral inequality," the kind of inequality in modern human societies that is based, on the one hand, on the excessive honor and respect given to some of their members and, on the other, on the resulting self-diminution felt by those who see themselves as lacking the qualities that make such honor and respect possible. Moral inequality occurs when the authorities are held in more esteem than one holds oneself and, vice versa, when the authorities hold others in less esteem than they hold themselves. In political terms, the psychological tendencies here reproduce the implied hierarchies, and thus inequality sustains itself within the internalized senses of self and value of a given society as much as through institutionalized forms of political and economic power. Rousseau defined the features of moral inequality this way: "different privileges enjoyed by some at the expense of others, such as being richer, more honored, more powerful than they, or even causing themselves to be obeyed by them" (1992, 16).

Kemal created ideological structures of political and moral inequality in Turkey. He expressed an undaunted belief in his own omnipotence, exhibited excessive self-righteousness, and placed his ego both in and above all things "national." He alone claimed to possess the cognitive and psychological tools necessary for creative and original action. He declared individual initiatives and associations formed by others to be unimportant and disempowered them with accusations of disloyalty and deception. Because his agency alone was important, he effectively displaced the powers of others—that is, he both excluded them and claimed to have embodied them in his own person.

Such displacement is not empowerment. Empowerment stems from being given power collectively by the consent of others. Empowerment is part of a democratic pattern that requires egalitarian respect for the input of others and a willingness to institutionalize inclusive and dynamic arrangements of power and authority. Kemal's displacement stemmed from claiming power, taking it as his own from others. For this maneuver to qualify as tutelary democratic, it must be accompanied by some democratic intent, and in Kemal's case such intent is not to be found. He intensified traditionalist moral inequalities by creating them anew in nationalist terms, and he enshrined the notion that all members of the nation, however great they were or were to be, stood below the eternal chief. Absent is the humility of reluctant charismatic leaders interested in democratic evolvement. Present is the hubris of those who seek to be permanently powerful at the expense of others' powers. Among these others, some will be held in esteem, the rest will be responsible to provide that esteem. Those judged highest, those held in most esteem, will (and must) command; the others will and must obey. Moral inequality thus structures thoroughgoing political inequality—that is, inequality in terms of power and agency. Kemalism provided no room for the autonomous development of standards different from its own nationalist ones, and it pre-emptively excluded political relations among equals. This is a fascistic corporatist tendency that, when coupled with the closure of political space itself, borders on the aspect of totalitarian regimes that aims to control the total life of a society through depoliticization.

Without autonomous space for individual and social norm development, without the rule of commonly generated laws, without respectful pluralist foundations, without contestation, without civic competition, without debate and discussion, and without procedures to reconcile differences among citizens, Kemalism impoverished and constrained rather than accelerated democratic political life in Turkey. It demanded energetic assertion and vitalistic action in support and defense of the nation's goals, but it denied the legitimacy of other sources for action and prevented their expression politically. The Assembly, for example, was not the place for debate about the people's business. It was the tool for the business of the RPP, creating a rootless parliamentarianism from the beginning, not a democratic one. The existence of a parliament alone is insufficient to denote democratic beginnings. For democracy, norms and procedures necessary to articulating the will of the politically active must be set in place. Despite a rhetoric of reason—"It is our first principle to act with reason, logic, intelligence. All the events that fill our life are proofs of this truth" (*SD* 5: 1925b, 210)—Kemalism early on closed itself off to rational challenges by considering all alternatives to be wayward. Despite a rhetoric of progress, it offered a narrowing, parochializing vision of corporatist economic and technological growth. Its own method even betrayed the reason of science, which demands self-criticism as part of the search for knowledge. Kemalism maintained its own truths dogmatically. It leaned in the direction of political rightism because it desired cultural homogenization, irrational exaltation of the national will, social organification, depoliticization, militarization, and the use of all apparatuses of the state for the conquest of conscience and belief. Despite its discourse of enlightenment, it shut down the bases of enlightenment by eliminating cultural critique and exchange.

Kemal himself was not unfamiliar with either autocracy or fascism. They were part of the Third Way "practices" in the developing and southern European domain. Indirect evidence of Kemal's—and Kemalism's—reconciliation with rightisms of his day can be seen in some of his recorded correspondence with several other noteworthy representatives of such currents in his time. In 1923, for example, he communicated "affectionate" "feelings of friendship" to the emperor of Ethiopia, whose rule he considered a "good omen" for the future of "the noble Ethiopians." The text reads as coming from one chief to another, one good shepherd to another, not from a serious modernizing revolutionary:

> August Sovereign [Hazretler]!
> In having itself represented in the ceremony of the enthronement of the Imperial Sovereign, the Government of the Republic [of Turkey] has wished to proffer distinct evidence of the feelings of friendship that the new Turkey has for your noble country. The Government of the Republic and I are following with affectionate interest the progress that the Ethiopian nation has succeeded in carrying out in a relatively short period thanks to the knowing and luminous administration of the Emperor, His Eminence. The brilliant onset of the dynastic rule of his Emperor the Eminence and the special abilities of his nation constitute a good omen for the realization of a near future that shall make the noble Ethiopians attain their ideals. (SD 6: 1932b, 244–45)

Similarly, after a high-level diplomatic meeting in Italy that İsmet İnönü had attended, Kemal wrote to the king of Italy in 1932, extending "feelings of sincere friendship," "wish[ing] happiness to his Majesty" and "prosperity for the great friendly country." He expressed sincere affinity for a "great friendly country." This is not simply diplomatic gobbledygook; it is what might be called true friendly fascism. In a telegram to Mussolini on the same date and occasion, Kemal wrote: "I am convinced that this visit and the hospitality shown by the great and noble Italian nation and our great friend the high and honorable Ducé will help further solidify the strong and sincere bonds of friendship that tie the two countries to each other" (SD 6: 1932c, 392).[3]

He wrote to many others, including the king of Sweden (in French), to

---

3. Several years earlier Kemal had written a warm note to Mussolini on the occasion of receiving Mussolini's sons as boy scouts in Turkey: "Mr. Mussolini Hazretleri Chief [Reis] of the Italian Government, The Turkish youth feels delighted in receiving the elite youth of Italy, amongst

whom he asserted that "the indelible stamps of the victories that have been achieved by the Swedish and Turkish nations are imprinted on history" (*SD* 2: 1934b, 278). The shah of Iran, who visited Turkey and emulated some of Kemalism's features, he called "Our great friend and my dear brother, the exalted chief of the brotherly Iranians" and to him conveyed a message of "a high will in civilizing, creating nations, [and] peace between the two remarkable nations" (*SD* 2: 1934a, 276–77). Finally, to Josef Stalin he wrote: "When in the coming hundred years the reputation and glory of all other dictators will have faded, history shall select Stalin in the Europe of the Twentieth Century and in the international field and among his contemporaries as a most important statesman [*devlet adamı*]" (*SD* 6: 1937, 267).

One may certainly interpret these communiques as part of realpolitik. But the implication, then, is that Kemal registered little revolutionary reservations about precisely those things at which he supposedly took aim with his six arrows: global monarchy and autocracy. In this regard, he is much less an exemplar than he is a representative of the norm in interwar relations of the global state system.

In assigning selective rightist traits to Kemalism, or even in classifying it as a solidaristic corporatist ideology, our analysis will surely encounter the charge of ethnocentrism, of imposing concepts from outside the context in order to make sense of and to criticize Kemalism. Our goal throughout, however, has been to bring out the central concepts of Kemalism. Along the way, we have identified the ideology's various conceptual innovations (e.g., laicism, transformationism), all of which are part of the original conceptual frame. Any fundamental reinterpretive effort requires that some terms external to the subject matter be used to capture dynamics present in it. Given the cross-cultural and transhistorical sociological background of Kemalism, including its roots in European corporatist and positivist traditions, we think—and show through the Kemalist documents— that concepts drawn from the ideological vocabulary of these traditions more compellingly capture the identity of crucial components of Kemalist discourse than do those concepts drawn from Europe's other traditions at the time, such as *liberalism, secularism,* or *democracy.* From the perspective of this study, the latter terms evince more imposition than the terms we have employed.

The anglophone interpretive milieu within which this study exists is compli-

---

whom are present your sons. Your esteemed excellency, I affirm my heartfelt respects to you" (*SD* 6: 1928, 388).

cated by the fact that many of Kemalism's self-representations—as modern, secular, revolutionary, and so on—clearly play off the ethnocentric sensibilities of many Westerners and confirm that Kemalism, in the eyes of its representatives today, has reproduced the West's own cherished enlightenment ideals. Whether or not the ideological or practical reality matches these principles often becomes another matter entirely. The account we offer here suggests that there are points of contact between Kemalism and the West, but that they involve Kemalism's rightist and reactionary currents, not its democratic and progressive ones. In this light, our analysis has been an attempt to correct for ethnocentrism and problematic self-representation by clarifying the category mistakes in the all-too-charitable equating of Kemalism and democracy. This untoward ethnocentrism underlies the West's granting to Kemalism the status of a democratizing ideology and its consequent acceptance of Kemalism's internal ideological totalization and institutional violence.

9

CONSEQUENCES AND PROSPECTS

Those who are studying the general situation of the world, the ideational new currents produced by the century and events, and with what skillful steps these [events] are marching toward the targets to which they are directed see clearly that it is definitely to their own detriment to object to Turkey's immediately attaining a state, order, and tranquillity. (*SD* 2: 1923n, 49–50)

All the measures we have taken can be summarized in one sentence: We declared our national sovereignty. Let us not play on words. Today's Turkish government is more or less [*az çok*] a Republic. This is our right, where is the badness in this? (*SD* 3: 1923b, 69)

In a short time we have accomplished much and great deeds. The greatest of these deeds is the Republic of Turkey whose foundation is Turkish heroism and the high Turkish culture. (*SD* 2: 1933, 275)

A country in ruins on the brink of the abyss . . . bloody skirmishes with all kinds of enemies . . . years of war . . . and then the new fatherland, the new society, the new state (applause) and in order to achieve these, uninterrupted transformations that are recognized with respect from within and abroad . . . here is a short expression of the Turkish general transformation . . . (*SD* 1: 1935, 380, ellipses in original)

The great services that the People's Party performed for the country can be examined in two respects: (1) the works done by the Grand National Assemblies formed by the elections that were guided by the Party and its governments, (2) the new principles, frames of thought, and concepts, in one word the political ideology. (RPP 1943b, Section 1, Paragraph 2)

The main principles in this program are the expressions of the path of "Kemalism" to which the party is always loyal. This path requires taking inspiration from the realities of the country and relying on the principles of freedom, unity, order, and progress. (RPP 1947, Introduction)

As we have suggested throughout this work, perhaps the most politically important element of contemporary Kemalism is the commonly held belief, created by its adherents, that Kemalism and democracy go hand in hand. Versions of this thesis differ. Some argue that the constitutive but unrealized intention of Kemalism was democratic or democratizing, others that Kemalism may be interpreted to support democracy or democratization. As we noted earlier, these views have been offered in both Turkish and English milieus since the founding of the Turkish Republic. They have appeared in various forms and contexts, for various thematic and political purposes. When, for example, Western political discourses expressed worry over the spread of atheistic communism or radical nationalism, Kemalism was understood as an exemplar of modern liberal and patriotic nationalism. Since the revolution in Iran in 1979, Kemalism has been the secular, modern, and democratic alternative to religious fundamentalism. Such views legitimize contemporary Kemalist ideological, institutional, and political cultural hegemony in Turkey, but they are, in our view, at odds with the original constitutive corporatist identity of Kemalist ideas and practices that inhibit democratization in classically rightist fashion. One may see the association between Kemalism and democracy promoted explicitly or implicitly in most political, social, and cultural milieus in Turkey today.

We are careful not to draw unwarranted conclusions from random observations, but the extent of the association in Turkey today between Kemal, Kemalism, and democracy is noteworthy from the perspective of ideological analysis. Political cultural expressions inside Turkey serve as indicators of popular political beliefs and values. Since the middle 1990s, it has been common, for example, to see various forms of the tutelary democratic thesis represented in public life in Turkey. One form, witnessed in the mid-1990s when the Kemalist establishment confronted challenges to its authority from Turkish-Islamist and Kurdish nationalist movements, was the proliferation of signs and symbols stressing the link between Mustafa Kemal, the republic, and democracy. In one rally in Istanbul, for example, crowds gathered and waved plastic flags picturing Kemal and reading, "We cherish the republic and democracy." Knowingly or not, they reproduced the core of the tutelary democratic thesis proffered by Kemalism and most of its interpreters throughout the history of the republic. The basic idea contained therein is that Atatürk originated, supported, and encouraged the development of democratic life in Turkey. This is the thrust of the tutelary democratic thesis.

Several category mistakes are at work in the association between Atatürk, republicanism, and democracy. For one, notwithstanding the seemingly constant and energetic efforts at constitutional and legal reform—many in the context of Turkey's application to become a member of the European Union—existing electoral, party, and parliamentary politics in Turkey today are not entirely democratic.[1] But the flaw in the conceptual association between Kemal, the Kemalist republic, and democracy most relevant to this work is the implied democratic theoretical accreditation given to Kemalism (and hence to Kemal) as the originator of whatever "democratic principles" do exist in Turkey. Indeed, the conceptual association between original Kemalism and democracy cultivates the national outlook that Kemal hoped to foster: the source and standards of national history and progress are to be found in the life of the *Kemalist national* experience. It produces the effect that Turkey had historically arrived with Kemalism, if not exactly at the end of history, certainly at the beginning of the end, and it conceals the constraints that Kemalism's ideological identity placed on democratic political development in Turkey. That is, the popular and scholarly conceptual association between Kemalism and democracy fails to illuminate the antidemocratic, solidaristic, and partly fascistic, corporatist tendencies of Kemalism, tendencies whose perpetual influence over political beliefs and values in Turkey have inhibited the development of social and political relations of egalitarian respect and liberty. It is certainly incumbent on us to concede rudimentary democratizing tendencies as they exist in Kemalism (e.g., popular sovereignty), but it is time for the promoters of Kemalism to concede its antidemocratic limitations so as to initiate deeper considerations about political-ideological and political-cultural necessities for a more democratic future. Our primary aim here is to summarize our case in systematic political-theoretical terms—democracy, solidarism, fascism, corporatism, and so on—to marshal a bit more evidence in that regard and to offer some final thoughts on democratic possibilities in Turkey.

1. For extensive analysis of the limits of these reforms, see Parla 2001.

RECAPITULATION OF INTERPRETIVE FINDINGS

Throughout this work, our interpretation has been governed by what might be called norms of interpretive charitability and restraint. Our criticisms of Kemalism have followed our earnest attempt to provide an account of what its primary expressions have articulated as its core political visions and concerns. We have built our critique on the basis of what we think to be the best—in the sense of most charitable—account of Kemalism's own explicit and implicit core ideological frame. In fact, it was because of our critical, democratic attitude toward Kemalism that we felt it was necessary to rebuild that framework and thus to have our criticism informed and restrained by it. Too much critical scholarly inquiry is inadequate in this regard. We have endeavored to develop our critique in conversation, if you will, with the central statements of Kemalism's central ideational viewpoints.

To this end, we have translated and reproduced a great deal of documentation. In order both to grasp and to criticize the ideational content of Kemalism, we allowed those who articulated it to speak in their own words. We sought to go beyond those aspects of their legacy that are reproduced as pithy maxims and messages in the common production of Kemalist hegemony. Folk and orthodox academic understandings of Kemalism occlude much of its political-ideological meaning, including its own self-conception as an ideology. It was important, therefore, to inquire further into its conceptual web in order to bring out its broader theoretical meanings and to begin to understand its lasting political effects in Turkey. This web evinces a particular outlook about society, economy, culture, and politics that cannot be garnered through casual observation of popular messages. Indeed, a new understanding of even the popular maxims and messages emerges once one looks beyond them into the larger framework in which they took shape and from which they have been extracted.

The reproduction of more original material here also reflects our sense of the need to present extensive evidence to counter the orthodox association of Kemalism and democracy. We believe that our account, although analytically exploratory and critical in its method, adds little either to the essential ideological thrust of the documents or to the intent within them. Those places where we identify a purpose in Kemal's utterances that is absent from his precise words, we try to locate that purpose within the conceptual meanings available more explicitly. Kemal was careful, for example, never to say that the nation's will was essentially his will for the nation, but his discourse on the "national secret"—which he held in his "conscience"—his rejection of the ideas of most compatriots, and so on, we think, suggest that he saw himself as singularly capable of and responsible for defining the nation's primary objectives. Hence, his will became the nation's will in the official ideology and his status that of the unchallengeable leader that it remains today. Where it was necessary to read unstated intentions into Kemalism, we have supported our decision to do so by establishing the relevant patterns in the materials.

Our interpretation is no doubt heavily shaped by our democratic political and political-theoretical concerns, but we have not simply looked for antidemocratic tendencies over other tendencies. We have approached our subject matter first and foremost with the concerns of political-ideological analysis, trying to bring out the central ideological terms of Kemalism and to conceptualize their precise ideological status. The process involves a give-and-take with the texts, and although democratic concerns have shaped our analytical energies, they have not been our only concerns. Our primary concern has been to provide the most accurate account of the evidence—that is, to explain the identity of Kemalism in as precise terms available in the repertoire of political theory. These terms, including solidaristic corporatism, laicism, and transformationism, go beyond many of the conventional terms of contemporary political discussion and debate, but they are the terms one must take seriously in order to understand Kemalism's core outlook. Some of them are indeed Kemalism's own terms. Our concern for democracy, therefore, is a primary, but not an exclusive concern, and we readily admit that other interpreters with other guiding questions will, no doubt, produce other interpretations. We believe that the ideological thrust of Kemalism is to frustrate democratic sensibilities radically and that this thrust is evident in its most honored documents, despite the professed commitment to building democracy that they contain.

In sum, ours is neither a mere retrospective reconstruction nor only a democratic political-theoretical critique. It is, rather, a three-level analysis that aims to provide (1) an account of the Kemalist ideology and its internal conceptual dynamics; (2) an account of the terms within political-ideological analysis that capture the central aims, presuppositions, and interests of that ideology; and (3) a critique of the tutelary democratic thesis both in Kemalism and in the arena of scholarly and popular interpretation of Kemalism. We have raised Kemalism's constitutive concepts to the foreground, analyzed them within the Kemalist frame, and considered their relation to democratic possibilities. Kemal's nonideological, pragmatic reputation notwithstanding, much was said by Kemal and the party that was in fact precisely intended to indicate a particular sense of what he and the party were "doing"; these words and the deeds shaped by them have had a lasting impact in Turkish society and politics. Our final thoughts here, then, are not simply a cynical rejection of what has been. Rather, they are an attempt to draw out the implications of Kemalism's embedded political judgments and to clarify in precise theoretical terms the ways in which they frustrate, rather than support, democratic practice and thought in Turkey. Some simplified summary of our account is in order. Here, we present both the terms of the received opinion regarding Kemalism's tutelary status (in subheadings) and a review of our case to the contrary. The summary of our case includes estimations of Kemalism's core values and its legacies in the context of democratic political practice, both in Turkey and in general.

Democratic Populism

Within Kemalism's own conceptual frame, its commitment to "populism" translates into a commitment to "democracy": "Our form of government is entirely democratic government. And in our language this government is called 'People's Government' " (*SD* 3: 1922a, 51). Kemalism's populism, though, was originally intended only to establish the new regime's popular sovereignty credentials, both internally and externally, not its democratic ones. Commitments to democracy and democratization throughout Kemalist discourse are not pervasive; more pervasive is a conscious postponement of democracy and, in that context, a rejection of democratic foundations. At its best, then, Kemalism sets itself to create "conditions for requirements" of democracy (*SD* 1: 1935, 380–83) without being democratic, but its antidemocratic practices and central views of leadership, society, and politics are hardly conducive to fulfilling even that more limited goal. Kemalist discourse contains very low estimations of the capacities of Turkey's residents to govern themselves ("until the day that the desirable result is yielded"—that is, until the citizen is "equipped with the qualities, prerequisites, and instruments with which he can recognize those whom he is going to elect" (RPP 1931, Section 1, Article 4). Although the single-party regime claimed to represent "the people," it did not trust the people's definition of its own interests, a trait somewhat antithetical to ideals of democratic populism. It exploited the symbolic terms of populist democracy in order to pursue antidemocratic politics—what it admits in its own frame are populist without necessarily being popular politics.

Kemalist populism thus distinguishes itself primarily as a guardian elite populism that also, consistent with solidaristic corporatism, denies class relations and individuals as the defining elements of the people. In this sense, it denies to all within society the rights to define society differently, including in terms, according to liberal and Marxian frameworks, conducive toward more pluralist and egalitarian politics. Kemalism reinforces its guardian elite populism with a charismatic hero, who disempowered "the people" by claiming all powers to himself, even at the expense of the other politically engaged persons at the time. The people's will was subordinated to the will of the monoleader, monoparty state, which claimed to be acting on behalf of the people (the "People's Party").

Was Kemalism, in its founding, appropriate to the time and conditions? Strong and persuasive arguments exist for many possible answers to this question. Those who believe that it was not appropriate point to the previous history of parliamentary and electoral experiments and to the existence of more democratic political thought in the ideologies of the time. It seems that alternatives to corporatism were possible, but they were shut out. How Turkey would have proceeded without Kemalism is very difficult to say.

Secularism

Kemalism is committed not to secularism, but rather to a partial and limited laicism insofar as it supports the official establishment and interpretation of the religious tradition of the majority of the population. Relative to past Ottoman practices, Kemalist laicism reduces the range of official support for religion, demoting Islam's role within specific spheres of governance and culture. But it also consciously expresses a commitment to a purified Islam as part of the hegemonic ideology, and it secures this form of Islam institutionally so as to cultivate a nationalist-Muslim conscience in the nation's members, whose "worldly" focus should be on national scientific and economic development. Rather than securing full freedom of conscience, therefore, Kemalist laicism accommodates Islam to the purposes of its transformation, even as it considers these developments to be part of its enlightened construction and "guiding" of new ideals (see *SD* 1: 1922a). "Enlightenment" refers to the scientific rationality embedded in the laicist program, but, again, this rationality never stands independent from the nationalizing project itself. Some further elaboration of the details on these sensitive matters seems useful.

In a strongly anticlerical fashion in the single-party period, Kemalism harshly denounced and repressed anti-Kemalist religiopolitical associations and interests. It also greatly reduced the role of Islam in politics (by abolishing the caliphate, banning parties and associations based on religion, instituting a new civil code, eliminating extensive reference to religious symbols and ideas in policies, and so on), but it did not entirely eliminate the role of Islam in official political ideology and practice. To the contrary, it offered its own interpretation of Islam and promulgated it in its own institutional framework, including in certain educational spheres. In place of Ottoman legitimacy symbols, the Kemalists offered a modern, nationalized version of pristine Islam, combining it with the virtues of the "noble" and "sublime," Central Asian, Turkish national "culture." This identity was formulated by Atatürk himself in his synthesis of aspects of contemporary Western civilization, the local assets of primordial Turkish national culture, and puritan Islam as interpreted by himself and the Kemalist Directorate of Religious Affairs.

Therefore, unlike other secular ideologies, whether they be neutral to or critical of religion, Kemalism did not fundamentally criticize or challenge religious norms in public or social policy, nor did it seriously question the role of God in personal or social morality. Indeed, the policy was a laicist "respect for religion." One of Kemal's most famous mottoes to this day is that "laicism does not mean not having a religion." No official or semiofficial academic Kemalist work during the single-party period questioned the central premises of religion or theism. Kemalism promoted Islam as a social morality system that, along with nationalism, also functioned to provide the social cement to bind the "nation" together. The emphasis on and mixture of the two dimensions would fluctuate historically, according to condition and circumstance. Kemal himself set this pattern, first constituting the independence struggle in religious terms and, before that, praising Islam greatly. Then he deemphasized it, while rejecting an association between Kemalism and "irreligious atheism" and securing a formal state structure for the management and governance of religion.

The alleged secularism of the ideology is further attenuated as a result of its commitment to creating "nationalist citizens." Its positivist scientistic proclamations notwithstanding, Kemalism aimed to socialize and indoctrinate an ideologically homogenous population so that it would be unwilling to question the fundamental premises of the regime and incapable of acting politically for anything but the vigilant defense of Kemalism's "sacred" goals. This legacy of original Kemalism persists in official governance today. The 1981 Law of Higher Education requires that university students be "imbued with a consciousness of service in loyalty to Atatürk's nationalism in the direction of Atatürk's reforms and principles" (Article 5, stipulating the "purposes of higher education"). Similarly, Article 42 of the 1982 Constitution, on education, states that "instruction and training are conducted under the supervision and control of the state, according to contemporary principles of science and education, in the direction of Atatürk's principles and reforms. No educational and instructional institutions contrary to these foundations may be opened." The deification of the Great Leader is crucial here; the articles show Kemalism's commitment to infusing the individual conscience and public life with its version of true Turkish nationalism. Kemalism, in short, was not committed to the principle that individuals should be free to examine, explore, choose, and cultivate the content of their own ethicopolitical principles. The hegemonic ideology began with an interest in infiltrating conscience, and the situation has not altered since the earliest days of the republic.[2] Indeed, Kemalism is not only a partial laicism; it is an obstacle to political and cultural secularization in this regard.

Revolutionism

The Kemalists explicitly distinguished their project from *revolution* as the term was used and understood in the interwar period. Revolution (*ihtilâl*) had negative connotations, connected to the Bolshevik and internationalist enemies of profit, property, religion, and the nation-state. Transformation (*inkılâp*) was the Kemalist term of preference, including Mustafa Kemal's, because *revolution* connoted forms of radical challenges to existing socioeconomic hierarchies and cultural priorities, different from the forms of change to which the RPP or Kemal were committed. Kemalism's revolutionary reputation is owing largely to the impression created by its republicanism (elimination of empire), its so-called secularism

2. To be sure, some Kemalists have modified their commitment to Islam in secularist ways, but only a very small number of them. Their departure from the pillars of Islam, moreover, does not logically follow from their Kemalism.

(with its abolition of the caliphate and Islamic legality), and its "Westerniza-tion/modernization" policies (e.g., sartorial, script, and calendar changes). From the perspective of liberal and Marxian accounts of revolution with which Kemalism has been identified, the Kemalist movement was nonrevolutionary or even counterrevolutionary. It committed itself neither to expanding the range of political liberty nor to fundamentally altering social and economic hierarchies. It did not seek to transform relations of power in egalitarian directions. It did not institutionalize mechanisms of regime change and leadership accountability. It did not frame its quest in terms of justice. Its primary goal was to elevate the "moral" and material status of the nation.

Socialist Statism

The statist arrow of Kemalism is one that has been taken as evidence of its so-cialist revolutionary politics. This view is especially common in Turkey among some Kemalist leftist circles—a designation that, from the perspective of the current study, is an oxymoron.[3] Kemalism's statist arrow, however, was consti-tuted by a commitment not to socialism, but to corporatist capitalism. According to Kemalism, there are no class inequalities of political relevance. Sometimes Kemal even maintained that in Turkey there were no classes. Moreover, in the transformation period, the state engaged in capital accumulation, investment, and reinvestment and offered support to a state-linked "entrepreneurial" class for the purposes of development, prosperity, riches, and happiness of the nation. This class enjoyed privileges and protections that were rationalized in the nation-developing discourse of "the high and general interests": the state was to be "en-gaged actively in those affairs—especially in the economic field—that are necessitated by the general and high interests" (RPP 1931, Section 2, Article 1, Paragraph Ç). This is not socialism or radical anti-imperialism. It is corporatism.

3. On Kemalism's association with "leftism" in Turkey, see Aksoy 1990 and Soysal 1984. Throughout the history of the republic, from the Kadro movement of the 1930s through the rev-olutionists of the 1960s to today's "left" groups, a "national left"—not a national-socialist left—has formed around Kemalist corporatism. An important representative today is Mümtaz Soysal, a member of the Constitutional Commission for the 1961 Constitution.

Antiabsolutism

The idea of antiabsolutism is central in the Kemalist conception of republicanism. Kemalism equated the replacement of the Ottoman Empire with the elimination of absolutism. It was part of the Kemalists' notion that, because of their movement, all that was old and bad had been relegated to the dustbin of history and all that was new and good had arrived. The "antiabsolutist" notion strategically occludes and legitimizes as populist Kemal's charismatic absolutism and his RPP's own absolute, closed grasp on power in the new republic. Thus, the idea that Kemalism eliminated absolutism is one of the most successful myths perpetuated by the hegemonic discourse, a myth that obviously feeds the popularity of the tutelary democratic interpretation.

Westernism

The West inspired some of the Kemalist project, but from a political-ideological standpoint it was neither the modern liberal nor the social democratic West that the Kemalists found very compelling. Kemalism did not, for example, initiate a strong parliamentary tradition characteristic of the liberal West. Its West was the nationalist, solidaristic corporatist West. Kemalism adopted, modified, and contributed to Third Way tendencies, and it brought along those cultural-structural (calendar, measurements, etc.) and cultural-stylistic changes it deemed desirable to ease economic, technological, and sociocultural integration with the capitalist West. But these were not the only "cultural" dimensions of the Kemalist project. Its interest in national and cultural homogenization in language, sentiment, and idea must be kept in view as well, as must the impact of the charismatic, amalgamate forms of pseudo-Western and Ottoman patrimonial authority adopted by Kemal. These preeminent features of Kemalism make it a very strong "Western" corporatist ideology with additional rightist tendencies, but distance it from the terms of the dominant Western ideological traditions of democratic modernity (from liberalism to Marxism to various forms of anticolonial and anti-imperial traditions informed by liberal, socialist, or other democratic ideals). The promotion of Kemalism as a model for other so-called developing countries amounts to the promotion of a right-wing ideology counter to democratization.

Modernism

In its development, Kemalism reinforced modernist bureaucratic and institutional commitments rhetorically, but it also extensively blurred lines of administration and obliterated social sphere boundaries in political culture. It sought to dominate all institutional spheres of authority and to constitute them according to its needs—from the political sphere through the educational, legal, and popular-culture spheres. The military became, for example, the military-civilian-educational-nationalist institution; the "free" press was to be "reared by the Republic," and so on. Kemalism legitimated the state's infiltration and domination of social and cultural spheres, while simultaneously restricting access to the decision-making arena. To this day, all legal organs reflect Kemalist solidaristic corporatist interests by design. These are not the institutional traits of modern differentiated governance carefully administered by a professional class engaged in their specific spheres of competence. The perceived need to mold society and to eliminate harmful currents enables the state to consider all within its rightful domain. Kemalism's intent to dominate all institutional space goes hand in hand with its interest in dominating all spheres of conscience and public morality and philosophy. It has from its inception sought to dominate political and ethical realms by creating persons and associations loyal to it and to it alone. This approach is neither modern nor rational because it is not careful about setting limits or distinctions, or about creating spaces for the consideration of alternatives. Kemalism considers all sociocultural space ultimately its own. It is thus undifferentiated at the level of culture just as it is undifferentiated at the level of institutional development.

"Reasonable," "Ethical," and "Egalitarian" Nationalism

Nationalist discourses are conducive to egalitarian ends only if they cultivate and inspire equal respect, both for all members of the nation and for other nations. This kind of respect may be based on various grounds, perhaps on assumptions of a universally shared and common rationality, perhaps on a common humanity for all sentient creatures. Whatever the terms, Kemalism fails to cultivate such respect: its nationalism implies internal hierarchies between members of the nation (the "top" and the "bottom"), and it offers an ambiguous, shifting depiction of hierarchical relations between the Turkish nation and other nations.

Kemalism's view of the nation was no doubt originally shaped in part by its solidaristic mobilization goals in the context of bringing the residents of the remaining Ottoman territories into a common nation-state project. But the ideological dimensions and consequences of Kemalism's formulation of the terms for this project must be considered as well. It asserts the need to lift people's confidences and energies so that they will make the nation great again. It therefore creates new standards that all should aspire to meet. These standards, however, were constructed by the few for the many and, in the context of the "domestic" conception of the nation, with little regard for the many. In its eyes, the RPP leadership knew better than others what must be done and how to do it. Thus, internally it created enduring hierarchies between the chiefs and subchiefs, on the one hand, and all leaders and the rest of the nation, on the other. It also laid the foundations for a structure of moral inequality by setting up processes through which one could be more equal than others in terms of honor, heroism, and esteem in the eyes of the nation, party, leader, and state.

Furthermore, vis-à-vis other nations Kemalism offers a mixed discourse of equality and superiority wherein the Turkish nation is depicted as the progenitor of all humanity. It invokes various ethnonational and racialist concepts to cultivate the expectation for a new Turkish greatness to thrive internationally, one that will enable Turkey to surpass all other civilized nations. In this way, the nation and its destiny became, in Kemalist Turkey, the dominant, if not the sole, reference point. There is little sense within Kemalism of a common humanity in which all nations participate or, more specifically, in which the Turkish nation participates equally with other collectivities. This absence compares starkly with the ideas of the previous Turkish national thinker, Ziya Gökalp, who, even as a corporatist, envisioned "civilization" as a shared sphere in which all nations participate in a common whole, much like different chapters compose a story in a book. Absent any emphasis on nation-to-nation egalitarian harmony, Kemalism's emphasis on the superiority of the Turkish nation vis-à-vis other nations takes on even greater significance. When questions regarding relations between nations arose in the transformation period, they were answered entirely from within the Turkish national frame. "This country belongs to the Turks"; "we are the masters"; and so on. In this discourse, racist and racialist Turkish nationalist tendencies were not sufficiently constrained. Domestic ideological homogenization policies lifted the nation without providing an egalitarian relational consciousness of enduring value vis-à-vis other nations. In general, little in

Kemalism stresses a universal or cosmopolitan outlook toward other collectivities or toward national differences as such.

Kemalism's homogenizing tendencies make it, to some extent, antirational. It demands that people not think about some things so that they fix their eyes and hearts squarely on a single goal. Turks should feel themselves to be part of the whole, they should feel that they have arrived at the most magnanimous point in the collective's history, that they are renovating the glorious potential of "Turkdom." This nationalist discourse was originally propagated to create a bond between the leader and the state, on the one hand, and loyal "citizens" on the other. It diminished, however, the relevance of the self and critical thinking just as it neglected the relevance of others. It thereby impoverished life in the nation for the members of the nation, even as it secured a certain form of solidarity. Depicting this sense of solidarity as the highest and most noble, Kemalism constrains examination of the political bases for this solidarity, its substantive limits, and its manipulated and manipulatable character.

Enlightened, Benevolent Leadership

Kemal self-consciously postured himself as an enlightened and benevolent leader. He and his followers depicted his unparalleled greatness. The entire leadership project amounted to promoting and sustaining Kemal's deified status as the "good shepherd." "I advised the people that they should not be deceived by the words of their bad shepherds" (*SD* 3: 1923a, 71). Considering his rule enlightened and benevolent, however, depends on assenting to his and the RPP's ideological goals. For whom and to whom was he "benevolent?" The idea of Kemal as enlightened also suggests commitments to the rational faculties and deliberative potentials of others, commitments that we have been hard pressed to find. Kemal's legacy is neither enlightened rule nor benevolence. It is, we think, more properly tagged as charismatic and autocratic selfishness. His rule was extremely personalistic. He claimed to have made all significant decisions, excluded others from making those decisions, and demanded that all answer to him. As chief, he infused himself unnecessarily and arbitrarily into everything, placed himself beyond rebuke and reproach, and sewed the seeds for his own personality cult by incessantly describing his bond with the "nation" as founder in terms of love, affection, and care.

Kemal thus cultivated atavism in Turkish political culture in several senses.

The term *atavism* invokes the idea of the reappearance of the ancestor. Contemporary social scientists use this term to describe the apparent contemporary resurgence of ethnonational and other so-called primordial ideas. The term loosely refers to a person or group of peoples who are throwbacks or reversions to a previous time.

Atatürk wanted those who loved him to believe that he was fully and energetically disposed to reviving the greatness of the Turkish nation on their behalf. He wanted them to understand that all his efforts were for them, just as a father's are for his sons and daughters, and that *he wanted them to be his sons and daughters*. He was successful in many ways in this regard. He certainly did not want them to think of themselves as equal to him. Nor did he want them to think of themselves as being dominated by him. He wanted them to follow him, to think what he thought, and to do so willingly. He wanted them to believe that he was good for them, a benevolent, loving and unselfish leader who did everything he could for them. In fact, he wanted them both to see his greatness and to understand his unselfishness so as not to find his greatness offensive. He wanted to be extraordinary in their minds without being insulting to them.

These were the strategic goals of the great charismatic leader, who, when he was not haranguing the nation with his congratulatory discourse, was castigating, demeaning, dismissing, and eliminating its voices and sentiments in politics and culture. The atavistic attachment to the great Ata—an attachment still felt profoundly and deeply in Turkish political life today—served Kemal's immediate goals of securing his and the RPP's sole grasp on power. It also had the effect of displacing power by creating the belief that Kemal (or, more generally, One Person alone) was responsible for all that was good, including the nation's very survival. Furthermore, it created what might be termed a politics of deferential reverence. Subsequent generations of leaders and "citizens" have viewed Kemal's way and model as the sole, single standard for legitimate political action and greatness. This phenomenon is not independent of Kemal's selfishness. Kemal consciously created and placed himself in a very irrational dynamic of love and hate, loyalty and treason, support and opposition, and then he replaced himself with republic, nation, and state so that the same dynamic existed between the people and Kemalism's (his) creations. The nation was to be "his great nation."

In analytical terms, this approach is totalizing, charismatic demagoguery and autocratic selfishness, not enlightened benevolence. And it has had the lasting effect of exaggerating the role of personality—especially Atatürk's—in leadership, while simultaneously undervaluing other personalities as well as the very institutions that are ostensibly those of "the people." Charismatic intentions aside, Kemal put his person into everything (his face is still nearly everywhere, in portrait, above the cash register, or behind and in front of the heads of every public official), thus denying alternative bases for a politics of enlightenment and benevolence.

The matter is actually quite simple: Kemal demanded deferential reverence from his followers. He cultivated their love and loyalty charismatically, and he sharply distinguished loyalty to him, which would be rewarded, from loyalty to traitorous forces, which would be punished. In this process, he demonstrated an inability to respect others and an unwillingness to share power or credit, even with those whose love and adoration he cultivated. Loyalty to Kemal was thus accompanied by a fundamental lack of respect for others and a weakened capacity among the "people" to respect themselves, collectively and individually, as possible sources of power. It almost goes without saying that the more people revere the One Leader, the less they fully—or even sufficiently, from the perspective of democratic possibilities—respect themselves. Kemal built this relationship, and the Kemalist state has perpetuated it through the various legal and institutional means designed to preserve and perpetuate Kemalism's hegemony. Kemal's offspring have assumed their role in the atavistic authority relations by making it their highest duty to preserve his legacy.

One final note on this point. Kemal's glorification of the military and his legitimation of violence and means of coercion—the implementation of "the initiatives that I gave the decision to undertake" should be "thorough and violent" (Atatürk 1960, 30)—have enabled the love/hate dynamic to take very coercive forms in the history of the republic. Embodying the ideals of their great Ata, many have exerted themselves coercively and violently not only out of loyalty to the republic, but also out of loyalty to Ata himself and to all that he stood for in the life of the nation.

Nonideological Pragmatism

To our minds and from the perspective of ideological analysis, pragmatism is not a very relevant evaluative category for Kemalism. A pragmatic disposition requires that one engage in gathering, evaluating, and reevaluating ideas in the context of changing experience in the world. Pragmatic decision making follows from thinking carefully not only about the so-called objective conditions and scenarios of political choice and action, but also about how the various people affected by those choices and actions may understand them. It requires taking the full pulse of a situation so that action within it conforms to what is known within that situation. Thus, the pragmatist's *ideas* must also evolve and grow in light of the circumstances of action and choice. Kemalism, however, posits clear and fixed ideological and ideational goals on the basis of which all action should be undertaken. Its commitment to problem solving without a rich engagement with worldly ideas is more an anti-intellectual component of its general mobilizational discursive strategy than a well-considered pragmatic doctrine. Kemal wanted people to become Kemalists, not pragmatists, which would mean subscribing to corporatism, not pragmatism. Kemal's statements made to the effect that actions are more important than ideas should be considered more *ideological pragmatism* than nonideological because the content of the ideas upon which he was acting were derived from Kemalism's central truths. He referred to these truths as the truths of civilization and the terms of the national secret, the content of which only he knew or could know. Kemal was dogmatic in a way that no committed philosophical pragmatist could be.

Kemal emphasized an apparent nonideological stance in part to occlude engagement with his own and his regime's ideological commitments. Kemalism is, however, the "ideology of the country's cause" (*SD* 1: 1937a, 402–3). As an alternative category to pragmatism, we suggest a "regulative and administrative" dogmatism: a combination of mechanical implementation and technical reason that seeks to order and arrange things according to a particular and exclusive vision of the right and good. Kemalism wants to regulate life, not simply to respond to it; it wants to shape thought, not simply guide it.

Originator of Turkish Humanism

Lacking any statement of the universal value of or respect for all nations and their members, Kemalism does not evince much humanism. Rather than the originator of Turkish humanism, it has been, especially against the political theoretical background of many available international humanist ideologies, more the originator and anchor for deeply Turkish-centric nationalism. Kemalism stands for the exaltation of Turkish culture, singularly defined, not for humanism, which asserts profound support for the equal worth and respect of all human be-ings. Indeed, Kemalism evinces little respect for the person as such or for collec-tivities formed by individuals. In this respect, it is Durkheimian, not Kantian, in its core. It views individuals as components of occupational groups, whose activ-ities are functional to the benefit of the whole, not as beings with intrinsic value deserving equal respect.

Originator of Turkish Rationalism and the Turkish Enlightenment

Kemalism's rhetorical support for reason as the standard of judgment in thought and action conflicts with its dogmatic absolutism regarding its truth and right-ness; and its profound commitment to administrative and technical rationality re-flects its social-engineering aims. That is, Kemalism narrows "enlightenment" to complement its interest in social engineering and the kind of national economic development that result from it. Otherwise, Kemalism is a highly enthusiastic nation-, land-, culture-, and leader-deifying ideology that promotes an unques-tioning reverence for sacred dogmas. Its leader's emotive enthusiasm and antire-flective practices of classifying, labeling, and rejecting those who disagree must also figure prominently in this estimation. As an ideologue, Kemal was quick to judge and draw conclusions from very limited evidence. Neither he nor his doc-trines demonstrated an interest in careful distinctions or a striving for terms of precise classification in relation to the evidence at hand. Reasoning by evidence and reflection about alternatives are virtually absent in the Great Leader's public speeches and statements. His *Great Speech* was intended to close the book on the history of the national struggle and the characters of the persons who took part in it by "enlightening" the nation to the only true perspective—but not to en-courage or support active research and further inquiry.

Kemalism's rationalist professions function in part to shield it from criticism as an irrational system, one that demands credulity, the suspension of rational ar-gumentation, and the abandonment of reasoned judgment. How can an ideology that professes to be guided by reason declare Kemalism to be the only valid "ism" and reject all other "isms" as "foreign and harmful"? Where is the encourage-ment of inquiry and speculation outside the realm of the nation-enhancing pos-itivist project? Thoroughly closed to questioning, Kemalism as a political ideology enshrines itself as the only legitimate idea for Turkey. Its primary goals in the domain of reason are technological progress and social engineering, goals essential to spur national economic development. Besides that, with its high doses of emotive nationalism, it retards the development of other critical and progressive traditions of rationality in Turkey.

The result of the hegemonic conquest of Turkey by Kemalism was a new, rigid, and stagnant tradition of sacred maxims in the Turkish political-cultural context. Kemalism's traditionalist characteristics are in need of further study. Suffice it to say here that it has created among its most loyal believers an attitude of blind and reactive attachment unencumbered by rational reconsideration.

Progressive in All Ways

Kemalism paints itself as a progressive ideology. "We shall go forward . . . [to-ward] the ideal of the most advanced and prosperous Turkey" (*SD* 1: 1937a, 401–2). "Advance" here draws attention to the new form of government insti-tuted by the Kemalists: "The present form of our state has become the most pro-gressive form that has eliminated the old forms that have persisted for centuries" (*SD* 2: 1925b, 236–37). But the progress achieved by the Kemalists must be eval-uated against other standards. Our standard in this analysis has been democracy, and in this sense, we suggest, Kemalism falls well short of significant political progress. Material progress—becoming "rich, prosperous, and happy" (*SD* 1: 1923a, 308)—may be an element of political progress, but it alone does not make Kemalism progressive, especially when inegalitarian political foundations are consciously reproduced and intensified. Selected cultural openings for the pur-poses of external economic and cultural integration do not amount to either po-litical or cultural progress. This is especially the case given the cult of hero love, the repressive and regressive constraints on politics, the narrowing of identity, and so on. In this regard, Kemalism often exploits progressive terminology ("be-coming modern," for example) to overstate its achievements. In the transforma-tion period, its primary progressive aims were those related to material and economic developmentalism, for which scientific and technological advance-ment was deemed necessary. Modern advancement entailed making the country prosperous. The Turk is "proud, confident, and industrious." "The future chil-dren of the republic shall be much more prosperous and happier than ourselves" (*SD* 1: 1923b, 326). On its own, this is a form of progress, but not in democratic terms—or in terms of the host of labels used to describe Kemalism by most ob-servers (*liberal, secular, radically modern,* etc.).

Orientation Toward Change

Kemalist corporatism gives precedence to stability in order to achieve its (not very) "progressive" aims of material development. Its discourse is pervaded by the need to create conditions of "tranquility and order," to find the "safe and secure path" in order to establish unfettered conditions for the transformation to proceed uninterrupted. "Condemned to be damned are those efforts directed at violating the social order of the nation" (*SD* 2: 1929a, 253). Its highest priorities are an ordered politics, an ordered legal system, an ordered socialization process, an ordered culture, and well-ordered consciences to produce and reproduce its essential political hegemony. Kemalism thus constructs barriers to creating and sustaining the dynamism essential to social and political progress in both institutional and human personal terms. It merely cultivates the perception that progress has been achieved. Because it obscures problems within itself by demanding full compliance and loyalty, it stifles possible additional changes according to alternative viewpoints.

Cure for Problems

Nor is Kemalism, as many of the most powerful sectors in Turkey believe today, a cure for present problems of nondemocratic practice. Rather, as the hegemonic ideology, it is more a contributing cause for present problems: the enduring political problems of entrenched hierarchies; toleration of authoritarian rule; reverence for militarism in society and education; racialist nationalism; arrogance of power; lack of open and effective political and participatory structures; a deferential, weakened, and disempowered political body; and persistent forms of moral and political inequality. More Kemalism is not going to rectify these problems because it is part of the political-cultural mix that enables them and allows them to endure.

A Permanent Guide for Action

Kemalism must therefore be abandoned as a permanent guide for political discourse and action. Perhaps aspects of its authoritarianism may be said to have been essential to initiating republican governance, but, *if* this is the case, it over-reached when it need not have. Whatever progressive goals it did achieve, it failed to initiate democratization or even fully republican structures of governance, for it shut down and shut out the people. Much of the responsibility for this must be placed with Kemal and other contemporaneous Kemalist ideologues. Their political practice set the pattern for antipolitical authoritarian control over a highly constrained public sphere permeated by the well connected and the military, and defined by highly constrained, often harsh, antireflective discourses and practices. Kemal himself engaged in a coercive politics of indictment, rejection, distaste, and removal. He set absolutely no example for future democrats to follow. He dismissed others' positions sometimes because they were simply the others' positions: "Let no one think otherwise." In this regard, Atatürk set unscrupulous expectations for thinking about the character of political life. Politics itself was to be understood as a mechanical and thoroughgoing implementation of the wills and exclusive plans of the powerful. Is this the path of future democrats or of future authoritarians?

Tutelary Democratic

The ideological building blocks for Kemalism were thus hardly tutelary democratic. The embedded ideological understandings of the Kemalist frame conditioned antidemocratic policies, attitudes, and values. Extremely slight insinuations of democratic, populist, and secularizing commitments and a postponement of democracy to the future under the deified rulership of a Great Father do not constitute the foundations for democracy. Kemalism's building blocks have made possible continued antidemocratic tutelage by a strata of chiefs and subchiefs empowered and emboldened to rule the nation absolutely and, when they deem necessary with the aid of the youth, harshly. In this way, Kemalism constitutes a dead end for Turkey in terms of its democratic possibilities, for reasons related both to Mustafa Kemal's direct impact and to the enduring rightist character of the Kemalist state and its kind of (anti-)politics. As a leader, Kemal fortified rather than undercut the inegalitarian and patrimonial tendencies within the culture of politics, and, as an ideology, Kemalism imposed constraints on the various forms of deliberative self-reflection, self-criticism, and regard for others that are necessary to democracy.

To Be Catechized with Reverence or Seen as a Dead End

These constraints appear in the static, reified character of the hegemonic ideology, and nothing has been done within established political discourses across the political spectrum in Turkey to analyze them. No attempts have been made to update, modify, or critically deconstruct or reconstruct Kemalism. It is taken and hailed again and again as the true and complete standard for modern governance. In this way, its static and constraining effects are constantly reproduced intact for each new generation.

The effects on the organization of power today are also profound. They include a persisting, strong central administrative statism (in some cases, in the form of a police-state statism); a strong military *and* civilian militarism; and hostility toward democratic, pluralistic, syndicalist, and class-based politics. Forms of political participation considered outside the bounds of appropriate corporatist politics are banned, both in the legal codes and in state policies. These forms include, for example, labor politics such as collective bargaining or organized trade union activities that do not comply with Kemalist corporatism's restrictions. They also include politics concerning national identity. Steps formally taken to address concerns of ethnonational heterogeneity are half-hearted and still unresolved owing to conflicting legal and penal measures that reinforce the insistent national homogeneity of Kemalist Turkish nationalism. This very strong nationalism, what we have described as its second face, continues to manifest itself as a hegemonic and effective sociocultural force. In this context, the ongoing personality cult of the Great Leader plays an important role, with the powerful Kemalist groups inside and outside the state forever recycling the basic ingredients of Kemalist identity and conscience under the watchful eyes of the eternal chief. The entire mix remains detrimental to democratic and progressive personality development.

As stressed earlier, the Kemalist state does not constitute the initial stages of the Turkish enlightenment. Those who maintain this view hope to link Kemalism to the European traditions of enlightenment, but they fail to observe (or to acknowledge) Kemalism's rejection of the West's dominant emancipatory traditions—liberalism and socialism. Indeed, in its development, Kemalism adamantly opposed both traditions and set in place a resistance to ongoing creative engagement with other emancipatory traditions that have evolved globally since the 1930s. Its West was the corporatist West, the postliberal, antiliberal, and antidemocratic West. For this reason, we maintain that Kemalism has always been an impediment to Turkish intellectual enlightenment and democratic politics. In suggesting that Kemalism has failed to embrace liberalism or socialism, we do not mean to suggest that these traditions should have been naïvely copied in the Turkish context. Our primary goal is to contest the idea that Kemalism did just that, a view extremely dominant among its observers. It is too imprecise for the interpreters of Kemalism to see it as having "argued that the cure for the ills of the Orient was the medicine of the West" (Sayyid 1997, 69) or to posit that Kemal "propelled the Turkish nation from halfhearted into wholehearted Westernization" (Rustow 1984, 351) or "infused [the Turkish people] with a belief in the values of Western democracy" (Kinross 1964, 504). We have tried to show in this book that thinking of Kemalism as Turkey's enlightenment mistakes Kemalism's historical identity and impact. Kemalism is therefore not to be catechized with reverence. It must be questioned, understood, and transcended.

PROSPECTS FOR DEMOCRACY

We acknowledge some difficulties in our interpretation of Kemalism as an ideology of mainly solidaristic and partly fascistic corporatism. For example, Kemalism is solidaristic, but it exhibits highly fractional dimensions as well. In the political realm, Kemal's castigating style stimulated a series of deep fractures within Turkish political culture. At times, solidarity was hardly his or the RPP's main objective. Indeed, the rhetoric was heavily solidaristic only in the realm of sociopolitical and economic relations. Kemalist solidarism required a heavier dosage of sincere humanism in order to cultivate its harmonious objectives throughout society. Its authoritarian aspects—the legitimate violence, the fascistic labor codes forbidding unions and strikes, the assaults on conscience and culture with its contested and particular vision of a Turkish nation—make whatever harmonies it achieved coerced, not even "free" in a solidaristic sense. So, one might argue, the sincere intention for solidarity is not there; in fact, solidarity is conditional on one's assent to hegemonic concerns. Indeed, we welcome further research on these matters.

In the end, what perhaps coheres the Kemalist ideological frame most is its infallible position on "the truth." Quite simply, it knows the truth, and others do not. From the Kemalist perspective, there is one true way, and then there is deviation. On one (their) side is logic, reason, rectitude, soundness, sincerity, legitimacy, safety, and the general interest. On the other side (or all other sides), there is deception, falsity, foolishness, ignorance, harm, danger, and division. On their side is truth; on the others, obscurantism and conniving. On their side, enlightenment; on the others, reactionarism, superstition, and threats of all kinds. Their leader is the savior of the nation and the carrier of the truth. His responsibility is unmatched, his path is right. He is the learner and finder of the nation's inclinations and needs. Critics are ignoramuses who seek to lead the nation astray.

As a final example, consider the subtext of the following Kemalist document from 1943 in which the party rejected alternative conceptions of sociopolitical change. In this case, the RPP stated that action had to be quick and anyone who suggested otherwise was wrong and dangerous:

> The idea that in social developments progressive advancements should definitely pass through certain stages and be related step by step in a gradual manner, is wrong. This wrong opinion is dangerous because it would also diminish the energy of those who are in the position of influencing social life. In matters that are necessary and compulsory in national life, it is a duty to destroy all kinds of obstacles that stand in the way of arriving at the target as soon as possible by taking advantage of all energies. (RPP 1943b, Section 1, Article 1, Paragraph F)

Kemalism has consistently represented its own views as nonmythological truths and declares alternative visions to be dangerous absurdities. In short, it lacks "fallibism," a sine qua non of democratic life. It has constantly produced the idea that there are no other reasonable ways than its own, generating a kind of righteous self-confidence that eliminates alternative possibilities. Kemalist self-confidence, in other words, confidently reassures itself with its truths. It does not propel a creative encounter with alternative ideas and novel approaches. In this way, it preempts the kind of open and alterable confidence necessary for modern democratic citizenship.

When trying to expose Kemalism's flaws and limitations from a democratic perspective, one must be prepared to confront its success in creating its own form of confidence. Its limits and shackles are not readily visible to the citizens and intellectuals of Turkey, where the hegemonic ideology remains in power, insinuating itself into the body politic in multifarious ways. The people often seem happy and secure as children of Atatürk, even as the politics of blame, threat, arrogance, stubbornness, exclusion, one-upmanship, and militarism pervade public relations. The fact that Kemalism has impoverished collective life is not yet sufficiently visible. In times of crisis, comfortable subchiefs, guardians, and true sons and daughters of the Kemalist order propose the model of their great Ata as the solution to persisting constitutional problems of power and accountability. But when the only escape is said to be the path of Kemal, what Kemalism lacks becomes starkly apparent. It offers no vision for a country that needs to find a way for all its citizens to live together as equals. It insists, always, on its own foundations, which themselves require its sustained hegemonic status. Kemal was consistent in leaving out of his discourse concerns for liberty, equality, and social justice. Turkey, he judged, needed a corporatist state and solidaristic society that could harmoniously integrate with the economically more developed world. An emphasis on political liberty and participation broadly conceived would surely threaten these goals. In fact, the absences in Kemalism derive logically from its core corporatist commitments. Under Kemalism, liberty and equality were (and are) not to flourish in Turkey and alternative conceptions of progress excluded.

During times of intense political competition in Turkey, Kemalist supporters sometimes gather under the auspices of political parties and politicians who still jockey for the position of the reigning subchief. Atatürk's face and logos adorn the settings at political rallies, from those of the solidarist "left" to those of the fascistic right.[4] At many of these rallies, the people hail Atatürk as the savior and great symbol of democracy in Turkey. Many of those waving the flags on which it is written "We cherish democracy and republicanism" hold the belief that by protecting the republic, they are protecting democracy. They believe that Kemalism provides the democratic *possibility*. Their expressions often suggest that they hold this belief with the certainty that Kemal wanted from those who loved him. As a result, they believe that they possess the truth and are on the correct path. They appear to see absolutely no tension between their hopes for democracy and the commitments they have absorbed as children of Atatürk.

Democracy in Turkey, however, requires that consciences and minds be set free in ways that Kemalism forbids. Democracy requires worldly attention and reflection—what might be called "worldly reason"—so that the construction of more equal, respectful, and humane relations may yet be attempted. It requires universalistic, egalitarian concepts and values, and, above all, openness to ques-

---

4. As evidence, consider the June 1999 coalition between the fascistic National Action Party and the "Democratic Left" Party.

tion and critique not only from without but also from within—that is, to autocritique, the basic rule of private and public enlightenment. In order to reach a more democratic society with fewer homogenizing and debilitating restrictions on public and political life as well as broader options, Turkey requires a *de*-Kemalization of both individual psychology and its overall political culture. De-Kemalization is distinct from anti-Kemalism: the former requires a self-conscious, reflective process of transcending the substance, effects, and concrete elements of Kemalist hegemony. It sees the effects of Kemalism as widespread and rejects the angry and resentful anti-Kemalist reaction that may reinscribe various injuries as a response to suffering Kemalism's condescension, if not insult. What may be called reactive anti-Kemalism fails to see that Kemalism has condescended not simply to certain portions of the political culture, but to the very people who have adopted it as their motto, who have subordinated themselves to its narrowing conceptions of reason, politics, society, nation, and popular rule. Kemalists and anti-Kemalists alike must become more critically self-aware of their common antidemocratic legacy.

This dilemma is, of course, not unique to Turkey. Many societies confront the same issue in differing degrees; all over the world there is much work to do if truly democratic futures are to emerge from what most think of as already democratic societies. The positive movement beyond the limitations of cherished antidemocratic doctrines and personalities requires a process of creative removal. In the Turkish context, it demands both the exposure of Kemalism's antidemocratic core and effects and the de-Kemalization of politics, society, and culture. The received opinion among nearly all interpreters and observers of the Turkish founding is of little help in this regard. It says that Kemalism was *and is* good and necessary. It repeats Kemalism's own mythology at the expense of an honest confrontation with and interrogation of its content and effects. We disagree with the received opinion. Kemalism was a mixed blessing, and its continuation is now a matter of choice.

WORKS CITED

INDEX

WORKS CITED

BOOKS AND ARTICLES

Abu-Rabi', Ibrahim M. 1996. *Intellectual Origins of Islamic Resurgence in the Modern Arab World.* Albany: State Univ. of New York Press.

Adıvar, Adnan. 1991. "Turkish Dictatorship: Position of Mustafa Kemal." Letter to *The Daily Telegraph,* 1928. Reprinted in *Atatürk'ün Büyük Söylevi Üzerine Belgeler,* compiled by Bilal N. Şimşir, 31–32. Ankara: Atatürk Kültür, Dil ve Tarih Yüksek Kurumu, Türk Tarih Kurumu Yayınları, 16:61.

Ahmad, Feroz. 1991. "Politics and Islam in Modern Turkey." *Middle East Studies* 27, no. 1: 3–21.

Aksoy, Muammer. 1990. *Atatürk ve Sosyal Demokrasi* (Atatürk and social democracy). Ankara: Gündoğan.

Altınay, Ayşe Gül, and Tanıl Bora. 2002. "Ordu, Militarizm ve Milliyetçilik" (Army, militarism, and nationalism). In *Milliyetçilik* (Militarism), edited by Tanıl Bora, 140–54. Istanbul: İletişim.

Arendt, Hannah. 1958. *Origins of Totalitarianism.* New York: Meridian Books.

———. 1986. "Communicative Power." In *Power,* edited by Steven Lukes, 59–74. New York: New York Univ. Press.

Atatürk, Mustafa Kemal. 1960. *1919–1920.* Vol. 1 of *Nutuk* (The great speech). Istanbul: Maarif Basımevi.

———. 1962. *1920–1927.* Vol. 2 of *Nutuk* (The great speech). Istanbul: Milli Eğitim Basımevi.

———. 1963. *Vesikalar* (Documents). Vol. 3 of *Nutuk* (The great speech). Istanbul: Milli Eğitim Basımevi.

Başgil, Ali Fuat. 1935. "Dördüncü Kurultay Münasebetiyle" (In connection with the Fourth Assembly). *Siyasal Bilgiler* 50: 3.

Bhargava, Rajeev, ed. 1998. *Secularism and Its Critics.* Delhi: Oxford Univ. Press.

Bianchi, Robert. 1984. *Interest Groups and Political Development in Turkey.* Princeton, N.J.: Princeton Univ. Press.

Bill, James A., and Robert Springborg. 2000. *Politics in the Middle East.* 5th ed. New York: Addison, Wesley, Longman.

Bocock, Robert. 1986. *Hegemony.* London: Ellis Horwood Limited.

Bora, Tanıl, ed. 2002. *Milliyetçilik* (Nationalism). Vol. 4 of the series *Modern Türkiye'de Siyasi Düşünce* (Political thought in modern Turkey). Istanbul: İletişim.

Bozkurt, Mahmut Esat. 1944a. *Atatürk İhtilâli.* Ankara: Kitaplar.

———. 1944b. "Türk Medenî Kanunu Nasıl Hazırlandı?" In *Medenî Kanunun XV. Yıldönümü,* edited by H. A. Yücel, 9–20. Istanbul: Kenan Matbaası.

Canovan, Margaret. 1987. "Republicanism." In *The Blackwell Encyclopedia of Political Thought,* edited by David Miller, 433–34. Cambridge: Blackwell.

Chadwick, Owen. 1975. *The Secularization of the European Mind in the Nineteenth Century.* Cambridge: Cambridge Univ. Press.

Comte, Auguste. 1975. *A General View of Positivism.* New York: Robert Speller and Sons.

Connolly, William E. 1999. *Why I Am Not a Secularist.* Minneapolis: Univ. of Minnesota Press.

Davison, Andrew. 1998. *Secularism and Revivalism in Turkey: A Hermeneutic Reconsideration.* New Haven, Conn.: Yale Univ. Press.

———. 2003. "Turkey, A 'Secular' State? The Challenge of Description." *South Atlantic Quarterly* 102, nos. 2–3: 333–50.

Dunn, John. 1969. *The Political Thought of John Locke.* Cambridge: Cambridge Univ. Press.

Durkheim, Emile. 1933. "Preface to the Second Edition." In *On the Division of Labor in Society,* 1–31. New York: Macmillan.

Esposito, John L. 2000. "Introduction: Islam and Secularism in the Twenty-first Century." In *Islam and Secularism in the Middle East,* edited by Azzam Tamimi and John Esposito, 1–12. New York: New York Univ. Press.

Gökalp, Ziya. 1959. *Turkish Nationalism and Western Civilization: Selected Essays of Ziya Gökalp.* New York: Columbia Univ. Press.

Goldie, Mark. 1983. "John Locke and Anglican Royalism." *Political Studies* 31, no. 1: 61–85.

Göle, Nilüfer. 1996. "Authoritarian Secularism and Islamist Politics: The Case of Turkey." In *Civil Society in the Middle East,* vol. 2, edited by A. R. Norton, 17–43. New York: E. J. Brill.

Gramsci, Antonio. 1990. *Selections from Political Writings, 1921–1926.* Minneapolis: Univ. of Minnesota Press.

Habermas, Jürgen. 1986. "Hannah Arendt's Communications Concept of Power." In *Power,* edited by Steven Lukes, 75–93. New York: New York Univ. Press.

Hakimiyeti Milliye. 1930. "Speech at Ödemiş by Mahmut Esat Bozkurt." September 19.

Heper, Metin. 2000. "The Ottoman Legacy and Turkish Politics." *Journal of International Affairs* 54, no. 1: 63–82.

Ingersoll, David E., Richard K. Matthews, and Andrew Davison. 2001. *The Philosophic Roots of Modern Ideology: Liberalism, Communism, Fascism, Islamism.* 3rd rev. ed. Englewood Cliffs, N.J.: Prentice Hall.

İnsel, Ahmed, ed. 2001. *Kemalizm* (Kemalism). Vol. 2 of the series *Modern Türkiye'de Siyasi Düşünce* (Political thought in modern Turkey). Istanbul: İletişim.

Jaeschke, Gothard. 1990. *Türkiye Kronolojisi (1938–1945)* (Chronology of Turkey [1938–1945]). Ankara: Türk Tarih Kurumu Basımevi.

Kaplan, İsmail. 1999. *Türkiye'de Milli Eğitim İdeolojisi* (The ideology of national education in Turkey and its implications for political socialization). Istanbul: İletişim Yayınları.

Karpat, Kemal H. 1959. *Turkey's Politics.* Princeton, N.J.: Princeton Univ. Press.

Keddie, Nikki R. 1983. *An Islamic Response to Imperialism: Political and Religious Writings of Sayyid Jamal ad-Din 'al-Afghani' (1839–1897).* Berkeley: Univ. of California Press.

————. 1988. "Ideology, Society, and the State in Post-colonial Muslim Societies." In *State and Ideology in the Middle East and Pakistan,* edited by Fred Halliday and Hamza Alavi, 9–30. New York: Monthly Review Press.

Keyder, Çağlar. 1979. "The Political Economy of Turkish Democracy." *New Left Review* 115: 3–44.

————. 1987. *State and Class in Turkey.* New York: Verso.

Kili, Suna. 1969. *Kemalizm* (Kemalism). Istanbul: Menteş.

————. 1984a. "Address." In *Papers and Discussion: International Symposium on Atatürk, 17–22 May 1981,* 17–22. Istanbul: Türkiye İş Bankası Cultural Publications.

————. 1984b. "The Turkish Revolution: The Developed and Developing Countries." In *Papers and Discussion: International Symposium on Atatürk, 17–22 May 1981,* 73–107. Istanbul: Türkiye İş Bankası Cultural Publications.

————, ed. 1996. *Dünya ve Türkiye Açısından Atatürk* (Atatürk from the perspective of the world and Turkey). Istanbul: Yapı Kredi.

Kinross, Patrick. 1964. *Atatürk: The Rebirth of a Nation.* London: Weidenfeld and Nicolson.

Kışlalı, Ahmed Taner. 1996. "Kemalist Devrim ve Türk Aydınlanması" (The Kemalist revolution and Turkish enlightenment). In *Dünya ve Türkiye Açısından Atatürk* (Atatürk from the perspective of the world and Turkey), edited by Suna Kili, 33–43. Istanbul: Yapı Kredi.

Kohn, Hans. 1933. "Ten Years of the Turkish Republic." *Foreign Affairs* (October): 154–55.

Köker, Levent. 1990. *Modernleşme, Kemalizm ve Demokrasi* (Modernization, Kemalism, and democracy). Istanbul: İletişim.

Kongar, Emre. 2001. *Küresel Terör ve Türkiye: Küreselleşme, Huntington, 11 Eylül* (Global terror and Turkey: Globalization, Huntington, and 11 September). Istanbul: Remzi Books.

Lerner, Daniel, and Richard Robinson. 1960. "Swords and Ploughshares: The Turkish Army as a Modernizing Force." *World Politics* 13, no. 1: 19–44.

Lewis, Bernard. 1961. *The Emergence of Modern Turkey.* London: Oxford Univ. Press.

——. 1998. *Multiple Identities of the Middle East.* New York: Schoken.

Locke, John. 1988. *Two Treatises on Government.* Cambridge: Cambridge Univ. Press.

Macpherson, C. B. 1962. *The Political Theory of Possessive Individualism: Hobbes to Locke.* Oxford: Oxford Univ. Press.

Mango, Andrew. 1999. *Atatürk.* London: John Murray.

Mardin, Şerif. 1962. *The Genesis of Young Ottoman Thought: A Study in the Modernization of Turkish Political Ideas.* Princeton, N.J.: Princeton Univ. Press.

——. 1983. *Jön Türklerin Siyasi Fikirleri 1895–1908* (The political ideas of the Young Turks 1895–1908). Istanbul: İletişim Yayınları.

——. 1989. *Religion and Social Change in Turkey: The Case of Bediüzzaman Said Nursi (1873–1960).* Albany: State Univ. of New York Press.

——. 1994. "Islam in Mass Society: Harmony versus Polarization." In *Politics in the Third Turkish Republic,* edited by Metin Heper and Ahmet Evin, 161–70. Boulder, Colo.: Westview.

Marx, Karl. 1994. *Selected Writings.* Edited by Lawrence H. Simon. Indianapolis: Hackett.

Mehta, Uday. 1999. *Liberalism and Empire: A Study in Nineteenth-Century British Liberal Thought.* Chicago: Univ. of Chicago Press.

Mill, John Stuart. 1988. *On Liberty.* Cambridge: Cambridge Univ. Press.

——. 1995. *On Liberty and Other Writings.* Cambridge: Cambridge Univ. Press.

Mitchell, Timothy. 2000. "Introduction." In *Questions of Modernity,* edited by Timothy Mitchell, xi-xxvii. Minneapolis: Univ. of Minnesota Press.

Mouffe, Chantall. 1995. "Democratic Politics and the Question of Identity." In *The Identity in Question,* edited by John Rachman, 33–45. New York: Routledge.

Nolte, Ernest. 1965. *Three Faces of Fascism: Action Française, Italian Fascism, National Socialism.* London: Weidenfeld and Nicolson.

"Ortadoğu'ya Atatürk Modeli" (The Atatürk model for the Middle East). *Sabah Gazetesi,* Feb. 17, 2003, 22.

Ozankay, Özer. 2000. *Dünya Düşünürleri Gözüyle Atatürk ve Cumhuriyet* (Atatürk and the republic in the view of world thinkers). Istanbul: Türkiye İş Bankası Yayınları.

Özbudun, Ergun. 1988. "Development of Democratic Government in Turkey: Crises, Interruptions, and Re-equilibriums." In *Perspectives on Democracy in Turkey,* edited by Ergun Özbudun, 1–58. Ankara: Turkish Political Science Association.

——. 2000. *Contemporary Turkish Politics: Challenges to Democratic Consolidation.* Boulder, Colo.: Lynne Rienner.

Özbudun, Ergun, and Ali Kazancıgil. 1981. "Introduction." In *Atatürk: The Founder of a Modern State,* edited by Ergun Özbudun and Ali Kazancıgil, 1–20. London: C. Hurst.

Parla, Taha. 1985. *The Social and Political Thought of Ziya Gökalp, 1876–1924.* Leiden: E. J. Brill.

———. 1991. *Türkiye'de Siyasal Kültürün Resmî Kaynakları: Atatürk'ün Nutuk'u* (The official sources of Turkish political culture: Atatürk's Nutuk). Vol. 1. Istanbul: İletişim Yayınları.

———. 1992a. *Türkiye'de Siyasal Kültürün Resmî Kaynakları: Atatürk'ün Söylev ve Demeçleri* (The official sources of Turkish political culture). Vol. 2. Istanbul: İletişim Yayınları.

———. 1992b. *Türkiye'de Siyasal Kültürün Resmî Kaynakları: Kemalist Tek-Parti İdeolojisi ve CHP'nin Altı Ok'u* (The official sources of Turkish political culture). Vol. 3. Istanbul: İletişim Yayınları.

———. 1996a. "Kemalism." In *Encyclopedia of the Modern Middle East,* 996–98. New York: Simon and Schuster.

———. 1996b. "Ziya Gökalp." In *Encyclopedia of the Modern Middle East,* 712–13. New York: Simon and Schuster.

———. 2001. *Türkiye'de Anayasalar, Genişletilmiş Yeni Baskı* (Constitutions in Turkey: Expanded new edition). Istanbul: İletişim.

Parla, Taha, and Andrew Davison. Forthcoming. "Secularism and Laicism in Turkey." In *World Secularisms at the Millennium,* edited by Janet R. Jakobsen and Ann Pellegrini. Chapel Hill, N.C.: Duke Univ. Press.

Parla, Taha, and Ayşe Öncü. 1990. "Militarism and Corporatism in Turkish Politics." In *Jahrbuch zur Geschichte und Gesellschaft des Vorderen und Mittleren Orients 1987–1988,* edited by J. Blaschke. Berlin: Parabolis.

Prakash, Gyan. 1995. "Postcolonial Criticism and Indian Historiography." In *Social Postmodernism: Beyond Identity Politics,* edited by Linda Nicholson and Steven Seidman, 87–100. Cambridge: Cambridge Univ. Press.

———. 2000. "Subaltern Studies as Post Colonial Criticism." In *Cultures of Empire: A Reader,* edited by Catherine Hall, 120–37. New York: Routledge.

Richards, Alan, and John Waterbury. 1996. *A Political Economy of the Middle East.* 2d ed. Boulder, Colo.: Westview.

Rousseau, Jean-Jacques. 1992. *Discourse on the Origin and Foundations of Inequality among Men.* Translated by Donald A. Cress. Indianapolis: Hackett.

Rustow, Dankwart. 1968. "Atatürk as Founder of a State." *Daedalus* 97: 793–828.

———. 1970. *Philosophers and Kings: Studies in Leadership.* New York: George Braziller.

———. 1984. "The Founding of a Nation State: Atatürk's Historical Achievement." In *Papers and Discussion: International Symposium on Atatürk, 17–22 May 1981,* 329–56. Istanbul: Türkiye İş Bankası Cultural Publications.

Ryan, Alan. 1965. "Locke and the Dictatorship of the Bourgeoisie." *Political Studies* 13: 219–30.

Sayyid, Bobby S. 1997. *A Fundamental Fear: Eurocentrism and the Emergence of Islamism.* London: Zed.

Schmitter, Philippe C. 1974. "Still the Century of Corporatism?" *Review of Politics* 36: 85–131.

Skinner, Quentin. 1978. *The Foundations of Modern Political Thought.* Cambridge: Cambridge Univ. Press.

Soysal, Mümtaz. 1984. "The Significance of the Kemalist Approach in Turkish Constitutionalism." In *Papers and Discussion: International Symposium on Atatürk, 17–22 May 1981,* 231–40. Istanbul: Türkiye İş Bankası Cultural Publications.

Stepan, Alfred. 1978. *State and Society: Peru in Comparative Perspective.* Princeton, N.J.: Princeton Univ. Press.

———. 2001. *Arguing Comparative Politics.* Oxford: Oxford Univ. Press.

Tully, James. 1980. *A Discourse on Property: John Locke and His Adversaries.* Cambridge: Cambridge Univ. Press.

Tunaya, Tarık Zafer. 2002. *Devrim Hareketleri İçinde: Atatürk ve Atatürkçülük* (Inside revolution movements: Atatürk and Atatürkism). 1964. Reprint. Istanbul: Bilgi Üniversitesi Yayınları.

Tunçay, Mete. 1992. *T.C.'nde Tek-Parti Yönetimi'nin Kurulması (1923–1931)* (The founding of the single-party regime in the Turkish Republic). 1981. Reprint. Istanbul: Cem Yayınevi.

Weber, Max. 1968. *Economy and Society.* Edited by G. Roth and C. Wittich. Los Angeles: Univ. of California Press.

Webster, Donald E. 1939. *The Turkey of Atatürk: Social Process in the Turkish Reformation.* Philadelphia: American Academy of Political and Social Science.

Wiarda, Howard J. 1997. *Corporatism and Comparative Politics: The Other Great "Ism."* Armonk, N.Y.: M. E. Sharp.

Zürcher, Eric J. 1993. *Turkey: A Modern History.* London: I. B. Tauris.

DOCUMENTS OF THE REPUBLICAN PEOPLE'S PARTY

Republican People's Party (RPP) [Cumhuriyet Halk Partisi (CHP)]. 1923. *Nizamnamesi* (Statutes). Istanbul and Ankara: RPP.

———. 1927. *Nizamnamesi* (Statutes). Istanbul and Ankara: RPP.

———. 1931. *Programı* (Program). Istanbul and Ankara: RPP.

———. 1935. *Programı* (Program). Istanbul and Ankara: RPP.

———. 1943a. *Programı* (Program). Istanbul and Ankara: RPP.

———. 1943b. "1943 Yirmi Yıl İcinde Cumhuriyet Halk Partisi" (RPP in twenty years). Ankara: Ulus Basımevi.

———. 1947. *Programı* (Program). Istanbul and Ankara: RPP.

CITATION GUIDE FOR *ATATÜRK'ÜN SÖYLEV VE DEMEÇLERİ*
(ATATÜRK'S PUBLIC ADDRESSES AND STATEMENTS)

Volume 1

Atatürk, Mustafa Kemal. 1961. *1919–1938*. Vol. 1 of *Söylev ve Demeçleri* (Public addresses and statements). 2d printing. Edited by Nimet Arsan. Ankara: Türk Tarih Kurumu Basımevi for the History of the Turkish Transformation Institute.

1920. "Hükümet Teşkilatı Hakkında" (On the organization of the government), 60–61.

1922a. "I. Meclis Üçüncü Toplanma Yılını Açarken" (Opening speech, 1st Assembly, 3rd year), 221–45.

1922b. "Saltanatın Yıkıldığına Daîr Verilen Karar Münasebetiyle" (On the decision given on the sultanate), 269–80.

1923a. "I. Meclis Dördüncü Toplanma Yılını Açarken" (Opening speech, 1st Assembly, 4th year), 282–309.

1923b. "II. Meclis Cumhurbaşkanlığına Seçilmesi Üzerine" (Upon being elected to the presidency, 2d Assembly), 325–26.

1923c. "II. Meclis İkinci Dönemi Açarken" (Opening speech, 2d Assembly, 2d year), 312–21.

1923d. "II. Meclis Subayların Aylıkları Münasebetiyle" (On the salary of military officers, 2d Assembly), 321–24.

1923e. "Seçim Yenilenmesi Hakkındaki Kanun Münasebetiyle" (On the occasion of the law on renewal of elections), 310–11.

1924. "II. Meclis II. Dönem II. Toplantı Yılını Açarken" (Opening speech, 2d Assembly, 2d year), 332–37.

1925a. "II. Meclis II. Dönem I. Toplantı Yılını Açarken" (Opening speech, 2d Assembly, 1st year), 326–31.

1925b. "II. Meclis II. Dönem III. Toplantı Yılını Açarken" (Opening speech, 2d Assembly, 3rd meeting), 337–43.

1926. "II. Meclis II. Dönem IV. Toplanma Yılını Açarken" (Opening speech, 2d Assembly, 4th year), 344–51.

1927a. "CHP II. Büyük Kongresini Açarken" (Opening the 2d Great Congress of the RPP), 351–53.

1927b. "III. Meclis II. Defa Cumhurbaşkanı Seçildikten Sonra III. Dönem I. Toplanma Yılını Açarken" (Opening speech, 3rd Assembly, 1st year), 353–54.

1931a. "CHP III. Büyük Kongresini Açarken" (Opening of the 3rd Great Congress of the RPP), 367–69.

1931b. "IV. Meclis III. Defa Cumhurbaşkanlığına Seçilmeleri Üzerine" (Upon being re-elected to the presidency, third time, 4th Assembly), 367.

1935. "CHP IV. Büyük Kurultayını Açarken" (Opening the 4th Great Congress of the RPP), 379–83.

1937a. "V. Meclis V. Dönem III. Toplanma Yılını Açarken" (Opening speech, 5th Assembly, 3rd year), 392–405.

1937b. "V. Meclis V. Dönem IV. Toplanma Yılını Açarken (açılışında)" (Opening speech, 5th Assembly, 4th year), 405–14.

1938. "V. Meclis V. Dönem III. Toplanma Yılını Açarken" (Opening speech, 5th Assembly, 3rd year), 41.

Volume 2

Atatürk, Mustafa Kemal. 1959. *1906–1938.* Vol. 2 of *Söylev ve Demeçleri* (Public addresses and statements). 2d printing. Edited by Nimet Arsan. Ankara: Türk Tarih Kurumu Basımevi for the History of the Turkish Transformation Institute.

1919. "Kırşehir Gençler Derneğindeki Hitabe" (Speech at Kırşehir Youth Association), 2–4.

1920. "Ankara İleri Gelenleriyle Bir Konuşma" (A talk with notables of Ankara), 4–15.

1922. "Halk Partisini Kurmak Hakkındaki Kararını Açıklaması" (Explaining the decision to found the People's Party), 46–48.

1923a. "Adana'da Çiftçilerle Konuşma" (A talk with farmers in Adana), 116–25.

1923b. "Adana'da Esnaflarla Konuşma" (A talk with artisans in Adana), 125–28.

1923c. "Adana'da Halkla Konuşma" (Addressing the people in Adana), 115–16.

1923d. "Afyonkarahisar Belediye Meclisi Üyeleriyle Konuşma" (A talk with the members of the Municipal Council in Afyonkarahisar), 159–63.

1923e. "Afyonkarahisar Gençleriyle Konuşma" (Addressing the Afyonkarahisar youth), 157–59.

1923f. "Balıkesir'de Halkla Konuşma" (Speech with the people of Balıkesir), 94–98.

1923g. "İstanbul Gazeteleri Temsilcilerine" (To the representatives of Istanbul newspapers), 54–62.

1923h. "İzmir'de Gazetecilerle Konuşma" (A talk with journalists in Izmir), 81–83.

1923i. "İzmir'de Halk İle Konuşma" (Talk with the people in Izmir), 83–91.

1923j. "İzmir İktisat Kongresini Açış Konuşması" (Opening speech, Izmir Economic Congress), 99–112.

1923k. "Konya'da Esnaf ve Tüccarlar İle Konuşma" (Addressing artisans and merchants in Konya), 134–37.

1923l. "Kütahya'da Öğretmenlerle Konuşma" (A talk with teachers in Kütahya), 163–65.

1923m. "Lise Öğretmen ve Öğrencileri İle Konuşma" (A talk with high school teachers and students), 153–56.

1923n. "Öğüt Gazetesi'ne" (To the Öğüt newspaper), 49–50.

1924a. "Dumlupınar'da Konuşma" (Talk in Dumlupınar), 173–82.

1924b. "Trabzon'da Halk Partililerle Konuşma" (To the party members in Trabzon), 189–90.

1925a. "Akhisar'da Bir Konuşma" (A talk in Akhisar), 223–24.

1925b. "Ankara Hukuk Fakültesinin Açılışında" (At the opening of the Ankara Law Faculty), 236–40.

1925c. "Bursa'da Bir Konuşma" (A talk in Bursa), 218–19.

1925d. "Kastamonu'da Bir Konuşma" (A talk in Kastamonu), 206–7.

1926. "Türk Sporcuları İle Bir Konuşma" (A talk with Turkish athletes), 242–46.

1927. "İstanbul Halkı Temsilcileriyle Konuşma" (A talk with representatives of the Istanbul people), 246–47.

1929a. "Eskişehir Halkı İle Bir Konuşma" (Addressing the people of Eskişehir), 253–54.

1929b. "Sıhhati Hakkında Bir Konuşma" (A talk on his health), 254.

1930a. "Serbest Cumhuriyet Fırkasının Kurulması Hakkında Bir Konuşma" (A statement on the foundation of the Free Republican Party), 255–56.

1930b. "Trabzon'da Bir Konuşma" (A talk in Trabzon), 256–57.

1931a. "İzmir'de Fırka Kongresinde Konuşma" (Speech in Party Congress in Izmir), 259–65.

1931b. "Konya'da Bir Konuşma" (A speech in Konya), 269–70.

1933. "Onuncu Yıl Söylevi" (Speech on the tenth anniversary of the establishment of the republic), 274–76.

1934a. "İran Şehinşahı ve Türkiye-İran Münasebetleri Hakkında Konuşma" (Speech on the Iranian shah and Turkish-Iranian relations), 276–77.

1934b. "İsveç Kralı ve Türkiye-İsveç Münasebetleri Hakkında Konuşma" (Speech on the Swedish king and Turkish-Swedish relations), 277–78.

1937. "Romanya Dışişleri Bakanı Antonescu İle Konuşma" (Talk with Antonescu, foreign minister of Romania), 280–83.

1938. "Türkiye Cumhuriyeti Ordularına Mesaj" (Message to the armed forces of the Turkish Republic), 286.

Volume 3

Atatürk, Mustafa Kemal. 1961. *1918–1937*. Vol. 3 of *Söylev ve Demeçleri* (Public addresses and statements). 2d printing. Edited by Nimet Arsan. Ankara: Türk Tarih Kurumu Basımevi for the History of the Turkish Transformation Institute.

1922a. "Sulh Şartları, İç ve Dış Meseleler" (Terms of peace, domestic, and international issues), 49–52.

1922b. "Sulh ve İnkılap" (Peace and transformation), 52–55.

1923a. "İstanbul Halkı ve Cumhuriyet" (People of Istanbul and the republic), 70–72.

1923b. "Kültür Hakkinda" (On culture), 66–70.

1923c. "Yeni Seçim ve İstanbul" (New elections and Istanbul), 61–62.

1924a. "Cumhuriyet Yıldönümü Münasebetiyle" (On the anniversary of the republic), 74–76.

1924b. "Hilafetin Lağvı" (The abolition of the caliphate), 74.

1924c. "Siyasî Fırkalar Hakkında" (On political parties), 77–78.

1926. "İzmir Suikast Teşebbüsü" (The Izmir assassination attempt), 80.

1930. "Atatürk ve İnkılap" (Atatürk and transformation), 84–89.

1931. "New York'tan İstanbul'a Uçan Amerikalı Tayyareciler Hakkında" (On the pilots who flew from New York to Istanbul), 90–92.

1932. "Keriman Halis'in Dünya Güzeli Seçilmesi" (On Keriman Halis's selection as world's beauty), 92–93.

1935. "Yeni Vaziyet" (The new situation), 97–100.

1937. "Yeni Hükümet Programı Hakkında " (On the new government program), 101–2.

Volume 4

Atatürk, Mustafa Kemal. 1991. *Atatürk'ün Tamim, Telgraf ve Beyannameleri: 1917–1938* (Atatürk's circulars, telegraphs, and written statements: 1917–1938). Vol. 4 of *Söylev ve Demeçleri* (Public addresses and statements). Edited by Nimet Arsan. 1964. Reprint. Ankara: Atatürk Research Institute.

1920. "BMM'nin Açılması Üzerine Padişaha Telegrafla Gönderilen Sadakat Arizası" (Message of loyalty sent to the sultan on the occasion of the opening of the GNA), 320–22.

1926. "Atatürk'e Teşebbüs Edilen Suikast Dolayısıyla Millete Beyanname" (Declaration to the nation upon the attempted assassination on Atatürk), 574.

1927a. "CHP Adayları Hakkında Vatandaşlara Yayınlanan Tamim" (The circular to the citizens concerning the RPP candidates), 534.

1927b. "II. Defa Cumhurbaşkanlığına Seçilmesi Üzerine Millete Beyanname" (Declaration to the nation upon being reelected to the presidency [second time]), 584.

1927c. "Seçimden Sonra Vatandaşlara Beyanname" (Declaration to citizens after the elections), 582–83.

1930. "Yeni Parti Çalışmaları Hakkında Paris Büyükelçisi Fethi Bey'e Verilen Cevap" (The answer given to Fethi Bey, ambassador to Paris, on the preparations for a new party), 598.

1931. "Seçim Dolayısıyla Millete Beyanname" (Declaration to the nation concerning elections), 553.

1935. "Milletvekili Seçimi Dolayısıyla Millete Beyanname" (Declaration to the nation concerning the deputy elections), 571–74.

1937. "Atatürk Diyarbakır'da" (Atatürk in Diyarbakır), 591.

Volume 5

Atatürk, Mustafa Kemal. 1972. *Atatürk'ün Sölev ve Demeçleri, Tamim ve Telgrafları* (Atatürk's public addresses and statements, circulars, and telegraphs). Vol. 5 of *Söylev ve Demeçleri* (Public addresses and statements). 1st printing. Edited by Sadi Borak and Utkan Kocatürk. Ankara: Ankara Üniversitesi Basımevi for the History of the Turkish Transformation Institute.

1923. "Napolyon, Harp ve Sulh" (Napoleon, war, and peace), 97.

1925a. "Milletin Kurtuluş ve Saadeti Hakkında" (On the salvation and happiness of the nation), 209.

1925b. "Umumi Efkârve Keyfi Hareket Edelir mi?" (The public opinion and arbitrary behavior), 210–11.

Volume 6

Atatürk, Mustafa Kemal. 1997. *Atatürk'ün Resmî Yayınlara Girmemiş; Söylev, Demeç, Yazışma ve Söyleşileri* (Atatürk's official unpublished public addresses, public statements, correspondences, and conversations. Vol. 6 of *Söylev ve Demeçleri* (Public addresses and statements). Edited by Sadi Borak. 1980. Reprint. Istanbul: Kaynak Yayınları.

1928. "Mussolini'ye Telgraf" (Telegraph to Mussolini), 387–88.

1931. "Köylü Milletvekillerinde Aranılan Nitelikler Üzerine" (On the qualities required in peasant deputies), 390–91.

1932a. "Balıkesirlilerle İltifat" (Greetings to the residents of Balıkesir), 393–94.

1932b. "Habeşistan İmparatorunun Mektubunu Sunan Elçiye Söylev" (Speech to the ambassador who presented the letter of the emperor of Ethiopia), 244–45.

1932c. "Türk-İtalyan İlişkileri Üzerine" (On Turkish Italian relations), 392.

1937. "Stalin'in Kişiliği Üzerine" (On the personality of Stalin), 267

INDEX

absolutism, 4, 179–80, 200, 202–4, 214, 277,
284. *See also* charismatic leadership; single-
party regime
Adıvar, Adnan, 47
advanced capitalism, 30–31
Ağaoğlu, Ahmed, 97
agriculture, 126
"Agriculture, Industry, Minerals, Forests,
Commerce, and Public Works," 63–64
Ahmad, Feroz, 45–46, 49
Altay, Fahrettin, 226
Amasya Accord, 44
anomie, 26–28, 30
Arendt, Hannah, 87, 246
Aristotle, 93
Armenia, 76–77
army: politics and, 231–43; role in education,
238–42; role of in Kemalism, 40–41, 248;
as watchdog of nation, 253–54
assassination attempt, 49, 158, 164–66, 181,
202, 252
Association for Defense of Rights of
Anatolia and Rumelia, 210, 211
Association for the Preservation of Sacred
Institutions, 47
Association Laws, 38–39
Atatürk, Mustafa Kemal: on abolition of
caliphate, 105, 108, 114; absolutism of, 4,
179–80, 202–4, 214, 277, 284;
antipolitical authoritarian control by, 287;

appeal to love, 162–65; as archpatriarch,
139; on assassination attempt, 49, 158,
164–66, 181, 202, 252; attitude toward
religion, 108–13; on citizen participation,
223–30; claims to RPP formation,
212–13; on class structure in Turkey, 60;
as commander in chief, 151–52; on
corporatist vision, 64; on democratic
Turkey, 140; development of ideology,
59–67; dogmatism of, 283; on economy,
70–71, 131–32, 258n. 2; elections and,
223–30; encouragement of agriculture,
126; equating of happiness/prosperity,
121, 130, 140, evidence of nondemocratic leadership, 148–59, 172–75;
expression of his infallibility, 192–204;
false humility of, 70, 160–62, 196–200,
202; on FRP, 115; goals for Assembly,
222–23; historical views about, 2–3, 4, 5,
8, 9; institutionalization of, 172–83;
justification for actions of, 198; as leader
of RPP, 66–67, 217; as leader of Turkey,
46–51, 143–44, 147, 159, 177–83,
280–82; on leadership of Turkey, 148–59,
162; leadership style, 170–77; legitimation
strategy, 59–60, 69–70, 116–24, 133–38,
220–21, 260; message to youth, 143,
204–8, 217–18; on military's role, 231–43;
on modernization, 124; on National
Assembly, 209; on national identity,

role of military in, 238, 242–43; separation of military/politics, 231; by single-party regime, 220–21; under totalitarianism/fascism, 246–47; treatment of Islam and, 91; Turkish elections and, 224–30

Gramsci, Antonio, 35–36n. 1

Grand National Assembly (GNA): candidates for, 226–29; First Assembly, 44–47, 223; Kemal on, 209; as Kemal's creation, 222–23; opposition to Kemal in, 70; purpose of, 263; Second Assembly, 48–49

Great Speech (Atatürk), 60, 284

Habermas, Jürgen, 36n. 1

happiness: anonymous service as, 199; commonality of, 80–81; as goal of RPP, 210–11; positive science as means to, 182; prosperity as means to, 121, 130, 140; social engineering as means to, 135–36; Turkish identity and, 80

harmony: classless society as, 211; as emphasis, 127, 129, 132; as way to freedom, 219

health care, 258

hegemony, 35–41. *See also* Kemalism/Kemalists

hero worship cult, 4, 144–45, 185–90, 200, 285, 288. *See also* charismatic leadership

Higher Education Law of 1981, 39

High Treason Laws, 45, 48, 49, 52

history: behind Kemalism, 41–50; Kemal as, 192; Kemal as reference point for eternity, 217–18; Kemalist view of, 139; Kemal's desire for control of, 217–18; Marxist revolution as end of, 95; positive stage of, 101; significance to nationalistic goals, 78–79, 122–23, 247–48; Turkey's role in, 127, 221–22; youth as, 204–8

hızır, 184–90

humanism, 3, 9

ideologues, 23, 24

ideology: analysis of, 25; analytical problems of study of, 19–21; articulation of, 23; components of, 23–25; concept of, 21; consequences of Kemalism, 260–65; hegemonic vs. pluralistic, 35–37; Kemalism as lacking, 7–11; practice vs., 22–23; tasks of, 24. *See also* corporatism; fascistic corporatism; Kemalism/Kemalists; *other specific ideologies;* solidaristic corporatism

"İhtilâl mı, İnkilâp mı?" (Ağaoğlu), 97

Independence Tribunals, 47, 49, 98, 115, 177

individuality/individualism: under Kemalism, 138, 256–57, 260–61; Kemal on, 62, 70, 211–12; liberalism and, 27, 28–29, 31, 32; limitations on, 90; peopleism and, 80–81; in republic, 87; transformation and, 97–98

individual rights, 29, 77–78, 131, 245–46

industry, 125–26

inferiority complex, 248–49

inkilâpçılık. See transformationism

İnönü, İsmet, 44, 183–85, 264

institutions: army, 231–43; elections, 223–30; National Assembly, 44–49, 70, 222–23, 226–29, 263; political party, 209–22 (*see also* Free Republican Party (FRP); Progressive Republican Party (PRP); Republican People's Party (RPP)); reform of, 50–53

interest representation, 31–33

international relations, 279–80

Iranian revolution, 6

ırk, 72–73

Islam: historical role of, 42, 45–46, 49; Kemalist reforms and, 50–53, 100, 132;

solidaristic government, 81; dismissal of
ideas of, 153–57; elections and, 152–53;
Independence Tribunals for, 177–78;
Kemal's view of, 148; of laicism, 111–12,
113–14; Law of Establishing of
Tranquility and, 145; press as, 178–79,
180; PRP as, 178–79; treatment of, 48–50,
70, 72–73, 99, 114–15, 133, 144, 159,
165–78
Orbay, Rauf, 181, 182–83
Ottoman Empire, 69, 102
Ottoman Parliament, 44, 45–46
Özbudun, Ergun, 5, 8, 121

parliament: corporate organization of, 33–34;
election of Ottoman Parliament, 44, 230;
Kemal's concept of, 222–23, 263;
principle of legitimacy of, 32; subordinate
role of, 253
paternalism, 182
patriarchal domination, 138–39, 183–92. *See
also* authoritarian rule; charismatic
leadership
peoplelsm. *See* populism
People's Faction, 47–48
Plato, 26
pluralism, 36–37
political action, 24
political candidates, 226–28
political corporatism, 33–34
political decision making, 32–34
political development, 223–30
Political Parties Law, 39–40
politics: consequences of nationalist identity,
261–62; constitutive meaning of, 14–15;
current trends, 269, 288; development of
inequality, 262, 287; effects of positivism
on, 101–2; elections, 223–30; etatism and,
131; fusing of state and party, 88–90;
hegemonic ideologies and, 35–37;

ideological basis of actions, 23, 24; of
Kemalist nationalist-populist republic, 84;
Kemalist understanding of leadership,
143–208; Kemalist view of state/society,
244–66; Kemal's view of, 61, 135; laicism
and, 57, 104–8; military's role in, 231–43;
models of organization of, 32; National
Assembly, 44–49, 70, 209, 222–23, 263;
obliteration of boundaries of, 278;
opposition within, 81; parties in Turkey,
209–22; of post-Kemal Turkey, 185–86;
presence of Kemal in, 38, 39, 41;
requirements of Kemalist tranquility, 182;
role of, 259; role of corporatism in, 26;
separation from religion, 100–101; of
single-party regime, 177–83; sovereignty,
115–24; study of ideologies, 19–21; in
totalitarian states, 191
populism: alternative translation of, 54;
charismatic authority and, 147;
declaration of republic and, 68; as form
of corporatism, 140; limits of received
view, 56; link to democracy, 136–37;
meaning of under Kemalism, 80–86,
272–73; relationship to nationalism, 80,
83, 85; relationship to other arrows, 58;
relationship to republicanism, 87–88;
relationship to transformationism, 98; use
as substitute for analysis, 1
positivism, 8, 13, 34, 101–5
positivist science: as basis of education,
100–105; definition of positive sciences,
101; elevation of above religion, 57;
legitimation strategy and, 118–22; as sole
creative thought needed, 217–18; as
source of prosperity, 130, 132
pragmatism, 7–11, 60, 192–95, 282–83
"Preface to Second Edition" of *Division of
Labor in Society* (Durkheim), 26
press: Kemalist limits on, 219, 254–55, 278;
Law for the Establishment of Tranquility

Atatürk, Mustafa Kemal;
Kemalism/Kemalists; solidaristic
corporatism

revolutionism, 91–96, 133–34, 275–76. *See
also* transformationism

rhetorical effect strategy, 137

Richards, Alan, 128

rightist tendencies, 244–47, 263–65. *See also*
fascism; fascistic corporatism; totalitarian
rule

Robinson, Richard, 8–9

Rousseau, Jean Jacques, 262

RPP. *See* Republican People's Party (RPP)

"RPP after Twenty Years, The," 64–65

Rustow, Dankwart, 3, 4, 49

sartorial regulations of 1925, 48

Second Group, 47–48

secularism: Kemalism viewed as, 5–7, 9–10,
273–75; Kemalist reforms and, 50–53;
Kemalist self-representation as, 1–2;
Kemalist version of, 5; laicism perceived
as, 118; laicism vs., 13–14, 108;
transformationism and, 275–76. *See also*
laicism

Sèvres, Treaty of, 42–43, 44–45, 76

shah of Iran, 265

Shariah, 48

single-party regime: cultural reforms,
215–16; democracy vs., 136; documents
of, 40, 88–89; goals of, 250; interest
articulation by, 32; leader of, 217; legal
reforms, 217–18; *Nutuk* account of, 145;
opposition to, 173–74; policies
established to maintain, 177, 218;
policymaking reference point of, 247–48;
role of Kemal, 189; RPP during, 209–15;
view of Islam, 274. *See also* Atatürk,
Mustafa Kemal; Republican People's
Party (RPP)

six arrows, 1–2, 7, 9, 54–60, 65. *See also*
laicism; nationalism; populism;
republicanism; statism;
transformationism

Skinner, Quentin, 20

social engineering, 135

socialism: corporatist view of, 30, 120;
etatism vs., 128; ideology vs. practice, 22;
Kemalist populism and, 81, 83–84, 138,
288–89

Societies for the Defense of National Rights,
43

society: corporatist model for, 28–30, 41,
244–45, 257–58; development of moral
inequality, 261–63, 279, 291; hegemonic
ideologies and, 35–38; homogenization
of, 251, 279–80; ideology as accounts of,
23; impact of Kemal's leadership, 251–52;
Kemalist progress in, 285; Kemalist
reforms, 50–53; Kemalist view of
members of, 247–48, 272; Kemalist views
of, 81–86; laicism and, 100; preservation
of Kemalism by, 41; public morality and,
26–28; regulation of youth of, 253–54;
relationship between individual/social
groups, 80–81; relationship to state,
254–56, 258; RPP goals for, 215–16

Society for the Defense of Rights of
Anatolia and Rumelia, 44

Society for the Study of the Turkish
Language, 78

Society of Turkish History, 78

solidaristic corporatism: capitalism and, 30;
class-based concepts and, 81; conception
of corporations, 12–13; concept of
leadership undergirding, 145; emphasis
of, 139; fascistic corporatism vs., 29–30,
245–46; formation of, 33, 60–65;
fractional dimensions of, 289–92;
individuality under, 70; Kemalist
achievements of, 257; Kemalistic